Complementary and Alternative Medicine and the Law

Complementary and Alternative Medicine and the Law

Lucinda E. Jesson
HAMLINE UNIVERSITY SCHOOL OF LAW

Stacey A. Tovino
WILLIAM S. BOYD SCHOOL OF LAW
UNIVERSITY OF NEVADA, LAS VEGAS

CAROLINA ACADEMIC PRESS
Durham, North Carolina

Copyright © 2010
Lucinda E. Jesson
Stacey A. Tovino
All Rights Reserved

Library of Congress Cataloging-in-Publication Data

Jesson, Lucinda E.
  Complementary and alternative medicine and the law / Lucinda E. Jesson and Stacey A. Tovino.
      p. cm.
  ISBN 978-1-59460-767-7 (alk. paper)
  1. Medical laws and legislation 2. Alternative medicine--Law and legislation--United States. I. Tovino, Stacey A. II. Title.

KF3821.J47 2010
344.7304'1--dc22

2009051502

Carolina Academic Press
700 Kent Street
Durham, North Carolina 27701
Telephone (919) 489-7486
Fax (919) 493-5668
www.cap-press.com

Printed in the United States of America

Contents

Acknowledgments	xi
Chapter One · Introduction to Complementary and Alternative Medicine	3
I. The Increased Presence of Complementary and Alternative Medicine in the United States	3
A. Evidence of Increased Use and Attention	3
B. Why Are More People Using CAM?	5
II. What Is Complementary and Alternative Medicine?	6
A. Definitions	6
B. Overview of CAM Modalities	9
Osteopathy	9
Chiropractic	11
Massage Therapy	12
Homeopathy	13
Naturopathy	14
Dietary and Herbal Supplements	14
Spirituality	15
Acupuncture	16
Midwifery	17
C. CAM in Cultural Context	18
III. Continued Tension between CAM and Conventional Medicine	19
Marcia Angell, M.D., Jerome P. Kassirer, M.D., *Alternative Medicine — The Risks of Untested and Unregulated Remedies* (1983)	21
Notes and Questions	24
IV. Legal Considerations	26
A. State Police Powers: Protecting Health and Safety	26
Jacobson v. Massachusetts	26
Notes and Questions	30
B. Overview of the Book	30
Chapter Two · The Gatekeeper Role of Licensure	33
I. Introduction to Licensure and the Practice of Medicine	33
A. The Status of Medical Practice in the Nineteenth Century	33
B. The Flexner Report: Expanding Physician Control over Health Care through Medical School Reform	35
C. Defining the Practice of Medicine	36
D. The Ongoing Struggle to Distinguish between Providers: A Role for Regulators, Patients, or the Professions?	37
Maxwell J. Mehlman, *Quackery*	37
Notes and Questions	39

II.	The Licensed Provider's Use of Complementary and Alternative Medicine	40
	In re George A. Guess, M.D.	42
	State Board of Medical Examiners of Florida, v. Robert J. Rogers, M.D.	45
	Robert C. Atkins, M.D. v. C. Maynard Guest, M.D., as Executive Secretary of the New York State Board for Professional Conduct	47
	Notes and Questions	50
	Comment: Complaint and Investigation Process	51
	Notes and Questions	53
	Problem	55
III.	Unlicensed Providers and the Practice of Medicine	56
	A. From Prayer to Healing Touch	57
	Curley v. State of Florida	58
	Board of Medical Quality Assurance v. Arthur Andrews	60
	Notes and Questions	63
	Michael H. Cohen, *Healing at the Borderland of Medicine and Religion: Regulating Potential Abuse of Authority by Spiritual Healers*	64
	Problem	65
	B. Midwifery	65
	Stacey A. Tovino, *American Midwifery Litigation and State Legislative Preference for Physician-Controlled Childbirth*	66
	The People of the State of Illinois Ex Rel. Leonard A. Sherman, Director of Professional Regulation v. Yvonne Cryns	67
	The State Board of Nursing and State of Kansas Ex Rel. State Board of Healing Arts v. E. Michelle Ruebke	71
	Notes and Questions	74
	Opening Statement of the Prosecutor in the Trial of a Midwife	77
	Opening Statement of the Defense Lawyer	78
	Problem	79

Chapter Three · Scope of Practice 81
I. Scope of Practice Disputes Outside the Courtroom 83
    A. Legislative Halls 83
        Maura Lerner, *A Bitter Fight Over Who Can Be Called "Doctor"* 84
        Notes and Questions 85
    B. Attorney General Opinions 86
        Nebraska Attorney General Opinion 87
        Recent Attorney General Scope of Practice Formal Opinions 88
        Comment: Statutory Interpretation 90
II. Scope of Practice Disputes in the Courtroom 91
    Foster v. Georgia Board of Chiropractic Examiners 91
    Crees v. California State Board of Medical Examiners 95
    Problem 99
    Notes and Questions 100
    Problem 101

Chapter Four · Malpractice 103
I. Standards of Care 103
    A. Common Law 103
        Kerkman v. Hintz 103
        Notes and Questions 111

		B. Statutes	112
		Notes and Questions	113
		C. Scope of Practice Statutes, Unprofessional Conduct Statutes, and Malpractice Standards of Care	114
		Wengel v. Herfert	114
	II.	Breach	116
		A. Foregoing Conventional Care	116
		Charell v. Gonzalez	117
		Charell v. Gonzalez	120
		Notes and Questions	121
		B. Failure to Refer	122
		Mostrom v. Pettibon	122
		Salazar v. Ehmann	127
		C. Not Amenable to CAM Care	128
		Tschirhart v. Pethtel	128
		D. Negligent Performance of a CAM Procedure	129
		Hinthorn v. Garrison	130
		E. Failure to Diagnose; Incorrect Diagnosis	131
		Wilcox v. Carroll	131
		Notes and Questions	137
		Sell v. Shore	138
		Notes and Questions	140
	III.	Causation	141
		A. Causal Link	141
		Ireland v. Eckerly, M.D.	141
		White v. Jones	142
		Notes and Questions	144
		B. Expert Testimony Regarding Causation	144
		Morgan v. Hill	144
	IV.	Malpractice Defenses	146
		A. Two Schools of Thought	146
		Jones v. Chidester	146
		Notes and Questions	151
		B. Assumption of the Risk	152
		Schneider v. Revici	152
		Charell v. Gonzalez	154

Chapter Five · Informed Consent 157
   I. Introduction 157
      A. Early Foundations 157
         Schloendorff v. The Society of New York Hospital 157
         Note and Questions 159
      B. The Patient Standard 160
         Canterbury v. Spence 160
         Notes and Questions 172
      C. The Professional Standard 174
         Culbertson v. Mernitz 174
   II. Informed Consent in the CAM Context 178
      A. Failure to Disclose Risks of Foregoing Conventional Medical Care 179
         Charell v. Gonzalez 179

	Schneider v. Revici	183
	Notes and Questions	189
	B. Failure to Inform the Patient of the Availability of CAM Care	190
	Moore v. Baker	190
	Notes and Questions	192
	C. Failure to Inform of the Risks of CAM Care	195
	Problem	195

Chapter Six · Regulation of Dietary Supplements by the Food and Drug Administration — 197

- I. Introduction — 197
- II. Organization and Authority of the Food and Drug Administration — 198
  - A. Overview — 198
    - Notes and Questions — 199
  - B. Regulation of Food — 199
    - 1. Label Requirements — 201
    - 2. Label Options — 201
  - C. Regulation of Drugs — 202
    - 1. Definition — 202
    - 2. Safety and Efficacy — 202
    - 3. Over the Counter Drugs — 203
- III. Regulation of Dietary Supplements — 204
  - A. Is It a Drug or a Food? — 204
    - *United States v. Nutrition Service, Inc.* — 204
    - Notes and Questions — 206
  - B. The Dietary Supplement Health and Education Act of 1994 (DSHEA) — 206
    - 1. Definition — 206
    - 2. Safety Standards — 207
    - *Nutraceutical Corporation v. Von Eschenbach* — 208
    - Notes and Questions — 211
    - Problem — 212
    - 3. Labeling — 212
    - *Pearson v. Donna E. Shalala, Secretary, United States Department of Health and Human Services* — 214
    - Summary Regarding Qualified Health Claims: B Vitamins & Vascular Disease — 217
    - Notes and Questions — 218
- IV. Rethinking the Regulation of Dietary Supplements — 219
  - Dietary Supplements: FDA Should Take Further Actions to Improve Oversight and Consumer Understanding — 219

Chapter Seven · Antitrust — 223

- I. Introduction — 223
  - A. Overview — 223
    - Department of Justice, Antitrust Division, Overview — 223
  - B. Federal and State Antitrust Authorities — 224
  - C. Antitrust Defenses — 226
  - D. A Policy Argument — 227
    - Caitlin Slessor, *The Right to Choose in Childbirth: Regulation of Midwifery in Iowa* — 227
    - Notes — 229

II.	Applying Antitrust Law	230
	A. An Antitrust Victory	230
	Wilk v. American Medical Association	230
	Notes	241
	B. An Antitrust Loss	241
	Solla v. Aetna Health Plans of New York, Inc.	242
	Notes	247
	Problem	247
III.	Antitrust Allegations in Other Contexts	248
	A. Denials of Clinical Privileges	248
	Welchlin v. Tenet Healthcare Corporation	248
	Notes and Problems	254
	B. Denial or Cancellation of Malpractice Insurance	254
	Nurse Midwifery Associates v. Hibbett	254
	C. Reimbursement Caps and Disparities in Reimbursement Rates	257
	American Chiropractic Association v. Trigon Healthcare, Inc.	258
	D. CAM Practitioners as Antitrust Defendants	260
	In the Matter of The Connecticut Chiropractic Association, The Connecticut Chiropractic Council, and Robert L. Hirtle, Esq.	261

Chapter Eight · Innovations in CAM Regulation — 267

I.	Medical Freedom Acts	268
	Notes and Questions	269
	Gonzalez v. New York State Dept. of Health	270
	Notes and Questions	271
II.	Striving for a Middle Ground on Regulation: Creation of Offices to Govern Unlicensed CAM Practitioners	273
	A. Defining CAM	274
	B. Establishing Minimal Standards of Conduct	274
	C. Creating a Bill of Rights	275
	Complementary and Alternative Health Care Client Bill of Rights	275
	Notes and Questions	277
III.	Rethinking the Need for Regulation	279

Index — 281

Acknowledgments

Lucinda Jesson would like to thank Jessica Kracl, a 2009 graduate of Hamline University School of Law, for her amazing research and writing assistance for Chapters One and Six of this text. In addition, she thanks Abigail Kozel and Maria Breu, Hamline University School of Law 2010 graduates, for their exemplary (and tactful) editing suggestions. Finally, Professor Jesson thanks Hamline University for the research stipend, which helped support the writing of this text.

Stacey Tovino would like to thank Heather Elliot-Heath, a December 2008 graduate of Hamline University School of Law, and Miguel Puentes, a May 2010 graduate of Drake University Law School, for their outstanding research assistance. Heather assisted in the preparation of six volumes of background material relating to contemporary and alternative medicine and Miguel prepared an exceptional manuscript entitled, "Fundamental Difficulties with Antitrust Litigation Pertaining to Complementary and Alternative Health: An Overview," from which much of the material in Chapter Seven was drawn.

Chapter One: Introduction to Complementary and Alternative Medicine

Expert from Anemona Hartocollis, *In Once Section of Beth Israel Hospital, Some Patients are Saying "Om", Not "Ah"*, N.Y. Times, Oct. 29, 2008, at A31. Copyright © 2008. Reprinted with permission of the New York Times.

Excerpts from Anne Fadiman, The Spirit Catches You and You Fall Down (Farrar, Straus, & Giroux, LLC 1997). Copyright ©1997 by Anne Fadiman. Reprinted by permission of Farrar, Straus and Giroux, LLC.

Marcia Angell, M.D., Jerome P. Kassirer, M.D., *Alternative Medicine—The Risks of Untested and Unregulated Remedies*, 339 New Eng. J. Med. 83 (1998). Copyright © 1998. Reprinted with permission by the New England Journal of Medicine.

Jill Mallory, M.D., *The Practice of Integrative Medicine*. Printed with permission by Jill Mallory, M.D.

Chapter Two: The Gatekeeper Role of Licensure

Maxwell J. Mehlman, *Quackery*, 31 Am. J.L. & Med. 349 (2005). Copyright © 2005. Reprinted with permission of the American Journal of Law & Medicine.

Stacey A. Tovino, *American Midwifery Litigation and State Legislative Preference for Physician-Controlled Childbirth*, 11 Cardozo Women's L.J. 61 (2004). Copyright © 2004. Reprinted with permission by the Cardozo Women's Law Journal.

Excerpts from Chris Bohjalian, Midwives (Random House 1997). Copyright © 1997. Reprinted with permission by Random House.

Chapter Three: Scope of Practice

Maura Lerner, *A Bitter Fight Over Who Can Be Called "Doctor"*, Minn.-S.P. Star Trib., June 8, 2008. Copyright © 2008. Reprinted with permission by Star Tribune.

Chapter Seven: Antitrust

Caitlin Slessor, *The Right to Choose in Childbirth: Regulation of Midwifery in Iowa*, 8 J. GENDER RACE & JUST. 511 (2004–05). Copyright © 2004–05. Reprinted with permission from the Journal of Gender, Race and Justice.

Complementary and Alternative Medicine and the Law

Chapter One

Introduction to Complementary and Alternative Medicine

A high school football player suffering from a herniated disc turns to acupuncture for treatment of his pain while still seeing a medical doctor for continued monitoring of his recovery. A fifty-year-old woman diagnosed with osteoarthritis in both of her knees regularly sees an orthopedic doctor, but also wears magnetic bracelets and places magnetic inserts in each of her shoes in an effort to use energy-healing to relieve her discomfort. A twenty-three-year-old pregnant woman chooses a midwife for the prenatal care and delivery of her child. These real life stories illustrate what oft-cited studies suggest: Americans are increasingly using the variety of therapies commonly referred to in the United States as Complementary and Alternative Medicine (CAM), either in conjunction with conventional medicine (complementary), or in place of it (alternative).

This book examines the place of CAM in the United States health care system primarily from a legal perspective, but also considers the history of CAM and the cultural and social implications of its growing presence. Not just for law students, this book has been designed with a variety of health professionals in mind, including practicing attorneys, health care providers and administrators, and consumers of complementary and alternative medicine. A central theme, which will be discussed throughout the book, is the tension between the government's interest in protecting the populous from "quackery," and the individual's interest in freedom to choose one's preferred method of health care.

I. The Increased Presence of Complementary and Alternative Medicine in the United States

A. Evidence of Increased Use and Attention

In 1998, David M. Eisenberg and colleagues published the results from nationwide telephone surveys conducted in 1990 and 1997 regarding the prevalence and cost of alternative therapy as well as disclosure of alternative therapy use to physicians. The results estimate that, in 1997, 42.1% of the U.S. population had used at least 1 of 16 alternative therapies listed in the past year, up from 33.8% in 1990. This research suggests that the total number of visits to CAM practitioners actually exceeded the total number of visits to primary care physicians in 1997. Use was higher in women; individuals aged 35–49 years of age; individuals with a college education; and those with an annual income above $50,000. The most commonly used therapies in 1997 were relaxation techniques, herbal medicine, massage therapy and chiropractic care. At an estimated $12.2 billion, Ameri-

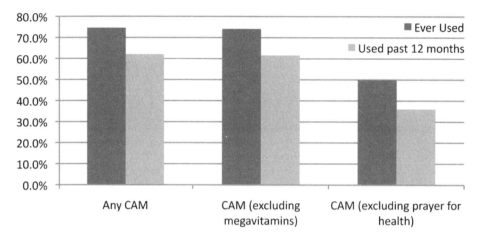

Figure 1.1 CAM Use by U.S. Adults: 2002

Graph created from information found at National Center for Complementary and Alternative Medicine, Complementary and Alternative Medicine Use in the United States, http://nccam.nih.gov/news/camstats/2002/graphics2002.htm (last visited Oct. 22, 2009).

cans paid more out-of-pocket for alternative medical care than for hospitalizations in 1997. *See* David M. Eisenberg et al., *Trends in Alternative Medicine Use in the United States, 1990–1997: Results of a Follow-Up National Survey*, 280 JAMA 1569 (1998). Limited to English-speaking individuals and now over ten years old, the study is just an estimate of CAM use in the U.S. Figure 1.1 illustrates more recent estimates of CAM use.

In addition to consumers, Congress was also increasingly aware of the presence of alternative medical therapies during the early to mid-1990s. In 1992, with a budget of just $2 million, the Office of Alternative Medicine (OAM) was created within the National Institutes of Health (NIH). That budget grew to $50 million in 1999 when the OAM was upgraded to an NIH center, the National Center for Complementary and Alternative Medicine (NCCAM). One of the twenty-seven centers making up the NIH, NCCAM's mission is to "explore complementary and alternative healing practices in the context of rigorous science, train complementary and alternative medicine researchers, and disseminate authoritative information to the public and professionals."

Some medical schools have also taken to teaching selected CAM therapies to future M.D.s, suggesting a relaxation of the historically tense relationship between conventional and unconventional medical practitioners. For example, the University of Arizona offers a full program in integrative medicine with a primary goal of contributing "rigorous scientific research on the integration of complementary and alternative therapies with conventional medicine." While the mission statements of both the NCCAM and the University of Arizona Program in Integrative Medicine propose inclusion of complementary and alternative medicine in the health care system, they also advocate for rigorous scientific testing. This remains a point of contention for some CAM practitioners who feel that their healing methods cannot be fully understood or explained using the scientific method.

One possible reason for the rise in required and elective CAM courses in medical schools is that, as consumers of health care continue to use a number of these therapies, medical doctors are pushed to learn more about them in order to educate their patients and avoid dangerous drug interactions. A more CAM-friendly position regarding its inclusion in medical schools goes beyond mere avoidance of its possible dangers and into acceptance that CAM may have something unique to offer, such as increased patient involvement in the healing process and heightened cultural competence on the part of the physician.

B. Why Are More People Using CAM?

What is responsible for the growing presence and increasing tolerance of CAM in the U.S. health care system? A common belief is that patients seek out complementary or alternative medicine because of dissatisfaction with traditional medical care. Somewhat surprisingly, current research has found no relationship between CAM use and discontent with conventional care. First, national studies show that in both 1990 and 1997, 96% of individuals who visited a CAM practitioner also saw a medical doctor during the previous year, suggesting that the use of different therapies is more complementary than it is alternative. This would indicate, at least, that while patients may be supplementing their traditional medical care, they are not dissatisfied enough to abandon it. Second, patients report that the use of complementary therapies is more about congruence with personal beliefs, values and life perspectives. In testing three hypotheses as to what sociocultural and personal factors might predict use of alternative therapies, researchers found that dissatisfaction with conventional care and a desire to be in control of their health were not indicative of alternative therapy use. Conversely, holistic views of health and a belief that the treatments promote health rather than just focusing on illness were strong predictors of alternative therapy use. *See* John A. Astin, *Why Patients Use Alternative Medicine: Results of a National Study*, 279 JAMA 1548 (1998).

A variety of core beliefs appear to draw people toward CAM, including holism, vitalism, spirituality, and different perspectives on the meanings of health and healing. Holism asserts that the whole is greater than the sum of its parts. The idea of holism as it applies to health is that the mind, body and spirit are all connected and that the health of one part cannot be viewed separately from the others. This concept is so central to many CAM therapies that CAM is often referred to as holistic medicine. Vitalism is the belief that there is a life-energy running through the body. In traditional Chinese medicine, this is known as the Qi (pronounced "chee"). Spirituality provides a source of motivation within human beings, which many CAM therapies view as crucial to the healing process. These core beliefs reinforce each other and produce a unique perspective on health and healing that many individuals find appealing. *See* Michael S. Goldstein, *The Emerging Socioeconomic and Political Support for Alternative Medicine in the United States*, 583 Annals Am. Acad. Pol. & Soc. Sci. 44, 47–48 (2002).

Another possible reason for the acceptance of CAM in the health care system is the need to reduce expenditures. Rising health care costs have prompted the government, insurance companies and physicians to encourage their patients to engage in healthier lifestyles. As Figure 1.2 reveals, many of the conditions for which CAM therapies are used are conditions that can be fairly unresponsive to conventional medicine. These chronic conditions cost the health care system billions of dollars annually. Many CAM practitioners and patients believe that CAM is both a more effective treatment for the patient and a more cost-effective route for the health care system.

The NCCAM's exponentially increasing budget is both evidence of CAM's rising popularity and one of the reasons behind it. As people gain confidence in the safety and efficacy of CAM therapies, they become more curious about giving them a try; as more people try them, the demand for evidence of their safety and efficacy rises.

Figure 1.2 Diseases/Conditions for Which CAM is Most Frequently Used: 2007
(These figures excluded the use of megavitamin therapy and prayer)

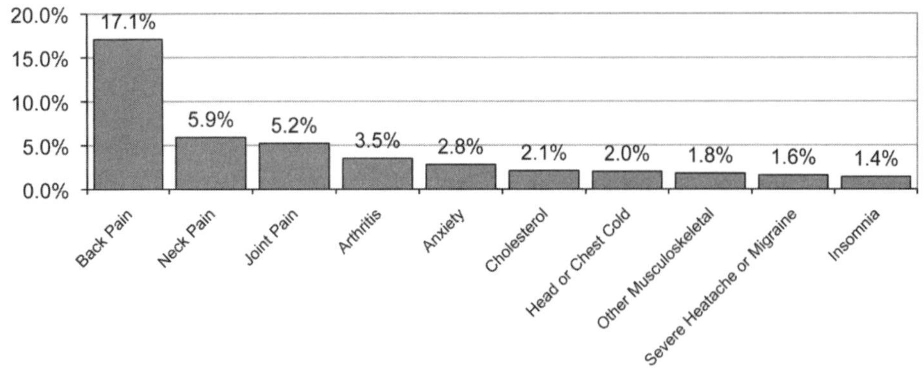

Condition	Percentage
Back Pain	17.1%
Neck Pain	5.9%
Joint Pain	5.2%
Arthritis	3.5%
Anxiety	2.8%
Cholesterol	2.1%
Head or Chest Cold	2.0%
Other Musculoskeletal	1.8%
Severe Headache or Migraine	1.6%
Insomnia	1.4%

Graph created from information found at National Center for Complementary and Alternative Medicine, Disease/Conditions for Which CAM is Most Frequently Used Among Adults—2002, http://nccam.nih.gov/news/camstats/2007/72_dpi_CHARTS/chart6.htm (last visited Oct. 22, 2009).

II. What Is Complementary and Alternative Medicine?

A. Definitions

In the beginning, complementary and alternative medical practitioners were called "irregulars"; their conventional counterparts were, of course, the "regulars." It has been called unorthodox, quackery, unconventional and holistic; today it is both complementary *and* alternative, with buzz-words like integrative. The ever-changing terminology elucidates the shifting perceptions toward this collection of healing philosophies and techniques. The less contentious names indicate a growing tolerance, if not acceptance, of CAM within part of the medical community.

The current terminology also denotes two different ways that individuals choose to use an unconventional healing modality: when used in collaboration with conventional medicine, the therapy is said to be *complementary*; when used in place of conventional medicine, the therapy is called *alternative*. The same therapy can be considered either complementary or alternative depending on the personal choice of the individual using that therapy, and the determination of whether something is complementary medicine or alternative medicine is always made based on whether conventional medicine is also being used to treat the individual. For example, in the introduction to this chapter we spoke of a young man using acupuncture along with conventional medical treatment for a herniated disc. The acupuncture in that scenario is complementary to the treatment of his medical doctor; remove the medical doctor from the situation and the acupuncture becomes an alternative treatment.

The term "CAM" encompasses a number of therapies that are highly diverse, both in their location and time of origin, as well as their philosophies of health and healing. Consider the practices of acupuncture and homeopathy: the former is an ancient healing art from East Asia which focuses on the free flow of vital life energy; the latter is

> **Box 1.1 CAM and Cancer Treatment**
>
> *When Olivia was diagnosed with breast cancer in 1990, she made the decision to include a number of "natural" therapies, along with conventional medicine, in her treatment plan. She used herbs, homeopathy, massage, and yoga. She turned to acupuncture to help with the nausea associated with chemotherapy and meditation to keep her thoughts positive. She described her use of integrative medicine as empowering and good for her spirit.*
>
> Olivia is not alone; some studies have shown that CAM use is particularly high in patients with cancer. Whole diets are a CAM modality frequently used by patients with cancer.
>
> One highly controversial treatment method is the **Gerson Therapy**, which includes:
>
> - a vegetarian diet with high consumption of raw fruit and vegetable juices,
> - vitamin supplements,
> - frequent detoxification of tissues and blood through the use of coffee enemas, and
> - a long list of restricted foods, including salt, coffee, tea, chocolate, alcohol, refined sugar, refined flour, canned and frozen foods, and all fats and oils.
>
> While a significant percentage of CAM use is unsupervised "self care" (which can be of particular risk with cancer patients), several nationally recognized cancer centers now integrate CAM therapies into treatment plans. The Dana-Faber Cancer Institute's Zalcim Center for Integrated Therapies, which treats with massage therapy, acupuncture, and nutritional guidance is one example.

traced back to Eighteenth-Century Germany and follows the belief that minute doses of substances, which would induce illness in a healthy individual, would actually cure a sick patient. The term "Complementary and Alternative Medicine" creates one very large umbrella in order to cover both of these distinct practices. The problem of defining CAM may account for some variation in studies regarding its prevalence. For example, some research studies include prayer or yoga in their definition of CAM, while others do not. Also, some surveys ask only about use of alternative therapies for a particular symptom or illness, thereby excluding discussion about use of alternative therapies for general wellness. For this reason, it is important when reading statistics about CAM use to recognize how the researcher established the scope of his study by what he included in his definition of CAM.

Perhaps the most useful definition of CAM comes from NCCAM, a part of the NIH which defines it as "a group of diverse medical and health care systems, practices, and products that are not presently considered to be part of conventional medicine." Conventional medicine is then defined as the kind practiced by Medical Doctors (M.D.s), Doctors of Osteopathy (D.O.s), and allied health professionals, such as physical therapists, psychologists, and registered nurses.

This definition creates a flexible dichotomy between conventional medicine and all other forms of healing by allowing therapies to transition from one group to the other. Moreover, the definition itself recognizes the importance of time and the possibility of transition; "not *presently* considered" indicates that a therapy may have previously been, or might in the future be, considered conventional medicine—it is the therapy's present characterization that matters. To illustrate, if chiropractors were to become viewed as al-

> **Box 1.2 In One Section of Beth Israel Hospital, Some Patients Are Saying 'Om,' Not 'Ah'**
>
> By Anemona Hartocollis
>
> Medical advances sometimes happen in strange ways. Someone finds a fungus in dirty lab dishes and—eureka!—Penicillin is born. Now a premier Manhattan hospital is turning a cancer-treatment floor over to a world famous fashion designer in the hope that serendipity, science and intuition will strike again.
>
> A foundation run by Donna Karan, creator of the "seven easy pieces" philosophy of women's wardrobes and founder of the much-imitated DKNY line of clothing, has donated $850,000 for a yearlong experiment combining Eastern and Western healing methods at Beth Israel Medical Center. Instead of just letting a celebrated donor adopt a hospital wing, renovate it and have her name embossed on a plaque, the Karan-Beth Israel project will have a celebrated donor turn a hospital into a testing ground for a trendy, medically controversial notion: that yoga, meditation and aromatherapy can enhance regimens of chemotherapy and radiation.
>
> On Wednesday, Dr. Shulkin, who had never done yoga before, joined Ms. Karan and about 60 Beth Israel employees on the floor of her late husband's West Village art studio for an hour of yoga poses, finishing off with "om" and the recorded sound of bells.
>
> "They didn't teach us that in medical school," Dr. Shulkin said afterward, still sitting barefoot on his black mat, swearing he had put his BlackBerry on "meditation mode" and had not checked it. Asked if the yoga had worked, he formed his answer carefully: "I think the personal touch and the personal attention to the patient absolutely works."
>
> N.Y. Times, Oct. 30, 2008, at A31.

lied health professionals, they would move from the CAM category to the conventional medicine category, regardless of their historical classification as CAM practitioners. Another example, which we will discuss in more detail later in this chapter, is osteopathy. Notice that, today, D.O.s are considered conventional medicine practitioners. This was not always the case. Osteopathy is an example of a formerly alternative practice that has become conventional.

A different approach to the CAM designation stems from the historic tension between homeopathy and conventional medicine. For instance, it is sometimes thought that CAM is any medical practice or philosophy other than allopathy. Allopathic medicine is a term used to refer to the system of medicine practiced by medical doctors (M.D.s). A definition of CAM which creates a CAM-allopathy dichotomy is problematic because not all non-allopathic practices are considered CAM. For example, osteopathy is not allopathy, nor is it properly categorized as CAM. The allopathy-CAM dichotomy is much more rigid than the conventional medicine-CAM distinction present in the NCCAM definition because allopathy cannot easily be re-defined, whereas the concept of conventional medicine can. Furthermore, use of the term "allopathy" to refer to traditional biomedicine was actually coined by the founder of homeopathy, Samuel Hahnemann, as part of the verbal warfare between homeopathy and conventional medicine. The word homeopathy comes from the Greek roots for "like" and "suffering," signifying the homeopathic principle of "like cures like." Hahnemann also coined the term allopathy for "other" and "suffering" to signify the two medical theories as distinct and exclusive doctrines. Although the term "allopath" may be used interchangeably with medical doctor in cases and commentary, it has not been widely accepted by the medical community because of this cultural subtext. The most common use of the term, as it is used here, is to distinguish this type of mainstream medicine from both osteopathy and all CAM therapies.

One final definition of alternative medicine sometime referenced in outside readings but that may be problematic is: "interventions neither taught widely in medical schools nor generally available in U.S. hospitals." First, note that this definition was written at a time when all of CAM was referred to simply as "alternative medicine;" it is not attempting to define alternative medicine as distinct from complementary medicine. Second, this definition appears outdated now that many U.S. medical schools do offer training in such therapies. Taken on its face, this definition might now exclude massage therapy or acupuncture from CAM, as those therapies are now available to patients in many U.S. hospitals.

In summary, CAM is a wide and varying category of healing methods which can be very difficult to define. For purposes of this text, we will use the NCCAM definition of CAM. Additionally, the NCCAM provides a few other definitions and breakdowns which are useful for understanding complementary and alternative medicine. *Whole Medical Systems* are complete systems of medical theory and practice. Naturopathy and homeopathy are examples of whole medical systems. The systems have unique philosophies regarding the cause and treatment of illness and are often used as alternatives to allopathy or osteopathy. Whole medical systems are in contrast to specific treatments or individual practices, such as the use of herbal teas or dietary supplements.

NCCAM divides CAM into four major categories: *manipulative* and *body-based practices*, *biologically based practices*, *mind-body medicine*, and *energy medicine*. These four categories may include whole medical systems or individual practices. See Table 1.1 on page 10 for explanations and examples of these categories.

B. Overview of CAM Modalities

While there may be hundreds of healing practices that fit under the NCCAM's definition of CAM, let us now explore the histories and philosophies of those practices that have developed a strong presence in the U.S. health care system.

Osteopathy

Osteopathic medicine is a whole medical system that emphasizes the musculoskeletal system, including the nerves, muscles and bones. Today, osteopathic medicine enjoys a place parallel to that of allopathic medicine in the U.S. health care system. The lack of mention in most current reference books on complementary and alternative medicine is just one piece of evidence to indicate osteopathy's transition to mainstream medicine. D.O.s, like M.D.s, go through rigorous post-graduate training and hold unrestricted licenses to perform surgery and prescribe medicine. As late as 1955, however, the American Medical Association (AMA) described the practice as "cultist healing." Not until 1973 were D.O.s licensed in all fifty states. The history of osteopathy and its rise to professionalism thus offer important insights into how a medical philosophy is rejected or accepted in the United States.

Table 1.1 The Four Domains of Complementary and Alternative Medicine

CAM Domain	Explanation	Examples
Manipulative, Body-Based Practices	Focus on the structure of the body, particularly the bones and joints	Osteopathy, chiropractic, massage therapy
Biologically Based Practices	Involves the use of naturally occurring substances, such as botanicals, vitamins, minerals and amino acids	Herbal and dietary supplements, megavitamins, whole diets, chelation therapy
Mind-Body Practices	Emphasizes the connection between the mind and the body and the importance of the mind in treating illness; also used to promote general wellness and to reduce stress	Spirituality, prayer, meditation, imagery
Energy Medicine	Veritable energy medicine works to affect the measurable energies surrounding the body, such as light, sound, and magnetism	Magnetic therapy, sound energy therapy, light therapy
	Putative energy medicine works to affect the seemingly immeasurable life-force energies surrounding the body, such as the Qi in traditional Chinese medicine or the Ki in Japanese Kampo	Reiki, therapeutic touch, acupuncture

Osteopathy (from the Greek words for "bone" and "sickness") was founded by Andrew Taylor Still, a self-taught healer who reportedly lost all confidence in conventional medicine after the deaths of three of his children to spinal meningitis. Still believed that disease was caused by misplaced bones interfering with blood flow and that the drugs and procedures used by allopaths were useless. He rejected all other forms of medicine and began practicing bone setting exclusively in 1874, believing it to be an effective treatment for asthma, headaches and kidney disease—essentially a wide variety of ailments. In 1892, Still established the American School of Osteopathy and helped found the American Osteopathic Association five years later. Enrollment in the school quickly grew to several hundred students and at least 10 more schools opened across the country by the turn of the century. Also spreading across the country were sham-schools, offering to teach osteopathy in just a few short lessons. This educational blemish did little to help D.O.s legitimize themselves in the eyes of allopathic physicians, who already viewed D.O.s as crude masseurs with no scientific rationale behind their practice.

Early on, osteopaths faced numerous legal battles, most commonly charged for the unlicensed practice of medicine. The first of these took place in 1893 in Red Wing, Minnesota, where Still's son, Charles, had been called to practice during the height of a diphtheria epidemic. Despite his reportedly successful treatment of dozens of children, the State Board of Health had him arrested for practicing without a license. The M.D. who brought the suit failed to appear in court and the issue was dropped. Matters of this kind persisted, but courts regularly rejected the idea that osteopathy constituted the practice of medicine, as it consisted primarily of manual manipulation at the time; the osteopaths were free to practice so long as they did not use drugs or surgery. It is difficult to say whether this was victory for the osteopaths because although they were allowed to continue their practice, their practice was not publicly recognized as medicine.

The most important occurrence in the recent history of osteopathy occurred in California in 1961. Compared to other states, D.O.s were highly successful in California in the decades before the 1960s. They were also highly segmented. A large group of osteopaths desiring equality with the allopathic physicians in the state regarded themselves as more scientific than traditional osteopaths. At the same time, M.D.s were developing the idea that the best way to beat the osteopaths would be to absorb them. After years of discussions between the California Osteopathic Association (COA) and the California Medical Association (CMA), the CMA converted the osteopathic school in Los Angeles to an allopathic school and authorized the school to grant the degree of Medical Doctor to past graduates who were licensed and practicing as D.O.s in the state. The desire to be seen as equals in the community made this a difficult offer for the osteopaths to refuse. That year, more than 2,000 D.O.s in California paid sixty-five dollars to change their title to M.D. This assertion of equality and the struggle to be accepted caused them to lose some of the unique identity that distinguished them from allopaths. For further discussion of the history of osteopathic medicine in the United States, *see* NORMAN GEVITZ, THE D.O.s: OSTEOPATHIC MEDICINE IN AMERICA (J. Hopkins Univ. Press 2004) (1982).

Osteopathy in its original form consisted mainly of manual manipulation of the spine. Today, the practice of osteopathy only slightly resembles the vision of its founder. Originally a drugless healing method, osteopaths now have full privileges to prescribe medication and perform surgery, and they have adopted a number of diagnostic and treatment procedures commonly used by allopathic physicians. Osteopaths, like allopaths, are also free to become board certified in specialty areas. The specialized training on the musculoskeletal system, the use of osteopathic manipulation therapy, and a focus on the whole body are now the primary characteristics distinguishing D.O.s from M.D.s. Many M.D.s would argue, however, that the latter is not a defining characteristic of D.O.s at all, as they too are concerned with the whole body. According to the American Osteopathic Association (AOA), there were approximately 53,000 practicing D.O.s in the United States in 2006. A majority of these were engaged in family medicine or primary care. There are currently 23 osteopathic medical colleges in the country.

Chiropractic

If there was one thing the osteopaths and the allopaths could agree on in the early Nineteenth Century, it was their mutual dislike of chiropractic therapy. Chiropractic (from the Greek words for "hand" and "practice") was founded in 1895 by Daniel David (D.D.) Palmer, who, like Still, believed that spinal manipulation was the key to wellness. Palmer, however, thought that disease was the result of nerve restriction rather than interference with blood flow. Known as "the Discoverer," Palmer opened the first Chiropractic School in 1897. In its second year, a handful of students were actually M.D.s seeking training in new techniques.

As with other therapies, internal dissension erupted over the purity of the practice. "Broad view" chiropractors, or "mixers," believed in a broader range of therapeutic practices and adopted a number of techniques, such as vibration and electrical stimulation, to use in conjunction with spinal manipulation. This outraged the purist chiropractors, called "straights," who believed solely in the simple manipulations done by hand, as first developed by Palmer. Also contributing to the internal discord was a bit of family rivalry. Palmer's son, Bartlett Joshua (B.J.), a.k.a. "the Developer," followed in his father's footsteps and, after his graduation from the original school in 1902, the two formed a partnership. B.J. then successfully maneuvered for complete control of the school and went so far as to not let his father set foot on the school grounds. B.J. had a strong interest in the commercial aspects of chiropractic and added business training to the school's curriculum. His encouragement that chiropractors should advertise their services helped to increase public awareness of the practice and ensure chiropractic's place in the American health care system. B.J.'s commercialism was also his downfall. Although he claimed to be a "straight" like his father, in 1924, B.J. introduced a device called the neurocalometer to the practice. The device supposedly measured the amount of heat released by nerves. B.J. leased the devices to chiropractors for an advance of $1,000 and monthly payments of $10 for a minimum of ten years. Although two-thousand chiropractors signed up for the device in the first year, many more saw the device as a money-grabbing ploy and rejected B.J. for it.

Despite a tumultuous history and attacks from both M.D.s and D.O.s, chiropractic practice persevered. Today, chiropractic practice enjoys greater insurance coverage than other CAM therapies, including Medicare coverage, Medicaid coverage in many states, and coverage under all state workers' compensation systems. A 2002 survey estimated that 20% of American adults had received chiropractic care at some time in their lives. Chiropractic care is sought mainly for treatment of lower back pain. Chiropractic care most often entails spinal adjustments using the hands, but sometimes involves other therapeutic treatments, such as heat and ice, dietary supplements, or electrical stimulation. Chiropractic practitioners must earn a Doctor of Chiropractic (D.C.) degree from a college accredited by the Council on Chiropractic Education, which is a 4-year postgraduate program. There are approximately 60,000 licensed chiropractic practitioners in the United States, outnumbering their conventional counterparts, the D.O.s, by approximately 7,000. For further examination of the history of chiropractic as well as its current unique place in the U.S. health care system, *see* Ted J. Kaptchuk & David M. Eisenberg, *Chiropractic: Origins, Controversies, and Contributions*, 158 ARCHIVES INTERNAL MED. 2215–2224 (1998); William C. Meeker & Scott Haldeman, *Chiropractic: A Profession at the Crossroads of Mainstream and Alternative Medicine*, 136 ANNALS INTERNAL MED. 216–227 (2002).

Massage Therapy

In addition to osteopathy and chiropractic, there is a third type of body manipulation practice which may fall under the purview of "CAM": massage therapy. This type of manipulation focuses on the muscles and soft tissues, rather than the bones and joints. The application of pressure to the tissue is intended to increase the flow of blood and oxygen to the area so as to decrease pain. In some forms of massage, such a shiatsu, pressure is applied in order to promote healthy circulation of the Qi, a vital life energy. The physiological effects of massage are not completely understood, but it is generally agreed that stress can worsen some diseases and conditions and that massage may improve health by reducing stress. Other biomedical theories regarding the effect of massage are also being studied, including blockage of pain signals, impact on the sympathetic (fight or flight) and the parasympathetic (rest and digest) nervous systems, stimulation of endorphins, and flow of the lymph (a fluid that travels through the lymphatic system carrying cells that fight disease).

Massage therapy has roots in countries around the world and dates back thousands of years. Consistent with its diverse origins, the term "massage" refers broadly to over 80 different techniques, including Swedish massage, shiatsu, deep tissue massage, and sports massage. Per Hendrik Ling, who, during the Eighteenth Century, developed what is now known as Swedish massage, believed that vigorous massage could improve blood circulation. During the late Nineteenth and early Twentieth Centuries, massage enjoyed a place within the medical community and was used in many different branches of medicine. As medicine grew more complex, however, it moved steadily away from massage. After a wane in interest in the mid Twentieth Century, massage regained popularity in the 1970s, particularly amongst athletes. This resurgence of massage took place outside of medicine in the form of specialized massage schools, professional organizations, and the development of private practices through independent entrepreneurs. Robert Noah Calvert, author of massage, argues that massage came into its golden age as a distinct healing art because of technological advances in medicine—as medicine and technology advanced, the need for human contact also grew.

Today, massage is used for a variety of conditions including sports injuries, stress, anxiety, pain, and to aid in general wellness through increased relaxation. Chair massages are often offered by schools and employers to improve the health of students and employees. Massage is sometimes accompanied with other therapies such as aromatherapy (the use of essential plant oils) and reflexology (in which it is believed that "reflex zones" of the foot correspond to different parts of the body and manipulation of those zones will relieve discomfort or disease in the matching body part). There are over 1,000 education and training programs for massage therapy in the United States today. These programs typically last six months to one year. Despite high numbers of graduates, it is estimated that about half of students who complete a massage training program do not go on to practice massage.

Regulation of the profession originated as an effort to control prostitution, which has been linked to massage for thousands of years. Some states have very little regulation of massage that go beyond this effort, while other states do go further by regulating the education standards and scope of practice for massage therapists. States require varying degrees of licensure or certification for massage therapists. For this reason, there are also a variety of names that one may see to refer to a massage therapist, including: Licensed Massage Therapist (LMT), Licensed Massage Practitioner (LMP), or Certified Massage Therapist (CMT).

Homeopathy

Perhaps the most difficult therapy for traditional medicine to accept or understand (and yet the most popular of the alternative therapies in the latter half of the Nineteenth Century) is homeopathy, a whole medical system based on the "law of similars." The principle philosophy of homeopathy is that illness can be cured by minuscule doses of a substance that would induce the same symptoms in a healthy individual. Dilution entails mixing one grain of the therapeutic substance with 99 grains of milk sugar and then mixing 1 grain of the resulting compound with another 99 grains of milk sugar. This process is performed a total of 30 times, until the diluted mixture contains only 1/1060 grain of the original therapeutic substance.

Homeopathy was introduced in the U.S. by Hans Gram in 1825. The concept of dilution attracted immediate ridicule from allopathic physicians for its implausibility. Despite this, homeopathy appealed to many at the time because it was cheaper than conventional medicine and considerably less repugnant than the conventional remedies of the time, such as bleeding or vomit-inducing tonics. After all but disappearing in the early 1900s, homeopathy resurged in the 1980s. Domestic homeopathy kits have allowed individuals to practice homeopathy in their homes by assisting them with the characterization of the symptoms and choosing the single substance that would best treat those symptoms. The individual can then go to a pharmacy or health food store, many of which have fairly extensive collections of homeopathic remedies, to purchase the remedy without a prescription. An increase in the number of people using homeopathy and the simultaneous decrease in the number visiting homeopathic practitioners suggests that home use is at least partially responsible for the revival of homeopathy in the U.S.

Currently, homeopathic practitioners receive training through diploma or certification programs. Homeopathy is often practiced in conjunction with other CAM therapies for which the practitioner is licensed, such as naturopathy or acupuncture. Three states, Arizona, Connecticut, and Nevada, license doctors for homeopathy.

Naturopathy

Naturopathy is a biologically-based practice that was developed by German-born Benedict Lust shortly after he contracted tuberculosis during his first visit to New York in the early 1890s. Fearing that the doctors in America would only make him worse, he returned to Germany where he met Sebastian Kneipp. Kneipp had developed the healing practice of "hardening," whereby vigor was restored through cold water baths and barefoot walks in the snow. Following this encounter with "Kneippism," Lust returned to New York in full health, vowing to bring the healing techniques he had learned in Germany to America. By 1901, he had come to call his collection of water-cures and diet and exercise programs "naturopathy" (literally meaning "nature disease"). The philosophy of naturopathy is that disease is an attack of the body on its self and that nature's innate healing power can be assisted by various activities such as hiking in the mountains before breakfast, consuming lacto-ovo vegetarian meals, and taking various baths, including mud baths.

Along with the early forms of osteopathy and chiropractic, naturopathy is considered a drugless healing method. It emphasizes use of the most natural, least invasive remedies for treating illness. Licensed naturopathic physicians in the U.S. earn a Doctor of Naturopathic Medicine (N.D.) degree from one of four accredited naturopathic medical schools in the country. During this program, naturopaths also study acupuncture and homeopathy. Fifteen states, the District of Columbia and the U.S. territories of Puerto Rico and the Virgin Islands formally regulate naturopathic physicians in varying capacities. Traditional naturopaths, as opposed to N.D.s, focus mainly on wellness and disease-prevention education. A 2002 survey estimated that only 0.9% of the adult population in the U.S. had ever used naturopathy.

Dietary and Herbal Supplements

Dietary Supplements, as defined under the Dietary Supplement Health and Education Act of 1994, are products "intended to supplement the diet" and that contain "one or more of the following: vitamins, minerals, herbs or other botanicals, amino acids, or any combination of the above ingredients." Some uses of dietary supplements are considered conventional medicine. For example, physicians have found that the vitamin folic acid prevents the birth defect spina bifida. Conventional physicians use vitamin supplements in the prenatal care of pregnant women. According to NCCAM, the use of supplements becomes CAM when the supplement has not been proven effective for a particular use through scientific study. One example of this is taking large doses of vitamin C to prevent a cold, even

> **Box 1.3 Whole Diets**
>
> Another dietary aspect of CAM is the use of special "whole diets" to achieve overall health. For some, whole diets are simply the decision not to eat meat or dairy for whatever reason. For others, a whole diet is a balance of the types of the foods they consume that is different from the average American and what is recommended in the "food pyramid." Some examples:
>
> Atkins Diet: 15% carbohydrate, 35% protein, 50% fat; recommended for weight loss only
>
> Ornish Diet: 75% carbohydrate, 15% protein, 10% fat; vegetarian
>
> Pritikin Diet: Similar to Ornish diet with increased emphasis on fiber and water consumption
>
> Zone Diet: 40% Carbohydrate, 30% protein, 30% fat; claims to help prevent heart disease, high blood pressure and diabetes
>
> Macrobiotic Diet: 50–60% whole grains; fish, beans, and local fruits are staples of this diet; low-fat, high fiber diet often followed by people with cancer or other chronic conditions

though such a "remedy" or preventative strategy has not been proven through scientific study. Consider how this fits with the NCCAM definition of CAM—in this case, evidence from scientific study is allowing some uses of dietary supplements to fit into the conventional medicine category, while the lack thereof is keeping other uses in the CAM category.

Spirituality

National health surveys reveal that while CAM is most often used for back and neck problems, head or chest colds, joint pain, anxiety and depression, the most commonly utilized CAM therapy is spiritual healing or prayer. While "spirituality" is typically defined as "the quality or state of being spiritual" and "spiritual" as "relating to sacred matters," spiritual CAM practices include both secular and religious modalities.

Secular practices include Transcendental Meditation (TM), Therapeutic Touch, self directed "mindfulness mediation," energy healing, Reiki Imagery, and other mind-body healing exercises. Of course, these practices can be used as part of a religious tradition as well. Transcendental Mediation, for example, is traditionally tied to oriental medicine, but practiced today by both secular and religious persons.

Religious CAM practices are widely accepted as well. These range from the prayers associated with mainline Western religions to the work of shaman, medicine men, and Christian Science healers. A Centers for Disease Control and Prevention (CDC) study found that nearly half of adults prayed for their own health during the preceding year. Almost five percent—which is roughly that same percent that utilize acupuncture—participated in a prayer based healing ritual during their lives. *See* Patricia M. Barnes et al., *Complementary and Alternative Medicine Among Adults; United States*, 2002 ADVANCED DATA FROM VITAL AND HEALTH STATISTICS No. 242 (May 2004). Definitions of the varied spiritual healing practices (as well as others CAM modalities) are described in NIH's ALTERNATIVE MEDICINE, EXPANDING MEDICAL HORIZONS: A REPORT TO THE NATIONAL INSTITUTES OF HEALTH ON ALTERNATIVE MEDICAL SYSTEMS AND PRACTICES IN THE

UNITED STATES 136–37 (Sept. 1992). For a broad discussion of spiritual healing, *see* Michael H. Cohen, *Healing at the Borderland of Medicine and Religion: Regulating Potential Abuse of Authority By Spiritual Healers*, 18 J.L. & RELIGION 373 (2002–03).

Recently, much has been written regarding whether there is an impact from spirituality on health outcomes. *See e.g.*, LARRY DOSSEY, HEALING WORDS: THE POWER OF PRAYER AND THE PRACTICE OF MEDICINE, 166–67 (Harper S.F. 1993); Dale Matthews et al., *Effects of Intercessory Prayer on Patients with Rheumatoid Arthritis*, 93 S. MED. J. 1138, 1177–86 (2000); Randolph C. Byrd, *Positive Therapeutic Effects of Intercessory Prayer in a Coronary Care Unit Population*, 81 S. MED. J. 815, 826–29 (July 1988). Pat Fosarelli, a physician and minister, summarized current literature in a recent article for the Journal of the American Medical Association (JAMA):

> There are numerous articles, both pro and con, about including spirituality in medical care. In addition, numerous studies have examined the association of spiritual beliefs and practices with health outcomes overall and for specific diseases. However, because of poorly defined variables, fluid end points, and confounding variables, some of these studies are so poorly conceived and executed that they provide little, if any, meaningful information. ... Because spirituality is non-logical and the science of medicine is highly logical, scientific ways of measuring "spirituality" (if it can be measured at all) can yield results that are confusing at best or erroneous at worst.

Pat Fosarelli, *Medicine, Spirituality, and Patient Care*, 300 JAMA 836–38 (2008).

Despite lack of scientific measurement, conventional medicine has increasingly integrated spiritual healing practices. A recent survey of 19 Integrative Health Care Centers found that nearly every one included a "mind-body" provider. While the term encompassed professionals ranging from psychologist to "healing touch therapist" and "spiritual counselor," the acceptance was far greater than that accorded chiropractors, massage therapists, and naturopaths. Michael H. Cohen & Andrea Hrbek et al., *Emerging Credentialing Practices*, 165 ARCHIVES INTERNAL MED. 289–95 (2005). Perhaps these health care practitioners are heeding the words of Hippocrates, who said, "Prayer indeed is good ... but while calling on the gods, a man should himself lend a hand."

Acupuncture

Acupuncture, an ancient form of energy medicine originating in China more than 2,000 years ago, was rediscovered by the American public after *New York Times* reporter James Reston wrote about his own experience with acupuncture during a visit to Peking in 1971. The front-page story documented Reston's appendectomy at a hospital in Beijing. Traditional anesthesia was used during the operation but, on the second night following the surgery, acupuncture was used to relieve Reston's abdominal discomfort. His report of its effective treatment of his pain peaked the interest of the American public. Intriguing photographs and stories of miraculous recovery proliferated in the popular media. When President Nixon visited China accompanied by his personal medical and osteopathic physicians, they returned with astounding reports of major surgeries being performed with nothing more than acupuncture to relieve the pain, American physicians took notice.

The most common form of acupuncture in the United States is the stimulation of points on the body with thin needles. The practice is based on the Chinese belief that health is maintained by the free circulation of a universal life energy called the Qi, which flows along pathways of the body called meridians. Accordingly, the needles are placed at intersections of the meridians in order to relieve blockages in the circulation of the Qi. Another central tenant of acupuncture is the yin-yang polarity theory, in which the body is seen as a balance between the yin, a cold and passive principle, and the yang, a hot and active principle. Health is maintained through proper internal balance of the yin and yang, which is achieved by a well-flowing Qi.

Today, acupuncture is not as firmly established in American medicine as the boom in the 1970s would have suggested. The concepts of yin and yang, meridians, and the Qi are not easily molded to fit the biomedical rubric to which American physicians adhere and attempts to explain the physiological effects of acupuncture through the placebo theory have been largely unsuccessful because of the difficulty in creating a double-blind test for the practice. Western science, however, has incorporated theories from neuroscience to explain the practice, arguing that the needles stimulate nerves and activate the body's natural painkillers. For the most part, the medical community has retained control over acupuncture, even if physicians are not the ones practicing it. Most states do require that acupuncture be performed under the supervision of a physician. In addition, most states require non-physician acupuncturists to pass an exam conducted by the National Certification Commission for Acupuncture and Oriental Medicine.

Midwifery

The topic of midwifery is unique in the discussion about complementary and alternative medicine because the practice is concerned solely with childbirth, a process that has long been considered "natural" or "non-medical," yet has been managed by medical practitioners since the early Twentieth Century. Unlike other conditions or ailments of the body, pregnancy can more readily be defined as outside the scope of medicine. So, how did childbirth come to be under the control of the medical community and where does that leave midwives today?

Scholars Dorothy and Richard Wertz recognize three distinct periods in the history of childbirth in America. First, there was "social childbirth." Running from the early Seventeenth to the mid-Eighteenth Century, this period involved a community responsibility for women to assist their family, friends, and neighbors in childbirth. The 1750s through much of the Nineteenth Century was a transitory period in which physicians began to enter the field of obstetrics. Finally, from the late Nineteenth Century to more recent times, the medical community affirmed their authority over childbirth. *See* RICHARD W. WERTZ & DOROTHY C. WERTZ, LYING-IN: A HISTORY OF CHILDBIRTH IN AMERICA (Expanded ed. Yale Univ. Press 1989).

Midwives in colonial America were not just accepted, but respected in the community. Some who were unfortunate to attend the birth of a stillborn or a baby with physical deformities, however, were thought to be practicing witchcraft. Midwives monopolized the area of childbirth both because the process was considered natural and not necessitating any medical or surgical expertise and because it was improper for a man to be present at the lying-in. Physicians were called upon only in the case of emergency. In fact, of the few regulations placed on midwives during the 1700s, one was that a man not be present unless necessity demanded. Midwives were informally educated at this time; a woman who had given birth herself and had witnessed and assisted in a few could then hold herself out as a midwife. In the spirit of community responsibility, midwives were to assist any woman in labor, rich or poor.

Perhaps the most pivotal moment in the history of midwifery in America was the popularization of the obstetric forceps around the 1750s. As childbirth became more "scientific," male physicians became more involved. Female midwives often could not afford the device or find a physician willing to train them in how to use it. Formal medical education being restricted to male students, female midwives were systematically excluded from the medical developments that would come to take over their practices. The opinion that pregnancy was riskier than previously thought gained momentum. As men came to be more included in the birthing process, particularly by urban middle and upper-class Americans, the argument that their presence was offensive or inappropriate lost its efficacy. In essence, safety trumped morality and physicians successfully argued that their presence was necessary for the safety of the mother and unborn child. This summary merely scratches the surface on the history of midwives and the tension between midwifery and obstetrics; for more on the subject, *see* JUDY BARRETT LITOFF, AMERICAN MIDWIVES: 1860 TO THE PRESENT (1978).

There are currently a few different types of midwives practicing in the United States. It is important to know how they are distinct from one another in order to understand the different licensing and scope of practice regulations that each face.

Certified Nurse Midwives (CNMs) hold at least a bachelor's degree and have completed both nursing and midwifery training. CNMs must pass national and state certification exams. Almost all CNMs practice in hospitals. The American College of Nurse Midwives (ACNM) is the professional organization covering CNMs.

Certified Midwives (CMs) must meet the same qualifications as a CNM, except that a CM is *not* a registered nurse. This is a new credential offered by the ACNM. As of 2007, it was recognized in only three states: New York, New Jersey, and Rhode Island.

Certified Professional Midwives (CPMs) are certified by the North American Registry of Midwives (NARM) after passing written exams and skill evaluations. This is not a degree or program-based credentialing process.

Direct-Entry or **Lay Midwives** may or may not be certified or have a college education. Their training may be through self-study, apprenticeship, workshops, formal instruction, or a combination. Direct-Entry midwives practice primarily in out-of-hospital settings or home births.

Doulas are birth companions who are with the family through the labor and birth and may even spend some time with the family during the days and weeks following the birth. Doulas are *not* midwives and do not perform any medical or clinical duties. The practice is worth mentioning, however, due to its growing popularity in the United States and the concerns that may arise with having a non-family member present at the delivery.

For an excellent discussion of the history of all of the above CAM modalities, *see* JAMES C. WHORTON, NATURE CURES: THE HISTORY OF ALTERNATIVE MEDICINE IN AMERICA (Oxford Univ. Press 2002).

C. CAM in Cultural Context

Healing practices from many different traditions are included in the broad definition of CAM. The World Health Organization estimates that between 65 and 80 percent of the world's health services constitute "traditional medicine." Examples of informal traditional medicine include body/mind medicine (including biofeedback and yoga), herbal medicine, traditional Chinese or Oriental medicine (including acupuncture), care provided by Tibetan and American Indian medicine people, and shamanism. While Complementary and Alternative Medicine courses may be new to American law and medical schools, many of these treatments long predate western medicine. Homeopathy remained essentially constant for 200 years. Acupuncture existed for 2,000.

Traditional healing only becomes "complementary" or "alternative" when introduced into conventional, western medicine. As the United States becomes increasingly diverse and immigrants and refugees who come here bring their traditional healing with them, our health care system faces a number of challenges. Health care outcomes for people of color are consistently worse than the outcomes of their white counterparts. Is this driven by use of CAM treatments rather than western medicine as some would argue? Or is part of the divide created by a lack of cultural competency and communication as others suggest? Perhaps CAM treatments continue to thrive because they cost less in a health care system that does not provide insurance for 16% of its population.

The legal issues which flow from these questions may involve First Amendment Freedom of Religion disputes because many traditional healing practices are intertwined with religious beliefs. We address some of these disputes in Chapter Two on Licensure. Insurance coverage for these treatments, often characterized as "experimental" and not "medically necessary" by payors, often results in legal disputes as well. Yet these same CAM providers, as we address in Chapter Four on Medical Malpractice, are far less likely to end up as a defendant in a negligence lawsuit. As you learn more about law governing CAM modalities, recall not only the provider who "stars" in the lawsuit or news story. Think of the patient, looking for options often grounded in culture and religion, yet needing protection against true fraud.

For background on the cultural differences which fuel CAM use, distrust within the western medical community and, occasional legal disputes, *see* Laura Howell et al., *Use of Herbal Remedies by Hispanic Patients: Do They Inform Their Physician*, 19 J. Am. Bd. Fam. Med. 566 (2006); Fredi Kronenberg et al., *Race/Ethnicity and Women's Use of Complementary and Alternative Medicine in the United States: Results of a National Survey*, 96 Am. J. Pub. Health 1236 (2006); Deepa Rao, *Choice of Medicine and Hierarchy of Resort to Different Health Alternatives Among Asian Indian Migrants in a Metropolitan City in the USA*, 11 Ethnicity & Health 153 (2006); Maria T. Chao et al., *Women's Reasons for Complementary and Alternative Medicine Use: Racial/Ethnic Differences*, 12 J. Alternative & Complementary Med. 719 (2006); Kamil M. Ariff & Khoo S. Beng, *Cultural Health Beliefs in a Rural Family Practice: A Malaysian Perspective*, 14 Austl. J. Rural Health 2 (2006); Gregory Juckett, *Cross-Cultural Medicine*, 72 Am. Fam. Physician 2267 (2005); Nancy E. Schoenberg et al., *Complementary and Alternative Medicine Use Among a Multiethnic Sample of Older Adults with Diabetes*, 10 J. Alternative & Complementary Med. 1061 (2004); Jeongseon Kim & Mabel M. Chan, *Factors Influencing Preferences for Alternative Medicine by Korean Americans*, 32 Am. J. Chinese Med. 321 (2004); Betsy Sleath et al., *Ethnicity and Physician-Older Patient Communication About Alternative Therapies*, 7 J. Alternative & Complementary Med. 329 (2001); Moon S. Chen, *Informal Care the Empowerment of Minority Communities: Comparisons between the USA and the UK*, 4 Ethnicity & Health 139 (1999).

III. Continued Tension between CAM and Conventional Medicine

CAM's presence in the health care industry has a number of social, political and legal implications stemming from concerns not only about the safety and efficacy of the therapies, but also about preserving the integrity of these historic, if not ancient, healing

> **Box 1.4 Cultural Divides and Traditional Healing**
>
> *When Lia was about three months old, her older sister Yer slammed the front door of the Lee's apartment. A few moments later, Lia's eyes rolled up, her arms jerked over her head, and she fainted. The Lees had little doubt what had happened. Despite the careful installation of Lia's soul during the hu plig ceremony, the noise of the door had been so profoundly frightening that her soul had fled her body and become lost. They recognized the resulting symptoms as quag dab peg, which means "the spirit catches you and you fall down." The spirit referred to in this phrase is a soul-stealing dab; peg means to catch or hit; and quag means to fall over with one's roots still in the ground, as grain might be beaten down by wind or rain.*
>
> *In Hmong-English dictionaries qua dab peg is generally translated as epilepsy.*
>
> ...
>
> *Looking over Lia's sparse medical records from the spring and summer of 1986, around the time of her fourth birthday, [Doctor] Peggy Philp summed up the first few months after her return [to her family] from foster care in three words: "Nothing interesting here." The Lees would disagree. Neil and Peggy [Lia's doctors] would spend hours recounting the details of medically complex periods in Lia's history that Foua and Nao Kao had summarized for me in a few minutes; now the tables were turned, and a period that seemed uneventful from the doctor's perspective was revealed, from the Lees' perspective, to be one of the richest in her life.*
>
> *The first thing Foua and Nao Kao did after Lia returned was to celebrate her homecoming and bolster her health by sacrificing a cow. In Laos, most of the chickens, pigs, cows, and buffalos kept by Hmong families were reserved for sacrifices to propitiate ancestors or cure illnesses by offering the souls of the slaughtered animals as ransom for fugitive souls. Even families too poor to keep animals of their own were guaranteed occasional meat in their diets by being invited to neeb ceremonies performed by wealthier villagers.*
>
> ...
>
> *When I told [the doctors, Neil and Peggy] that Foua and Nao Kao, in their willingness to travel down the middle road of "a little medicine and a little neeb," viewed themselves as eminently reasonable and their doctors as incapable of compromise, Neil and Peggy shook their heads in puzzlement and consternation.*
>
> *In order to keep Lia's condition from deteriorating further, the Lees stepped up their program of traditional medicine.... For example, the Lees spent $1,000 on amulets filled with sacred healing herbs from Thailand, which Lia wore constantly around her neck. They also tried a host of less costly but time-consuming therapies. Foua inserted a silver coin that said "1936 Indochine Fançaise" into the yolk of a boiled egg, wrapped the egg in a cloth, and rubbed Lia's body with it; when the egg turned black, that meant the sickness had been absorbed. She massaged Lia with the bowl of a spoon. She sucked the "pressure" out of Lia's body by pressing a small cup heated with ashes against her skin, creating a temporary vacuum as the oxygen-depleted air inside the cup cooled. She pinched Lia to draw out the noxious winds. She dosed Lia with tisanes infused from gleanings of her parking-lot herb garden.*
>
> ...
>
> *Neil and Peggy had no idea what the Lees were doing to heal Lia because they never thought to ask.*
>
> From Anne Fadiman, A Spirit Catches You and You Fall Down (Farrar, Straus and Giroux, 1997)

philosophies. The costs and benefits of increased integration between CAM and conventional medicine weigh on both sides, but the primary concern for conventional practitioners, as you will see in the following excerpt, is the problem of evidence. As you read the article and following notes, consider the possible outcomes of following their recommendations for the future of medicine.

Marcia Angell, M.D., Jerome P. Kassirer, M.D., *Alternative Medicine—The Risks of Untested and Unregulated Remedies* (1983)
339 New Eng. J. Med. 83

What is there about alternative medicine that sets it apart from ordinary medicine? The term refers to a remarkably heterogeneous group of theories and practices—as disparate as homeopathy, therapeutic touch, imagery, and herbal medicine. What unites them? Eisenberg et al. defined alternative medicine (now often called complementary medicine) as "medical interventions not taught widely at U.S. medical schools or generally available at U.S. hospitals." That is not a very satisfactory definition, especially since many alternative remedies have recently found their way into the medical mainstream. Medical schools teach alternative medicine, hospitals and health maintenance organizations offer it, and laws in some states require health plans to cover it. It also constitutes a huge and rapidly growing industry, in which major pharmaceutical companies are now participating.

What most sets alternative medicine apart, in our view, is that it has not been scientifically tested and its advocates largely deny the need for such testing. By testing, we mean the marshaling of rigorous evidence of safety and efficacy, as required by the Food and Drug Administration (FDA) for the approval of drugs and by the best peer-reviewed medical journals for the publication of research reports. Of course, many treatments used in conventional medicine have not been rigorously tested, either, but the scientific community generally acknowledges that this is a failing that needs to be remedied. Many advocates of alternative medicine, in contrast, believe the scientific method is simply not applicable to their remedies. They rely instead on anecdotes and theories.

In 1992, Congress established within the National Institutes of Health an Office of Alternative Medicine to evaluate alternative remedies. So far, the results have been disappointing. For example, of the 30 research grants the office awarded in 1993, 28 have resulted in "final reports" (abstracts) that are listed in the office's public on-line data base. But a Medline search almost six years after the grants were awarded revealed that only 9 of the 28 resulted in published papers. Five were in two journals not included among the 3500 journal titles in the Countway Library of Medicine's collection. Of the other four studies, none was a controlled clinical trial that would allow any conclusions to be drawn about the efficacy of an alternative treatment.

It might be argued that conventional medicine relies on anecdotes, too, some of which are published as case reports in peer-reviewed journals. But these case reports differ from the anecdotes of alternative medicine. They describe a well-documented new finding in a defined setting. If, for example, the Journal were to receive a paper describing a patient's recovery from cancer of the pancreas after he had ingested a rhubarb diet, we would require documentation of the disease and its extent, we would ask about other, similar patients who did not recover after eating rhubarb, and we might suggest trying the diet on other patients. If the answers to these and other questions were satisfactory, we might publish a case report—not to announce a remedy, but only to suggest a hypothesis that should be tested in a proper clinical trial. In contrast, anecdotes about alternative remedies (usually published in books and magazines for the public) have no such documentation and are considered sufficient in themselves as support for therapeutic claims.

Alternative medicine also distinguishes itself by an ideology that largely ignores biologic mechanisms, often disparages modern science, and relies on what are purported to be ancient practices and natural remedies (which are seen as somehow being simultaneously more potent and less toxic than conventional medicine). Accordingly, herbs or mixtures of herbs are considered superior to the active compounds isolated in the laboratory. And healing methods such as homeopathy and therapeutic touch are fervently promoted despite not only the lack of good clinical evidence of effectiveness, but the presence of a rationale that violates fundamental scientific laws—surely a circumstance that requires more, rather than less, evidence.

Of all forms of alternative treatment, the most common is herbal medicine. Until the 20th century, most remedies were botanicals, a few of which were found through trial and error to be helpful. For example, purple foxglove was found to be helpful for dropsy, the opium poppy for pain, cough, and diarrhea, and cinchona bark for fever. But therapeutic successes with botanicals came at great human cost. The indications for using a given botanical were ill defined, dosage was arbitrary because the concentrations of the active ingredient were unknown, and all manner of contaminants were often present. More important, many of the remedies simply did not work, and some were harmful or even deadly. The only way to separate the beneficial from the useless or hazardous was through anecdotes relayed mainly by word of mouth.

All that began to change in the Twentieth century as a result of rapid advances in medical science. The emergence of sophisticated chemical and pharmacologic methods meant that we could identify and purify the active ingredients in botanicals and study them. Digitalis was extracted from the purple foxglove, morphine from the opium poppy, and quinine from cinchona bark. Furthermore, once the chemistry was understood, it was possible to synthesize related molecules with more desirable properties. For example, penicillin was fortuitously discovered when penicillium mold contaminated some bacterial cultures. Isolating and characterizing it permitted the synthesis of a wide variety of related antibiotics with different spectrums of activity.

In addition, powerful epidemiologic tools were developed for testing potential remedies. In particular, the evolution of the randomized, controlled clinical trial enabled researchers to study with precision the safety, efficacy, and dose effects of proposed treatments and the indications for them. No longer do we have to rely on trial and error and anecdotes. We have learned to ask for and expect statistically reliable evidence before accepting conclusions about remedies. Without such evidence, the FDA will not permit a drug to be marketed.

The results of these advances have been spectacular. As examples, we now know that treatment with aspirin, heparin, thrombolytic agents, and beta-adrenergic blockers greatly reduces mortality from myocardial infarction; a combination of nucleoside analogues and a protease inhibitor can stave off the onset of AIDS in people with human immunodeficiency virus infection; antibiotics heal peptic ulcers; and a cocktail of cytotoxic drugs can cure most cases of childhood leukemia. Also in this century, we have developed and tested vaccines against a great many infectious scourges, including measles, poliomyelitis, pertussis, diphtheria, hepatitis B, some forms of meningitis, and pneumococcal pneumonia, and we have a vast arsenal of effective antibiotics for many others. In less than a century, life expectancy in the United States has increased by three decades, in part because of better sanitation and living standards, but in large part because of advances in medicine realized through rigorous testing. Other countries lagged behind, but as scientific medicine became universal, all countries affluent enough to afford it saw the same benefits.

Now, with the increased interest in alternative medicine, we see a reversion to irrational approaches to medical practice, even while scientific medicine is making some of its most dramatic advances. Exploring the reasons for this paradox is outside the scope of this editorial, but it is probably in part a matter of disillusionment with the often hurried and impersonal care delivered by conventional physicians, as well as the harsh treatments that may be necessary for life-threatening diseases.

Fortunately, most untested herbal remedies are probably harmless. In addition, they seem to be used primarily by people who are healthy and believe the remedies will help them stay that way, or by people who have common, relatively minor problems, such as backache or fatigue. Most such people would probably seek out conventional doctors if they had indications of serious disease, such as crushing chest pain, a mass in the breast, or blood in the urine. Still, uncertainty about whether symptoms are serious could result in a harmful delay in getting treatment that has been proved effective. And some people may embrace alternative medicine exclusively, putting themselves in great danger. In this issue of the Journal, Coppes et al. describe two such instances.

Also in this issue, we see that there are risks of alternative medicine in addition to that of failing to receive effective treatment. Slifman and her colleagues report a case of digitalis toxicity in a young woman who had ingested a contaminated herbal concoction. Ko reports finding widespread inconsistencies and adulterations in his analysis of Asian patent medicines. LoVecchio et al. report on a patient who suffered central nervous system depression after ingesting a substance sold in health-food stores as a growth hormone stimulator, and Beigel and colleagues describe the puzzling clinical course of a patient in whom lead poisoning developed after he took an Indian herbal remedy for his diabetes. These are without doubt simply examples of what will be a rapidly growing problem.

What about the FDA? Shouldn't it be monitoring the safety and efficacy of these remedies? Not any longer, according to the U.S. Congress. In response to the lobbying efforts of the multibillion-dollar "dietary supplement" industry, Congress in 1994 exempted their products from FDA regulation. (Homeopathic remedies have been exempted since 1938.) Since then, these products have flooded the market, subject only to the scruples of their manufacturers. They may contain the substances listed on the label in the amounts claimed, but they need not, and there is no one to prevent their sale if they don't. In analyses of ginseng products, for example, the amount of the active ingredient in each pill varied by as much as a factor of 10 among brands that were labeled as containing the same amount. Some brands contained none at all.

Herbal remedies may also be sold without any knowledge of their mechanism of action. In this issue of the Journal, DiPaola and his colleagues report that the herbal mixture called PC-SPES (PC for prostate cancer, and *spes* the Latin for "hope") has substantial estrogenic activity. Yet this substance is promoted as bolstering the immune system in patients with prostate cancer that is refractory to treatment with estrogen. Many men taking PC-SPES have thus received varying amounts of hormonal treatment without knowing it, some in addition to the estrogen treatments given to them by their conventional physicians.

The only legal requirement in the sale of such products is that they not be promoted as preventing or treating disease. To comply with that stipulation, their labeling has risen to an art form of doublespeak (witness the name PC-SPES). Not only are they sold under the euphemistic rubric "dietary supplements," but also the medical uses for which they are sold are merely insinuated. Nevertheless, it is clear what is meant. Shark cartilage (priced in a local drugstore at more than $3 for a day's dose) is promoted on its label "to maintain proper bone and joint function," saw palmetto to "promote prostate health," and horse-chestnut seed extract to "promote ... leg vein health." Anyone can walk into a health-food store and unwittingly buy PC-SPES with unknown amounts of estrogenic activity, plantain laced with digitalis, or Indian herbs contaminated with heavy metals. Caveat emptor. The FDA can intervene only after the fact, when it is shown that a product is harmful.

It is time for the scientific community to stop giving alternative medicine a free ride. There cannot be two kinds of medicine—conventional and alternative. There is only medicine that has been adequately tested and medicine that has not, medicine that works and medicine that may or may not work. Once a treatment has been tested rigorously, it no longer matters whether it was considered alternative at the outset. If it is found to be reasonably safe and effective, it will be accepted. But assertions, speculation, and testimonials do not substitute for evidence. Alternative treatments should be subjected to scientific testing no less rigorous than that required for conventional treatments.

Notes and Questions

1. In a contrasting piece, *Alternative Medicine—Learning from the Past, Examining the Present, Advancing to the Future*, Wayne Jonas briefly describes the history of CAM and its relation to mainstream medicine. He finds that CAM has always been shunned by the mainstream, but eventually integrated into its treatment. More recently, its popularity in usage went up along side overarching concerns surrounding the ability for mainstream medicine to effectively treat chronic conditions while keeping costs low for medical consumers. Because of the increase in public interest and usage, CAM therapies have become wrapped into mainstream medical education.

But Jonas is wary about the new interest in integration. He pushes for a critical assessment of the pros and cons of CAM care. In the future, Jonas sees that CAM may become a large part of the commonplace medical community. However, to utilize the good aspects of CAM while weeding out the "quackery," he advises the integration of CAM into mainstream medicine with research, reason, and logic.

For Jonas' full article, *see* Wayne B. Jonas, M.D., *Alternative Medicine—Learning from the Past, Examining the Present, Advancing to the Future*, 280 JAMA 1616 (1998).

2. What is at risk to be lost in the "scientification" of CAM? What could be gained?

3. One safety concern regarding the use of CAM is that of non-disclosure to regular physicians. While national studies indicate that a vast majority of CAM users are also seeing a medical doctor, leading to fewer than 40% of respondents who used a CAM therapy disclosed that use to a physician; concerns about possible contraindications with prescribed medications as well as increased health care costs due to the lack of coordinated care. In a 2001 study, many respondents reported that they did not disclose their use of complementary medicine because they felt it was not important for the doctor to know (61%) or the doctor did not ask (60%). Some patients reported feeling that use of complementary medicine was none of the doctor's business (31%), or that the doctor would not understand (20%). Few patients reported feeling that the doctor would disapprove (14%). *See* David M. Eisenberg et al., *Perceptions About Complementary Therapies Relative to Conventional Therapies Among Adults Who Use Both: Results from a National Survey*, 135 ANNALS OF INTERNAL MED. 344 (2001). Is "integration" the answer to this problem?

Box 1.5 Integrative Medicine

The term "Integrative Medicine" encompasses a broad array of practice styles which share certain themes. The definition by the National Center for Complementary and Alternative Medicine at the National Institutes of Health is: Integrative Medicine "combines mainstream medical therapies and complementary and alternative medicine therapies for which there is some high-quality scientific evidence of safety and effectiveness." Integrative medicine is defined by Dr. Andrew Weil, founder of the Arizona program in Integrative Medicine, as "healing-oriented medicine that takes account of the whole person (body, mind and spirit), including all aspects of lifestyle. It emphasizes the therapeutic relationship and makes use of all appropriate therapies, both conventional and alternative." These definitions serve to guide the understanding of the general public, but what does Integrative Medicine mean to the practicing physician and why are so many doctors and patients being drawn to this type of practice?

For physicians, adapting to an Integrative Medicine practice model provides a structure for focusing on prevention, empowering patients to be partners in their own healthcare, and avoiding unnecessary pharmaceuticals and interventions. This model represents a shift in the standard Western healthcare model, which primarily focuses on the use of technology to treat existing conditions and modulate the adverse effects of poor lifestyle choices. Although scientific advances in the practice of medicine have reduced the burden of infectious disease and improved the survival of trauma patients, it has minimized the importance of prevention and devalued the connection between the mind and the body. In the age of pharmaceuticals, surgery, and high-tech medical imaging, the practice of Integrative Medicine seeks to focus on those aspects of medicine which are less quantifiable.

One of the least quantifiable, yet most powerful, aspects of an Integrative practice is the doctor-patient relationship. The Integrative physician takes the extra time to learn about the whole patient: body, mind, and spirit. The doctor gets to know the patient much as a close friend or family member would know them. Interviews are typically longer than the standard fifteen minute patient encounter, and explore topics such as the patient's diet, sense of spiritual connection, belief systems, sources of stress, and goals for the future. Instead of the traditional model of care, where the physician hears the complaint and responds with a prescription or list of diagnostic tests, the Integrative model prioritizes the improvement of nutrition, stress-reduction, and natural therapies with low potential for harm. In short, the doctor becomes more intimate with the patient, and offers lifestyle advice, in addition to appropriate standard medical care. All of this is done within a context of acceptance of all forms of healing and respect for the patient's preferences and belief system.

It is this intimate relationship that also opens patient encounters to discussion of non-traditional forms of healing. Since the Integrative physician is usually trained in alternative therapies such as mind-body medicine, meditation, and spiritual practices in medicine, the patient tends to feel more comfortable discussing alternative forms of healing they may practice. Studies show us that patients in traditional medical practices do not tell their physicians about alternative therapies, herbs, and supplements they use. Integrative physicians, by contracts, commonly explore these options with patients and as a result of create an accepting, open-minded environment. As a result, Integrative physicians often hear stories not traditionally heard in the medical interview, such as stories of spontaneous healing, spiritual experiences, or prior work with alternative practitioners. It is this open-minded and more personalized style that draws many patients into Integrative practices.

In summary, a solid foundation in nutrition, supplements, herbs, alternative systems of healing, mind-body medicine, spirituality, and manual therapies are essential for the physician practicing Integrative medicine, but the this style of practice means much more. The Integrative physician uses an intimate and flexible version of the doctor-patient relationship as the primary platform for offering lifestyle and therapeutic advice. Recommendations are individualized and chosen within the context of the patient's belief system. It is a welcoming style of practice, where patients and physicians explore healing through many avenues and find it in many forms.

Jill Mallory, M.D., The University of Wisconsin Integrative Medicine

IV. Legal Considerations

A. State Police Powers: Protecting Health and Safety

When examining the regulation of CAM, it is important to understand the power of the state to regulate providers in order to protect the public health. The Tenth Amendment to the Constitution provides that "the powers not delegated to the United States, nor prohibited by it to the States, are reserved to the states respectively, or to the people." The ability of the *federal* government to act is limited by the powers granted to it in the Constitution; all other powers are reserved to the states. These are often called "state police powers." The following excerpt is thought to be the first discussion of these powers from the Supreme Court:

> [There is] an immense mass of legislation, which embraces every thing within the territory of a State, not surrendered to the general government: all which can be most advantageously exercised by the States themselves. Inspection laws, quarantine laws, *health laws of every description*, as well as laws for regulating the internal commerce of State.... No direct general power over these objects is granted to Congress; and, consequently, they remain subject to State legislation. If the legislative power of the Union can reach them, it must be for national purposes....

Chief Justice John Marshall, *Gibbons v. Ogden*, 22 U.S. 1, 78 (1824) (emphasis added).

The most significant case to examine the police powers of the state with regard to public health and safety was *Jacobson v. Massachusetts*, 197 U.S. 11 (1905). The case addresses the refusal of Mr. Jacobson to comply with a local ordinance requiring small pox vaccination. In upholding the ordinance, the Court defers to the public health authority despite Mr. Jacobson's claim that his liberty interests were violated by the compulsory vaccination law. As you read the excerpt below, consider the scope of the states' power and the possibility for judicial interference.

Jacobson v. Massachusetts
Supreme Court of the United States, 1905
197 U.S. 11

Mr. Justice Harlan delivered the opinion of the court.

* * *

[T]he board of health of the city of Cambridge, Massachusetts, on the 27th day of February, 1902, adopted the following regulation: 'Whereas, smallpox has been prevalent to some extent in the city of Cambridge, and still continues to increase; and whereas, it is necessary for the speedy extermination of the disease that all persons not protected by vaccination should be vaccinated; and whereas, in the opinion of the board, the public health and safety require the vaccination or revaccination of all the inhabitants of Cambridge; be it ordered, that all the inhabitants of the city who have not been successfully vaccinated since March 1st, 1897, be vaccinated or revaccinated.'

Subsequently, the board adopted an additional regulation empowering a named physician to enforce the vaccination of persons as directed by the board at its special meeting of February 27th.

The above regulations being in force, the plaintiff in error, Jacobson, was proceeded against by a criminal complaint in one of the inferior courts of Massachusetts. The complaint charged that on the 17th day of July, 1902, the board of health of Cambridge, being of the opinion that it was necessary for the public health and safety, required the vaccination and revaccination of all the inhabitants thereof who had not been successfully vaccinated since the 1st day of March, 1897, and provided them with the means of free vaccination; and that the defendant, being over twenty-one years of age and not under guardianship, refused and neglected to comply with such requirement.

The defendant, having been arraigned, pleaded not guilty. The government put in evidence the above regulations adopted by the board of health, and made proof tending to show that its chairman informed the defendant that, by refusing to be vaccinated, he would incur the penalty provided by the statute, and would be prosecuted therefor; that he offered to vaccinate the defendant without expense to him; and that the offer was declined, and defendant refused to be vaccinated.

* * *

The authority of the state to enact this statute is to be referred to what is commonly called the police power, a power which the state did not surrender when becoming a member of the Union under the Constitution. Although this court has refrained from any attempt to define the limits of that power, yet it has distinctly recognized the authority of a state to enact quarantine laws and 'health laws of every description;' indeed, all laws that relate to matters completely within its territory and which do not by their necessary operation affect the people of other states. According to settled principles, the police power of a state must be held to embrace, at least, such reasonable regulations established directly by legislative enactment as will protect the public health and the public safety. [Citations omitted]. It is equally true that the state may invest local bodies called into existence for purposes of local administration with authority in some appropriate way to safeguard the public health and the public safety.

We come, then, to inquire whether any right given or secured by the Constitution is invaded by the statute as interpreted by the state court. The defendant insists that his liberty is invaded when the state subjects him to fine or imprisonment for neglecting or refusing to submit to vaccination; that a compulsory vaccination law is unreasonable, arbitrary, and oppressive, and, therefore, hostile to the inherent right of freeman to care for his own body and health in such way as to him seems best; and that the execution of such a law against one who objects to vaccination, no matter for what reason, is nothing short of an assault upon his person. But the liberty secured by the Constitution of the United States to every person within its jurisdiction does not import an absolute right in each person to be, at all times and in all circumstances, wholly freed from restraint. There are manifold restraints to which every person is necessarily subject for the common good. On any other basis organized society could not exist with safety to its members. Society based on the rule that each one is a law unto himself would soon be confronted with disorder and anarchy. Real liberty for all could not exist under the operation of a principle which recognizes the right of each individual person to use his own, whether in respect of his person or his property, regardless of the injury that may be done to others. This court has more than once recognized it as a fundamental principle that 'persons and property are subjected to all kinds of restraints and burdens in order to secure the general comfort, health, and prosperity of the state; of the perfect right of the legislature to do which no question ever was, or upon acknowledged general principles ever can be, made, so far as natural persons are concerned.' [Citations omitted.]... The good and welfare of the commonwealth, of which the legislature is primarily the judge, is the basis on which the police power rests in Massachusetts. [Citation omitted.]

Applying these principles to the present case, it is to be observed that the legislature of Massachusetts required the inhabitants of a city or town to be vaccinated only when, in the opinion of the board of health, that was necessary for the public health or the public safety. The authority to determine for all what ought to be done in such an emergency must have been lodged somewhere or in some body; and surely it was appropriate for the legislature to refer that question, in the first instance, to a board of health composed of persons residing in the locality affected, and appointed, presumably, because of their fitness to determine such questions. To invest such a body with authority over such matters was not an unusual, nor an unreasonable or arbitrary, requirement. Upon the principle of self-defense, of paramount necessity, a community has the right to protect itself against an epidemic of disease which threatens the safety of its members. It is to be observed that when the regulation in question was adopted smallpox, according to the recitals in the regulation adopted by the board of health, was prevalent to some extent in the city of Cambridge, and the disease was increasing. If such was the situation, — and nothing is asserted or appears in the record to the contrary, — if we are to attach, any value whatever to the knowledge which, it is safe to affirm, in common to all civilized peoples touching smallpox and the methods most usually employed to eradicate that disease, it cannot be adjudged that the present regulation of the board of health was not necessary in order to protect the public health and secure the public safety. Smallpox being prevalent and increasing at Cambridge, the court would usurp the functions of another branch of government if it adjudged, as matter of law, that the mode adopted under the sanction of the state, to protect the people at large was arbitrary, and not justified by the necessities of the case. We say necessities of the case, because it might be that an acknowledged power of a local community to protect itself against an epidemic threatening the safety of all might be exercised in particular circumstances and in reference to particular persons in such an arbitrary, unreasonable manner, or might go so far beyond what was reasonably required for the safety of the public, as to authorize or compel the courts to interfere for the protection of such persons. [Citations omitted.]

* * *

There is, of course, a sphere within which the individual may assert the supremacy of his own will, and rightfully dispute the authority of any human government, — especially of any free government existing under a written constitution, to interfere with the exercise of that will. But it is equally true that in every well-ordered society charged with the duty of conserving the safety of its members the rights of the individual in respect of his liberty may at times, under the pressure of great dangers, be subjected to such restraint, to be enforced by reasonable regulations, as the safety of the general public may demand. An American citizen arriving at an American port on a vessel in which, during the voyage, there had been cases of yellow fever or Asiatic cholera, he, although apparently free from disease himself, may yet, in some circumstances, be held in quarantine against his will on board of such vessel or in a quarantine station, until it be ascertained by inspection, conducted with due diligence, that the danger of the spread of the disease among the community at large has disappeared. The liberty secured by the 14th Amendment, this court has said, consists, in part, in the right of a person 'to live and work where he will' (*Allgeyer v. Louisiana*, 165 U. S. 578, 41 L. ed. 832, 17 Sup. Ct. Rep. 427); and yet he may be compelled, by force if need be, against his will and without regard to his personal wishes or his pecuniary interests, or even his religious or political convictions, to take his place in the ranks of the army of his country, and risk the chance of being shot down in its defense. It is not, therefore, true that the power of the public to guard itself against imminent danger depends in every case involving the control of one's body upon his willingness to submit to reasonable regulations established by the constituted authorities, under the sanction of the state, for the purpose of protecting the public collectively against such danger.

* * *

The latest case upon the subject of which we are aware is *Viemester v. White*, decided very recently by the court of appeals of New York. That case involved the validity of a statute excluding from the public schools all children who had not been vaccinated. One contention was that the statute and the regulation adopted in exercise of provisions was inconsistent with the rights, privileges, and liberties of the citizens. The contention was overruled. The court saying, among other things: 'Smallpox is known of all to be a dangerous and contagious disease. If vaccination strongly tends to prevent the transmission or spread of this disease, it logically follows that children may be refused admission to the public schools until they have been vaccinated.

The appellant claims that vaccination does not tend to prevent smallpox, but tends to bring about other diseases, and that it does much harm, with no good. It must be conceded that some laymen, both learned and unlearned, and some physicians of great skill and repute, do not believe that vaccination is a preventive of smallpox. The common belief, however, is that it has a decided tendency to prevent the spread of this fearful disease, and to render it less dangerous to those who contract it. While not accepted by all, it is accepted by the mass of the people, as well as by most members of the medical profession. It has been general in our state, and in most civilized nations for generations. It is generally accepted in theory, and generally applied in practice, both by the voluntary action of the people, and in obedience to the command of law. Nearly every state in the Union has statutes to encourage, or directly or indirectly to require, vaccination; and this is true of most nations of Europe.... A common belief, like common knowledge, does not require evidence to establish its existence, but may be acted upon without proof by the legislature and the courts.... The fact that the belief is not universal is not controlling, for there is scarcely any belief that is accepted by everyone. The possibility that the belief may be wrong, and that science may yet show it to be wrong, is not conclusive; for the legislature has the right to pass laws which, according to the common belief of the people, are adapted to prevent the spread of contagious diseases. In a free country, where the government is by the people, through their chosen representatives, practical legislation admits of no other standard of action, for what the people believe is for the common welfare must be accepted as tending to promote the common welfare, whether it does in fact or not. Any other basis would conflict with the spirit of the Constitution, and would sanction measures opposed to a Republican form of government. While we do not decide, and cannot decide, that vaccination is a preventive of smallpox, we take judicial notice of the fact that this is the common belief of the people of the state, and, with this fact as a foundation, we hold that the statute in question is a health law, enacted in a reasonable and proper exercise of the police power.' 179 N. Y. 235, 72 N. E. 97.

Since, then, vaccination, as a means of protecting a community against smallpox, finds stong support in the experience of this and other countries, no court, much less a jury, is justified in disregarding the action of the legislature simply because in its or their opinion that particular method was—perhaps, or possibly—not the best either for children or adults.

* * *

We now decide only that the statute covers the present case, and that nothing clearly appears that would justify this court in holding it to be unconstitutional and inoperative in its application to the plaintiff in error.

Notes and Questions

1. In his opinion, Justice Harlan expresses judicial deference to the state police power. What language in the opinion indicates this to you? Under what limited circumstances does he say the Court is able to intervene in the exercise of state police power?

2. One of Jacobson's arguments was that smallpox vaccination tended to bring about other dangers. How did the Court respond to this argument? The role of the state in weighing competing scientific theories is an important concept we will refer to throughout this book.

3. Another important point one can take from *Jacobson* regarding the state police power is the ability of the state to delegate that power to other authorities. What reasons does the Court give in deciding that it was appropriate for the legislature to refer to the board of health on the question of whether vaccination was a necessary and proper course of action?

4. Consider whether *Jacobson*, which was decided in the early Twentieth Century, is still relevant now, in the Twenty-First Century. Do advances in science change the analysis of how the state should balance competing scientific theories? What about the Court's consideration of the tension between individual liberties and the common welfare—has the general philosophy espoused by the Court changed over time?

B. Overview of the Book

Although not specifically about the use of complementary or alternative medicine, *Jacobson* presents the central theme of this book: what power does the state have to regulate personal health care decisions? The next two chapters examine the power of the state to regulate the medical profession through **licensure** and **scope of practice** regulations. By determining which health care professions may be licensed to practice, the state acts as a gatekeeper. And by setting parameters around what those practitioners may do, the state can limit the extent to which certain professions become integrated in the health care system. Each of these kinds of regulations impact the ability of individuals to access CAM practitioners.

The next two chapters look at two different approaches for regulating CAM: **medical malpractice** and **informed consent**. Under these models, the state regulates the profession by allowing individuals more access to CAM practitioners but protecting them, either through malpractice litigation in the event that something goes wrong, or through informed consent regulations, so that the individual knows and understands the decision they are making for their medical care.

The sixth chapter considers the authority of the **Food and Drug Administration** to regulate medicinal drugs. In the context of CAM, the FDA is most involved with dietary supplements. The chapter considers the extent to which the FDA is involved with protecting the public from potentially harmful substances and restricting access to those substances. These decisions, like many in this text, harken back to the dilemma faced in *Jacobson*: how far can the state proceed in constraining individual liberties (to treat oneself with unconventional treatments, for example), in the name of preserving the public health? While the answer with regard to contagious diseases like smallpox is answered by *Jacobson*, what about treatments for noncontiguous diseases? Should the balance between individual liberties and state police power be different? Using the Court's phrase, should "a sphere within which the individual may assert the supremacy to his own will" be drawn more widely?

After examining FDA actions, we turn to address the **antitrust** laws. These statutes (which regulate contracts, conspiracies and other activities in restraint of trade) have been used by CAM providers against medical association members who refuse to deal with them and, in some cases, seek to destroy nonallopathic professions. Finally, the text explores new **emerging approaches to regulation** of Complementary and Alternative Medicine such as Health Freedom Acts, creation of offices specifically designed to regulate unlicensed CAM providers, and statutory requirements to consult unconventional medical physicians during investigations of licensed CAM providers.

Chapter Two

The Gatekeeper Role of Licensure

I. Introduction to Licensure and the Practice of Medicine

History sheds light on both the tensions between allopathic and CAM providers and the legal concepts of licensure and scope of practice addressed in this and the following chapter. Much of the tension can be traced to the American Medical Association's ("AMA") efforts to professionalize medical practitioners beginning in the Nineteenth Century. In order to gain the status of a "profession"—an occupation that distinguishes itself, in part, by setting its own rules and standards—the members of the profession must agree on two matters: who is admitted to professional status and what the rules are that govern those members. That agreement did not come easily. The process took almost 70 years. It featured ongoing battles between a broad spectrum of regular, irregular, and CAM providers that reverberates in our current legal battles.

Today, many CAM providers viewed as "irregulars" a century ago have achieved status as licensed professionals. But most of these practitioners face strict limits on their scope of practice, as discussed in the following chapter. Still others practice in uncharted waters as unlicensed providers, not knowing if they will be prosecuted for the unlicensed practice of medicine.

A. The Status of Medical Practice in the Nineteenth Century

In the Nineteenth Century, physicians struggled to be recognized as professionals. They competed not only with homeopaths (many of whom were highly educated with a following of well-to-do patients), but with psychic curers and medicine makers who advertised their medicines and advice in the popular press. It was difficult to differentiate between these Nineteenth Century medical professionals. Their relative numbers outpaced population growth. Few barriers to entry existed and medical schools proliferated, offering quick degrees. While select late Nineteenth Century physicians trained at Johns Hopkins and abroad, serious academic study largely was thought unnecessary for private practice. As Paul Starr points out in his highly readable text, The Social Transformation of American Medicine, while a few doctors graduated from medical school, the vast majority had only taken a series of lectures or a two term medical course and then served as an apprentice. The majority did not earn money significantly above the pay of public employees and many found themselves, salary wise, in the lower end of the middle class. In short, the doctor was not substantially different from the traveling salesperson, spending much time in the homes of patients, and often facing both unregulated competition and underemployment.

In 1846, the AMA was established with the explicit goal of distinguishing the "regular" medical professional from sectarianism and quackery. Sectarians included a variety of dissident groups including Thomsonianism (a system of botanic medicine popular in the mid-Nineteenth Century); Eclectics (successors to the Thomsonians who combined herbal medicine with conventional science and a campaign against excessive bleeding and drugging); Christian Scientists; and homeopaths. The approach taken by the AMA was to adopt a Code of Ethics and to enlist members who would practice under that code. That first Code of Ethics prohibited member physicians from promoting secret remedies, engaging in advertising, and engaging in any consultation with "irregular" providers. The AMA's early efforts sought voluntary compliance with its goal of establishing a self-regulated, respected and exclusive profession—at first. But its efforts at limiting access to medical associations and reforming education largely failed.

One of the largest, longest battles occurred between physician "regulars" and homeopaths. As Starr describes it:

> The avoidance of contact with homeopaths took on all the gravity of a pollution taboo ... A New York doctor was expelled [from the medical society] for buying milk sugar at a homeopathic pharmacy. The Surgeon General of the United States was denounced for having taken part in the treatment of Secretary of State William Seward, the night he was stabbed and President Lincoln was shot, because Seward's personal physician was a homeopath ... Despite these attacks, homeopathy enjoyed wide popularity in the two decades after the Civil War ... [It] fought itself to a position almost of parity with the regular profession in legal entitlements and public respectability, though not in numbers of practitioners.

PAUL STARR, THE SOCIAL TRANSFORMATION OF AMERICAN MEDICINE 98–99 (1982).

As voluntary efforts failed, AMA physicians joined forces with some of the more educated healing sects (particularly eclectics, who practiced healing through the use of medicines made from plants, and homeopaths) to lobby state legislatures for licensure in the 1870s and 1880s. States began to adopt licensing laws which required a state conferred license in order to "practice medicine." At first, these medical practice acts (which then, as now, were dominated by allopathic physicians) set forth only minimal requirements for licensure: the practitioner must have received a diploma or have a long established practice. Slowly, states began to appoint boards (typically composed of AMA members) to "pass" on the qualification of candidates. Few states regulated medical schools, however, so "diploma mills" proliferated. For further discussion of this history, *see* Peter J. Van Hemel, *A Way Out of the Maze: Federal Agency Preemption of State Licensing and Regulations of Complementary and Alternative Medicine Practices*, 27 AM. J.L. & MED. 329 (2001); Jeffrey F. Chase-Lubitz, *The Corporate Practice of Medicine Doctrine: An Anachronism in the Modern Health Care Industry*, 40 VAND. L. REV. 445, 450–53 (1987); and Walter Gellhorn, *The Abuse of Occupational Licensure*, 44 U. CHI. L. REV. 6 (1976).

A licensure requirement without an enforcement mechanism would be meaningless. Then, as now, licensure was based on and enforced by the state's police power to protect the health, safety and welfare of its citizens. In 1888, in *Dent v. West Virginia*, 129 U.S. 114, 122 (1889), the United States Supreme Court upheld a state's licensure mandate, stating:

The power of the state to provide for the general welfare of its people authorizes it to prescribe all such regulations as in its judgment will secure or try to secure them against the consequences of ignorance and incapability, as well as of deception and fraud. As one means to this end it has been the practice of states, from time to immemorial, to exact in many pursuits a certain degree of skill and learning upon which the community may confidently rely; their possession being generally ascertained upon an examination of parties by competent persons or inferred from a certificate to them in the forum of a diploma.... Few professions require more careful preparation by one who seeks to enter it than that of medicine.

B. The Flexner Report: Expanding Physician Control over Health Care through Medical School Reform

At the turn of the century, the AMA made medical school reform a priority. It invited the Carnegie Foundation for the Advancement of Teaching to investigate medical education and Carnegie turned to educator Abraham Flexner. Flexner visited each medical school in turn, and, in 1910, issued the Flexner Report. It reported missing laboratories, libraries with no books, reeking corpses and admission requirements which were waived for anyone who paid tuition. Flexner's recommendations were breathtakingly simple: build the few first class and middle rank schools to the standard set by Johns Hopkins and disband the great majority of schools. The country was overrun with too many badly trained doctors. The Flexner Report—and the AMA—set out to remedy this.

Their efforts paid off.

Five years after the report, the number of medical schools dramatically dropped, as did the number of physicians. Licensing boards raised their standards to demand college coursework and graduation from an accredited medical school. The AMA effectively became that national accrediting agency and the number of physicians plummeted. At the turn of the Twentieth Century, there were 173 physicians per 100,000 of population. By 1930, that number dropped to 125 per 100,000.

While the AMA sought stricter licensure laws, at the dawn of the Twentieth Century the approach of other individual health professionals was divided. Chiropractors and osteopaths jumped aboard the licensure bandwagon but many professions did not. Even where non-physicians won licensing privileges, the prize was limited. Few were able to prescribe drugs and even fewer gained access to the newly invigorated hospital.

As Paul Starr explains:

> According to a survey of nine thousand families carried out over the years 1928 to 1931, all the non-M.D. practitioner combined—osteopaths, chiropractors, Christian Scientists and other faith healers, midwives, and chiropodists—took care of only 5.1 percent of all attended cases of illness. Physicians finally had medical practice pretty much to themselves.
>
> PAUL STARR, THE SOCIAL TRANSFORMATION OF AMERICAN MEDICINE 127 (1982).

Nowhere was the post-Flexner Report contrast more evident than in the practice of homeopathy. In 1898, homeopaths had nine national societies, 66 general homeopathic hospitals, 74 specialty homeopathic hospitals, 20 homeopathic medical colleges and 31 medical journals. In 1902, there were 15,000 practitioners. By 1980, there were

128 practitioners and no homeopathic hospitals. *See* John Lunstroth, *Voluntary Self-Regulation of Complementary and Alternative Medicine Practitioners*, 70 Alb. L. Rev. 209 (2006).

C. Defining the Practice of Medicine

In order to limit the practice of medicine to licensed professionals, states also had to define the parameters of that practice. Many of the statutes passed in the early Twentieth Century remain largely intact. Consider the following definitions:

New York: N.Y. Educ. Law §6521

The practice of the profession of medicine is defined as diagnosing, treating, operating or prescribing for any human disease, pain, injury, deformity or physical condition.

California: Cal. Bus. & Prof. Code 2052(a)

[A]ny person who practices or attempts to practice, or who advertises or holds himself or herself out as practicing, any system or mode of treating the sick or afflicted in this state, or who diagnoses, treats, operates for, or prescribes for any ailment, blemish, deformity, disease, disfigurement, disorder, injury, or other physical or mental condition of any person, without having at the time of so doing a valid, unrevoked, or unsuspended certificate as provided in this chapter or without being authorized to perform the act pursuant to a certificate obtained in accordance with some other provision of the law is guilty of a public offense, punishable by a fine not exceeding ten thousand dollars ($10,000), by imprisonment in the state prison, by imprisonment in a county jail not exceeding one year, or by both the fine and either imprisonment.

Licensed physicians can perform any of the procedures and tasks identified as "the practice of medicine" in these statutes. And the definitions are undeniably broad. They seemingly suggest that every parent who held a hand to the forehead of a flushed child, declared that the child had a fever and then gave the child aspirin was "practicing medicine." After all, wouldn't this qualify as "diagnosis" and "prescribing?"

The breadth of the New York and California statutes describing the "practice of medicine" are not exceptions. Most states have broad prohibitions on the unlicensed practice of medicine—and the breadth of these statues frequently overlap with treatments and consultations by CAM providers.

Of course, legislatures also create numerous exceptions to the prohibition against the unlicensed practice of medicine. Chief among the exceptions are those for individuals (such as students and physician's assistants) acting under the direct supervision of a licensed physician and individuals licensed by another health related licensing board (such as Boards of Nursing and Dentistry) who confine their activities to those within the scope of the license (the next chapter of our text will address the disputes over what, exactly, is within the "scope of practice" for non-physician licensed providers). Other exceptions are narrower, including limited exceptions for out-of-state licensed practitioners. Consider whether any of these exceptions would address any public policy concerns you had over the breadth of the definition of the "practice of medicine."

> **Box 2.1**
>
> Consider the following acts and decide, first, whether they could constitute the practice of medicine under the literal reading of these statutes, and, second, whether limiting these acts to the purview of licensed providers is a sensible public policy choice:
>
> - Use of an ultrasonic machine on a patient
> - Administration of a massage for chronic neck pain
> - Conducting a pap smear and sending the specimen to a lab for analysis
> - Administering a x-ray
> - Taking a patient's blood pressure
> - Incision and drainage of a cyst
> - Prescribing birth control pills
> - Taking a patient's medical and emotional history and suggesting that the patient purchase St. John's Wort (describe) at the local natural health store
> - Taking a patient's medical and emotional history and suggesting that the patient try a herbal remedy, then offering to sell that remedy to the patient
> - Prenatal care

D. The Ongoing Struggle to Distinguish between Providers: A Role for Regulators, Patients, or the Professions?

An internet website promotes a cure for prostate cancer: Come to Mexico for vacation and treatment! The aisles at the local health food store promote herbal remedies, if you can afford it. The TV evangelist offers healing as he lays on hands.

Is it for consumers to differentiate between healers and charlatans? Or do we leave this to the somewhat economically conflicted medical profession and/or the state? As Maxwell Mehlman points out, this is hardly an issue we have left behind in the Nineteenth and Twentieth centuries.

Maxwell J. Mehlman, *Quackery*
31 Am. J.L. & Med. 349 (2005)

Everyone condemns medical quackery. Government regulators seek to protect us from it. Alternative providers strive to distance themselves from it. Orthodox medicine wants to stamp it out.

The question is: What constitutes "quackery"? How do we distinguish quacks from mainstream practitioners? Even more problematic, how do we distinguish between quackery, which everyone agrees is beyond the pale and therefore should be fair game for sanction, and practices that, while unorthodox, should be tolerated in the interests of promoting medical progress and patient choice?

* * *

I. Quackery Past and Present

The origin of the term "quackery" is obscure. One theory is that it comes from the Dutch word "quacksalver," which means "quackery" in Dutch. The term became widely used in the United States during the Nineteenth Century. Then, as now, it was derogatory. It described hucksters, charlatans, and snake oil salesmen.... Yet the Nineteenth Century quacks were not simply unscrupulous entrepreneurs who took advantage of gullible patients. They emerged in response to serious shortcomings of mainstream American medicine. In the early Nineteenth Century, orthodox practitioners emulated Dr. Benjamin Rush, a signer of the Declaration of Independence. Rush and his disciples advocated three principal remedies for whatever ailed the patient: phlebotomy or bleeding, the use of purgatives, and blistering with caustic poultices. Bleeding was necessary, Rush believed, because disease resulted from "morbid excitement caused by capillary tension." In fact, bleeding just served to weaken patients, often hastening or assuring their deaths. Purging was accomplished with calomel, a powder of mercury chloride, which caused a "heavy flow of saliva, bleeding gums, mouth sores, tooth loss, and an unfettered, bloody evacuation of the bowels." Rather than aiding patients, it caused dehydration. Blistering simply caused pain. In the words of one historian of quackery, "Rush's medical theories were unfortunately both archaic and lethal."

* * *

Faced with unresolved disease and horrific standard treatments, it is not surprising that many people sought relief by going to what might be considered quacks. Patent medicines were milder than the purgatives, and often contained soothing ingredients like alcohol and opium. Homeopathy used tiny amounts of active substances that produced few ill effects. Even the electrical gadgetry that captivated the public toward the end of the Nineteenth Century usually did not cause serious injury. Moreover, the quacks ventured into rural areas and frontier lands devoid of trained physicians.

* * *

What is striking is that so many of the conditions that gave rise to quackery in the Nineteenth Century are present today. After a half-century of major therapeutic breakthroughs in the form of antibiotics and vaccines, medical progress seems to have slowed. No cures have been found for the major killer diseases. Treatments, such as invasive surgery and chemotherapy, can be harsh. Promised advances in genomic medicine remain elusive. Patients who have tried standard approaches to no avail or who are skeptical or frightened of them may feel they have nothing to lose by trying unorthodox alternatives.

Another factor that may drive patients toward quackery is the commercialization of mainstream medicine. *** The premium placed on patient volume by managed care produces assembly-line medicine where physicians spend little time with patients. In contrast, observes Michael Young, "[m]ost quacks manage a superb 'bedside manner.' Since they can't really provide a cure if major disease is present, they specialize in promises, sympathy, consideration, concerns, and reassurance. The patient responds to such attention."

* * *

Finally, just as Nineteenth-Century quacks saw themselves as champions of free-market entrepreneurship, the anti-regulatory, neo-conservative economic philosophy that prevails inside the Beltway creates conditions conducive to modern quackery. For example, Republican lawmakers in Congress repeatedly (though unsuccessfully) have introduced a bill entitled the "Access to Medical Treatment Act" that would broaden the ability of licensed health care professionals to treat patients with alternative approaches. As one of the original sponsors, Senator Robert Dole (R-Kan.), stated: "In a free market system, it seems to make sense to make available non-harmful alternative medical treatments to individuals who desire such treatments, without the Federal Government standing in the way."

* * *

III. Where to Draw the Line

[W]hy is quackery so persistent? Why do people fall for it if it does not work or if it harms them? Certainly people can be gullible, and arguably a person who is ill and desperate for help is likely to be especially susceptible to the wiles of the charlatan. But one would expect that patients eventually would realize they were being duped. It is perhaps understandable that the proverbial snake-oil salesman could pull into a Nineteenth Century village, make a killing, and skedaddle before anyone made a fuss, but surely the townspeople would lynch the next con artist who rode into town. Why is quackery not so self-destructive?

The answer is twofold. First, quack remedies may appear to work when the patient's improvement is caused by the natural course of the illness. As one prominent critic of quackery points out, "most remedies are self-limiting and improve with time regardless of treatment." But quack remedies also may actually "work." That is, they may generate a placebo effect, which can make the patient feel better or even improve the patient's health by triggering the patient's own disease-fighting capabilities.

* * *

The gravamen of quackery therefore may boil down to a question of intent. If the purveyor intends to provide net benefit to the patient, then the purveyor is not a quack, even though the benefit is produced by a placebo effect that is itself the result of knowing deception. On the other hand, a person who hawks a nostrum *knowing* that it does not produce a placebo effect or that, although it may produce one, it ends up causing net harm to the patient, is a quack.

There are two problems with this approach, however. First, it is difficult to determine a person's intent. Clever quacks would take pains to avoid admitting that they knew that their products provided no patient benefit or caused net harm. Second, this approach would reward intentional ignorance, a head-in-the-sand attitude in which quacks simply avoided learning whether or not their products worked.

The alternative is to adopt an objective standard to identify when someone can be said to know that a product does not produce patient benefit. One option is to consider something quackery when it flies in the face of currently accepted medical and scientific knowledge. But the history of medicine shows that this test can easily become a means of cementing a prevailing school of thought and armoring it against valid criticism and needed progress. Consider peptic ulcers. It took ten years for the mainstream medical community to accept the results of Australian research that showed that most ulcers were caused by bacteria, not by stress or spicy foods.

A practice also could be deemed to be quackery when it had been tested and not found to produce net patient benefit. But this option would result in very few practices being considered quackery, since so few have been tested, and even fewer tested properly so that a benefit would have been detected if one actually had been produced.

In short, we are left with no handy, *a priori* way to identify quackery.

Notes and Questions

1. *Challenges to the breadth and vagueness of state medical practice acts.* There have been frequent challenges to the breadth of the state definitions of the "practice of medicine." *See e.g.*, *People v. Rogers*, 641 N.W.2d 595 (Mich. App. 2001) (defendant chal-

lenged the definition as facially broad and unconstitutionally vague; court denied claims stating that the statute created exceptions for gracious and humane acts and can be limited by application); *Pinkus v. MacMahon*, 29 A.2d 885 (N.J. 1943) (owner of a food store argued that the definition of the practice of medicine was so broad as to not allow a suggestion from one person to another regarding treatment of a condition); W.R. Habeeb, *Constitutionality and Construction of Statutes or Regulations Prohibiting One Who Has No License to Practice Dentistry or Medicine From Owning, Maintaining, or Operating an Office Therefor*, 20 A.L.R.2d 808 (1952). As demonstrated in the following case, *In re Guess*, 393 S.E.2d 833 (1990), these cases almost uniformly are resolved in favor of the constitutionality of the statute.

Several states, however, have revised their medical practice acts to place parameters on the broadness. For example, Oklahoma's practice act explicitly states that it shall not "prohibit services rendered by any person ... practicing any nonallopathic healing practice." 59 Okla. Stat. Ann. § 492. The Minnesota Practice Act exempts from "unlicensed practice" those unlicensed complementary and alternative health care providers practicing according to a newly enacted statutory provision Minn. Stat. Ann. § 146A.

2. *To protect the public health or the health of the profession?* State regulation of health professionals is based on the states' rights to regulate to "protect the public health" pursuant to its police power and the Tenth Amendment. Historically, this police power has been broadly defined to trump an individual's right to make autonomous health care choices when invoked to protect the public health. See *Jacobson v. Massachusetts*, 197 U.S. 11, 26 (1905) (upholding state's right to order compulsory vaccination against argument that compulsory vaccination violated the individual's right to care for his own body and health "in such way as to him seems best").

However, state licensure laws differ from traditional forms of public health regulation (which include laws such as mandatory testing, treatment, quarantine and isolation used to fight infectious diseases) in that they are a form of professional self-regulation. The state, through its licensing and practice acts, sets standards for entry to the licensed profession, but then delegates authority to interpret and enforce those standards to boards largely drawn from the regulated profession. While protecting the public health is the primary stated mission of licensing boards, these agencies are also in the position of protecting the economic interests of their licensees. Whether a board acts to protect the public, as opposed to the interests of the licensed profession, is a matter of frequent debate. *See* Sue A. Blevins, The Medical Monopoly: Protecting Consumers or Limiting Competition?, Policy Analysis No. 246 (Cato Instit. 1995); Carl F. Ameringer, State Medical Boards and the Politics of Public Protection (1999); Edwin A. Locke et al., *The Case Against Medical Licensing*, 8 Medicolegal News 13, 15 (1980).

II. The Licensed Provider's Use of Complimentary and Alternative Medicine

While a licensed physician does not face prosecution for the unlicensed practice of medicine, with the license come standards of conduct derived from state statutes generally referred to as "medical practice acts." These statutes define unprofessional conduct and provide direction to the physician-dominated medical boards (often referred to as a "Board of Medical Practice" or "Board of Healing Arts") charged with regulating both physician conduct and the practice of medicine. These medical practice acts authorize boards to investigate and discipline physicians on quality-related grounds and/or impairment because of chemical abuse or other reasons. Even where a physician charged with illegal conduct is found "not guilty" of criminal conduct, that individual may still face a civil investigation and discipline by a medical board.

Typical professional standards of conduct set out in medical practice acts, violation of which is cause for "discipline," include the following:

- Conviction of a felony reasonably related to the practice of medicine;
- False or misleading advertising;
- Engaging in any unethical conduct; conduct likely to deceive, defraud, or harm the public, or demonstrating a willful or careless disregard for the health, welfare or safety of a patient;
- Failure to supervise a physician's assistant;
- Aiding or abetting an unlicensed person in the practice of medicine;
- Adjudication as mentally incompetent;
- Engaging in unprofessional conduct. Unprofessional conduct shall include any departure from or the failure to conform to the minimal standards of acceptable and prevailing medical practice;
- Inability to practice medicine with reasonable skill and safety to patients by reason of illness, drunkenness, use of drugs, narcotics, chemicals;
- Revealing a privileged communication;
- Improper management of medical records;
- Engaging in abusive or fraudulent billing practices;
- Becoming addicted or habituated to a drug or intoxicant;
- Prescribing a drug or device for other than medically accepted therapeutic or experimental or investigative purposes; and
- Engaging in conduct with a patient which is sexual or may reasonably be interpreted by the patient as sexual.

Where a medical board finds that one or more of these standards of conduct have been violated, boards generally have broad authority to discipline the licensee. Disciplinary action can range from a simple reprimand and/or fine, to revocation of the license. Intermediate discipline measures include license suspension or placement of conditions (such as supervision, completion of training, and practice monitoring) on the individual practice. For an overview of the physician discipline process, *see* TIMOTHY JOST, OVERSIGHT OF THE COMPETENCE OF HEALTHCARE PROFESSIONALS 17–44 (Health Administration Press 1997).

When licensed physicians face discipline over use of CAM modalities, the standards of conduct most often at issue are "engaging in unprofessional conduct" (which includes the failure to conform to standards of acceptable and prevailing practice) and aiding and abetting the unlicensed practice of medicine by others. Of course, it is not just physicians who are licensed. Dentists, nurses, pharmacists and, in many states, physical therapists, psychologists, and podiatrists are licensed although the standards and scope of practice vary among the professions and states. Similarly, some CAM providers are licensed. Chiropractors, for example, are licensed in all 50 states whereas acupuncture is licensed in

37 and homeopaths in 3 states (see chart at page 56 for further description). But the largest controversies over the use of CAM therapies by licensed providers involve disputes between physicians and medical practice boards skeptical of alternative treatments.

When reading the following cases, consider how use of the CAM treatment came to the attention of the medical board; what evidence the court relied upon to make its decision; what deference the Court awarded the largely "self governing" board; and which discipline ultimately was imposed.

In re George A. Guess, M.D.
Supreme Court of North Carolina
393 S.E.2d 833 (1990)

Mitchell, Justice.

The facts of this case are essentially uncontested. The record evidence tends to show that Dr. George Albert Guess is a licensed physician practicing family medicine in Asheville. In his practice, Guess regularly administers homeopathic medical treatments to his patients. Homeopathy has been defined as:

> A system of therapy developed by Samuel Hahnermann on the theory that large doses of a certain drug given to a healthy person will produce certain conditions which, when occurring spontaneously as symptoms of a disease, are relieved by the same drug in small doses. This [is] ... a sort of "fighting fire with fire" therapy.

* * *

The Board of Medical Examiners of the State of North Carolina (herein Board) is legislatively created body established "to properly regulate the practice of medicine and surgery." N.C.G.S. § 90-2 (1985). On 25 June 1985, the Board charged Dr. Guess with unprofessional conduct, pursuant to N.C.G.S. § 90-14(a)(6), specifically based upon his practice of homeopathy.

* * *

Following notice, a hearing was held by the Board on the charge against Dr. Guess. The hearing evidence chiefly consisted of testimony by a number of physicians. Several physicians licensed to practice in North Carolina testified that homeopathy was not an acceptable and prevailing system of medical practice in North Carolina. In fact, there was evidence indicating that Guess is the only homeopath openly practicing in the State. Guess presented evidence that homeopathy is a recognized system of practice in at least three other states and many foreign countries. There was no evidence that Guess' homeopathic treatment had ever harmed a patient, and there was anecdotal evidence that Guess' homeopathic remedies had provided relief to several patients who were apparently unable to obtain relief through allopathic medicine.

Following its hearing, the Board revoked Dr. Guess' license to practice medicine in North Carolina, based upon findings and conclusions that Guess' practice of homeopathy "departs from and does not conform to the standards of acceptable and prevailing medical practice in this State," thus constituting unprofessional conduct as defined and prohibited by N.C.G.S. § 90-14(a)(6).

The Superior Court found and concluded that Guess' substantial rights had been violated because the Board's findings, conclusions and decision were "not supported by competent, material and substantial evidence and [were] arbitrary and capricious."

[T]he Court of Appeals rejected the Superior Court's reasoning to the effect that the Board's findings, conclusions and decision were not supported by competent evidence. [Citation omitted.] The Court of Appeals, nonetheless, affirmed the Superior Court's order reversing the Board's decision[.]

* * *

The statute central to the resolution of this case provides in relevant part:

§ 90-14. Revocation, suspension, annulment or denial of license.

(a) The Board shall have the power to deny, annul, suspend, or revoke a license ... issued by the Board to any person who has been found by the Board to have committed any of the following acts or conduct, or for any of the following reasons:

* * *

(6) Unprofessional conduct, including, but not limited to, *any departure* from, or the failure to conform to, *the standards of acceptable and prevailing medical practice*, or the ethics of the medical profession, *irrespective of whether or not a patient is injured thereby*....

N.C.G.S. § 90-14 (1985) ...

[T]he Court of Appeals reasoned that, in order to be a valid exercise of the police power, the statute must be construed as giving the Board authority to prohibit or punish the action of a physician only when it can be shown that *the particular action in question* poses a danger of harm to the patient or the public.

The Board argues, and we agree, that the Court of Appeals erred in construing the statute to add a requirement that each particular practice prohibited by the statute must pose an actual threat of harm. Our analysis begins with a basic constitutional principle: the General Assembly, in exercising the state's police power, may legislate to protect the public health, safety and general welfare. [Citations omitted.] When a statute is challenged as being beyond the scope of the police power, the statute will be upheld unless it has no rational relationship to such a legitimate public purpose. [Citations omitted.]

Turning to the subject of this case, regulation of the medical profession is plainly related to the legitimate public purpose of protecting the public health and safety. *See* Board of Medical Examiners v. Gardner, 201 N.C. 123, 127, 159 S.E. 8, 10 (1931). State regulation of the medical profession has long been recognized as a legitimate exercise of the police power.

* * *

The provision of the statute in question here is reasonably related to the public health. We conclude that the legislature, in enacting N.C.G.S. § 90-14(a)(6), reasonably believed that a general risk of endangering the public is *inherent* in any practices which fail to conform to the standards of "acceptable and prevailing" medical practice in North Carolina. We further conclude that the legislative intent was to prohibit any practice departing from acceptable and prevailing medical standards without regard to whether the particular practice itself could be shown to endanger the public.

* * *

Certain aspects of regulating the medical profession plainly require expertise beyond that of a layman. Our legislature recognized that need for expertise when it created a Board of Medical Examiners composed of seven licensed physicians and one additional member. N.C.G.S. § 90-2 (1985). Examining the language of N.C.G.S. § 90-14(a)(6), we conclude that the legislature clearly wished to protect the public from "unprofessional conduct" by physicians, and gave as an example of such conduct that which does not conform to the "standards of acceptable and prevailing medical practice." The statutory phrase "standards of acceptable and prevailing medical practice" is sufficiently specific to provide the Board-comprised overwhelmingly of expert physicians—with the "adequate guiding standards" necessary to support the legislature's delegation of authority.

The statute in question is a valid regulation which generally tends to secure the public health, safety, and general welfare, and the legislature has permissibly delegated certain regulatory functions connected with that valid exercise of the police power to the Board.... The Court of Appeals thus erred in requiring a showing of potential harm from the particular practices engaged in by Dr. Guess as a prerequisite to Board action, and for that reason the Court of Appeals' decision is reversed.

* * *

Dr. Guess strenuously argues that many countries and at least three states recognize the legitimacy of homeopathy. While some physicians may value the homeopathic system of practice, it seems that others consider homeopathy an outmoded and ineffective system of practice. This conflict, however interesting, simply is irrelevant here in light of the uncontroverted evidence and the Board's findings and conclusion that homeopathy is not currently an "acceptable and prevailing" system of medical practice in North Carolina.

While questions as to the efficacy of homeopathy and whether its practice should be allowed in North Carolina may be open to valid debate among members of the medical profession, the courts are not the proper forum for that debate. The legislature may one day choose to recognize the homeopathic system of treatment, or homeopathy may evolve by proper experimentation and research to the point of being recognized by the medical profession as an acceptable and prevailing form of medical practice in our state; such choices, however, are not for the courts to make.

We stress that we do not intend for our opinion in this case to retard the ongoing research and development of the healing arts in any way. The Board argues, and we agree within our admittedly limited scope of medical knowledge, that preventing the practice of homeopathy will not restrict the development and acceptance of new and beneficial medical practices. Instead, the development and acceptance of such new practices simply must be achieved by "acceptable and prevailing" methods of medical research, experimentation, testing, and approval by the appropriate regulatory or professional bodies.

REVERSED and REMANDED.

Frye, Justice, dissenting.

The underlying and essential question in this case is whether the Board may revoke a physician's license to practice medicine for "unprofessional conduct" under N.C.G.S. § 90-14(a)(6) based on a deviation from "the standards of acceptable and prevailing medical practice" without a finding that the deviation carries with it a potential for harm to the physician's patients or to the public. The Court of Appeals held that the Board may not do so. I agree and therefore dissent from the majority's holding to the contrary.

Even a cursory review of subsection (6) shows that it is directed to protecting the health and safety of patients and the public. The common thread running through each of these reasons for revocation of a license is the threat or potential for harm to patients and the public.

The majority treats the language "irrespective of whether or not a patient is injured thereby" as meaning irrespective of whether there is an injury or threat of injury caused by the deviation. I do not believe that the legislature so intended.... [T]his language gives the Board authority to act before injury occurs, but does not eliminate the public purpose requirement that the medical practice pose some threat or potential for harm to the public. The phrase "unprofessional conduct" connotes dishonorable or unethical behavior, [citation omitted] and, in the context of the statute, means substandard medical practice that cannot be tolerated because of the risk of harm such treatment poses to the public. [It] was enacted for the purpose of regulating the medical profession to protect the public health and safety and not simply to prevent a doctor from being the first one in the State to use a particular medicine or form of healing.

* * *

A careful examination of the evidence presented before the Board shows that Dr. Guess' practice of homeopathy is not unprofessional conduct within the meaning of N.C.G.S. §90-14(a)(6). All of the evidence tended to show that Dr. Guess is a highly qualified practicing physician who uses homeopathic medicines as a last resort when allopathic medicines are not successful. He takes 150 credits of continuing medical education approved by the American Medical Association every three years and from fifty to eighty hours of homeopathic continuing medical education each year.... This is not a case of a quack beguiling the public with snake oil and drums, but a dedicated physician seeking to find new ways to relieve human suffering. The legislature could hardly have intended this practice to be considered "unprofessional conduct" so as to revoke a physician's license in the absence of some evidence of harm or potential harm to the patients or to the public....

I also disagree with the majority's conclusion that Dr. Guess's evidence presented to the Board concerning the efficacy of homeopathy and its use outside North Carolina was not relevant to the issue before the Board. North Carolina does not and should not exist as an island to itself. The evidence that homeopathy is accepted in other states and in other countries of the world and that it has a beneficial rather than harmful effect certainly ought to be of some significance to the Board and to the citizens of this State concerned about the public health and safety. The majority rejects evidence of the legitimacy of homeopathy in other states and countries throughout the world as being irrelevant because homeopathy is not currently an acceptable and prevailing system of medical practice in North Carolina. This raises the legitimate question of how the acceptable and prevailing practice can be improved in North Carolina if we do not even consider what happens in other states and countries.

* * *

State Board of Medical Examiners of Florida v. Robert J. Rogers, M.D.

Supreme Court of Florida
387 So. 2d 937 (1980)

Alderman, Justice.

This cause is before us on direct appeal to review the decision of the District Court of Appeal, First District, in Rogers v. State Board of Medical Examiners of Florida, 371 So.2d 1037 (Fla. 1st DCA 1979), which construed a provision of the Florida Constitution.... [W]e affirm the result of the district court's decision because, under the particular facts of this case, it appears that the action of the Board of Medical Examiners restraining Dr. Rogers

> **Box 2.2**
>
> Chelation therapy is a chemical process in which a man-made animo acid, EDTA (ethylene diamine tetra-acetic acid), is delivered intravenously to bind molecules, such as metals and minerals, so they can be removed from the body. First used in the 1940s for the treatment of heavy metal poisoning, EDTA chelation removes heavy metals and minerals such as lead, iron, copper, and calcium from the blood and is approved by the FDA for use in treating lead poisoning and toxicity from other heavy metals.
>
> Although it is not approved by the FDA to treat coronary artery disease (CAD), some physicians and alternative medicine practitioners have recommended EDTA chelation as a way to treat this disorder. Several theories have been suggested for the use of this process in CAD. One theory suggests that EDTA chelation might work by removing calcium found in fatty plaques that block the arteries. Another suggests that chelation may stimulate the release of a hormone that in turn causes the calcium to break up or decreases cholesterol levels. Finally, a third theory suggests that chelation may reduce oxidative stress, which in turn would reduce inflammation in the arteries and improve blood vessel function. For additional information, see National Center for Complementary and Alternative Medicine (NCCAM), Chelation Therapy, http://nccam.nih.gov/chelation/q-and-a.htm#3.
>
> Several controversies exist surrounding the use of chelation therapy. For an overview of these disputes, *see* Michael H. Cohen, *Holistic Health Care: Including Alternative and Complementary Medicine in Insurance and Regulatory Schemes*, 38 Ariz. L. Rev. 83 (1996).

from further utilization of chelation treatment was an arbitrary and unreasonable exercise of the state's police power.

Dr. Rogers, a practicing physician in Brevard County, was ordered by the Brevard County Medical Association to discontinue the use of chelation therapy in the treatment of arteriosclerosis. As a result of his refusal to discontinue its use, Dr. Rogers was expelled from the association. Subsequently, pursuant to section 458.1201(1)(p), Florida Statutes (1975), the Florida State Board of Medical Examiners filed an administrative complaint charging Dr. Rogers with unprofessional conduct as defined by section 458.1201(1)(m), Florida Statutes (1975).... The hearing officer, whose findings and conclusions were adopted by the Board, concluded that chelation therapy can best be classified as investigational, that it more likely can be classified as quackery, and that its use outside a controlled environment such as a research institute fails to conform to acceptable and prevailing medical practice. Although not finding that chelation therapy is in any manner harmful to the patient or that Dr. Rogers misled his patients into believing that this methodology of treatment was a cure for arteriosclerosis, the hearing officer determined that Dr. Rogers failed to demonstrate that chelation therapy results in any patient benefit in terms of organic process and recommended that Dr. Rogers be reprimanded, be ordered to cease and desist from employing this treatment, and be placed on probation for one year during which time he should demonstrate the type of exemplary conduct required of a duly licensed physician.

Although the state has the power to regulate the practice of medicine for the benefit of the public health and welfare, this power is not unrestricted. The regulations imposed must be reasonably related to the public health and welfare and must not amount to an arbitrary or unreasonable interference with the right to practice one's profession which is a valuable property right protected by the due process clause.

Under the particular facts of this case, we conclude that the Board's action unreasonably interferes with Dr. Rogers' right to practice medicine by curtailing the exercise of his professional judgment to administer chelation therapy. The record before us fails to evidence harmfulness as a reasonable basis for the Board's action in restricting use of this treatment. Cf. Golden v. McCarty, 337 So.2d 388 (Fla.1976). Furthermore, the evidence demonstrates that no fraud or deception was exercised by Dr. Rogers upon his patients who were fully informed of the nature of the procedure and the possibility of no improvement. Sanctions were imposed against Dr. Rogers because he utilized a modality not accepted by the Board as having been proven effective, not because the Board found that the treatment was harmful or that Dr. Rogers had defrauded his patients into believing that chelation treatment was a cure for their conditions. The Board's findings do not support a conclusion of quackery, and the state-imposed limitation on the administration of chelation treatment has not been shown by the evidence to have a reasonable relationship to the protection of the health and welfare of the public.

Accordingly, based upon the record in this case, we hold that the Board's action is an unreasonable exercise of the police power, and we affirm the result of the decision of the district court quashing the order of the Board.

Robert C. Atkins, M.D., v. C. Maynard Guest, M.D., as Executive Secretary of the New York State Board for Professional Conduct

Supreme Court, New York County, New York
158 Misc.2d 426, 601 N.Y.S.2d 234 (1993)

Peter Tom, Justice.

In this motion, petitioner Robert C. Atkins ("Atkins"), a physician, seeks to challenge the authority of the New York State Board for Professional Medical Conduct (the "Board") to subpoena the file and records of one of his patients being treated by a controversial modality of treatment which allegedly controls and confines the spread of cancer.

The modality of treatment, which is the subject of this controversy, is known as "ozone therapy." Petitioner alleges that ozone, a naturally occurring substance, is a powerful oxidative agent that is bactericidal and virucidal, and when introduced into the body is useful in the management and control of cancer. Petitioner asserts that ozone therapy is not taught in United States medical schools and is not available in United States hospitals, but is widely used in Germany, where it was discovered and developed. The ozone therapy protocols used by petitioner were allegedly developed by Dr. Rudy Falk, the former head of oncological surgery at Toronto General Hospital.

The within proceeding concerns the records of a certain patient of Atkins who shall be referred to herein as "Jane Doe" or the "Patient". * * * Jane Doe was originally diagnosed with breast cancer in 1986 and subsequently underwent a left mastectomy. The Patient thereafter endured six months of chemotherapy and, since her surgery, regularly sees Dr. Ronald A. Primus, an oncologist. Jane Doe maintains that she was cancer-free for approximately four years until in or around December 1990 when Dr. Primus informed her that a blood test indicated the presence of cancer cells.

It is at this juncture that Jane Doe began to use Atkins who commenced the ozone therapy and concomitant nutritional guidelines. The Patient contends that she also continued to see Dr. Primus on Atkins' advice.

On or about September 14, 1992, during her second ozone treatment, Jane Doe felt weak and, after being observed for approximately four hours by Atkins and his staff, was sent to New York Hospital and was thereafter transferred to the emergency room of Jacobi Hospital. The Patient was, inter alia, treated in a hyperbaric chamber and was eventually released with no apparent side effects or injuries. The hyperbaric chamber is more commonly known as the decompression chamber, and is most often used to treat scuba divers suffering from the "bends," which is the presence of nitrogen in the blood stream (the Merck Manual, p. 2381 [15th ed. 1987]).

On or about September 15, 1992, the Board, through the Office of Professional Medical Conduct ("OPMC") received a complaint concerning Atkins' therapy from an emergency room doctor who had treated Jane Doe. Respondent maintains that on September 22, 1992, an internal committee on professional conduct met to review the complaint and determined, inter alia, that: the complaint was authentic; an investigation was warranted; and subpoenas should be issued to aid the investigation. On or about January 13, 1993, a subpoena (the "Subpoena") was issued and served on Atkins the following day. The Subpoena sought the production by Atkins of Jane Doe's entire file.... Petitioner seeks in this motion an order quashing the Subpoena Duces Tecum issued by respondent dated January 13, 1993 and compelling respondent to produce the complaint filed against him. Respondent cross-moves to enforce the Subpoena.

Atkins, a licensed physician in the State of New York, is a self-described "leading medical author, lecturer and radio host" with a medical practice estimated at over 5,000 patients. Petitioner claims to be one of the leading proponents of alternative medicine in the United States, which recognizes the limits of conventional medicine for treating cancer and other degenerative diseases through harsh drugs and invasive surgery, and the need for alternative methods of treatment. One such alternative method utilized by Atkins is ozone therapy.

In the instant motion, Atkins argues that respondent has failed to establish the minimum threshold requirement for the issuance of the Subpoena pursuant to the Public Health Law and that his patient who is not the complaining party has specifically asked not to permit respondent access to her personal medical records. Petitioner maintains that the mere fact that he utilizes ozone therapy is legally insufficient for OPMC to obtain the patient's medical records and that the patient's statutorily guaranteed confidentiality of her treatment with the doctor of her choice must be considered. In this motion, Atkins also seeks an order directing the release of the complaint made by the emergency room doctor on the ground that the cloak of confidentiality of the report has been waived since the complaining doctor has publicized in the press his news about Dr. Atkins and his controversial medical therapy.

[Enforceability of Subpoena]

The Board, through OPMC, is a State Agency vested with the authority and responsibility to investigate professional misconduct against physicians. The Board is empowered to bring charges, subpoena records, hold hearings and discipline physicians (Public Health Law § 230, 230-a).

* * *

In Matter of Levin v. Murawski, 59 N.Y.2d 35, 462 N.Y.S.2d 836, 449 N.E.2d 730, the Court of Appeals held that:

> To warrant the issue of a subpoena in furtherance of an investigation, undertaken in consequence of receipt of a complaint or otherwise ... there must be a showing that there exists '*some basis for inquisitorial action.*' (emphasis added)
>
> What is required when investigation is triggered by receipt of a complaint is a threshold showing of the authenticity of the complaint as warranting investigation, not a threshold substantiation of the charges made in the complaint ... the disclosure compelled by a subpoena is ordered in aid of investigation of the merits of the charges. (emphasis added) (citations omitted).

In an endeavor to establish the foregoing threshold, respondent submits an in camera affidavit, along with supporting documentation including hospital records.... A review of the in camera submissions made by respondent makes it clear that there exists a threshold showing warranting the issuance of the Subpoena.

* * *

[Confidentiality Issues re: medical records and complaint]

Petitioner argues that the rights of the patient, and the confidentiality of the physician-patient relationship, should act as a bar to the release of the Patient's records to the Board. The patient states:

> I unequivocally and categorically reject any attempt by the State to gain access to my privileged and confidential medical records.

In reviewing the legislative history of Public Health Law § 230, it is clear that the Legislature took note of the fact that the Board, during the first year of its existence, was frustrated in its ability to properly conduct investigations of physicians due to the unavailability of facts. The Board was therefore given subpoena power specifically designed to override the physician-patient privilege for the limited purpose of carrying out the Board's function and otherwise protected the confidentiality of that relationship.

* * *

The language of Public Health Law § 230(10)(*l*) leaves little doubt of the Legislature's intention:

> The board or its representatives may examine and obtain records of patients in any investigation or proceeding by the board....

* * *

The overriding Legislative intent of Public Health Law § 230 to promote and protect public health, and the statutory provision which guarantees confidentiality, permit OPMC to subpoena medical records of a physician under investigation without impinging upon the patient's constitutional rights despite claims that it invaded the patient's right of privileged confidentiality to receive a particular medical treatment and from a physician of her choice. See Schachter v. Whalen, 581 F.2d 35 (2d Cir. 1978).

In view of all of the foregoing, this Court concludes that despite the Patient's assertion of the physician-patient privilege, the subpoena should stand.

In addition, that branch of the petition which seeks the release of the complaint made to the Board is denied. The petitioner requests the complaint so that it may be used as a basis for an action in defamation, but both the release of the complaint, and its admission in any administrative or judicial proceeding, are prohibited by Public Health Law § 230(11)(a).

Accordingly, the petition is denied. Respondent's cross-motion is granted and petitioner is directed to comply with the Subpoena within thirty days of the service of a copy of this judgment with notice of entry.

Notes and Questions

1. Following the *Guess* decision, the North Carolina legislature amended the section under which Dr. Guess was penalized, limiting the grounds for discipline, stating: "The Board shall not revoke the license of or deny a license to a person solely because of that person's practice of a therapy that is experimental, nontraditional, or that departs from acceptable and prevailing medical practices unless, by competent evidence, the Board can establish that the treatment has a safety risk greater than the prevailing." N.C. GEN. STAT. 90-14(a)(6).

According to the North Carolina Medical Board, Dr. Guess is still licensed to practice medicine in the state of North Carolina, although his practice is in Charlottesville, Virginia, specializing in family practice. He also had out of state licenses in California (license cancelled either voluntarily or not renewed for five or more years), and Washington (expired in 1993). N.C. Med. Bd., License No.: 22573 (Issued: Jun. 13, 1978), *available at* http://www apps.ncmedboard.org/Clients/NCBOM/Public/Licensee_Details.aspx?&EntityID=81556&PublicFile=1 (North Carolina); Va. Dep't of Health Prof'l, License No. 0101027745 (Issued: Dec. 6, 1976, Expiration: Nov. 30, 2010), *available at* https://secure01.virginiainteractive.org/dhp/cgi-bin/search_publicdb.cgi?search_type=4&license_no=0101027745 (Virginia); Med. Bd. of Cal., License No. G 51720 (Originally Issued: Dec. 5, 1983), *available at* http://licenselookup.mbc.ca.gov/licenselookup/lookup.php?LicenseType=G&LicenseNumber=51720 (California); Wash. State Dep't of Health, Credential No. MD00022262 (Expiration Date: Nov. 1, 1993), *available at* https://fortress.wa.gov/doh/providercredentialsearch/ProviderDetail_1.aspx?CredentialIdnt=384454 (Washington).

Dr. Atkins is the author of the bestselling diet book, Dr. Atkins' Diet Revolution (1972), and the follow-up, Dr. Atkins' New Diet Revolution (2002), detailing the benefits and ease of a high calorie, low-carbohydrate diet ("Atkins Diet"). Dr. Atkins died on April 17, 2003, from complications resulting from a head injury after falling on ice on his way to work on a New York City sidewalk. CNN Health, *Diet Guru Dr. Robert Atkins Dead at 72* (Apr. 17, 2003), *available at* http://www.bmj.com /cgi/reprint/326/7398/1090.pdf (obituary). N.Y. Bd. of Med, License No. 081022 (Issued: Aug. 5, 1958), *available at* http://www.nysed.gov/coms/op001/opsc2a?profcd=60&plicno=081022&namechk=ATK.

In early 2008, the State of Florida Department of Health filed an administrative complaint against Dr. Rogers. Three charges were made against Dr. Rogers including medical malpractice, fraudulent representations in the practice of medicine, and inappropriate prescribing of the drug Westhroid. In December 2009, Dr. Rogers applied for and was granted a Voluntary Relinquishment of License in order to avoid further administrative action against him. With that, Dr. Rogers is no longer licensed to practice medicine in the state of Florida, nor can he apply for licensure in Florida in the future.

2. The *Guess* court noted that "homeopathy may evolve by proper experimentation and research to the point of being recognized by the medical profession as an acceptable and prevailing form of medical practice in our state" and states that "preventing the practice of homeopathy will not restrict the development and acceptance of new and beneficial medical practices." Do you agree with the court? How can experimentation and research proceed on homeopathy if its practice is out of bounds for licensed physicians? Is the approach of the *Rogers* Court—to permit use of an unproved modality if there is not evidence of harm and patients are not defrauded—preferable?

3. Are there factual distinctions between the chelation practices of Dr. Rogers and the homeopathic practices of Dr. Guess which justify the different holdings of the Florida and North Carolina courts? If not, what else might explain the divergent opinions?

4. In *Rogers*, the court appeared to give weight to the fact that Dr. Rogers' patients were "fully informed" of the nature of chelation and of the "possibility of no improvement." Should physicians be able to use "informed consent" of patients as a defense in a licensing case? If you were advising Dr. Rogers, what would you suggest that he tell patients prior to chelation treatment?

5. None of the patients in these three cases claimed harm of any sort. Several patients claimed that the CAM treatments relieved pain. Should patient harm be a prerequisite to Board imposed discipline? Most state boards do not require harm, although, recently Alaska and Washington revised their healing arts statutes to require "demonstrable physical harm" to a patient, even if the remedy is unconventional. *See* Kristen J. Josefek, *The Changing Face of Law and Medicine in the New Millennium*, 26 AM. J.L. & MED. 295, 302 (2000).

6. In 2009, the Washington Supreme Court visited the state's CAM. In *Ames v. Washington State Health Department Medical Quality Health Assurance Commission*, 208 P.3d 549 (Wash. 2009), the court examined whether "expert testimony should have been offered on the standard of care with regard to Ames's techniques or on the efficacy (or lack thereof) of LISTEN." The petitioner, Dr. Geoffrey Ames, used the LISTEN device on Patient One (P1) to diagnose and treat the cause of P1's sluggishness and fatigue. LISTEN is a bio-feedback machine that measures sweat on the skin to determine how the skin reacts to various stimuli. The machine is not FDA approved for detecting or treating allergies, the reason Dr. Ames was using it. Nor had Dr. Ames been properly trained on the machine. The Washington State Health Department's Medical Quality Health Assurance Commission (MQAC), during a hearing prompted from P1's complaint, found that Dr. Ames "engaged in unprofessional conduct in violation" of state law and suspended his license.

Dr. Ames appealed the Commissions decision. The Washington Supreme Court ruled that Washington law does not require expert testimony in MQAC hearings and that the members of the Commission may use their own expert understanding in evaluating a factual claim presented to them under the substantial evidence standard. The court acknowledged that, in certain bare-bones cases where little evidence is available to support a factual finding by the Commission, the substantial evidence standard would vacate the Commissions' ruling. However, in this case, the court found that the expert testimony on the record was substantial enough to pass the test. Two experts, including the creator of LISTEN and another physician with understanding of bio-feedback machines, along with Dr. Ames testified to the Commission.

Ames examined the evidentiary nature of Medical Practice Board proceedings. In the Comment below, that process is examined in more detail.

Comment: Complaint and Investigation Process

State health licensing boards are responsible not only for determining who meets the standards for licensure, but also for investigating complaints and disciplining licensees whom they find to have violated the statutes or rules governing the profession. While the complaint and investigation process differs among states, the following process is fairly typical.

a. Initial Processing

The process begins with the receipt of a complaint by the licensing board. The board is typically comprised of a majority of licensees, although most today also include consumer (non-licensee) members as well. Much of the initial work is done by board staff, (typically state employees), and the state's Attorney General's Office. Upon receipt, board staff will first look to see if the complaint is jurisdictional: that is, whether the complaint alleges a violation of a statute or rule that the board is empowered to enforce. A complaint about personality, for example, typically would be dismissed. Most licensing boards have at least one complaint committee. Typically, this committee is made up of at least two board members and board staff. The committee evaluates the complaint and decides on the best way to purse it. Some complaints do not require much investigation at all. With most, however, board staff will subpoena relevant medical records. The board may also hire a consultant to help the complaint committee assess a particular complaint. On occasion, a complaint may be referred to either the Attorney General's Office or similar agency for a field investigation which would include more extensive document retrieval and formal interviews with the licensee and witnesses.

b. Committee Deliberations

After the investigation is complete, the complaint committee typically chooses one of several alternatives: 1) dismiss the complaint; 2) seek temporary suspension of the licensee if there is an immediate, serious threat to patient health; 3) conduct an information conference; and 4) hold an informal evidentiary hearing. Temporary suspensions are rare, so most licensees involved in the process face either an informal conference or hearing.

The "informational" or "educational" conference typically is to educate a licensee on a problem that does not rise to the level of requiring disciplinary action. The informal evidentiary hearing, however, typically begins with a written notice that explains the conduct that arguably violates the board's practice act.

The informal evidentiary hearing (or "conference") is usually attended by complaint committee members, the board's attorney (often a member of the state Attorney General's Office), the board staff, and the licensee. The licensee may be represented by counsel. The hearing often will be recorded. It may include questioning of the licensee by complaint committee and counsel about the allegations found in the notice. In some states, negotiation and conciliation, as well as education of the licensee, may take place as well.

c. Negotiation of a Resolution

After the initial informal hearing (sometimes at the very end of the hearing itself), the complaint committee will present a recommended resolution. If the resolution involves disciplinary action of any sort, the terms typically will be set forth in a proposed stipulation and order. The proposed stipulation and order not only will spell out the disciplinary action sought, but will also describe the underlying conduct in many states. The rationale behind the factual specificity is due to the confidentiality of the complaint process. Often, until there is resolution through either a negotiated agreement or other final board action, even the complainant will not be aware of the status of the proceedings.

In negotiating the agreement, three important considerations should be understood. *First,* the primary mission of the board should be to protect the public. Whether serious harm has occurred to date is not as critical as the question of potential harm in the future. *Second,* the licensee should be concerned about what constitutes "discipline." Discipline includes revocation or suspension of a license or placing limitations or conditions on a license. Limitations may include having one's practice supervised or the areas of practice restricted. A civil penalty to reimburse the board for costs and an agreement to take additional classes, on the other hand, are not typically considered "discipline." One reason the distinction is important is because state disciplinary and licensure boards are required to report certain disciplinary actions against physicians to the National Practitioner Data Bank (NPDB). While the general public is not allowed access to the NPDB, hospitals and licensure boards do have access and, indeed, hospitals must check the NPDB for physicians applying for staff privileges, thus providing a system for preventing doctors with a poor disciplinary track record from moving from state to state and hospital to hospital. *Third,* the licensee should consider the implications (beyond licensure) of discipline and the facts admitted to the stipulation. Does the agreement affect the ability to qualify as a Medicare provider? Are there possible criminal implications? Finally, what exposure might exist for a potential malpractice claim?

d. Administration Hearing and Board Decision

If the settlement negotiations are unsuccessful, the case will go to a contested case hearing, typically before an administrative law judge. The hearings (which are closed to the public in most states) often involve extensive expert testimony and can spread across several months. After the hearing, the administrative law judge will make factual findings and a recommendation to the full board as to whether violation of the statutes or rules occurred. The board may accept the recommendations either in whole or in part and it is the board that ultimately decides whether or not to impose discipline. The board's decision (which is usually public if discipline is imposed) may then be appealed to either district or an appellate court.

Notes and Questions

1. Licensees have a property right in the state issued license to practice. As a result, due process considerations come into play during the complaint, investigation and hearing process. Simply stated, due process requires appropriate notice and the opportunity to be heard. With regard to "notice," two types of notice are critical. First, licensees should have individualized notice of the specific questioned acts — in essence the charges against the licensee. Second, licensees must have generalized advanced notice (through the governing statute or rule) that the type of conduct at issue may lead to discipline.

Looking at the generic complaint and investigation process described above, consider whether this process is: 1) too lengthy and cumbersome; 2) affords about the right amount of due process; or 3) does not provide sufficient due process to the licensee. Also, consider how the process described above compares to the process used in the *Guess* case. Did Dr. Guess have the appropriate amount of due process? Was the statutory prohibition against "unprofessional conduct" sufficient notice to Dr. Guess that the practice of homeopathy was "unprofessional conduct?" *See Dommisse v. Napolitano*, 474 F. Supp. 2d 1121 (D. Ariz. 2007) (rejecting constitutional claim by M.D. who argued the Medical Board violated his rights by subjecting him to discipline under standards of care applicable to practitioners of allopathic medicine rather than naturopathic); *Hoffman v. State Board of Registration for the Healing Art*, 936 S.W.2d 182 (Mo. Ct. App. 1996) (pushing nurse in the operating room was unprofessional conduct); *Ward v. Oregon State Board*, 226 Or. 128, 510 P.2d 554 (1973) (upholding revocation of license for unprofessional conduct where nurse had permitted her daughter to serve as a registered nurse although her daughter had no license). *But see Tuma v. Board of Nursing*, 593 P.2d 711 (Idaho 1979) (reversing Board of Nursing order which disciplined nurse for discussing treatment options without physician approval, holding that the prohibition against "unprofessional conduct" did not give adequate notice that this specific conduct was prohibited). For a critical discussion of the investigation and discipline process, as applied to physicians who utilize CAM therapies, *see* Joseph A. Barrette, *The Alternative Medical Practice Act: Does it Adequately Protect the Rights of Physicians to Use Complementary and Alternative Medicine?*, 77 St. John's L. Rev. 75 (2003).

2. Dr. Atkins argued (unsuccessfully) for a copy of the complaint filed by the Emergency Room doctor against him. While Dr. Atkins sought the complaint as evidence in a defamation lawsuit, could he have argued that his right to due process entitled him to the complaint? If you represented the Board, how would you respond to this argument?

3. Legal disputes over medical board access to patient records in a licensing investigation (as occurred in *Atkins*) are frequent. *See In re Doe*, 711 F.2d 1187 (2d Cir. 1983) (Board can access patient records in any investigation and proceeding by the board acting within the scope of its authorization); *Schachter v. Whalen*, 581 F.2d 35 (2d Cir. 1978) (access to patient medical records for investigation of licensed physician for misconduct are crucial for implementation of public policy). Typically patients are unaware that their records have been either subpoenaed or produced. See 45 C.F.R § 164.512 (HIPPA allows uses and disclosures of protected health information without the written authorization of the individual, if required by law or for purposes of public health activity).

4. In *Atkins*, the Court conducted an "in camera" examination of hospital and other unidentified records submitted by the Board to determine whether there was a "threshold showing of the authenticity of the complaint" justifying a subpoena. The court found that the threshold showing had been made without disclosing the facts or records to support this finding. Nor did Dr. Atkins have the opportunity to review what the Board submitted, in camera, to the court. What minimal facts and allegations do you believe would have been necessary to justify a Board subpoena? What—beyond the fact that Jane Doe underwent ozone therapy—would be necessary?

5. In *State Bd. of Registration for Healing Arts v. McDonagh*, 123 S.W.3d 146 (Mo. 2003), the Board brought a disciplinary complaint against Dr. McDonagh alleging violation of Missouri Healing Arts Practice Act through his use of chelation therapy in the treatment of patients with vascular disease. The Administrative Hearing Committee (AHC) heard expert testimony from the Board that the use of chelation therapy to treat vascular disease is not generally accepted and does not meet the standard of care, as well as expert testimony that supported Dr. McDonagh's off-label use of chelation to treat vascular disease. The Board objected to this expert testimony supporting Dr. McDonagh. The AHC did not rule on the objection. Based on all the evidence, the AHC admitted the testimony, found no evidence of harm from chelation therapy and found no cause to discipline McDonagh. The circuit court affirmed.

The Board appealed alleging that the AHC failed to apply the appropriate standard for admission of expert testimony, and that the testimony of McDonagh's experts should have been excluded. The Supreme Court of Missouri concluded that facts and data on which an expert relies must be those reasonably relied on by experts in the relevant field. In this case, the Court concluded that the relevant field is physicians treating persons with vascular disease and because the AHC failed to properly apply this standard, the Court reversed and remanded to the AHC for reconsideration.

6. Licensed CAM providers also face the complaint, investigation and hearing process described above. For example, in *Filkoff N.D. v. Conn. Board of Naturopathic Examiners*, 1999 Conn. Super. LEXIS 2388 (Conn. Super. Dec. 1, 1999) the Court affirmed the Board's decision to revoke the naturopath's license for what the court described as a "bizarre scenario" where the licensee, Dr. Filkoff, made repeated sexually suggestive remarks to a female patient (which included a "tour" of his residence, suggestions of tantric exercises

and massages, and locking her into his office); falsified a medical record; submitted fraudulent claims to an insurance carrier; and violated doctor/patient confidentiality. *See Faulkenstein v. District of Columbia Bd. of Med.*, 727 A.2d 302 (D.C. 1999) (acupuncturist's license was revoked where he failed to complete apprenticeship, did not have a collaborating physician and used the initials "M.D."); *Zabrecky v. Conn. Bd. of Chiropractors*, No. 0702118, 1991 Conn. Super. LEXIS 2682 (Conn. Super. Nov. 15, 1991) (chiropractor's license was suspended and civil penalty imposed where licensee found to have rendered negligent care in prescribing and dispensing substances "Neythymin" and "Neytumorin"). For a thoughtful discussion of the ethical dilemmas which may face attorneys representing CAM practitioners in licensing disputes, *see* Emerson Lee, *Attorney Professional Responsibility Implications of a Fraudulent CAM Licensing Application*, 21 Geo. J. Legal Ethics 881 (2008).

Problem

Assume that you are Executive Director of a State Medical Board with a statutory code of conduct similar to the one summarized at page 41 of this text. You have received complaints about the following conduct by four separate licensed physicians. Outline what steps, if any, you would take to investigate the complaints and on what statutory basis.

- A surgeon teaches cardiac patients self-hypnosis to reduce post-operative depression and pain.
- An anesthesiologist dangles a pendulum to test a patient's chakras, or vortices of energy, and employs energy healing, while reducing anesthesia levels as appropriate just prior to surgery.
- A psychiatrist treating a depressed, suicidal patient not only prescribes appropriate medication, but also mentions the Tibetan Book of the Dead for contemplation of what might happen immediately following suicide.
- A general practitioner treating a patient with anxiety tells the patient that "celery juice has a calming effect on the nervous system."

[These issues were taken from a comprehensive article on holistic health care: Michael H. Cohen, *Holistic Health Care: Including Alternative and Complementary Medicine in Insurance and Regulatory Schemes*, 38 Ariz. L. Rev. 83, 121 (1996).]

The Federation of State Medical Boards issued guidelines to be used by boards concerning potential discipline of physicians for use of CAM therapies. The guidelines suggest that a medical board evaluate whether the treatment is:

- Effective and safe: having adequate scientific evidence of efficacy and/or safety or greater safety than other established treatment models for the same condition;
- Effective, but with some real or potential danger: having evidence of efficacy, but also of adverse side effects;
- Inadequately studied, but safe: having insufficient evidence of clinical efficacy, but reasonable evidence to suggest relative safety; or
- Ineffective and dangerous: proven to be ineffective or unsafe through controlled trials or documented evidence or as measured by a risk/benefit assessment.

House of Delegation of the Federation of State Medical Boards of the United States, Model Guidelines for the Use of Complimentary and Alternative Therapies in Medical Practice (April 2002), *available at* http://www.fsmb.org/pdf/2002_grpol_Complementary_Alternative_Therapies.pdf.

Table 2.1 Overview of Licensing Requirements for Select CAM Practitioners

Profession	States with Licensure	Training	Notes
Chiropractors (D.C.)	50 and District of Columbia	4–5 years or 4200 hours; includes medical sciences and clinical experiences	None
Non-M.D. acupuncturists	37 and District of Columbia	3 years or 1800 hours; includes 300 hours Chinese herbology and 500 clinical hours; some (but not all) states require anatomy	Additionally three states have certification and two require registration. One state (Oklahoma) explicitly limits acupuncture to licensed M.D./D.O.s
Naturopathic doctors (N.D.)	17	4-year postgraduate program	Two states specifically prohibit practice
Massage therapists	36 states and District of Columbia	100–1000 hours; most states specify a minimum of 500 hours; states may specify graduation from an accredited program	Two additional states require certification or registration
Homeopathic physicians	3; Licensure as a homeopathic physician is available only to MDs and DOs in Nevada, Arizona, and Connecticut	Nevada specified 6 months of postgraduate training; Arizona requires 300 hours; Connecticut does not specify any educational requirements	In two additional states homeopathy falls within the scope of practice for licensed chiropractors; three states with Health Freedom statutes may permit unlicensed practice with certain training/disclosures

In your role as Executive Director, are these guidelines helpful in assessing potential next steps in the four complaints?

III. Unlicensed Providers and the Practice of Medicine

While licensed providers utilizing CAM modalities (such as Doctors Guess, Atkins and Rogers) may face allegations of unprofessional conduct and failure to meet professional standards, unlicensed providers face even more uncertain terrain. In this section, we explore practitioners facing charges of practicing medicine without a license. These individuals may face either the threat of injunctive relief (a court order to stop providing the patient service), criminal prosecution, or both.

Typically it is the state medical board which polices the prohibition against the unlicensed practice of medicine. While boards usually are complaint-driven (in that they respond to and investigate complaints), state medical boards are often more proactive where the unlicensed practice of medicine is concerned. For example, many medical boards use undercover investigators posing as patients.

In addition to enforcement by medical boards, you will also find, but less frequently, other health licensing boards attempt to exclude unlicensed providers from practicing. *People and Sherman v. Cryns* is an example of this in the nursing context. Finally, because the unlicensed practice of medicine is a crime (most often a gross misdemeanor) criminal prosecution by the district attorney and/or state Attorney General may occur.

The breadth of the definition of the "practice of medicine" provides prosecutors and the medical board levying charges with a great deal of latitude in selecting cases. The other way to view this (from the perspective of the unlicensed practitioner) is that, simply stated, much is uncertain. When does the lay midwife move from simply "catching" the baby to "delivering" the child? When is the naturopath providing education about herbal products as opposed to diagnosis and prescribing? While a number of states provide for licensure or registration of certain CAM providers (see illustrative chart on p. 56), most practice in an uncertain world. Chief among these are "healing touch" and spiritual providers, as well as lay midwives.

Examining these three areas highlight the themes underlying many cases involving unlicensed CAM providers: the parameters of patient choice in providers and place of treatment; the concern that by allowing CAM modalities, patients will not avail themselves of "scientifically proven" remedies; the age old dilemma of distinguishing between health care providers and, simply put, quacks; the deference (if any) we should give to different cultures and their faith-based practitioners; and the underlying question of whether regulation through licensure is motivated by public protection or economic protection of allopathic physicians. Consider these issues as you review the following cases and commentary selections, as well as when you engage in the role-play exercise at the end of this section.

A. From Prayer to Healing Touch

Religious healing was one of the earliest exceptions to the prohibition on the unlicensed practice of medicine. Defining the parameters of the exception proved a challenge in the mid Twentieth Century. On one hand, the First Amendment to the Constitution guarantees freedom of religion. On the other hand, the Tenth Amendment reserves to the states the power to protect the public health through its policy power.

One difficult question is when religious leaders' words become a "diagnosis" and their acts "treatment." A second is when the state should intervene to end religious healing or insist upon supplementing it with conventional medicine in the name of public health. In the cases that follow, we see courts struggle with this tension between religious freedom and state power to protect public health. As you read the cases, think about how the legal analysis applied in *Curley* and *Andrews* would address the issues raised by CAM practices known today as "healing touch." For as the Twentieth Century waned, the country saw a movement from religious healing (as defined by the system of beliefs of the various mainstream religions) to a broad spectrum of spiritual practices, many of which were not connected with organized religion. Consider the following CAM therapy (as generally described by the Office of CAM and Alternative Health at NIH) and the potential legal status of its practitioners:

> **Energy Medicine** is a domain in CAM that includes putative energy fields, also called biofields. These energy fields have defied measurement to date. Therapies

involving putative energy fields are based on the concept that human beings are infused with a subtle form of energy. This vital energy or life force is known under different names in different cultures, such as "qi" in traditional Chinese medicine (TCM), "ki" in the Japanese Kampo system, "doshas" in Ayurvedic medicine, and elsewhere as "prana," "etheric energy," "fohat," "orgone," "odic force," "mana," and "homeopathic resonance." Vital energy is believed to flow throughout the material human body. Therapists claim that they can work with this subtle energy, see it with their own eyes and use it to effect changes in the physical body and influence health.

Examples of practices involving putative energy fields include Reiki and Johrei (both of Japanese origin), and healing (or therapeutic) touch, in which the therapist is purported to identify imbalances and correct a client's energy by passing his or her hands over the patient. Both of these modalities involve movement of the practitioner's hands over the patient's body to become attuned to the condition of the patient, with the idea that by so doing, the practitioner is able to strengthen and reorient the patient's energies.

Many small studies of therapeutic touch have suggested its effectiveness in a wide variety of conditions, including wound healing, osteoarthritis, migraine headaches, and anxiety in burn patients. However, there has been little rigorous scientific research. Overall, these therapies have impressive anecdotal evidence, but none has been proven scientifically to be effective.

Another example of a popular CAM therapy with spiritual overtones is the field of **mind-body interventions**. The Office of CAM and Alternative Health reports that there is evidence that mind-body interventions can be effective in the treatment of coronary artery disease, enhancing the effect of standard cardiac rehabilitation in reducing all-cause mortality and cardiac event recurrences for up to two years. Certainly, mind-body techniques, including relaxation, meditation, guided imagery, biofeedback and hypnosis are popular modalities—and utilized by about 17 percent of the population.

When these and similar CAM therapies (with the exception of intercessory prayer) are provided by non-clergy, they do not fit neatly into a religious exception to the prohibition against the unlicensed practice of medicine. Nor are they supported by consensus scientific evidence regarding their safety and efficacy. Yet these spiritual approaches to healing, whether described as the "yin and yang" in oriental medicine or "centering" process used in mind-body medicine, are used by a variety of CAM providers. As you read the following cases, consider 1) when does a spiritual advisor cross the line between religious care and the practice of medicine; and 2) given the dictates of the cases and the broad parameters of the "practice of medicine," whether secular "spiritual healing" practices, when undertaken by a non-physician, may subject the practitioner to prosecution for the unlicensed practice of medicine.

Curley v. State of Florida
Supreme Court of Florida, en Banc
16 So. 2d 440 (1943)

PER CURIAM.

An information was filed against the defendant on April 21, 1942, in the Circuit Court of Walton County, in two counts.... The second count on which the defendant was convicted, charged that the defendant 'did practice medicine, he the said E. C. Curley not being then and there lawfully licensed and authorized to practice medicine in the State of Florida, by the State Board of Medical Examiners,' etc. The defendant pled not guilty.

Section 458.15, Florida Statutes 1941, F.S.A. §458.15, makes it a criminal offense for any person, not being then lawfully licensed or authorized to practice medicine in this state, to 'practice or advertise to practice medicine.'

Section 458.13 defines the practice of medicine in these words: 'A person is practicing medicine within the meaning of this chapter, except as hereinafter stated, who holds himself out as being able to diagnose, treat, operate or prescribe for any human disease, pain, injury, deformity or physical condition, or who shall offer or undertake by any means or method to diagnose, treat, operate or prescribe for any human disease, pain, injury, deformity or physical condition.' Then follow numerous exceptions. It is provided that this statute shall not be construed to affect the furnishing of medical assistance in cases of emergency or the domestic administration of family remedies 'or the practice of the religious tenets of any church'....

* * *

Taking the testimony as a whole, including that of the State, our conclusion is that the testimony did not show that this defendant was practicing medicine within the meaning of the statute. He never used or prescribed any drugs, nor did he use any instruments. About all that he usually did was to touch the body of persons who came to him, as many did, with his fingers at various points on the body, some times at one or two, some times at several points, meanwhile praying silently to himself. He believed that he had some marvelous power from on High to heal practically all of the ills of the flesh. In some instances he would tell people what he thought was the matter with them, and in some few instances he did resort to massage in addition to the touching of the body with his fingers. But the state as well as defense witnesses testified that they did not go to him as a medical doctor or for medical treatment.

* * *

We recognize the wisdom and constitutional validity of the legislative policy of protecting the public by penal laws against ignorant quacks and scheming charlatans who would attempt to pose as members of the great medical profession and assume the ability to diagnose diseases and prescribe drugs or perform operations for their cure. The proper practice of medicine and surgery require years of study and training, and the qualifications of those who are allowed to enter this noble profession must be evidenced by licenses issued by the State Board of Medical Examiners, who have endeavored to maintain a high standard of mental and moral qualifications in the profession. The overwhelming majority of our people depend entirely upon the medical profession to diagnose and cure their ills and to restore them to health and vigor and are very skeptical of the merit of any other means.

But the legislature has also recognized the fact that from ancient times down to this modern and so called materialistic age there have always been quite a large percentage of people who believed in the efficacy and availability of Divine power, not only to save the souls but also the bodies and lives of men and to heal all the ills that flesh is heir to, if one but has sufficient faith to invoke the interposition of that Supreme power. And if this class of people hear and believe that some person can and does invoke the power of Most High to heal people of their ills, or that in his own person such individual possesses some strange mental, magnetic or psychic power to banish disease from the human body, people entertaining that belief will seek him out. And it is not the policy of our laws to prevent them; nor to punish those to whom they go, and who endeavor to heal the ills of men by such mental or spiritual means-so long as they do not invade the province of the medical profession and assume the ability to diagnose diseases and prescribe drugs or other medical or surgical or mechanical means to restore the health of those who go to them. The reason for this policy is founded upon the liberty of the individual citizen under our bill of rights, and the fact that so long as these faith healers or spirit mediums rely upon their power, by prayer or faith, to invoke the exercise of the power of the Almighty, if indeed they fail to cure, they at least can do no harm. On the other hand, the ignorant and unlicensed quack who poses as a physician and attempts to diagnose diseases and to prescribe drugs or perform operations, etc., may, and probably will, do a great deal of harm and is dangerous to the community.

* * *

Now this appellant testified that the power which he invoked was not his own, but that it was the power of God. And if some of the uncontradicted witnesses are to be believed, he was instrumental in accomplishing some remarkable cures. And there is no evidence to show that he ever did anyone any harm or injury. Now, to most of us, this matter of healing 'by faith and the laying on of hands,' ancient as it is, is still beyond us. But according to Shakespeare's Hamlet, 'There are more things in heaven and earth, Horatio, than are dreamt of in your philosophy.' And in that magnificent speech of St. Paul's before King Agrippa, he said to the king: 'Why should it be thought a thing incredible with you, that God should raise the dead?' So the legislature and the courts might well accord our citizens the liberty to decide such questions as these for themselves.

* * *

Board of Medical Quality Assurance v. Arthur Andrews
Court of Appeal, Sixth District, California
211 Cal. App. 3d 1346 (1989)

Record

Board [of Medical Quality Assurance] initiated this proceeding September 12, 1986, by a petition requesting a temporary restraining order and a permanent injunction pursuant to section 125.5 and sections 2052 and 2053. The petition alleged that appellants (hereafter collectively "RSNH") were engaging in the unlawful practice of medicine without a license and that their conduct had injured named individuals.

Board's evidence included an advertisement for RSNH from a periodical. This advertisement did not mention religion. It was entitled "The California Health Sanctuary" and claimed to offer supervised fasting, natural diet, rest, and instruction in natural hygiene.

Also offered was a document published by the Religious School of Natural Hygiene entitled "The Major Tenets-Heed My Words." This document stated that the Religious School of Natural Hygiene is a healing church which operates the California Health Sanctuary near Hollister, California, for those "who seek health restoration, knowledge of health maintenance and experience in healthful living." This document described the philosophy of the RSNH. Among other things it stated that prayer, rest and fasting, along with the laying on of hands are activities which permit God's healing power to be implemented. It also recommended consumption of raw foods or foods in their natural state.

A card given to members of the RSNH states that the practices of this organization preclude use of drugs, medicines, vaccinations, blood transfusions, x-rays "and all other such practices." The RSNH encourages prayer and fasting, often for long periods of time, as instruments to promote healing and eliminate disease. It further recommends organic and uncooked foods.

Board further presented evidence of practices of RSNH which included promulgating a doctrine that many physical conditions can be cured by undergoing supervised periods of fasting; persuading certain individuals to participate in such fasts, under supervision of appellant Andrews, who received compensation; advising some persons to stop taking medications prescribed by a physician; and performing diagnostic procedures such as physical examinations with a stethoscope, taking blood pressures and pulses, feeling parts of the body, examining the mouth and eyes, and in one case attempting to remove a colonic blockage by hand. Specifically, Board presented declarations and testimonial evidence of five individuals who had fasted under Andrews' supervision and who claimed to have been injured, as well as evidence concerning another individual who had died immediately after undergoing a lengthy supervised fast. Each of the surviving witnesses claimed severe and persistent physical injury as a result of a prolonged fast. Also, each of these witnesses claims to have consulted Andrews in order to correct a physical ailment, not for religious or spiritual purposes. * * *

[Patient] Nettle came to Andrews to lose weight. Andrews said he was a healer and held himself out as having special skill and knowledge to treat obesity by supervised fasting. [Nettle] paid him to supervise her fasts, which he did for payment. She fasted as much as 30 days at a stretch, receiving only water. During these fasts she had such symptoms as multiple vomiting without relief, irregular menstruation, bloody urine, and amnesia, and lost the ability to work and developed great mental confusion. When she was delirious Andrews said things to her concerning religion. She was at the Health Sanctuary for 10 months and lost 160 pounds. To the present day she suffers adverse physical and mental symptoms which her doctors attribute to the starvation. * * *

Evidence was also presented regarding Sara Roundtree, an individual who died after fasting at RSNH. She fasted several times, each fast lasting from 10 to 30 days. A doctor reviewed her history and data sheet prepared by a student at the RSNH which indicated she went to Andrews to lose weight.... Eventually during a fast she developed severe diarrhea; Andrews took her to the hospital and she died there five hours later. The cause of death on the autopsy report was sepsis, probable, due to "inanition" (starvation). * * *

Both doctors who testified as expert witnesses, Dr. Sampson and Dr. Margen, gave the opinions that prolonged fasting is dangerous to life. In addition, Dr. Sampson testified that Andrews' practices with respect to all the witnesses who fasted constituted the practice of medicine.

RSNH presented evidence that supervised fasting is integral to its religious beliefs. It also offered evidence that it is a religious organization exempt from Federal and California income taxes and that a decision of the same superior court which issued the injunction here determined that RSNH is using its property for church purposes within a zoning ordinance.

* * *

Discussion

The issue here is not whether RSNH engaged in activities which constitute the practice of medicine. Ample evidence in the record supports the trial court's findings that they did do so, and they do not challenge those findings.

Nor is there a serious argument made that the injunction infringes appellants' constitutional rights to free exercise of religion under the First Amendment. Cases are legion which hold that freedom of religious belief may be absolute but freedom of action is not (Cantwell v. Conn., 310 U.S. 296, 304; 60 S.Ct. 900, 903; 84 L.Ed. 1213 (1940)). The state may legitimately regulate dangerous conduct regardless of religious content. It is therefore universally held that in the interests of protecting its citizens' health, the state may regulate health treatments which are potentially dangerous to the patient.

* * *

The United States Supreme Court states the test of secular laws which impinge on religious belief as follows: "[I]f the State regulates conduct by enacting a general law within its power, the purpose and effect of which is to advance the State's secular goals, the statute is valid despite its indirect burden on religious observance unless the State may accomplish its purpose by means which do not impose such a burden." (*Braunfeld v. Brown* (1961) 366 U.S. 599, 607, 81 S.Ct. 1144, 1148, 6 L.Ed.2d 563.) Applying this test to the unauthorized practice of medicine, we conclude in agreement with all the authorities cited above that the state may proscribe that dangerous conduct despite its asserted centrality to a religious creed. It cannot seriously be argued that the State of California lacks the power to regulate the practice of medicine in the interest of public safety. (Citations omitted)

Accordingly we find no constitutional issue of free exercise of religion in this case. The issue is rather the scope of the exemption provided by section 2063. Assuming, arguendo, that the fasting practices of RSNH constitute the practice of religion, are these practices ipso facto exempt under the statute which prevents regulation which would "interfere in any way with the practice of religion?"

One case to date has construed the scope of this exemption and has held, in a prosecution for practicing midwifery without a certificate, that where such practice was pursuant to a bona fide tenet of a religious faith, the exemption applied. (*Northrup v. Superior Court, supra,* 192 Cal.App.3d 276, 237 Cal.Rptr. 255 (1987)). *Northrup's* reasoning was that a literal reading of the statute required this result. *Id.* at 283. The court said "From the face of the statute, it is clear the Legislature determined that in the licensing context, the state's interests are subservient to its citizens' religious beliefs." (*Ibid.*) ... This result was reached in the face of the demonstrated dangerousness of the practices which the State sought to regulate; the record in *Northrup* showed that two of the three deliveries involved had resulted in stillbirths.

With due respect, we believe it is far from clear that the legislature intended by this exemption statute to offer special protection to dangerous medical practices.

* * * Here what is involved is not faith healing but the practice of medicine, and therefore the exemption does not apply. The record here is replete with examples of appellants' conduct in purporting to have special knowledge of the body's physical symptoms and needs and further undertaking to diagnose ailments and to prescribe treatment for those ills. The conduct and the treatment goes far beyond prayer and reliance on divine intervention.

We do not agree with the *Northrup* court that the phrase "interfere in any way with the practice of religion" has any greater or different meaning than the free exercise clause of the first amendment as it has been interpreted by the judiciary. That protection clearly does not extend to dangerous religious practices including unauthorized practice of medicine. Appellants can find no case other than *Northrup* which holds that there is an exemption for dangerous practices based on religious belief.

The People argue that we need not disagree with *Northrup* to decide this case because a point of distinction from *Northrup* is the presence in this case of evidence that the medical practices employed were not bona fide expressions of religion, whereas in *Northrup* the court noted there was no evidence that the church there was not genuine nor that midwifery of the sort there practiced was not genuinely integral to the belief.... We agree that the exemption does not apply to religious practices that are not bona fide. Also it is true that here, unlike *Northrup,* there is evidence that the victims did not come to appellants for religious purposes but to have their physical ailments treated. Thus this record would support a finding that the medical practices were not promulgated for true religious purposes.

Unfortunately, we have no such unambiguous finding. The trial court did not plainly say that the medical practices here are not bona fide religious practices. There is the rather cryptic finding that "the practice of natural hygiene does not require a belief system based on religion." That finding is followed by the finding that the fasts of three victims were not religious experiences nor religious practices but were solely for therapeutic reasons. That finding comes close to saying that appellants engaged in these practices not for basic religious purposes but to avoid the licensing restrictions, but it does not precisely say so. We hesitate to premise our judgment solely on the proposition that the practices of appellants here were not bona fide expressions of religion absent an unambiguous finding to that effect by the trial court.

It is our conclusion that upon the facts presented by this record, the court had the power to enjoin appellants from engaging in the unauthorized practice of medicine, as it did. There is no question that the described activities constitute the practice of medicine; that the Board has a substantial interest in preventing such activities, which are demonstrably harmful on this record; that there is no constitutional protection for such activities; and that there is no exemption for such activity, either because the exemption does not purport to go beyond the constitutional protection for freedom of religion, or alternatively because the record does not show that these practices are basic or central to a religion. In reaching this decision we do not deem it necessary to question the bona fides of appellant Andrews' religious faith; that fact is not relevant.... The Board may obtain an injunction preventing appellants from practicing medicine without a license.

Notes and Questions

1. *Unlicensed practice and faith healers.* As noted in the preceding cases, medical practice acts typically create an exception for certain religious practices. Some exceptions, such as the California exception preventing regulation which would "interfere in any way with the practice of religion" in *Andrews*, are broad. Others carve out narrower exceptions. Ohio exempts Christian Science practitioners, stating "the treatment of human ills through prayer alone by a practitioner of the Christian Science church in accordance with the tenets and creed of such church, shall not be regarded as the practice of medicine provided that sanitary and public health laws shall be complied with, no practices shall be used that may be dangerous or detrimental to life or health, and no person shall be denied the benefits of accepted medical and surgical practices." OHIO REV. CODE ANN. §4731.34(B). Minnesota exempts "a person who practices ritual circumcision" and "a Christian Scientist or other person who endeavors to prevent or cure disease exclusively by mental or spiritual means or by prayer." MINN. STAT. ANN. §147.09. Missouri created an exception to the practice of medicine for Christian Science Practitioners through case law. *Kansas City v. Baird*, 92 Mo. App. 204 (Mo. App. 1902).

While these exceptions address healing through prayer, they are of more limited use when the spiritual healing practices also involve diagnosis. As discussed earlier in this chapter, diagnosis and treatment are "the practice of medicine" reserved for licensed practitioners. *See* Michael H.Cohen, *Healing at the Borderland of Medicine and Religion: Regulating Potential Abuse of Authority by Spiritual Healers*, 18 J.L. & RELIGION 373 (2002–03); Barry Nobel, *Religious Healing in the Courts: The Liberties and Liabilities of Patients, Parents, and Healers*, 16 U. PUGET SOUND L. REV. 599 (1993). As noted above, some states specifically state that a practitioner of the Christian Science church, through prayer alone, shall not be regarded as the practice of medicine. *See* OHIO REV. CODE § 4731.34. More recently, after the Medicare Act permitted Christian Science healers to receive Medicare payments, one commentator advanced the argument that acceptance of payment as a provider suggests that these healers should indeed be subject to licensing laws. Lauren A. Greenberg, *In God We Trust; Faith Healing Subject to Liability*, 14 J. CONTEMP. HEALTH L. & POL'Y 451, 469 (1998).

2. A few states directly address spiritual healing therapies, including therapeutic touch, imagery and Reiki, within the scope of practice of certain licensed practitioners. *See e.g.*, Mass Bd. of Registration in Nursing, Holistic Nursing Practice and Complementary Therapies, Advisory Ruling No. 9801. While this ruling provides clarity for licensed nurses that use of these modalities is professionally acceptable, it raises a concern for non-nurses in that it infers that use is limited to licensed medical professionals.

3. Review the following commentary in light of these cases and ask yourself if licensure of energy healers and therapeutic touch is the best regulatory answer, given the porous boundary between medicine and faith.

Michael H. Cohen, *Healing at the Borderland of Medicine and Religion: Regulating Potential Abuse of Authority by Spiritual Healers*

18 J.L. & Religion 373, 397–99 (2002–03)

With many states licensing a variety of CAM providers, it may seem inevitable that new CAM professions, including those based largely on spiritual healing practices, will seek licensure. But in fact, although a current trend is toward increasing licensure of health care providers and toward increasing administrative involvement in the licensing process, licensing is not uniformly favored as a mechanism to control dangerous and deviant practices. The critique of occupational licensure hold that licensure tends to be ineffective and tends to protect the entrenched interests of those judging candidates for licensure, rather than the public, therefore by and large failing to serve the interests it portends to present.

But even if it were effective as a means to control fraud, licensure has other implication in terms of its limits on practitioners' ability to rely on intuitive aspects of their craft—the so-called dark side of regulation. Particularly in the case of CAM therapies, licensure presents a potential "dark side" in terms of increased regulatory control and bureaucratic hurdles, and unnecessary intrusion into the therapeutic relationship. For this reason, many CAM providers fear that the "heart and soul" of their profession will be lost once they are subject to professional regulatory boards.

If practices involving energy healing remain at the crossroads of touch, intention, therapeutic contact, and caring—that is, they are practiced in good faith, with genuine regard for patient boundaries—then practitioners might have a genuine fear that regulation would be intrusive and have an overall destructive effect on morale in practice. Many providers, in fact, prefer that practices such as energy healing remain unregulated and beyond the requirements of uniform examinations and educational criteria.

But even in the absence of licensing mechanisms, spiritual healers remain at risk of prosecution when their practices purport to involve (or are understood by the patient to involve) a potential effect on physical health. Once the line between religion and medicine is crossed, the state arguably has the right (and many would argue, the duty) to intervene. Certainly, as noted, the police power pursuant to the Tenth Amendment authorizes such intervention, once practices aim not only at belief, faith and doctrine, but also at facilitating physical health. And states, as noted, have not hesitated to prosecute healers in situations involving the patient's physical health.

Problem

Consider again the actions taken by providers in the problem at page 55 of the text. If these acts (*i.e.*, teaching cardiac patients self-hypnosis to reduce depression and pain; employing energy healing prior to surgery; invoking the Tibetan Book of the Dead for contemplation of what might happen following suicide; and telling a patient with anxiety that "celery juice has a calming effect") were taken by unlicensed providers, would these CAM practitioners be subject to prosecution for the unlicensed practice of medicine?

B. Midwifery

In the past century, science has driven historic transformations: infectious diseases conquered by antibiotics, small pox eradicated, and lives lengthened by new drugs and technologies. At the same time, science drove health care from the home to the hospital. In the Nineteenth Century, hospitals served the poor while well-to-do patients were cared for by physicians in their homes. Beginning in the early Twentieth Century, however, hospitals, with a focus on surgery, cleanliness, ventilation and professional medical staffs, became the preferred place for treatment. Along the way, many came to believe that the newer, the more technologically advanced the medical procedure, the better the outcome. Nowhere was this more pronounced than with babies and childbirth. Infant formula must be an improvement over breastfeeding. A birth with anesthesia and labor inducers must be superior to natural childbirth. Obstetricians and hospital deliveries must be an improvement over home deliveries—deliveries that until the Twentieth Century were predominantly overseen by midwives.

In short, the landscape dramatically changed between 1900 and today. Physicians saw birthing as "obstetrics," and therefore, imbedded in "the practice of medicine." They lobbied state legislatures to provide them with exclusive control over prenatal care, delivery and childbirth. Home births became a rare exception. At the turn of the Twentieth Century, more than half of births took place at home, attended by midwives. By 1940, 55% of births were physician attended hospital births. By 1950, that percentage grew to 88%. In 2000, 99% of women gave birth in a hospital. Lay midwives (sometimes referred to as "direct entry midwives" because they relied upon experience, not formal education, for their expertise and entry into the profession) have become a rarity. Most openly practicing midwives today are licensed nurse-midwives, who practice in hospitals under the supervision of physicians.

Yet a closer look at maternal mortality rates and the safety studies regarding elective home births reveal an interesting statistic: midwifery is just as safe, if not safer, than hospital/physician based care where low risk childbirth is involved. It certainly is a less expensive option. And for many women concerned about the proliferation of cesarean sections, episiotomies and labor induction techniques, home births beckon them as a less intrusive, more family friendly option. While hospital deliveries, with physicians in attendance and neonatal specialists just a ward away, are the best alternatives for the high-risk pregnancy, women not designated as "high risk" argue that the choice of birthplace and birthing attendant should be theirs. For an interesting review of the debate about the safety data of midwife versus physician-attended births, *see* Laura D. Hermer, *Midwifery: Strategies on the Road to Universal Legalization*, 13 HEALTH MATRIX 325, 339–348 (2003).

In the later part of the Twentieth Century, it was not just rural mothers without access to obstetricians who turned to lay midwives. A minority of women across economic, geographic and racial divides sought access to home births and/or "natural childbirth." Indeed, beginning in the 1980s, hospitals began to respond to women's concerns about the medicalization of childbirth, by offering birthing rooms and centers, "rooming in" for the baby, and increased access by fathers and other family members.

The changes in attitudes about lay midwifery (from acceptance to outcast status to mixed views today) played out in legislative battles across the country. In the early Twentieth Century, many states began to regulate midwifery in response to physician pressure. Some, either by statute or judicial interpretation, deemed it the "unlicensed practice" of medicine or nursing. Still others, differentiated between lay midwives and certified nurse midwives.

Because of the resurgence of interest in home births in the late Twentieth Century, several states began to refine their decades old policies regarding midwifery. Today, each state regulates the practice of lay midwifery somewhat differently. Some deem lay midwifery (depending on the specific acts performed in the delivery process) as the unlicensed practice of medicine. Others permit midwifery only by if practiced by licensed nurse-midwives. Others specifically permit practice by lay midwives, typically within a limited scope of practice.

In the excerpt below regarding the practice of midwifery in Alabama and in the two cases from Kansas and Illinois, consider how the approaches of these three states differ and how you would craft regulation of lay midwifery (if any) for one of the several states that have yet to directly address this issue.

Stacey A. Tovino, *American Midwifery Litigation and State Legislative Preference for Physician-Controlled Childbirth*
11 Cardozo Women's L.J. 61, 76–78 (2004)

Despite lay midwives' safe delivery of thousands of Alabama babies and the improvement of health outcomes in the women who received prenatal care at the local health departments' prenatal clinics, the Alabama legislature passed a new law in 1976 that ended the legal practice of lay midwifery. The relevant portion of this law, initially set forth in Alabama's session laws at Acts 1976, No. 499, p. 624, §1, and currently codified at Alabama Code §34-19-3 (hereinafter "Act 499"), provides:

(a) It shall be unlawful for any person other than a licensed professional nurse who has received a license from the State Board of Nursing and the Board of

Medical Examiners to practice nurse midwifery in this state. Any person violating this subsection shall be guilty of a misdemeanor.

(b) Nothing in subsection (a) of this section shall be construed as to prevent lay midwives holding valid health department permits from engaging in the practice of lay midwifery as heretofore provided until such time as said permit may be revoked by the county board of health. Paragraph (a) of Act 499 continued to allow nurse-midwives to practice hospital-based midwifery in Alabama as long as they obtained and maintained the appropriate licensure. However, paragraph (b) "grandfathered in" lay midwives who had been issued permits by local boards of health and allowed them to continue to engage in the practice of lay midwifery, but only "until such time as said permit may be revoked by the county board of health." Accordingly, to the extent the local boards of health refused to renew lay midwives' old permits, or to issue new permits, lay midwives' practices became illegal.

Indeed, lay midwives' non-underground practices all but ended within five years of the passage of Act 499. "[C]ounty health departments made renewal of lay midwife permits extremely difficult." Some physicians refused to sign lay midwives' new permits, and some local health boards effectively retired currently registered lay midwives by refusing to renew their registrations. No Alabama county health department issued a lay midwife permit after 1977. In addition, Alabama counties began enforcing old, ignored rules that prohibited any individual over the age of sixty-five from practicing midwifery.

After decades of practice, more than 150 Alabama midwives, all of whom were black, received letters or visits from physicians or nurses informing them that they could no longer practice midwifery. In one case, a nurse simply "dropped by" the home of a lay midwife who had been practicing in Mobile County since the 1920s and told her that "she was no longer a midwife." Mrs. Smith remembers that, "They wrote me at the health department that I couldn't be no more midwife[sic]. I had to bring my bag and my equipment in, not only me, but all of them that were delivering."

The elimination of lay midwifery in Alabama was effectuated with little organized resistance. Alvin Holmes, the legislator who co-sponsored the bill that became Act 499, remembers "little controversy" surrounding 499's enactment. Even though lay midwives had worked under the auspices of local health departments since 1918, the midwives did not have the political clout to organize opposition to Act 499. By the 1980s, the majority of Alabama women delivered their babies in the hospital setting and, today, Alabama women do not have the legal right to choose any type of midwife (even a nurse-midwife) to attend a home delivery.

The People of the State of Illinois Ex Rel. Leonard A. Sherman, Director of Professional Regulation v. Yvonne Cryns

Supreme Court of Illinois
786 N.E. 2d 139 (2003)

Chief Justice McMorrow delivered the opinion of the court:

At issue in this case is the narrow question of whether plaintiff, the People of the State of Illinois *ex rel.* Leonard Sherman, Director of the Illinois Department of Professional Regulation (Department), established a *prima facie* case that defendant, Yvonne Cryns, a lay midwife, violated provisions of the Nursing and Advanced Practice Nursing Act (Act) (225 ILCS 65/20-75(a) (West 2000)) when she participated in the August 19, 2000, birth of Spencer Verzi.

* * *

BACKGROUND

On October 5, 2000, the circuit court entered a temporary restraining order against defendant's practice of nursing and midwifery, pending a hearing on plaintiff's complaint for preliminary injunction. The circuit court conducted a hearing on the preliminary injunction complaint on October 13, 2000. Plaintiff called Louis Verzi, the father of Spencer Verzi, to testify with respect to Spencer's birth. Verzi stated that he and his wife, Heather, hold "alternative ideas on health that are not shared with most doctors in hospitals." Accordingly, the Verzis decided that it was best that they have their child at home without the presence of a doctor or nurse. The Verzis desired to take a natural approach to childbirth and decided on a "water birth," wherein the mother gives birth while being partially submerged in a birthing pool. Verzi stated that the water-birth option was not available at any nearby hospitals, and that he and his wife hired defendant to work with them to accomplish a home water birth. According to Verzi, defendant never claimed to be a nurse, and he and his wife did not view defendant as a nurse. Rather, Verzi testified, the purpose of defendant being in their home during Spencer's birth was "to give us advice and to help us through the birth of our child, to help us in things that we didn't know." According to Verzi, defendant discussed with him and his wife the fact that if complications were to arise during the birth, medical assistance would not be immediately available.

According to Verzi, defendant had Heather fill out a "client form," in which Heather indicated that the Verzis believed in "natural health" and did not believe in prescriptions or over-the-counter medications. The responses on this form also indicated that the Verzis viewed Heather's mother as their "doctor," meaning that they relied on her for advice with respect to their health. According to Verzi, Heather had several prenatal visits with defendant, during which defendant monitored the baby's heartbeat using both a specially designed stethoscope known as a "fetoscope," and also a device known as a "Doppler," in which reflected sound waves are used to estimate the speed and direction of blood flow.

Verzi testified that at mid-morning on August 19, 2000, his wife's water broke, and that defendant arrived at their home between 1 and 1:30 p.m. Several family members and friends had gathered at the Verzi house to witness the birth. At approximately 3:45 p.m., Heather began to deliver the baby when his left foot emerged from the birth canal. According to Verzi, during the delivery defendant used the fetoscope "four or five times" to listen to the baby's heartbeat, and also used the Doppler device. Verzi recalled that at one point during the birthing process, Heather asked defendant to physically pull the baby out, and that defendant refused Heather's request. Verzi stated that defendant instead told Heather to push the baby out, and that Heather's body would know the right thing to do. However, Verzi testified that Heather continued to have difficulty in delivering the baby and that "when matters became urgent" defendant did attempt to physically extract the baby. By 4:30 p.m., the baby was born. However, upon his birth Spencer was not breathing. Verzi stated that although defendant administered CPR to Spencer for approximately 10 minutes using an "Ambu bag," which is a device used to push air into a baby's lungs after birth, the baby was not responsive. Verzi testified that at that point defendant requested that 911 be called. According to Verzi, defendant was still at their home, attempting to resuscitate Spencer, when the ambulance and paramedics arrived ...

* * *

Plaintiff next called defendant to testify. Defendant invoked her fifth amendment (U.S. Const., amend. V) privilege against self-incrimination because of criminal charges pending against her as a result of Spencer Verzi's death, and refused to answer any questions.

* * *

ANALYSIS

The question of whether the conduct of defendant on August 19, 2000, falls within the scope of the Act requires us to interpret the provisions found within that statute.

It is well settled that the General Assembly has wide regulatory power with respect to the health-care professions, and it is within the broad discretion of the legislature "'to determine not only what the public interest and welfare require, but to determine the measures needed to secure such interest.'" *Burger,* 198 Ill. 2d at 41, 259 Ill.Dec. 753, 759 N.E.2d 533, quoting Chicago National League Ball Club, Inc. v. Thompson, 108 Ill.2d 357, 364, 91 Ill.Dec. 610, 483 N.E.2d 1245 (1985). An example of the legislature's exercise of these broad regulatory powers is its enactment of the Nursing and Advanced Practice Nursing Act (225 ILCS 65/5-1 *et seq.* (West 2000)).

* * *

A nurse who specializes in the delivery of babies is referred to as a "certified nurse midwife" in the Act and is characterized as an "[a]dvanced practice nurse." [Citation omitted.] ... Advanced practice nursing licenses are granted for four categories of APNs, only one of which is relevant here: certified nurse midwife. Pursuant to section 15-10 of the Act, a registered nurse shall be qualified for licensure as a certified nurse midwife if that person has applied in writing to the Department; holds a current license to practice as a registered nurse in this state; has successfully completed requirements to practice as, and holds a current, national certification as, a nurse midwife; has paid the required fees; and has successfully completed a post-basic advanced practice formal education program in nurse midwifery. 225 ILCS 65/15-10 (West 2000). In addition, pursuant to section 15-15 of the Act (225 ILCS 65/15-15 (West 2000)), a certified nurse midwife must enter into a written collaborative agreement with a physician who provides medical direction as authorized in the collaborative agreement.

[W]e conclude that the conduct of defendant on August 19, 2000, during the birth of Spencer Verzi constituted *prima facie* evidence of "professional nursing" within the meaning of the Act.... It is clear that the General Assembly passed the Act as a comprehensive regulation of the practice of nursing, and that the Act reflects serious policy concerns about the detrimental effect to the public health and safety when unlicensed individuals engage in the conduct described in, and regulated by, the Act. To this end, the legislature explicitly provided in section 5-15 (225 ILCS 65/5-15 (West 2000)) that only those persons qualified and licensed under the Act are authorized to engage in the conduct defined as "professional nursing" in section 5-10(l) of the Act. 225 ILCS 65/5-10(l) (West 2000). The legislature chose broad language to define those individuals covered by the Act, stating that "any person" who practices or offers to practice professional nursing in this state must abide by the rules and regulations set forth in this statute. 225 ILCS 65/5-15 (West 2000). * * *

The General Assembly, however, also deemed it appropriate to enumerate certain limited and explicit exceptions to the coverage of the Act. For example, the Act does not apply to individuals who "furnish[ ] * * * nursing assistance in an emergency" (225 ILCS 65/5-15(c) (West 2000)) or to instances where "[t]he incidental care of the sick [is performed] by members of the family, domestic servants or housekeepers" (225 ILCS 65/5-15(e) (West 2000)). The Act also excludes from coverage those individuals who care for the sick "where treatment is by prayer or spiritual means" (225 ILCS 65/5-15(e) (West 2000)) and exempts from its coverage persons "employed as nursing aides, attendants, orderlies, and other auxiliary workers in private homes, long term care facilities, nurseries, hospitals or other institutions" (225 ILCS 65/5-15(f) (West 2000)). Under the principle of *expressio unius est exclusio alterius,* the enumeration of exceptions in a statute is construed as an exclusion of all other exceptions....

Applying this rule of construction to the matter before us, we conclude that the General Assembly intended to exempt from the coverage of the Act only those instances specifically enumerated. We discern no contrary legislative intent which would overcome this rule of construction and support defendant's contention that traditional midwives, as a class, were intended by the General Assembly to be excluded from coverage under the Act. [Citation omitted.]

In addition to broadly defining the class of individuals subject to regulation under the Act, the General Assembly also employed broad language to define the conduct to which the Act applies. Section 5-10(*l*) of the Act defines "professional nursing practice" to include "the assessment of healthcare needs, nursing diagnosis, planning, implementation, and nursing evaluation," the "promotion, maintenance, and restoration of health," and "counseling, patient education, health education, and patient advocacy." 225 ILCS 65/5-10(*l*) (West 2000). The record establishes that plaintiff proffered sufficient evidence to establish a *prima facie* case that defendant's conduct with respect to the Verzi birth constituted the practice of "professional nursing" and was therefore prohibited for an individual without a nursing license.

Louis Verzi testified that he and his wife hired defendant "to give us advice and to help us through the birth of our child, to help us in things that we didn't know." Verzi stated that Heather had several prenatal visits with defendant, during which defendant monitored the status of the baby's health by using a fetoscope and Doppler to listen for the baby's heartbeat. On the date of Spencer's birth, August 19, 2000, defendant arrived at the Verzi home shortly after Heather began her labor. After Heather delivered the baby's left foot, she experienced difficulty in delivering any more of the baby. Verzi testified that during the labor process, defendant, on several occasions, used the fetoscope and Doppler to check the baby's heartbeat while the baby was still in Heather's uterus. Once Spencer was born, defendant attempted to resuscitate him with the aid of an Ambu bag to push air into his lungs. Defendant attempted resuscitation in this manner for approximately 10 minutes, stopping every minute or so to listen to Spencer's heartbeat with the fetoscope.

We conclude that the above described evidence is sufficient to establish a *prima* facie case that defendant engaged in the practice of nursing without a license. We agree with the appellate court below that throughout her interaction with the Verzis, defendant was assessing the "healthcare needs" of both Heather and the baby, and making "nursing evaluation [s]" in violation of section 5-10(*l*) of the Act (225 ILCS 65/5-10(*l*) (West 2000)). ... Finally, we agree with the appellate court that defendant's actions in attempting to resuscitate the baby constituted "corrective measures" to improve his health status and constituted additional violations of the Act (225 ILCS 65/15-5 (West 2000)).

Were we to accept defendant's argument that those persons who label themselves as traditional nonnurse midwives are not regulated by the Act, an absurd result would occur. An individual would be able to bypass the licensing and training requirements of the Act simply by referring to herself as a "traditional nonnurse midwife," even if that person provided exactly the same type of nursing care as a certified nurse midwife. This would mean that a person's status under the Act would depend merely upon how she labeled herself, and the conduct in which that person engaged would become irrelevant. In construing statutes, we presume that the General Assembly, in enacting the legislation, did not intend absurdity or injustice. *Burger,* 198 Ill. 2d at 40, 259 Ill. Dec. 753, 759 N.E.2d 533. The stringent training and licensing requirements for a certified nurse midwife demonstrate the legislature's intent to regulate this specific area of nursing practice. Defendant's interpretation of the Act would render a certified nurse midwife's license meaningless. Certainly, the General Assembly could not have intended such an absurd result.

* * *

The State Board of Nursing and State of Kansas Ex Rel. State Board of Healing Arts v. E. Michelle Ruebke
Supreme Court of Kansas
913 P.2d 142 (1996)

The hearing on the temporary injunction revealed that Ruebke acts as a lay midwife comprehensively assisting pregnant women with prenatal care, delivery, and post-partum care. She is president of the Kansas Midwives Association and follows its promulgated standards, which include a risk screening assessment based upon family medical history; establishing prenatal care plans, including monthly visitations; examinations and assistance in birth; and post-partum care. She works with supervising physicians who are made aware of her mode of practice and who are available for consultation and perform many of the medical tests incident to pregnancy.

Ruebke does not advertise her services but is available to members of her church, friends, and Christians who hear about her by word of mouth. She delivers babies throughout the state and has supervising physicians in many different regions.

Ruebke does not charge for her services and considers them to be a ministry. Some families have given her money, others goods, and many have given her nothing.

* * *

Dr. Debra L. Messamore, an obstetrician/gynecologist, testified she had reviewed the Kansas Midwives Association standards of care and opined those standards were similar to the assessments incident to her practice as an OB/GYN. Dr. Messamore concluded that in her judgment the prenatal assessments made by Ruebke were obstetrical diagnoses.

Dr. Messamore testified that the prescriptions Ruebke has women obtain from their physicians are used in obstetrics to produce uterine contractions. She further testified the Kansas Midwives Association standard of care relating to post-delivery conditions of the mother and baby involved obstetrical judgments. She reviewed the birth records of [a] birth [attended by Ruebke] and testified that obstetrical or medical judgments were reflected. Although admitting that many procedures at issue could be performed by a nurse rather than a physician, she opined:

> "Obstetrics includes taking care of the normal process and making sure that it's as normal as possible for the mother and the baby, but also checking to make sure if there's any complications that develop and then treating those complications as they arise, or trying to prevent them if the mother has certain risk factors."

She also stated her opinion that, so defined, obstetrics is a branch of medicine or surgery.

Ginger Breedlove, a Kansas certified advanced registered nurse practitioner and nurse-midwife, testified on behalf of Nursing. She reviewed [delivery] records [from three pregnancies where Ruebke was the midwife] and testified nursing functions were involved. She admitted she could not tell from the records who had engaged in certain practices and that taking notes, giving enemas, and administering oxygen is often done by people who are not nurses, although education, experience, and minimum competency are required.

After the hearing, the trial court adopted, with two minor exceptions, the proposed findings of fact and conclusions of law submitted by Ruebke's counsel. The court held that provisions of both acts were unconstitutionally vague, Ruebke's midwifery practices did not and were not intended to come within the healing arts act or the nursing act, and her activities fell within exceptions to the two acts even if the acts did apply and were constitutional.

The factual findings, highly summarized, were that Ruebke had not been shown to hold herself out as anything other than a lay midwife; has routinely used and consulted with supervising physicians; was not shown to administer any prescription drugs; was not shown to do any suturing or episiotomies, make cervical or vaginal lacerations, or diagnose blood type; and had engaged only in activities routinely and properly done by people who are not physicians.

Regulatory history of midwifery

One of the specific statutory provisions we deal with, K.S.A. 65-2802(a), defines the healing arts as follows:

> "The healing arts include any system, treatment, operation, diagnosis, prescription, or practice for the ascertainment, cure, relief, palliation, adjustment, or correction of any human disease, ailment, deformity, or injury, and includes specifically but not by way of limitation the practice of medicine and surgery; the practice of osteopathic medicine and surgery; and the practice of chiropractic."

K.S.A. 65-2869 specifically provides that for the purpose of the healing arts act, the following persons shall be deemed to be engaged in the practice of medicine and surgery:

> (a) Persons who publicly profess to be physicians or surgeons, or publicly profess to assume the duties incident to the practice of medicine or surgery or any of their branches.
>
> (b) Persons who prescribe, recommend or furnish medicine or drugs, or perform any surgical operation of whatever nature by the use of any surgical instrument, procedure, equipment or mechanical device for the diagnosis, cure or relief of any wounds, fractures, bodily injury, infirmity, disease, physical or mental illness or psychological disorder, of human beings.

With the two applicable healing arts statutes above set forth in mind, it will be helpful in establishing the basis for our decision to relate a brief history of the regulation of midwifery and the healing arts, first generally, then more specifically the particular history in Kansas.

When midwives emigrated to America, they occupied positions of great prestige. Some communities licensed midwives and others did not. This continued until the end of the 19th century. In the 19th and 20th centuries, medical practice became more standardized. Economically and socially well-placed doctors pressed for more restrictive licensing laws and for penalties against those who violated them....

Although obstetricians held themselves out as a medical specialty in United States as early as 1868, midwives were not seen as engaged in the practice of obstetrics, nor was obstetrics universally viewed as being a branch of medicine. In 1901, North Carolina recognized obstetricians as engaged in the practice of medicine but women midwives, as a separate discipline, were exempted from the licensure act. State v. Welch, 129 N.C. 579, 40 S.E. 120 (1901)....

The popularity of midwifery declined significantly during the first third of the 20th Century. By 1930, births attended by nonphysicians had declined to 15 percent of all births. 30 St. Louis U. L.J. at 993. This trend continued, and by 1975 the percentage of births attended by midwives had dropped to less than 1 percent. Note, Kristin McIntosh, *Regulation of Midwives as Home Birth Attendants*, 30 B.C. L. Rev. 477, 484 (1989).

The 1978 Kansas Legislature created a new classification of nurses, Advanced Registered Nurse Practitioner ("ARNP"). L.1978, ch. 240, §1. One classification of ARNP is certified nurse midwives. Although the regulations permitting the practice of certified nurse midwives might be argued to show additional legislative intent to prohibit the practice of lay midwives, this argument has been rejected elsewhere. See Leigh v. Bd. of Registration in Nursing, 395 Mass. 670, 679–81, 481 N.E.2d 1347 (1985).

* * *

A 1986 review of the laws of every state found that lay midwifery was specifically statutorily permitted, subject to licensing or regulation, in 25 jurisdictions. Twelve states, including Kansas, had no legislation governing or prohibiting lay midwifery directly or by direct implication. Several states recognized both lay and nurse midwives. Some issued new licensing only for nurse midwives, while others regulated and recognized both, often as separate professions, subject to separate standards and restrictions. Note, Kerry E. Reilley, *Midwifery in America: The Need for Uniform and Modernized State Law*, 20 Suffolk U. L. Rev. 1117, 1125, 1127–29 (1986).

* * *

This historical background brings us to the question of whether the healing arts act is unconstitutionally vague and if Ruebke's midwifery practices, as a matter of law, come within the act's scope. In making this determination, we first consider the parties' diametrically opposed views as to our scope of review on appeal....

[Court addresses scope of review and arguments regarding constitutionality of Healing Arts Act finding that the act is not unconstitutionally vague]. * * *

Although we hold the act not to be unconstitutionally vague, we also hold the definitional provisions do not cover midwifery. In their ordinary usage the terms in K.S.A. 65-2802(a) used to define healing arts clearly and unequivocally focus exclusively on pathologies (*i.e.,* diseases) and abnormal human conditions (*i.e.,* ailments, deformities, or injuries). Pregnancy and childbirth are neither pathologies nor abnormalities. * * *

The specific terms in the statutory definition of the healing arts are not unconstitutionally vague, but they do not include the normal delivery of children.

Having addressed the issue of whether the specific words of the statutory definition of the healing arts are vague and include midwifery, we must also consider whether the definition as a whole is rendered vague, or broad enough to include midwifery, by the inclusion of the general words "the practice of medicine and surgery" in the definition of the healing arts.

The term "the practice of medicine and surgery," which is included in the statutory definition of the healing arts is not unconstitutionally vague because it has an established legal meaning in this state—a meaning which does not include a midwife's aiding in childbirth.

"Medicine is defined as 'the science and art of dealing with the prevention, cure, or alleviation of disease; in a narrower sense, that part of the science and art of restoring and preserving health which is the province of the physician as distinguished from the surgeon and obstetrician.' (Webster's New Inter. Dict.) The same authority defines surgery as the "art or practice of healing by manual operations; that branch of medical science which treats of mechanical or operative measures for healing diseases, deformities or injuries.'" State v. Johnson, 84 Kan. at 417, 114 Pac. 390 (Kan. 1911).

At least as early as 1915, it is clear that medicine was understood by its nature to be concerned with disease and infirmities. See American Medical Association, *Regulation of the Practice of Medicine*, 78 (1915) ("[A]ny regulation of the practice of medicine should be taken to be directed against any unauthorized person who attempts to treat any physical ailment by whatsoever system he may choose.") Similarly, there is no indication contemporaneous with the enactment of a healing arts regulatory scheme that unlicensed midwifery was being illegalized; nor, from a practical standpoint, could it have been. As we earlier explained, midwifery remained prominent in the earlier part of this century. The services of midwives were needed, and it is abundantly clear that early regulation of Kansas medical practice made no mention of, nor could in any manner be considered to have altered or changed, midwifery.

[The Board of] Healing Arts argues that the "practice of medicine" includes the practice of obstetrics. It reasons, in turn, that obstetrics includes the practices traditionally performed by midwives. From this, it concludes midwifery is the practice of medicine.

However, equating midwifery with obstetrics, and thus with the practice of medicine, ignores the historical reality, discussed above, that midwives and obstetricians coexisted for many years quite separately. From the time of our statehood, the relationship between obstetricians and midwives changed from that of harmonious coexistence, cooperation, and collaboration, to open market competition and hostility. See 20 Suffolk U. L. Rev. at 1119–20.

We will not engage in speculation or osmotic reasoning that while obstetrics and midwifery were not in the technical or narrow sense the "practice of medicine" 80 years ago, they have now subliminally so become. Such questionable logic should not be the underpinning of the prohibition of midwifery when, if the Kansas Legislature had wanted to specifically equate midwifery to the practice of medicine, it could have done so as the Missouri Legislature did. See Mo.Rev.Stat. § 334.010 (1994).

To even the most casual observer of the history of assistance to childbirth, it is clear that over the course of this century the medical profession has extended its reach so deeply into area of birthing as to almost completely occupy the field. The introduction of medical advances to the childbirth process drew women to physicians to assist during the birth of their children. Yet, this widespread preference for physicians as birth attendants hardly mandates the conclusion that only physicians may assist with births.

Neither logic nor experience suggests this conclusion. At the time the legislature chose to commence to regulate practitioners of medicine and surgery, the delivery of children, although sometimes assisted by physicians, was not the practice of medicine or surgery.

* * *

Notes and Questions

1. Conflict in state legislators over the licensure of midwives continues almost unabated. In 2007, Illinois, Delaware, and Alabama (the state addressed in the article by Professor Tovino) all addressed midwifery legislation, with sobering results for licensure advocates. In Illinois, a bill promoted by the Illinois Families For Midwifery passed the Senate, but was ultimately unsuccessful. Ill. S.B. 385, 96th General Assembly (2007). Delaware, facing a shortage of prenatal services, saw the introduction of Del. H.B. 106, 144th General Assembly (2007), which met a similar fate. Alabama midwifery proponents introduced legislation to certify professional midwives without requiring nursing degrees, but with requirements for informed consent. The bill was not made law.

In contrast, the 2007 Missouri legislature amended the medical practice act to legalize midwifery and to establish a board for licensing Certified Professional Midwives. Shortly after the bill became law (Mo. Ann. Stat. §376.1753), it was declared unconstitutional by the Cole County Circuit Court. Midwifery advocates and the State Attorney General appealed the district court ruling to the Missouri Supreme Court. In *Missouri State Med. Ass'n v. State*, 256 S.W.3d 85 (Mo. 2008), the Missouri Supreme Court reversed the circuit court, holding that the Medical Association lacked standing and third party standing to challenge the validity of the statute.

2. Legislatures determining whether—and, if so, how—to regulate lay midwives are often confronted be the need to balance public protection against a woman's right to choose the place, process and attendant for the birth of her baby. In short, to balance the protection of the public health against the rights to privacy and choice. As the previous materials demonstrate, there is controversy over how much (if at all) the public health is put at risk by home births attended by midwives. A 1993 study, for example, found that 75% of births in European countries with lower infant mortality rates than the United States are attended principally by midwives, most of whom are not nurse midwives. (Alan Guttmacher Institute, Annual Report 1993). But this is far from the only disagreement over how to balance public health against a woman's right to choose. There also is disagreement over what "rights" to privacy and choice women have. Should medical privacy and a woman's right to reproductive decision making found in *Roe v. Wade* also confer a right to choose the place and provider for the birth of a baby? To date, courts have consistently rejected constitutional claims of a right to choice of health care provider and place of birth in this context. *See e.g., Lange-Kessler v. Dep't of Educ.*, 109 F.3d 137 (2d Cir. 1997).

3. Legislation is an important vehicle for improved access to midwifery because courts, historically, have taken a dim view of midwifery where it is not a separately licensed activity. Typically, the lay midwife will be found to be "practicing medicine" illegally without a license. *See e.g., Smith v. State of Indiana, ex. rel. Med. Licensing Bd. of Indiana*, 459 N.E. 2d 401 (Ind. 1984); *Commonwealth v. Porn*, 82 N.E. 31 (Mass. 1907); Amy F. Cohen, *The Midwifery Stalemate and Childbirth Choice: Recognizing Mothers-to-Be As the Best Late Pregnancy Decisionmakers*, 80 Ind. L.J. 849 (2005); Laura D. Hermer, *Midwifery: Strategies on the Road to Universal Legalization*, 13 Health Matrix 325 (2003); Chris Hafner-Eaton and Laurie K. Pearce, *Birth Choices, The Law, and Medicine: Balancing Individual Freedoms and Protection of the Public's Health*, 19 J. Health Pol. Pol'y & L. 813 (1994). Many courts, in making the assessment over whether midwifery is the practice of medicine will look critically at the specific actions of and instruments used by the midwife. In *Leigh v. Bd. of Reg. in Nursing*, 395 Mass. 670, 481 N.E.2d 1347 (Mass. 1985), the Court found that a lay midwife who used "obstetrical instruments" and "prescriptions or formulas" was engaged in the practice of medicine. *See People v. Jihan*, 127 Ill.2d 379, 537 N.E.2d 751 (Ill. 1989) (differentiating between "assisting" during delivery and "delivering" the baby). Several states that permit the practice of lay midwives set out parameters in the authorizing statutes. Often these parameters also exclude the use of surgical instruments or drugs from the midwives scope of practice.

4. In *Ruebke* the court noted that the lay midwife neither advertised, nor charged for her services. For purposes of determining whether lay midwifery constitutes the "practice of medicine" should payment, or lack thereof, be a relevant factor? Is a profit motive part of what differentiates a quack from a health care provider?

5. In *Cryns*, the lawsuit against the lay midwife was instigated by the Board of Nursing. Could this also have been brought by the Board of Medical Practice alleging that the conduct was the unlicensed practice of medicine?

6. It is not only courts which are called upon to interpret ambiguous legislation to determine whether a midwifery is the unlicensed practice of medicine. Most states also give the state attorney general authority to give formal opinions upon the law by request of elected officials. Typically, courts give some deference to these formal opinions interpreting a statute. Consider the following formal opinion from the Attorney General of Mississippi:

Governor Ray Mabus
P.O. Box 139
Jackson Mississippi 39205

Dear Governor Mabus:

Attorney General Mike Moore has received your opinion request and has assigned it to me for research and reply. In your letter, you state:

Midwifery has historically been practiced both by registered nurses, who are referred to as nurse practitioners, and by people who are not registered nurses, who are referred to as direct entry or traditional midwives.

This letter requests an official opinion with respect to the proper interpretation of Section 73-25-35 of the Mississippi Code of 1972, Annotated, as applied to midwives who are not nurse practitioners. The question presented is whether Section 73-25-35 precludes the practice of midwifery for compensation by direct entry midwives.

As amended in 1990, Section 73-25-35 read as follows:

Registered nurses who are licensed and certified by the Mississippi Board of Nursing as nurse practitioners are not prohibited from such practice, but are entitled to engage therein without a physician's license.

Prior to 1990, Section 73-25-35 reads as follows:

Females engaged in practice of midwifery are not prohibited from such practice, but are entitled to engage therein without a license.

There has been some confusion as to the amendment of Section 73-25-35 regarding how it affects the practice of midwifery by direct entry midwives. In one instance, direct entry midwives were informally told that they could still practice, but could not accept payment for their services.

Section 73-25-33 of the Mississippi Code of 1972, Annotated, defines the practice of medicine to include the practice of midwifery for compensation. It then goes on to provide that nothing in that section is intended to apply to females engaged solely in the practice of midwifery.

Thus, it would appear that both nurse practitioners and direct entry midwives are excluded from the class of people who are defined as being engaged in the practice of medicine. Arguably, Section 72-25-35 would, therefore, not preclude the practice of midwifery by either nurse practitioners or direct entry midwives who are engaged solely in the practice.

In summation, your question is whether or not persons who are not licensed nurses can practice midwifery for compensation.

Miss. Code Ann. Section 73-25-33 states:

The practice of medicine shall mean to suggest, recommend, prescribe, or direct for the use of any person, any drug, medicine, appliance, or other agency, whether material or not material, for the cure, relief, or palliation of any ailment or disease of the mind or body, or for the cure or relief of any wound or fracture or other bodily injury or deformity, or the practice of obstetrics or midwifery, after having received, or with the intent of receiving therefore, either directly or indirectly, any bonus, gift, profit or compensation; provided, that nothing in this section shall apply to females engaged solely in the practice of midwifery.

By its express terms, the practice of medicine as defined in Miss. Code Ann. Section 730-25-33 specifically excludes the practice of midwifery. Thus, it is the opinion of this office that those persons otherwise not licensed as nurses may engage in the practice of midwifery with licensure as a physician and for compensation.

Sincerely,

MIKE MOORE, ATTORNEY GENERAL

Sara E. DeLoach
Special Assistant General

Governor Ray Mabus, 1991 WL 577650 (Miss. A.G. June 28, 1991)

How much deference should a legal opinion like this one be accorded by a court? Why would an elected official seek such as opinion?

> ### Opening Statement of the Prosecutor in the Trial of a Midwife
> Chris Bohjalian, Midwives, 266 (1997)
>
> "No one is going to tell you that Sibyl Danforth is an evil person. No one is going to tell you that she is a cold-blooded murderer," [the Prosecutor Bill] Tanner said. "If anything, you're going to hear from the defense what a fine person she is... what a remarkable person she is.... For your purposes, however, none of that matters.
>
> "Sibyl Danforth has been charged with practicing medicine without a license, and she has been charged with involuntary manslaughter. No one is saying she murdered anybody. But she did kill someone. That's a fact, and that's what matters."
>
> * * *
>
> Tanner shook his head and sighed before continuing. "Charlotte Fugett Bedford is dead because of Sibyl Danforth. Undeniably. Indisputably. Incontrovertibly. A twenty-nine-year-old woman is dead because of Sibyl Danforth's criminal recklessness. And if Mrs. Danforth is not the sort of person who would take a handgun and shoot one of you over money or drugs or... or in a crime of passion, it is upon her shoulders that the death of Charlotte Bedford rests. Sibyl Danforth killed her. Pure and simple: Sibyl Danforth killed her. That's why we're all here right now."
>
> The [prosecutor] looked at specific jurors as he spoke, as if he were eulogizing a river they'd once fished together that was now dry or polluted beyond use. For emphasis, he would occasionally pause and look out the window at the storm clouds, but he always seemed to turn back toward the jury when he had a particularly dramatic point he wanted to make.
>
> * * *
>
> "We will show you that from the moment Charlotte and Asa Bedford sat down with Sibyl Danforth to discuss the notion of having their baby in their home, Mrs. Danforth behaved with the sort of gross irresponsibility that could only result in tragedy.
>
> "Should Charlotte Bedford have even been allowed to have her baby in her bedroom in the first place? We will show that other midwives—as well as probably every single reasonable physician on this planet—would have said no. The risk was too great."

"Did Charlotte and Asa understand this risk? It is clear they did not. Either Mrs. Danforth did not appreciate the risk herself or she chose not to share her knowledge of the risk with her clients; either way, she never warned the Bedfords of the dangers of their decision.

"On the day that Charlotte Bedford went into labor, did Sibyl Danforth even demonstrate the common sense order to consider the weather? No, she did not. Did a woman born and raised right here in Vermont, a woman who must know the ... orneriness and capriciousness and downright uncertainty of Vermont weather, discuss with the Bedfords the chance that they'd be trapped in their home in the event that something went wrong? No. She did not."

"And then that night," he said, "when she realized that because of her own astonishing lack of foresight she and a woman in labor were cornered in a bedroom miles and miles from the help a hospital would have provided, what did Mrs. Danforth do? She had Charlotte push ... and push ... and push. Hours beyond what any doctor would have allowed, she had Charlotte push. Hours beyond what a healthy woman could have endured, she had her push. Without anesthesia. Without painkillers. She had her push."

* * *

"Sibyl Danforth had the poor woman push for so long that she thought she had killed her! She actually believed she had had one of her mothers push for so long, so nightmarishly long, that the woman had finally died. Pushed to death, so to speak. The irony? Sibyl Danforth hadn't pushed her to death. She almost had. But not quite. Charlotte Bedford did not die from pushing. It took a ten-inch knife with a sparkling six-inch blade to do that."

Opening Statement of the Defense Lawyer
Chris Bohjalian, Midwives, 273–78 (1997)

"That's how it's always been with midwives," [Stephen Hastings, the defense attorney] said with dignified authority, pacing calmly before the jurors. "To some people, they're witches—or, these days, strange and somehow dangerous throwbacks to another era. But in the eyes of other people, they're healers. Not surprisingly, it always seems to be the women who see them as healers, and the men who are quick to cry witch. Or shaman. Or meddler. Midwives, by their very nature and profession, have always challenged authority; they've always been a bit too independent—in the eyes of men, anyway. The history of midwifery in America is filled with the names of women lionized by their own gender and ostracized by men. Names like Anne Hutchinson. That's right, Anne Hutchinson. The first religious leader in Colonial America who was a woman was also a midwife.

* * *

"My point? The people who are prosecuting Mrs. Danforth are going to be insisting home birth is not merely irresponsible, it's insane. Well, you're going to see that they're wrong. It may not be the right choice for some women, but it's no more dangerous for most than a hospital birth. Let's face it, women have been having babies in their homes since, well, since the beginning of time. And until recently, they were cared for by the likes of Priscilla Mayhew: knowledgeable, tireless, loving midwives. Women who dedicated their lives to their sisters in labor. Who were these women?

> "There's one sitting right before you. Sibyl Danforth. As you know, Sibyl Danforth is a midwife. You will learn that she is a knowledgeable midwife. A tireless midwife. A loving midwife.
>
> "Most important, you will learn that she is an excellent midwife.
>
> "You will learn that statistically her babies did every bit as well as babies born at North Country Hospital, and her mothers actually did better. That's right, her mothers did better. They had fewer episiotomies, fewer lacerations, and fewer surgical interventions"....
>
> "In all of her years of delivering babies and tending to mothers, only one woman died. Charlotte Bedford.
>
> "And please understand, we are not going to tell you that her death isn't a tragedy. It is, my God, of course it is," Stephen said, and he ran his hand over the lacquered wood at the edge of the court reporter's desk ...
>
> "And no one is sadder about that fact than Sibyl Danforth. Is Charlotte Bedford's family devastated by the loss? Yes. Any family would be. But Sibyl Danforth is devastated, too. After all, Sibyl Danforth saw her die. She was there, she was present in the room. She saw the woman die.
>
> * * *
>
> "For God's sake, Sibyl Danforth didn't kill someone," [Stephen] said, "she saved someone. Sibyl Danforth didn't take the life of one young woman that morning in Lawson, she saved the life of one baby boy. That's what happened, that's the truth: She rescued a baby from his dead mother.
>
> "The State, of course, is claiming otherwise, insisting that Charlotte Bedford was alive when Sibyl Danforth performed the rescue. Where did this allegation come from? The opinion of a terrified exhausted, and naïve twenty-two-year-old woman, that's where: a woman who hadn't yet seen a dozen births, but had just endured the drama of her young life....
>
> "Make no mistake: Sibyl Danforth knows about birth, but she also knows about death. She is too well trained to confuse a live person with a dead one. Charlotte Fugett Bedford was dead when Sibyl Danforth saved the life of the child in her womb."
>
> He turned toward [the defendant midwife] and pointed at her: "This woman isn't a felon, she's a hero! Her actions weren't criminally negligent, they were courageous! She's courageous!"

Problem

In a state where naturopaths are not licensed, the Board of Medical Practice initiated an undercover investigation of a practicing naturopath, Dr. Miller. No patient has ever complained about Dr. Miller. After the investigation, the Board filed a lawsuit asking that Dr. Miller be enjoined from the unlicensed practice of medicine. Assume that the practice of medicine is as defined by the State of New York at page 36 of your text.

In preparation for the hearing, the parties met and agreed to the following stipulated facts:

1. Miller is a doctor of naturopathy who practices at the Happy Hills Naturopathic Clinic. Miller has an undergraduate degree from Smith College and a four-year postgraduate degree from the National College of Naturopathic Medicine, in Portland, Ore-

gon. Miller is currently licensed as a naturopathic physician by the State of Oregon Board of Naturopathic Examiners; however, Miller does not hold and never has held a valid license to practice medicine in this state.

2. Miller's business card notes she has a "Family Practice." On her letterhead, Miller refers to herself as a "Naturopathic Physician" and to her office as a "Naturopathic Clinic." In addition, as part of a short biography Miller uses for her speaking engagements, she refers to herself as "Dr. Miller" and notes that she has "her own holistic practice."

3. Patients go to Miller's clinic for just about everything for which they would go to a medical doctor, such as cancer, arthritis, acute sinusitis, premenstrual and menstrual complaints, earaches, colds, and Acquired Immune Deficiency Syndrome (AIDS). Miller sees patients of all ages and both sexes. Miller's practice includes what she calls "cursory" or "pertinent" physical examinations, gynecological examinations, homeopathic medicine, botanical medicine, Oriental medicine, and clinical nutrition. Miller is the primary health care practitioner for some of her patients.

4. Miller reviews patients' health histories, reported symptoms, and diet, and she may examine them. Miller uses this information to decide whether each person is healthy, in need of consultation, or in need of a referral to another health care professional.

5. Miller considers her examinations to be "screenings." Miller will perform screens upon a patient's request or to examine a health-related condition or problem for which the person is seeing Miller. For example, Miller may use a stethoscope to listen to patients' hearts, lungs, and abdomens; she may use an otoscope to examine patients' ears; she may use a sphygmomanometer to obtain patients' blood pressure; she may perform a urinalysis; and she may examine their mouths and their eyes. Miller may use methods of Chinese diagnosing to asses a patient's energy.

6. Miller may take samples from patients to send to a laboratory for analysis. The laboratory analyzes the sample and sends Miller the results. Miller then makes assessments based on the laboratory report.

7. Miller describes her practice from a "vitalistic" point of view. She states she educates her patients to attempt to remove the "obstacles to cure," thus assisting the inherent self-healing forces within each person and returning the individual to a state of balance.

8. The recommendation Miller makes depends on her individualized evaluation of the patient. Miller stated: "[E]very patient is treated differently and treated as an individual...." Miller sometimes makes recommendations regarding a particular course of action, including the use of an ultrasound machine to relieve muscle tension, "trigger point" therapy, and acupuncture. Miller also recommends therapy to patients, such as homeopathic remedies, herbal remedies, nutritional supplements, vitamins and minerals, exercise, and dietary advice. Miller counsels patients on the overuse of toxicity of vitamins, minerals, and botanicals.

9. Miller states that, while she has been in this state, she has never practiced the full range of health care services that she has been educated and trained to provide.

Prior to the court hearing, the judge orders the parties to meet and try and negotiate a settlement agreement. Take the side of either the Board or Miller and prepare for, then role play the settlement negotiation which should begin with each side presenting it's version of why Miller should or should not be subject to injunctive relief.

If a settlement is not reached, assume the role of the judge and make a ruling on the Board's request for injunctive relief assessing each of Miller's practices to determine which, if any, cross the line into the unlicensed practice of medicine.

Chapter Three

Scope of Practice

While licensure of a profession may avoid some legal problems, it is far from a panacea for CAM providers. In contrast to physicians who are licensed to broadly diagnose and treat illness, non-physician providers are only granted a specific "scope of practice" with state licensure. This professional scope of practice is carved out of the universal scope of practice accorded all physicians and defines the legal authority of the practitioner. In theory, the scope of practice restrictions limit practitioners to the services they are skilled and trained to perform. Typically, scopes of practice for non-M.D./D.O.s restrict practice to either a subset of functions/body parts (such as restricting chiropractors to treat the human spine) or subject the practitioner to those duties delegated/ supervised by a physician (such as the delegation provided to a physician's assistant). Like licensure, scope of practice parameters vary from state to state. And the battles defining the varying rules are legendary.

The initial legislative battles in most CAM licensure efforts feature very different opponents: the less educated, lay members of the putative profession on one hand and highly educated physicians on the other. The initial challenge for a profession seeking licensure is to define who is entitled to licensure and the practice parameters which must be observed by the newly licensed practitioner. Should the parameters be liberal, such as that for physicians who benefit from practice acts that cover all health care services? Or should they be restrictive, such as the scope of practice for lay midwives in states that permit licensure? What should be the educational requirements for the licensee?

In setting these initial standards, proponents of licensure face skeptics from within and without the profession, as well as within the legislature itself. Let us use naturopaths seeking licensure as an example. The first set of skeptics often is a coalition of less educated, lay naturopaths who may not meet the proposed education requirements for license and who oppose licensing standards they might not meet. As a result, they may oppose licensure altogether, preferring the risk of prosecution for unlicensed practice of medicine to the certainty of exclusion from a more exclusive licensed profession. The second battle is between the naturopaths seeking licensure and the members of established professions (nurses and physicians, perhaps) who view creation or expansions of scope of practice for others as an encroachment of their turf.

These battles play out in legislative halls as well as in campaign contributions and lobbying marathons. The Pew Commission reports that in 1995, over 800 bills that would either regulate emerging health professions or change their scope of practice were introduced in state legislatures. Over 300 passed. Two years later, the number of bill introductions doubled to 1600. Not all of these bills related to CAM providers, of course. Many scope of practice fights occur between physicians and other established professions (nurse practitioners, physician assistants, certified nurse midwives) who seek to change their practice acts to permit them to provide additional care that is consistent with their growing education and training. Almost uniformly these scope of practice expansions are opposed by physician organizations, as are most licensure proposals by previously unregulated CAM professions.

Much of the tension between CAM providers and the medical profession is natural—both in economic and philosophical terms. Nonphysician providers typically charge less, given their lower training costs, and thereby provide economic competition for the medical profession. More fundamentally, many established physicians are troubled by the paucity of scientific testing for many CAM interventions, believing them to be based on anecdotes rather than double-blind peer review studies. Which motivation is most prevalent (economic or patient safety) was a central dispute in the landmark case, *Wilk v. American Medical Ass'n*, 719 F. 2d 207 (7th Cir. 1983).

Wilk was an antitrust case brought by nonphysician providers alleging that the AMA sought to "eliminate chiropractic." The antitrust aspects of *Wilk* are addressed in Chapter 7. The motivation behind physician skepticism of chiropractors, however, relates to scope of practice disputes as well.

In response to *Wilk*, the AMA argued that its doctors "genuinely entertained a concern for what they perceive as scientific method in the care of each person" and that this objectively based concern was the "dominant motivating factor" behind the AMA rule preventing physicians from teaching at chiropractic colleges, engaging in joint research with chiropractors, and preventing any cooperation between the two groups. In evaluating the AMA's "refusal to deal" with chiropractors, the Court of Appeals stated as follows:

> Although doubting the AMA's genuineness regarding its concern for scientific method in patient care, the district court concluded that the AMA established that element. While it was attacking chiropractic as unscientific, the AMA simultaneously was attacking other unscientific methods of disease treatment (e.g., the Krebiozen treatment of cancer), and, as the district court noted, the existence of medical standards of guidelines against unscientific practices was relatively common. ... The court, however, found that the AMA failed to carry its burden of persuasion as to whether its concern for scientific method in patient care was objectively reasonable.
>
> The [district] court acknowledged that during the period that the Committee on Quackery [which focused on practices of providers of alternative medicine] was operating, there was plenty of material supporting the belief that all chiropractic was unscientific. But, according to the court (and this is unchallenged), at the same time, there was evidence before the Committee that chiropractic was effective, indeed more effective than the medical profession, in treating certain kinds of problems, such as back injuries. The Committee was also aware, the court found, that some medical physicians believed chiropractic could be effective and that chiropractors were better trained to deal with musculoskeletal problems than most medical physicians. Moreover, the AMA's own evidence suggested that at some point during its lengthy boycott, there was no longer an objectively reasonable concern that would support a boycott of the entire chiropractic profession. Also important was the fact that "it was very clear" that the Committee's members did not have open minds to pro-chiropractic arguments or evidence.

* * *

> Next, the court found that the AMA met its burden in establishing that its concern about scientific method was the dominant motivating factor for promulgating [the rule] and in the conduct undertaken and intended to implement it.

* * *

> But even so, the court acknowledged there was evidence showing that the AMA was motivated by economic concerns, as well.

While the chiropractors prevailed against the AMA in *Wilk*, the distrust of alternative providers which initially led to the AMA's Committee on Quackery still exists among many mainstream practitioners. But not all physicians oppose all CAM therapies. Approximately 60% of medical school offer courses in CAM today. Nearly 60% of allopathic physicians have either made referrals to CAM practitioners or are willing to do so. *See* Miriam S. Wetzel et al., *Course Involving Complementary and Alternative Medicine at U.S. Medical Schools*, 280 JAMA 784 (1998).

I. Scope of Practice Disputes Outside the Courtroom

A. Legislative Halls

It is state law that defines medical practice, limiting it to licensed allopathic physicians, and state law that carves out exceptions for nonphysician providers. Understandably, when any set of providers wants to expand or clarify its scope of practice, they first turn to the legislature. In theory, lawmakers look to see what set of therapies the provider has the skills and training to perform. In reality, campaign endorsements, contributions, lobbyists, the public sway of the AMA, the number of lawn signs pounded in by chiropractors, a heart wrenching story about a failed home birth, and even voters come into play.

A 1998 Task Force on Health Care Workforce Regulation expressed the dilemma as follows:

> The legal authority to provide and be reimbursed for healthcare services is tied to state statutes generally referred to as practice acts, which established professional "scopes of practice." These practice acts, often different from state to state, are the source of considerable tension among the professions; the resulting "turf battles" clog legislative agendas across the country. Caught in the middle of these battles, legislators must decide whether new or unregulated disciplines and occupations should be regulated and whether professions currently regulated should be granted expanded practice of authority.
>
> These battles are costly and time-consuming for the professions and the state legislature was involved. The more critical problem, however, is a decision-making process itself which is distorted by campaign contributions, lobbying efforts and political power struggles. In this environment, practice act decisions may not be based on evidence regarding quality of care and the potential impact on health care costs and access. Such decisions (regarding who concomitantly provide what types of care) demand a more empirical foundation and a less political venue.

Karen Sisco et al., *Strengthening Consumer Protection: Priorities for Health Care Workforce Regulation*, PEW HEALTH PROFESSIONS COMMISSION, 1998.

Let us examine one example of a decade long licensure battle over whether to license naturopaths in Minnesota and the scope of practice debate which was part and parcel of the contentious debate.

Maura Lerner, *A Bitter Fight Over Who Can Be Called "Doctor"*
Star Tribune June 8, 2008

It took 99 years, but Minnesota has finally given official recognition to the practice of naturopathic medicine, which relies on the body's powers to heal itself.

Under a new state law, naturopaths—who use everything from herbal remedies to biofeedback—will be allowed to register with the state and call themselves doctors without fear of running afoul of the medical establishment.

You might think that would be a cause for celebration throughout Minnesota's alternative-health community.

But you'd be wrong.

Instead, the new law has triggered a bitter rift among the vast array of people who practice alternative medicine, from homeopaths to folk healers to massage therapists.

To those covered by the new law, it's simply a way to get more respect and professional freedom for a particular brand of holistic medicine. But others see it as an assault in a turf war that could benefit a few highly trained practitioners at the expense of others.

"What they're trying to do is become the gatekeeper for natural health, so nobody else can practice," said Greg Schmidt, who runs the Minnesota Natural Health Legal Reform Project, which led a pitched battle to sink the law.

Despite assurances to the contrary, the fissure remains.

"I didn't realize how much of an issue it was going to be," said Rep. Neva Walker, DFL-Minneapolis, who championed the bill for years before it finally passed and was signed into law in May. "[I] didn't realize somebody who had supported all forms of alternative healing for years was going to be an enemy."

The quest for recognition

Naturopathic doctors call their work a mix of modern and traditional medicine.

In some states, they are licensed professionals, much like medical doctors. The main difference, they say, is that they rely on herbs, vitamins and other natural, low-tech remedies to treat ailments that, they believe, are often caused by stress and lifestyle.

"It's blending the best of what we know in science with the best of what we know in natural medicine," said Leslie Vilensky, of New Prague, president of the Minnesota Association of Naturopathic Physicians.

In Minnesota, supporters have tried, on and off, to pass a naturopathic law since 1909. But they have been lumped in with other folk healers, allowed to work with patients as long as they didn't cross into territory reserved for doctors or other licensed professionals.

Sometimes, that's been tricky.

In 1996, Helen Healy, a St. Paul naturopath, was accused by the state Board of Medical Practice of practicing medicine without a license. Her case instantly became a *cause célèbre* for alternative medicine supporters. Natural healers of all stripes, from herbalists to homeopaths, protested in the streets over her treatment. Eventually the medical board compromised, allowing Healy to see patients within certain limits.

At that point, Healy, who runs the Wellspring Naturopathic Clinic, vowed to try to change state law to allow naturopathic doctors to practice freely. She never imagined that the biggest resistance would come from former allies.

"We're not trying to take away anybody's rights to use these gifts from nature," she said last week. "We just need to have a place … for naturopathic physicians."

A divide among healers

For years, Healy and her colleagues pushed futilely for a law to license naturopathic doctors. This year, they changed strategy and proposed a less-formal registration.

It allows those who qualify to use the title "naturopathic doctor" and expand their "scope of practice" to include such things as ordering blood tests and MRIs, and admitting patients to hospitals.

It only applies, however, to graduates of four-year naturopathic medical schools — about 26 people now practicing in Minnesota, according to the naturopathic group.

At first, they ran into flak from both sides. The Minnesota Medical Association (MMA), representing conventional doctors, objected to allowing naturopaths to prescribe drugs and perform minor surgery. When those items were dropped, the MMA withdrew its opposition.

But the alternative-medicine groups dug in their heels. Boyd Landry, who heads the Coalition for Natural Health in Washington, D.C., argued that it could lead to restrictions on other people practicing alternative medicine. "This is about market share. This is about turf," he said.

Schmidt, of the Minnesota group, agreed. "Regulatory schemes create boxes, and boxes fence people in as much as they fence people out," he said. Schmidt worried what would happen to naturopaths who are self-taught or took correspondence courses and don't qualify under this law.

"Why should they be denied a title?" he asked.

Supporters, though, say the new law doesn't interfere with anyone's right to practice alternative medicine. "Take a look at the bill; it's not there. The bill doesn't prohibit anybody," Healy said. "We are not trying to control the universe of natural health care."

The debate isn't over. The new law, which takes effect in July 2009, calls for a work group of both sides to hammer out the details. Both sides said that's a good thing.

Meanwhile, after nearly a century of trying, naturopaths are relishing their victory.

"It's not necessarily as complete or thorough as other laws, where naturopaths practice in other states," said Vilensky, president of the Minnesota group. "But we're very happy that we're able to do what we can do under this law."

Notes and Questions

1. The new Minnesota law which permits naturopaths who meet certain education and training requirements to register with the state and hold themselves out as "doctors" is an example of a growing trend toward graduated levels of regulation. The Minnesota naturopathic registration law describes the scope of naturopathic medicine as follows:

> (1) ordering, administering, prescribing, or dispensing for preventive and therapeutic purposes: food, extracts of food, nutraceuticals, vitamins, minerals, amino acids, enzymes, botanicals and their extracts, botanical medicines, herbal remedies, homeopathic medicines, dietary supplements and nonprescription

drugs as defined by the federal Food, Drug, and Cosmetic Act, glandulars, protomorphogens, lifestyle counseling, hypnotherapy, biofeedback, dietary therapy, electrotherapy, galvanic therapy, oxygen, therapeutic devices, barrier devices for contraception, and minor office procedures, including obtaining specimens to assess and treat disease;

(2) performing or ordering physical examinations and physiological function tests;

(3) ordering clinical laboratory tests and performing waived tests as defined by the Untied States Food and Drug Administration Clinical Laboratory Improvement Amendments of 1988 (CLIA);

(4) referring a patient for diagnostic imaging including x-ray, CT scan, MRI, ultrasound, mammogram, and bone densitometry to an appropriately licensed health care professional to conduct the test and interpret the results;

(5) prescribing nonprescription medications and therapeutic devices or ordering noninvasive diagnostic procedures commonly used by physicians in general practice; and

(6) prescribing or performing naturopathic physical medicine.

MINN. STAT. ANN. § 147E.05 (2008).

Graduates from an approved naturopathic education program may register with the state and hold themselves out as "doctors" but the law does not prohibit unregistered naturopaths from the practice of naturopathy. This law is similar in approach to the innovative Colorado law which provides for gradations of regulation for mental health professionals depending upon the profession's potential for public harm. For an explanation of the Colorado approach, *see* Barbara Safriet, *Closing The Gap Between Can and May in Health Care Providers' Scopes of Practice: A Primer for Policy Makers*, 19 YALE J. ON REG. 301, 325–26 (Summer 2002).

B. Attorney General Opinions

Attorney Generals are the chief legal advisors for state officials. In this role, they are often called upon to advise executive heads of government as well as local officials. Moreover, at least the 43 independently elected Attorney Generals serve not only as the lawyer for the executive branch but also as the people's lawyer. In this role the official is responsible for serving the public interest, as well as the governor, commissioners and state agencies. *See* William P. Marshall, *Break Up the Presidency? Governors, State Attorney Generals, and Lessons From the Divided Executive*, 115 YALE L.J. 2446 (2006).

One of the areas where state Attorney Generals wear two hats is the provision of formal legal opinions. While informal opinions are frequently provided to agency clients, where a formal opinion is requested by a state agency or local government and the issue is one of statewide significance, the Attorney General may agree to render and sign a formal opinion. While the criteria for and weight given these opinions varies by state, generally they are deemed persuasive but not binding.

When struggling with a difficult scope of practice dispute, a health licensing board may seek guidance from the state Attorney General. Below is one such opinion and a chart summarizing recent CAM scope of practice Attorney General opinions.

As you read this material, consider why one might seek such an opinion rather than either clarifying legislation or a more definitive declaratory judgment action in court.

Nebraska Attorney General Opinion
Opinion 91055 (June 17, 1991)

SUBJECT: Scope of Practice of Chiropractors
REQUESTED By: Gregg F. Wright, M.D., M.Ed. Director of Health

You have asked whether the scope of practice of a chiropractor licensed by the Department to practice chiropractic in this state includes:

1. Performing internal pelvic examinations to determine whether the patient should be referred for treatment elsewhere;

2. Performing electrocardiograms (EKGs) to determine whether a patient's cardiac status is the cause of the reported symptoms or whether chiropractic treatment can be safely performed; or

3. Performing rectal examinations other than one performed prior to performing colonic irrigation.

We have concluded the answer to each of your questions is yes, as discussed below.

Chiropractic practice is defined by statute as follows:

> For purposes of the Uniform Licensing Law, the practice of chiropractic is defined as being one or a combination of the following, without the use of drugs or surgery:
>
> (1) The diagnosis and analysis of the living human body for the purpose of detecting ailments, disorders, and disease by the use of diagnostic X-ray, physical and clinical examination, and routine procedures including urine analysis; or (2) the science and art of treating human ailments, disorders, and disease by locating and removing any interference with the transmission and expression of nerve energy in the human body by chiropractic adjustment, chiropractic physiotherapy, and the use of exercise, nutrition, dietary guidance, and colonic irrigation. The use of X-rays beyond the axial skeleton shall be solely for diagnostic purposes and shall not expand the practice of chiropractic to include the treatment of human ailments, disorders, and disease not permitted when the use of X-rays was limited to the axial skeleton. Neb.Rev. Stat. §71-177 (Reissue 1990).

Thus, under the clear language of the statute, the practice of chiropractic includes "the diagnosis and analysis of the living human body for the purpose of detecting ailments, disorders, and disease by the use of diagnostic X-ray, physical and clinical examination, and routine procedures including urine analysis ..."

Under Nebraska law, where the words of a statute are plain and unambiguous, no interpretation is needed to ascertain their meaning. In the absence of anything to indicate the contrary, words will be given their ordinary meaning. Kellogg Co. v. Herrington, 216 Neb. 138, 343 N.W.2d 326 (1984). We fail to see how the above quoted statutory language could be susceptible of more than one reasonable but conflicting interpretation or meaning with regard to the diagnostic procedures in question. See Wurst. Blue River Bank, 235 Neb. 197, 454 N.W.2d 665 (1990). It is Our opinion a court would find as a matter of law the words in question are not ambiguous. Thus, no interpretation or resort to legislative history for the purpose of discovering legislative intent is necessary. In any event, we find the legislative history of §71-177 to be inconclusive on this point, especially in light of the broad language adopted by the legislature.

Thus, the performance of internal pelvic exams, electrocardiograms and rectal examinations by chiropractors is within the scope of chiropractic practice to the extent such procedures are part of a "physical and clinical examination or routine procedure" which is conducted for the "diagnosis and analysis of the living human body for the purpose of detecting ailments, disorders and disease."

We would note the clear distinction in the statute between the scope of permissible "diagnosis and analysis", as outlined above, and the permissible method of treatment authorized by § 71-177(2). We also note the statutory definition of chiropractic practice contained in § 71-177(1) is much broader than the historic definition. See e.g., Malory's Medical Dictionary for Lawyers, Second Edition. Two prior informal opinions, dated November 22, 1983 and August 30, 1984 respectively, were issued subsequent to the amendment of § 71-177 in 1983. Nonetheless, they were based upon historical concepts of chiropractic practice which have been superseded by the enactment of § 71-177(1) by the Nebraska legislature. To the extent these opinions are inconsistent with the clear language of § 71-177 or this opinion they are no longer valid. The proper statutory definition of chiropractic practice is for the legislature to determine and our opinion is based solely on the clear language adopted by the legislature.

Sincerely yours,

DON STENBERG

Attorney General

Recent Attorney General Scope of Practice Formal Opinions

Acupuncture

Montana	48 Mont. Att'y Gen. Op. 7 (1999).	The State Board of Medical Examiners requested an opinion as to whether a physician may practice acupuncture using solid needles without first being licensed to practice acupuncture. The Attorney General's Office opined that before a physician may represent himself as being a licensed acupuncturist he must first obtain a license to practice acupuncture. However, the A.G. also opined that physicians who do not have a license to practice acupuncture may still use solid needles to perform "therapeutic modalities."
Nebraska	Neb. Att'y Gen. Op. No. 99026 (May 28, 1999).	The Dept. of Health and Human Services asked whether the scope of practice for chiropractors includes acupuncture. The A.G.'s office opined that because no state laws or cases described acupuncture as surgery it could be regarded as a form of chiropractic physiotherapy. Therefore acupuncture falls within a chiropractor's scope of practice for the purposes of Nebraska law.
Hawaii	Haw. Att'y Gen. Op. No. 03-5 (Aug. 18, 2003).	The state's Director of Commerce and Consumer Affairs requested an opinion as to whether medical acupuncture sufficiently differs from traditional acupuncture as to fall outside acupuncturists' scope of practice, and whether a physician licensed by the Board of Medical Examiners may practice medical acupuncture without licensure from the Board of Acupuncture. The A.G. opined: 1) Medical acupuncture is not sufficiently distinct from traditional acupuncture to fall outside acupuncturists' scope of practice. 2) Physicians cannot practice medical acupuncture without licensure by the Board of Acupuncture.

Chiropractic

Kansas	Kan. Att'y Gen. Op. No. 96-12 (Feb. 20,	A State Representative requested an opinion as to whether physicians had the authority under K.S.A. 65-2869 to perform manual

	1996).	manipulation. The A.G. opined that chiropractic manual manipulation does not fall within a physician's scope of practice.
Tennessee	Tenn. Att'y Gen. Op. No. 00-131 (Aug. 15, 2000).	The Tennessee Board of Chiropractic Examiners requested an opinion as to whether the Chiropractic Practice Act (1999) permitted chiropractors to order and receive results of diagnosis tests including urinalysis, arthritis panel, urine count, glucose tolerance test, male-female endocrine profile, standard blood profile and pregnancy testing.
		The A.G.'s office opined that a chiropractor would exceed the chiropractic scope of practice by collecting and analyzing human specimens or ordering such analysis. Additional legislation would be needed before a chiropractor could order and receive the results of such diagnostic tests.
Georgia	Ga. Att'y Gen. Op. U2006-1 (June 6, 2006).	The A.G.'s office opined that a licensed chiropractor had the authority to refer a patient for X-ray or MRI to determine whether the patient's condition is appropriate for chiropractic treatment. This supersedes 1993 Op. Att'y Gen. 93-11, which held that MRI referral falls outside the chiropractic scope of practice.
Louisiana	La. Att'y Gen. Op. No. 79-745 (July 24, 1979).	The attorney for the state's Board of Chiropractic Examiners requested an opinion as to whether chiropractors had the legal authority to: 1. Draw blood from a vein via finger puncture? 2. Perform an internal pelvic examination?
		The A.G. opined that drawing blood or conducting a pelvic exam did not constitute reasonable means of discovering spinal alignment and therefore neither fell within a chiropractor's scope of practice.
		This opinion was reaffirmed in Louisiana Op. Att'y Gen. No. 84-290 (March 30, 1984).

Homeopathy

Nevada	1999 Nev. Att'y Gen. Op. 24 (1999).	The Nevada Board of Pharmacy requested an opinion as to whether a licensed homeopathic physician could prescribe controlled substances. The A.G.'s office concluded that under current statures homeopathic physicians did not have the authority to prescribe controlled substances or dangerous drugs. If members of the profession needed to prescribe such drugs they should seek the statutory authority to do so.

Massage Therapy

Alabama	Ala. Att'y Gen. Op. No. 2004-166 (June 24, 2004).	The Board of Massage Therapy asked the extent to which a cosmetologist could practice massage therapy. The A.G.'s office opined that a cosmetologist could only practice massage therapy to the extent that the scope of practice of cosmetology overlapped with that of massage therapy (the A.G. did not provide guidance as to what that might mean). A cosmetologist could not represent himself or herself as a massage therapist without obtaining a separate massage therapy license.

Midwifery

Missouri	Mo. Att'y Gen. Op. No. 87-86 (Sept. 4, 1986).	The A.G. opined that nurse-midwives were authorized to practice nurse-midwifery under current Missouri law and were exempted from laws prohibited non-physicians from practicing obstetrics.
Texas	Tex. Att'y Gen. Op. No. H-1293 (Dec.	The A.G. opined that the practice of midwifery was not the practice of medicine. Midwives could perform any services necessary for the

19, 1978). delivering of a baby, but could not render a diagnosis on a disease or obstetrical complication. This authority was explicitly limited to registered nurses who are nurse midwives and certified nurse midwives.

Comment: Statutory Interpretation

A straightforward reason a profession may first turn to the legislature to expand its scope of practice is simple: legislation is more authoritative. Judges cannot disregard a statute without ruling it unconstitutional. Attorney Generals do not possess this latitude in providing formal opinions. They, like the judiciary in most cases, are restricted to interpreting ambiguous statutes.

Despite this restriction, plenty of statutory interpretation work remains for judges and, when they agree to render an opinion, state attorney generals. When a statute is enacted, its purpose is often cloaked in ambiguous language and imprecise drafting, the result of a series of protracted compromises. Simply put, a plain and unambiguous law is rare indeed. Yet the goal of statutory interpretation is to first discern that legislature purpose and then to effectuate it.

This goal assumes that there is one "intent" or "purpose." Consider the following comment on legislative interest:

> That the intention of the legislature is undiscoverable in any real sense is almost an immediate inference from a statement of the proposition. The chances that of several hundred men each will have exactly the same determinate situations in mind as possible reductions of a given determinable, are infinitesimally small. The chance is still smaller that a given determinate, the litigated issue, will not only be within the minds of all these men but will be certain to be selected by all of them as the present limit to which the determinable should be narrowed. In an extreme case, it might be that we could learn all that was in the mind of the draftsman, or of a committee of half a dozen men who completely approved of every word. But when this draft is submitted to the legislature and at once accepted without a dissentient voice and without debate, what have we then learned of the intentions of the four or five hundred approvers?

Max Radin, *Statutory Interpretation*, 43 HARV. L. REV. 863, 870 (1930).

Assuming that legislative intent can be found, what tools are available to seek it out? The first place to look to interpret a phrase is often the language of law as a whole. Justice Scalia described this in *West Virginia University Hospitals, Inc. v. Case*, 499 U.S. 83, 100 (1991), where he wrote for the majority: "[w]hen a statutory term presented to us for the first time is ambiguous, we construe it to contain that permissible meaning which fits most logically and comfortably with the body of both previously and subsequently enacted law." But where that inquiry arrives at a dead-end, two additional avenues for construction may be use: canons of statutory construction and legislative history.

Judicial canons for statutory construction are interpretive rules which are inconsistent and derided by commentators yet continually cited by courts. Consider the following examples:

- The expression of one thing is the exclusion of another. [One application of this canon is the argument that when a statute creates a list of specific themes, the implication is that items not listed are excluded]

- The "particular" limits the "general," [Typically applied so that when particular words of description are followed by general words, the general are limited to the class of particular items.]
- The legislature does not intend a result that is absurd, impossible of execution or unreasonable.
- No law shall be constructed to be retroactive unless clearly and manifestly so intended by the legislature.

Legislative history is often turned to when the statute is ambiguous and canons of interpretation yield no clear answer. But where to turn in the process of legislation is also unclear. Certainly after-the-fact pronouncements of intent by individual law makers are afforded little weight, but consider the following avenues:

- Conference committee reports
- Statements made during floor debate by the bill's author
- Bill reports compiled by legislative staff
- Earlier bill drafts
- Findings set forth in the bill's preamble
- Statements by the governor upon signing the bill

Which of these would you find most indicative of the collective intent of the legislature?

II. Scope of Practice Disputes in the Courtroom

As noted in the last chapter, chiropractors sought to quickly follow physicians in seeking licensure in all 50 states in the early Twentieth Century. But they came to learn that with those licenses came restricted scopes of practice and years of disputes with physicians. As you read the following descriptions of disputes between chiropractors and physicians, as they play out in both the courtroom and the halls of state legislatures, consider how a new profession with less income and acceptance might handle concerted efforts to limit its scope of practice.

Foster v. Georgia Board of Chiropractic Examiners
Supreme Court of Georgia
359 S.E. 2d 877 (1987)

Marshall, Chief Justice.

The appellant, Charles Foster, is a licensed chiropractor in the State of Georgia. The state instituted administrative proceedings against him, seeking the imposition of sanctions on grounds that in dispensing certain nutritional substances for treatment of a patient, he engaged in the prescribing of drugs and thereby exceeded the statutorily authorized scope of his license to practice chiropractic in this state. The hearing officer concluded that the appellant had exceeded the scope of his chiropractic license, and sanctions were imposed. In reviewing the hearing officer's decision, the appellee, the Georgia Board of Chiropractic Examiners, agreed that the appellant was not authorized to prescribe the nutritional treatment, but the Board modified the sanctions imposed by the hearing officer. The superior court summarily affirmed the decision of the Board. The appellant filed an application for discretionary appeal in this court, challenging the constitutionality of the applicable statutory provisions as construed by the tribunals below. We granted the appellant's application for discretionary appeal, for the purpose of deciding "[w]hether the Georgia Code allows chiropractors to prescribe nutritional treatment for their patients, and if so, to what extent." For reasons which follow, we hold that, at least under the circumstances here, the chiropractor was not authorized to prescribe the nutritional treatment. We, therefore, affirm.

Facts

Based upon facts stipulated by counsel for the parties, the hearing officer found and concluded as follows:

On September 19, 1984, a patient, referred to as L.R. (who was, in fact, an undercover agent for the state), visited the appellant's office. The patient completed a medical history form, indicating that he was generally feeling tired and run down and that he was taking "Corgard," a heart medication. The appellant indicated to the patient that a complete blood history and urinalysis would be needed.

The appellant consulted with a licensed medical doctor regarding the patient's condition and the advisability of having a blood history done by a laboratory. The licensed medical doctor concurred that a blood history should be done on the patient and instructed the appellant to have a licensed practical nurse withdraw the blood from the patient, which was done. The blood samples were sent to a laboratory for analysis, and a blood-analysis report was sent by the laboratory to the appellant.

From the blood-analysis report, the appellant prepared a report, entitled a "Bio-Chemical Interpretation," for the patient. From this, the appellant prescribed a course of treatment for the patient's condition, which included taking the following substances, pursuant to specific instructions as to the amount and timing of the substances to be taken:

1. Samolinic
2. Digestaid
3. Prostadyn
4. Supra Renal 220
5. Organamin
6. Free Amino

These substances may be sold without prescription and are, in fact, sold in food stores by merchants and other lay persons; in addition, the substances are not habit-forming and do not require medical supervision for use. The substances are used by the appellant to treat dietary deficiencies and to enhance the well-being of the patient.

The hearing officer concluded that the use of the substances in question by the appellant to treat the patient constitutes the prescribing or use of drugs, in violation of the Georgia Chiropractic Practices Act. OCGA § 43-9-1 et seq. (referred to hereinafter as the Georgia CPA).

Based on this, the hearing officer, likewise, concluded that the appellant's conduct constitutes unprofessional conduct harmful to the public and of a nature likely to jeopardize the interest of the public, in violation of OCGA § 43-9-12(a)(6). The hearing officer further concluded that the appellant's conduct also constitutes a violation of OCGA §§ 43-9-12(a)(8) and 43-34-46, in that the appellant has practiced medicine in Georgia without a license. The hearing officer ordered that the appellant's license to practice chiropractic in Georgia be suspended for a period of three years, but that said sanction be suspended and the appellant's license be put on probation for the three-year period.

[The Board of Chiropractic Examiners, hereinafter "Board," adopted the hearing officer's findings of fact and conclusions of law.]

Georgia's Statutory Scheme

As defined by OCGA §43-9-1..., "'(c)hiropractic means the adjustment of the articulation of the human body, including ilium, sacrum, and coccyx, and the use of electric X-ray photography, provided that the X-ray shall not be used for therapeutical purposes.' This definition has existed unchanged since its original enactment by Ga.L.1921, pp. 166, 167. The following language was, however, added to the statute in 1977: 'The term "chiropractic" shall also mean that separate and distinct branch of the healing arts whose science and art utilize the inherent recuperative powers of the body and the relationship between the musculoskeletal structures and functions of the body, particularly of the spinal column and the nervous system, in the restoration and maintenance of health. Chiropractic is a learned profession which teaches that the relationship between structure and function in the human body is a significant health factor and that such relationships between the spinal column and the nervous system are most significant, since the normal transmission and expression of nerve energy are essential to the restoration and maintenance of health. However, the term "chiropractic" shall not include the use of drugs or surgery.' Ga.L.1977, p. 232. See OCGA §43-9-1(2), supra.

Basic Arguments Advanced By The Appellant

The appellant's basic argument, as a matter of statutory construction, is that, based on the status of chiropractic in 1921, the General Assembly defined it as an adjustment of the articulation of the human body. However, the appellant asserts that subsequent developments in chiropractic education and training embrace nutrition, among other modalities, as a proper part of chiropractic, and the 1977 redefinition of chiropractic was intended to embrace such modalities within the official, extremely broad definition of chiropractic. In support of this argument, the appellant further contends that in all accredited chiropractic colleges in this country, students are specifically instructed in the diagnostic essentials of how nutrition relates to human health and the recuperative powers of the human body.

More specifically, referring to the language employed in the 1977 statutory redefinition of chiropractic in Georgia, the appellant argues that "the inherent recuperative powers of the body" can be altered by neurological dysfunction and cannot be restored without providing man with proper vitamins and minerals, which are necessary for "the normal transmission and expression of nerve energy ... essential to the restoration and maintenance of health." So this argument proceeds, nutrition also aids the process of spinal adjustment. The appellant seeks to distinguish vitamins from drugs by arguing that vitamins are naturally occurring substances that promote the free flow of energy, whereas drugs "insult the totally mobile and free-flowing expression of nerve energy."

Cases From Other Jurisdictions Interpreting Their Chiropractic Statutes

In *King v. Bd. of Med. Examiners,* 65 Cal.App.2d 644, 151 P.2d 282(5) (1944), vitamins and other non-prescription substances were prescribed by a practitioner of a drugless health profession for a patient, but not for the treatment of a disease or ailment. There, it was held that the defendant was not guilty of practicing medicine without a license.

In *State v. Baker,* 229 N.C. 73, 48 S.E.2d 61 (1948), an osteopath was convicted of practicing medicine without a license by prescribing drugs for the treatment of ailments.

Under North Carolina law, osteopathy, like chiropractic, is a system of treating diseases of the human body without drugs or surgery.

In *Baker,* the defendant had advised a patient, a nursing mother, to feed her baby a certain type of milk. He also advised the patient to procure for herself various patent and proprietary preparations, including vitamin preparations, with directions as to the mode of administration. These preparations were obtainable without a prescription from a physician.

The North Carolina Supreme Court, stating that the lexicographers are in agreement, held that a drug is "any substance or preparation used in treating disease." 48 S.E.2d at p. 66. Consequently, the court concluded, "[w]hether a vitamin preparation is a drug or a food is ordinarily a question of fact. The same substance may be a drug under one set of circumstances, and not a drug under another. The test is whether it is administered or employed as a medicine. *Stewart v. Robertson,* 45 Ariz. 143 (40 P2d 979, 40 C.J. 625)." *Id.*

On this basis, the court concluded that the defendant did not exceed the bounds of his osteopathic license by advising the nursing mother with respect to the child's nourishment, or by prescribing the vitamin preparations "used solely for nourishment." *Id.* However, the court held that other preparations, although available to the general public without prescription, were administered by the defendant in the treatment of his patient's ailments and were, therefore, drugs "within the meaning of the law." *Id.* at p. 67.

* * *

In *State v. Winterich,* 157 Ohio St. 414, 105 N.E.2d 857 (1952), the Ohio Supreme Court held that substances, although classifiable as foods, become "drugs" within legal contemplation if prescribed by chiropractors for patients and if such substances are "intended for use in the diagnosis, cure, mitigation, treatment or prevention of disease * * *" 105 N.E.2d at p. 861. However, the chiropractor's conviction for engaging in the practice of medicine without a license was reversed because of an error in the trial court's jury charge.

In *People v. Bovee,* 92 Mich.App. 42, 285 N.W.2d 53, 16 A.L.R.4th 48, (1979), the Michigan Court of Appeals was called upon to interpret Michigan's chiropractic statute, which, at the time, defined chiropractic as "the locating of misaligned or displaced vertebrae of the human spine," but also included within that definition "the procedure preparatory to and the adjustment by hand of such misaligned or displaced vertebrae ..." M.C.L. § 338.156; M.S.A. § 14.596. Citing *State v. Wilson,* 11 Wash.App. 916, 528 P.2d 279 (1974), and *Attorney General v. Raguckas,* 84 Mich.App. 618, 270 N.W.2d 665, 668–669. (1978), the Michigan Court of Appeals in *Bovee* held that to allow chiropractors to dispense nonprescription drugs as part of a procedure preparatory to a spinal manipulation would be "'directly contrary to the philosophical foundation of the chiropractic profession ... [and] ... the universally accepted view that the chiropractic profession is limited to the manual adjustment of the spine. Drugs play no part in the chiropractor's approach to health.'" 285 N.W.2d at p. 59.

The Michigan legislature subsequently amended that state's chiropractic statute to provide that the "[p]ractice of chiropractic includes ... (iii) [t]he use of analytical instruments, *nutritional advice,* rehabilitative exercise and adjustment apparatus ... for the purpose of locating spinal subluxations or misaligned vertebrae of the human spine. The practice of chiropractic does not include ... the dispensing or prescribing of drugs or medicine." (Emphasis supplied.) M.C.L. § 331.16401(1)(b); M.S.A. § 14.15(16401)(1)(b).

In *Attorney General v. Beno,* 422 Mich. 293, 373 N.W.2d 544 (1985), the Michigan Supreme Court, citing *Attorney General v. Recorder's Court Judge,* 92 Mich.App. 42, 285 N.W.2d 53 (1979), held that the Michigan legislature's inclusion of the foregoing statutory provision on nutritional advice did not authorize the use of vitamins and food supplements for treatment of disease or other human ailment, but only authorized chiropractors to dispense vitamins or food supplements when employed as part of a program to correct a subluxation or misalignment of the spine.

* * *

Georgia Case Law

In *Metoyer v. Woodward,* 176 Ga.App. 826, 338 S.E.2d 286, supra, the Georgia Court of Appeals, agreeing with an opinion rendered by the Attorney General of the State of Georgia (Opinions of the Attorney General, 1984, p. 116), held that the 1977 statutory redefinition of chiropractic in Georgia, including the legislative determination contained therein that chiropractic is a learned profession, did not expand its authorized scope of practice beyond the existing statutory authorization to adjust the articulation of the human body according to specific chiropractic methods.

Holding With Respect to the Construction of the Georgia CPA

We are in agreement with the Georgia Court of Appeals' decision in *Metoyer v. Woodward,* supra, as well as the previously cited decisions rendered by the courts of other states.

Consequently, we hold that since the Georgia CPA does not authorize chiropractors to prescribe or dispense vitamins, minerals, or nutritional substances, and since the appellant here did prescribe such items for treatment of a patient's ailments, such conduct constituted the unauthorized practice of medicine in this state.

* * *

Judgment affirmed.

Crees v. California State Board of Medical Examiners

Second District Court of Appeal for the State of California
213 Cal. App. 2d195 (1963)

Fox, P. J.

This is an appeal by plaintiffs from a judgment in an action for a declaration of rights.

Plaintiffs are a California nonprofit corporation composed of practicing doctors of chiropractic and seven individual licentiates of the chiropractic board. They brought this action for declaratory and injunctive relief against defendants, who are the California State Board of Medical Examiners, five members of that board, the California State Board of Chiropractic Examiners and two members of that board. Plaintiffs sought to have certain rights, immunities, and privileges, claimed by plaintiff doctors of chiropractic under the Medical Practice Act (Bus. and Prof. Code, §2000–2490) and the Chiropractic Initiative Act, defined and declared. Plaintiffs also sought injunctions against the two defendant boards to enjoin them from interfering with said asserted rights.

* * *

The trial court made findings of fact and conclusions of law, and gave judgment for the defendants. The pertinent portions of the judgment are:

"It is Ordered, Adjudged and Decreed that the respective rights and duties of the parties are as follows:

* * *

"A. Duly licensed chiropractors who do not hold themselves out as physicians and surgeons, but only as 'doctors of chiropractic' or 'D.C.' may, nevertheless, be in violation of the State Medical Practice Act.

"B. Licensed chiropractors are not authorized by their license to use any drugs or medicines in materia medica or the dangerous or hypnotic drugs mentioned in section 4211 of the Business and Professions Code or the narcotics referred to in section 11500 of the Health and Safety Code for: (1) diagnosis; (2) as an aid in the practice of chiropractic; (3) for emergencies; or (4) for clinical research.

"C. Licensed chiropractors are not authorized by their license to practice obstetrics or to sever the umbilical cord in any childbirth or to perform episiotomy.

"D. A duly licensed chiropractor may only practice or attempt to practice or hold himself out as practicing a system of treatment by manipulation of the joints of the human body by manipulation of anatomical displacements, articulation of the spinal column, including its vertebrae and cord, and he may use all necessary, mechanical, hygienic and sanitary measures incident to the care of the body in connection with said system of treatment, but not for the purpose of treatment, and not including measures as would constitute the practice of medicine, surgery, osteopathy, dentistry, or optometry, and without the use of any drug or medicine included in materia medica.

"A duly licensed chiropractor may make use of light, air, water, rest, heat, diet, exercise, massage and physical culture, but only in connection with and incident to the practice of chiropractic as hereinabove set forth.

"E. It is true that chiropractic is not a static system of healing and that it may advance and change in technique, teaching, learning, and mode of treatment within the limits of chiropractic as set forth in paragraph H above. It may not advance into the fields of medicine, surgery, osteopathy, dentistry, or optometry.

"F. Plaintiffs have failed to state facts sufficient to constitute a cause of action for injunction against defendants.["]

* * *

Plaintiffs contend on appeal that the trial court erred in (1) refusing to permit introduction of evidence by plaintiffs in support of their contentions and claims; (2) granting the motion of defendants for a declaration of rights and duties of the parties based on the pleadings and stipulations; (3) in making the declarations set forth in paragraphs B, C, E, F, G, H, J, and K of the judgment, *supra*; and (4) failing to make a declaration as to the meaning of the term "practice" as contained in the last part of section 7 of the Chiropractic Act.[2]

* * *

---

2. The pertinent portion of the section provides that the "... 'License to practice chiropractic'... shall authorize the holder thereof to practice chiropractic in the State of California as taught in chiropractic schools or colleges; and, also, to use all necessary mechanical, and hygienic and sanitary measures incident to the care of the body, but shall not authorize the practice of medicine, surgery, osteopathy, dentistry or optometry, nor the use of any drug or medicine now or hereafter included in materia medica."

Introduction of Evidence

Plaintiffs base their contention that evidence concerning practices in the science of chiropractic and present and past curricula at colleges of chiropractic should have been heard by the trial court on section 1000-7 of the [West's] Business and Professions Code [Deering's Bus. & Prof. Code, Appendix I, § 7], which provides that a license issued by the Board of Chiropractic Examiners shall authorize the holder thereof "to practice chiropractic in the State of California *as taught in chiropractic schools or colleges....*" (Italics added.) (1) They contend that to establish what is chiropractic, it is necessary, *inter alia,* to take extrinsic evidence as to what is and has been taught in chiropractic educational institutions, and the practices that have developed in the profession.

Their position, however, is not sustained by the prevailing authorities. Section 7 of the Chiropractic Act (West's Bus. and Prof. Code, § 1000-7 [Deering's Bus. & Prof. Code, Appendix I, § 7]) contains the only provision which undertakes either to define or describe chiropractic or to declare what is authorized by a license issued under the act. (2) The authorization is in two parts: (1) "to practice chiropractic ... as taught in chiropractic schools or colleges"; and (2) "to use all necessary mechanical, and hygienic and sanitary measures incident to the care of the body."

The first part of this authorization, plaintiffs contend, authorizes the practice by a licensed chiropractor of anything that he has been taught in chiropractic schools. As said in *People v. Fowler,* 32 Cal.App.2d Supp. 737, 745 [84 P.2d 326]: "This is too broad an interpretation of the provision. It contains two expressions, each of which has a limiting, as well as an authorizing effect. The practice authorized must be 'chiropractic', and it must also be 'as taught in chiropractic schools or colleges.' Neither of these expressions can rule the meaning of the statute, to the exclusion of the other." The court pointed out (pp. 746–747) that there was a "general consensus of definitions, current at and before the time the Chiropractic Act was adopted [which] shows what was meant by the term 'Chiropractic' when used in this act;" also, that "'[t]he words of a statute must be taken in the sense in which they were understood at the time when the statute was enacted.' [Citations.]"; and that "[w]ords of common use, when found in a statute, are to be taken in their ordinary and general sense. [Citations omitted.]" The court explained that "[t]he effect of the words 'as taught in chiropractic schools or colleges' is not to set at large the signification of 'chiropractic', leaving the schools and colleges to fix upon it any meaning they choose. Were the word 'chiropractic' of unknown, ambiguous or doubtful meaning, this clause ... might serve to provide a means of defining or fixing its signification, but there is here no such lack of clarity. The scope of chiropractic being well known, the schools and colleges, so far as the authorization of the chiropractor's license is concerned, must stay within its boundaries; they cannot exceed or enlarge them. The matter left to them [the schools and colleges] is merely the ascertainment and selection of such among the possible modes of doing what is comprehended within that term, as may seem to them best and most desirable, and so the fixing of the standards of action in that respect to be followed by chiropractic licensees."

The principle enunciated in the *Fowler* case, *viz.,* that the "... general consensus of definitions, current at and before the time the Chiropractic Act was adopted, shows what was meant by the term 'chiropractic' when used in that act" (*People v. Fowler, supra,* at 746), has been cited and followed by the courts of this state through the intervening years.

* * *

This principle of the *Fowler* case has also been adopted by courts in other jurisdictions, which have also cited *Fowler* with approval. In *State* ex rel. *Wheat v. Moore,* 154

Kan. 193 [117 P.2d 598], the phrase "as taught and practiced in ... colleges of osteopathy" was involved. The Kansas Supreme Court stated (117 P.2d at 604): "The words of a statute must be taken in the sense in which they were understood at the time when the statute was enacted ... (*People v. Fowler, supra.*)" At the same page, the Kansas court also cites *Fowler* as a "well-considered" opinion for its distinguishing of various forms of the healing arts. One year earlier, in *Burke v. Kansas State Osteopathic Assn.* (1940) 111 F.2d 250, the Circuit Court of Appeals for the Tenth Circuit had dealt with the same question of construction as involved in the *Moore* case. In *Burke,* the federal court stated (p. 256): "[T]he mere fact that these subjects were taught in the osteopathic college is not evidence that the graduates of that college had a right to practice anything but osteopathy. In many of the leading schools of America today, the principles of communism, fascisms [*sic*] and other isms inimical to our form of government are examined and discussed. Not that these schools desire their students to believe these isms but that the students may know what they are and discern between these objectionable theories of government and proper forms of government."

The Supreme Court of Wisconsin cited *Fowler* in *State v. Grayson,* 5 Wis.2d 203 [92 N.W. 2d 272]. In that case, the court was called upon to rule with respect to a definition of "chiropractic" similar to that in *Fowler.* In holding the definition to be "fully consistent" with those found in dictionaries and encyclopedias, the court said (92 N.W. 2d at 277): "In *People v. Fowler* ... a California intermediate appellate court was called upon to determine the meaning of the word 'chiropractic'... The court arrived at a definition very similar in scope to that [in this case] ... We can perceive no clear cut legislative intent that ... [the] definition [of 'chiropractic'] must ... [be] so broad in scope as to permit every practice or procedure that may be taught in any chiropractic college."

In *Smith v. State Board of Medicine of Idaho,* 74 Idaho 191 [259 P.2d 1033] the Idaho Supreme Court cited *Fowler* as support for affirming a conviction of a "naturopath" for practicing medicine. *Fowler* and *In re Hartman, supra,* are cited by the Nebraska Supreme Court in *State* ex rel. *Johnson v. Wagner,* 139 Neb. 471 [297 N.W. 906], where the scope of "osteopathy" was in question. There, the court stated (p. 910): "The scope of osteopathy is well known and schools and colleges of osteopathy must stay within its boundaries, they cannot enlarge them. (*People v. Fowler* ...)" The statute involved in *Wagner* contained the phrase "as taught in ... Osteopathic colleges ..." The Nebraska court pointed out that "[t]he fact that branches of medicine and surgery may be taught to increase the knowledge of the student ... will not warrant him to invade those fields on the theory that they constitute the practice of osteopathy."

There is patently no merit in plaintiffs' claim that the practices that have developed in this profession are admissible in evidence to determine the acts and procedures they may properly perform under their chiropractic license.

[Court addresses procedural arguments]

Does a License to Practice Chiropractic Authorize the Holder Thereof: (1) To Use Drugs or Medicines: Or (2) To Practice Obstetrics, Sever the Umbilical Cord, or Perform Episiotomy?

The initial answer to this question is found in section 7 of the Chiropractic Act as adopted by the people at the general election in November 1922. That section provides that the "License to practice chiropractic'... shall not authorize the practice of medicine, surgery ... nor the use of any drug or medicine now or hereafter included in materia medica." In this connection it is appropriate to point out that in the official argument presented to the voters prior to the November 1922 election, in favor of the adoption of the Chiropractic Act, it was stated that the proposed act "prohibits the use of drugs, surgery or the practice of obstetrics by chiropractors...." The official argument may be considered as an aid to an interpretation of an act. (*Beneficial Loan Society, Ltd. v. Haight*, 215 Cal. 506, 515 [11 P.2d 857]; *People v. Fowler, supra*, pp. 744–745.) In *People v. Augusto*, 193 Cal.App.2d 253 [14 Cal.Rptr. 284], the court points out (pp. 257–258) that a chiropractor administers his treatment "'... with the hands, no drugs being administered.' [Citations.]" Thus it is crystal clear from the plain wording of the initiative act and the decisions in this state that a chiropractor is not authorized to use drugs or medicines and it was not intended that he should be so authorized. It is likewise equally clear that the holder of a chiropractic license is not authorized to perform surgery. The Chiropractic Act expressly so provides (§7), and the decisions so hold (*People v. Fowler, supra*; *People v. Nunn, supra*).

* * *

It will be recalled that section 7 of the Chiropractic Act also provides that a license to practice chiropractic shall not authorize the practice of medicine. It is apparent that these provisions do not authorize the practice of obstetrics, the severance of the umbilical cord or the performance of an episiotomy. These procedures all fall in the medical-surgical field (see, e.g., *In re Hartman, supra*; *People v. Nunn, supra*) which chiropractors may not invade.

In an effort to fortify their position, plaintiffs emphasize the portion of section 7 which provides that the holder of a license to practice chiropractic may "use all necessary mechanical, and hygienic and sanitary measures incident to the care of the body ..." But this language does not authorize either the use of drugs, medicines, the severance of tissues, or the practice of obstetrics. In this connection it should be noted that the last provision of section 7 (following the last quoted authorization) sets forth two very specific limitations: (1) that the license to practice chiropractic "shall not authorize the practice" of medicine or surgery; (2) "nor the use of any drug or medicine now or hereafter included in materia medica."

* * *

Although the Chiropractic Act provides that a license to practice chiropractic does not authorize the use of "any drug or medicine now or hereafter included in materia medica," plaintiffs nevertheless contend that a chiropractor may use such drugs or medicines for: (1) diagnosis; (2) as an aid in the practice of chiropractic; (3) for emergencies; or (4) for clinical research. But since a chiropractor is not authorized to use drugs and medicines at all, it follows that his license does not authorize him to use them in any of the above areas of his professional activities.

* * *

From the foregoing it is manifest that the court's declaration of the rights of the parties in paragraphs F and G of the judgment is correct.

* * *

The Judgment is Affirmed.

Problem

Applying the definition of chiropractic set out in the Georgia statutes described in *Foster*, determine whether the following activity is inside or outside the scope of chiropractic practice:

- Testing of a patient's urine for sugar and albumin because the presence of sugar could mean "malformality of several organ dysfunctions" and could implicate the "general health picture" while albumin could show there was a "protein missing in the metabolism" which it could in turn "show that there are problems with the kidneys." The chiropractor states that conducting urinalysis provides him or her with information about whether the patient is susceptible to chiropractic care at all, or whether the patient should be referred to another health care provider.
- A general physical examination including the taking of blood pressure and examining the heart, lungs, throat and mouth, all to determine the overall health of the patient. The chiropractor uses a tongue depressor, stethoscope, and blood pressure measure to determine whether the patient should be referred elsewhere or is susceptible to chiropractic treatment. Moreover, chiropractors often prescribe an exercise regime as part of the treatment of low back pain, and it would be dangerous to prescribe any type of exercise regime without knowing the patient's overall health condition.
- Collecting laboratory specimens including urine, blood and hair samples. Using an ultrasound machine as part of making chiropractic diagnosis.
- Examination and x-ray of an elbow. The chiropractor states that the x-ray can be used to rule out a localized problem with the elbow as a cause of the patient's pain.

Notes and Questions

1. By limiting chiropractic to practice as it existed in 1922, as the court did in *Crees*, it virtually guarantees that the growth of a profession is determined not by science or academic learning centers, but by legislators. Even assuming that legislators are the best qualified to determine the appropriate scope-of-practice, upon what evidence do they have to make these decisions? Legislators surely would like to see that the practitioner can safely and effectively engage in the disputed practice. But how can a health care provider demonstrate this when the provider is not authorized to engage in practice in the first place?

Barbara Safriet describes this conundrum in her essay:

> Health care-related knowledge continues to expand as research yields new inventions and improves old ones. And just as physician's skills have evolved as a consequence, so too have those of other providers. Yet, when these other professionals seek a corresponding expansion of their legal authority, as reflected in their statutorily defined scopes of practice, they are stymied by both the inertia of the legislative process and the medical-preemption dynamic described earlier. As a result, what they are able to do is always several years (or more) ahead of what they are permitted to do. The sum total of wasted professional assets represented by this disparity is staggering—and growing.

> Another legal problem intrinsic to overly restrictive scope-of-practice laws borders on the absurd: How are providers to achieve expanded scopes of practice by demonstrating that they can safely and effectively do what they are not yet authorized to do? Few would be willing to follow the obvious but perilous path of demonstrating that they have competently done something that is clearly beyond the scope of their current legal authority. This conundrum is especially acute when the asked-for expansion would eliminate mandatory physician's supervision or direction. No matter how well-educated or capable of independent

practice, the provider in such a situation is likely to encounter a predictable response from organized medicine to any study data mustered as evidence: "Since the data must reflect legally 'supervised' practices, they prove nothing with respect to your capacity to practice safely and effectively on your own license."

Barbara Safriet, *Closing the Gap Between Can and May in Health-Care Provider's Scopes of Practice: A Primer for Policymakers*, 19 Yale J. on Reg. 301 (Summer 2002):

Because non-physician health care providers charge less for their services, to what extent should there be overlap between a physician and chiropractor scope-of-practice? For example, does rigid adherence to legislatively prescribed scopes-of-practice results in overall higher health care costs?

For further discussion on this dilemma, *see* Rebecca Burg, Note, *HMO Exclusion of Chiropractors*, 66 S. Cal. L. Rev. 807, 833–34 (1993) (concluding that chiropractor provided services are less costly then physician provided services); Barbara J. Safriet, *Health Care Dollars and Regulatory Expense: The Role of Advanced Practice Nursing*, 9 Yale J. on Reg. 417 (Summer 1992) (addressing training costs of physicians virus nurse practitioners), For an excellent overall review of this issue *see* Lori Andrews, *The Shadow Health Care Systems: Regulation of Alternative Health Care Providers*, 32 Hous. L. Rev. 1273 (1996).

2. Would having non-physician CAM professionals practice under the supervision of physicians either solve or exacerbate the tensions between physician and CAM providers? On one hand, physician supervision could expand the scope-of-practice for many providers. Increased supervision, however, increases costs and (depending upon the supervising physician) may limit the discretion of the CAM provider. Consider the activities (ultrasound, x-ray, physical exams, and laboratory services) proposed in the problem preceding these notes and think about whether physician oversight would elevate any concern you have about a chiropractor engaging in the activity.

3. A frequently litigated scope-of-practice dispute involves the ability of chiropractors to perform pre-employment and physical exams (particularly those required for truck drivers) as well as exams for athletics. The results vary, as do the underlying practice acts. For an interesting review of the lengthy dispute in Minnesota, *see* Minnesota Board of Chiropractic Examiners, The Authority of Chiropractors to Perform Certain Physical Examinations, http://www.mn-chiroboard.state.mn.us/issue-article-1.htm (last updated Mar. 20, 2000); *but see Attorney General on behalf of the people of Michigan v. Beno*, 373 N.W.2d 544 (Mich. 1985) (diagnosis of a patient's health by means of a complete examination for a pre-employment physical is outside the scope of chiropractic).

4. While many of the reported cases involving scope-of-practice disputes involve physicians and non-physicians, scope-of-practice disputes between different non-physician providers proliferate. Rather than turning to the courts, many of these disputes fall into the laps of state legislators. For an interesting account of the clash between chiropractors and physical therapists regarding a treatment known as spinal manipulation, *see* James W. Hillard & Marjorie B. Johnson, *State Practice Acts of Licensed Health Professions: Scope-of-Practice*, 8 DePaul J. Health Care L. 237 (2004).

Problem

Assume that after the *Foster* case was decided, a bill was proposed to the Georgia legislature to amend the Georgia Chiropractic Practice Act to read "nothing herein shall be construed to prohibit the rendering of dietary advice."

- If you were a legislator, would you vote in favor of the amendment? Why or why not?
- If you were a lobbyist representing the Medical Association, what position would you take with regard to this bill?
- Assume the legislation passed. You are an Assistant Attorney General preparing an AG Opinion responding to the following Board of Chiropractic examiners question: "In the course of providing dietary advice can licensed Chiropractors dispense vitamins, minerals and food supplements?" What information would you want to review in order to respond? What would your opinion read and why?

Chapter Four

Malpractice

I. Standards of Care

A. Common Law

In the context of conventional medical malpractice, a major issue facing the courts over the last century has been the standard of care that should apply to defendant physicians. A number of judicial opinions traditionally are used to illustrate the courts' transition from the 'local rule,' which holds physicians to the standard of other reasonably prudent physicians in the same or similar geographic area, to the 'national rule,' which holds physicians to the standard of other reasonably prudent physicians in the same specialty across the nation. *See e.g.*, FURROW ET AL., HEALTH LAW: CASES, MATERIALS AND PROBLEMS 327–342 (6th ed., Thomson West 2008).

In the context of CAM malpractice, the question becomes: What standards apply to CAM practitioners? What standards should apply to CAM practitioners? Should a CAM practitioner be held to the same standard as a conventional physician?

In *Kerkman v. Hintz*, reprinted in part below, the Supreme Court of Wisconsin answered some of these questions when it established a new standard of care for chiropractors in the State of Wisconsin. The Court also examined several related questions, including whether a non-chiropractor's expert testimony may be used to establish the standard of care applicable to chiropractors.

Kerkman v. Hintz

Supreme Court of Wisconsin

418 N.W.2d 795 (1988)

William G. Callow, JUSTICE.

This is a review of a published decision of the court of appeals, Kerkman v. Hintz, 138 Wis. 2d 131, 406 N.W.2d 156 (Ct. App. 1987), reversing a judgment of the circuit court for Racine county, Judge John C. Ahlgrimm, which found Dr. Max A. Hintz, Chiropractor, liable for malpractice.

There are two issues presented on review. First, did the circuit court instruct the jury correctly on the appropriate standard of care by which to measure a chiropractor's diagnosis, treatment, or referral of a patient? Second, in light of an award of $241,000 in damages to Mr. Kerkman for past and future pain, suffering and disability, past medical expenses, and loss of earning capacity, should an award of no damages to Mrs. Kerkman for loss of consortium be reversed in the interest of justice? Because we conclude that a chiropractor should be held to a standard of care which requires the chiropractor to exercise the same degree of skill which is usually exercised by a reasonable chiropractor in the same or similar circumstances, we hold that the circuit court's instruction to the jury on the appropriate standard of care was erroneous. Accordingly, we affirm that part of the decision of the court of appeals which remanded the cause for a new trial on negligence. We further conclude that a new trial on the question of Mrs. Kerkman's damages is not required. Accordingly, we reverse that part of the decision of the court of appeals which remanded the question of Mrs. Kerkman's damages to the circuit court for further consideration.

In September, 1982, Jerome Kerkman (Kerkman) consulted Dr. Max A. Hintz, Chiropractor (Hintz), with complaints of soreness in the upper shoulders and neck and numbness in his hands. Kerkman had previously consulted Hintz in 1979 regarding pain in his lower back. In 1979 Hintz had taken an X-ray of Kerkman's spinal column and adjusted Kerkman's back. Hintz is a graduate of the Palmer College of Chiropractic (Palmer College) located in Davenport, Iowa, and his specialty is upper cervical chiropractic. Upper cervical chiropractic concentrates treatment on the top two vertebrae of the spine — the atlas and the axis.

At the initial visit in September, 1982, Hintz took a history from Kerkman, analyzed a subluxation of the C-1 vertebra, and performed an adjustment. In the two weeks following the initial visit, Hintz saw Kerkman three times and performed two, possibly three, additional adjustments of Kerkman's back. Following these adjustments, Kerkman's condition deteriorated.

In November, 1982, Kerkman went to his family medical physician, Dr. Baker. During the course of Dr. Baker's examination of Kerkman, Dr. Baker called in a neurosurgeon, Dr. Harry H. Lippman (Lippman). Lippman diagnosed a compressed spinal column and thereafter performed an operation to relieve the compression. Following the surgery, Kerkman felt better temporarily. However, Kerkman's condition began to deteriorate, and a second operation was performed to remove a herniated disc at the C-5/C-6 level of the cervical spine. Following the second operation, Kerkman still had problems with numbness in his hands, walking, and bladder control.

In May of 1984, Kerkman commenced this action against Hintz, alleging negligent treatment. In addition, Mrs. Kerkman joined the action with a claim for loss of consortium. At trial, the evidence presented by Kerkman, concerning whether Hintz had met the required standard of care, focused on whether Hintz had exercised the care and skill exercised by a recognized school of the medical profession. Specifically, Kerkman introduced the testimony of two neurosurgeons, Dr. Lavern Herman and Dr. Harry Lippman, both of whom testified that from a medical standpoint Hintz had not conducted a proper diagnosis of Kerkman. In opposition to the evidence presented by Kerkman, the evidence introduced by Hintz focused on Hintz's assertion that he had exercised the same degree of care which is usually exercised by a reasonable chiropractor.

At the close of evidence, Hintz requested Wisconsin Civil Jury Instruction 1023, modified to reflect the fact that the claim was for chiropractic malpractice.[1] In essence, Hintz

---

1. Dr. Hintz's requested instruction stated in pertinent part: "It was the duty of the defendant chiropractor, in rendering chiropractor services to the plaintiff in treatment of his complaints, to exercise that degree of care, skill, and judgment which is usually exercised, under like or similar circumstances, by the average chiropractor, who practices the specialty which the defendant practices, having due regard for the advanced state of chiropractic at the time in question."

requested an instruction that, as a chiropractor, he was required to exercise the same degree of care which is usually exercised by a reasonable chiropractor. The trial court declined to give the proposed instruction and, instead, instructed the jury that a chiropractor must exercise the same degree of care and skill which is usually exercised by a recognized school of the medical profession.[2] On August 16, 1985, the jury returned a verdict awarding Kerkman $241,000 in damages. The jury verdict further provided that nothing be awarded to Mrs. Kerkman for loss of consortium.

Following trial, Hintz filed several motions after verdict, alleging primarily that the circuit court had erred when it instructed the jury that Hintz was to be held to the same degree of care and skill which is usually exercised by a recognized school of medicine. Hintz further alleged that the circuit court erred in permitting medical doctors to testify that the medical standard of care was breached by Hintz. Kerkman also filed motions after verdict requesting: (1) judgment on the verdict and (2) that the circuit court change the award of no damages for loss of consortium to an award of $15,000.

In denying Hintz's motions, the circuit court noted that its instruction to the jury was based on Kuechler v. Volgmann, 180 Wis. 238, 192 N.W. 1015 (1923), in which it was held that, in evaluating a patient's condition prior to treatment, a chiropractor must exercise the same degree of care and skill which is usually exercised by a recognized school of the medical profession.[3] The circuit court further ruled that, because the chiropractor's treatment had invaded the field of medicine, it was appropriate to permit medical doctors to testify that the medical standard of care was breached. After denying Kerkman's request to change the loss of consortium jury determination, the circuit court granted Kerkman's motion for judgment on the verdict.

Both Kerkman and Hintz appealed from the order and judgment of the circuit court, each raising substantially the same issues which were before the circuit court. The court of appeals reversed the judgment of the circuit court. According to the court of appeals, the standard of care articulated in Kuechler had been abrogated through subsequent legislative action which recognized chiropractic care and provided for the licensing of chiropractors. Kerkman, 138 Wis. 2d at 139, 142. The court of appeals then established a new standard of care which required chiropractors "to (1) recognize a medical problem as contrasted with a chiropractic problem; (2) refrain from further chiropractic treatment when a reasonable chiropractor should be aware that the patient's condition is not amenable to chiropractic treatment and the continuation of the treatment may aggravate the condition; and (3) refer the patient to a medical doctor when a medical mode of treatment is indicated." Id. at 144. The court of appeals further held that, in determining whether a chiropractor has breached his or her duty, that the chiropractor "is held to the same standard of care as the reasonable chiropractor in the same or similar circumstances." Id.

---

2. The trial court's instruction to the jury provided in pertinent part: "You are instructed that in the State of Wisconsin, a licensed Chiropractor is obligated to conduct a competent assessment and evaluation of a patient's condition before chiropractic treatment or consultation. In performing this duty, a chiropractor must exercise the same degree of care and skill that is usually exercised by a recognized school of the medical profession. In this regard, you are instructed that ignorance in the practice of medicine does not lessen a chiropractor's liability for failure to perform this duty. If you determine that the defendant, Max A. Hintz, failed to perform this duty by exercising the same degree of care and skill that is usually exercised by a recognized school of the medical profession, you will find Max A. Hintz to be negligent."

3. Hintz's other motions, alleging that Kerkman failed to prove a causal connection between the care and the injury, that the award was excessive and contrary to public policy, that the verdict unconstitutionally deprived Hintz of his rights, and that the verdict was against the great weight of the evidence, were also denied by the circuit court.

Because the jury was improperly instructed, the court of appeals reversed the judgment of the circuit court and remanded for a new trial on the issue of negligence, with instructions for the circuit court to determine whether the erroneous instruction affected the determination of damages as to both Mr. and Mrs. Kerkman, and whether a new trial on the issue of damages was required.

The court of appeals also addressed the question of whether non-chiropractic experts could be used to establish a breach of the chiropractor's standard of care. In this regard, the court of appeals held that, because of the overlap between the chiropractic and medical professions, a medical doctor's testimony is admissible if there is a sufficient factual showing that the medical witness is qualified by knowledge, skill, experience, training, or education to give the requested opinion. Id. at 149 (citing sec. 907.02, Stats.). On May 7, 1987, this court granted Kerkman's petition for review.

Kerkman, in asserting that it was error for the court of appeals to conclude that the Kuechler holding had been abrogated, contends that the legislative enactment of separate licensure for chiropractors emphasizes the legislature's recognition of the need for a chiropractor to be held to a medical standard of care when diagnosing a patient's condition before rendering chiropractic treatment. According to Kerkman, instead of liberating chiropractors from being held to a standard for diagnosing a patient's condition consistent with medical knowledge, the codification and recodification of the administrative regulation of the Chiropractic Examining Board has served to underscore the recognition that the safety of the patient is paramount and that the chiropractor must know when the patient's problem is beyond the bounds of the chiropractor's training and education. It is Kerkman's position that the circuit court properly relied upon Kuechler and properly instructed the jury to assess Hintz's conduct in light of the degree of care usually exercised by a recognized school of the medical profession. Although the codification of the administrative regulation of the Chiropractic Examining Board may have served to underscore the recognition that the safety of the patient is paramount, we disagree that this compels the conclusion that a chiropractor must be held to a medical standard of care.

For the reasons listed below, we conclude that the holding in Kuechler—that a chiropractor must be held to a medical standard when diagnosing or analyzing a patient's ailment—has been abrogated. In Kuechler, this court addressed the question of the appropriate standard of care to apply to a chiropractor's analysis and diagnosis of a patient's ailment. According to the court, when a chiropractor undertakes to analyze or diagnose a patient's ailment, the chiropractor "must exercise the care and skill ... usually exercised by a recognized school of the medical profession." Kuechler, 180 Wis. at 244. Underlying this holding was the court's conclusion that "the practice of chiropractic is the practice of medicine." Id.

However, at the time Kuechler was decided, chiropractors were not licensed professionals. Since that time, the legislature has enacted numerous provisions for the licensure and regulation of chiropractors. Specifically, in 1925 the legislature for the first time provided that a person must be licensed before practicing chiropractic. Sec. 147.23, Stats. (1925).... By 1956, administrative regulations had been adopted which included a definition of chiropractic.... Wis. Admin. Code, Chapter Chir 1 (1956). The validity of these administrative regulations were subsequently affirmed by this court. State v. Grayson, 5 Wis. 2d 203, 211, 92 N.W.2d 272 (1958).

In 1982, at the time Kerkman sought chiropractic care from Hintz, the Wisconsin statutes provided that no person may engage in the practice of chiropractic unless licensed by the Chiropractic Examining Board. In addition, all applicants for a license to practice chiropractic must have completed two years of study towards a bachelor of arts or science degree and must have graduated from a reputable school of chiropractic. Sec. 446.02, Stats. (1981–82). Applicants must also have passed both a written examination on subjects taught in approved chiropractic schools and a clinical examination. Wis. Admin. Code, sec. Chir 1.03 (1982). (All references in this opinion are to the Wisconsin Administrative Code in effect in 1982 unless otherwise noted.)

The statutes further provided that the practice of chiropractic means:

"(a) To examine into the fact, condition, or cause of departure from complete health and proper condition of the human; to treat without the use of drugs ... or surgery; to counsel; to advise for the same for the restoration and preservation of health or to undertake ... to do any of the aforementioned acts, for compensation ...; and

"(b) To employ or apply chiropractic adjustments and the principles or techniques of chiropractic science in the diagnosis, treatment or prevention of any of the conditions described in s. 448.01(10)." Sec. 446.01(2), Stats. (1981–82).

Section 448.01(10), Stats. (1981–82), pertaining to medical practices, provided that to "[t]reat the sick" meant "to examine into the fact, condition or cause of human health or disease, or to treat, operate, prescribe or advise for the same."

According to the Administrative Code, the practice of chiropractic included "examination, counsel and advice with respect to the diagnosis and/or analysis of any interference with normal nerve transmission, expression and the correction thereof by a chiropractic adjustment to remove the interference as a cause of disease, without the use of drugs or surgery." Wis. Admin. Code, sec. Chir 3.02(1). Diagnosis and/or analysis included "the use of diagnostic and analytical instruments and procedures approved by the [chiropractic examining] board and within the scope of the practice of chiropractic in which the licensee can show proof of proficiency to the board." Id. at 3.02(2). The use of "instruments or machines such as colonic irrigators, diathermy, plasmatic, short wave, radionics..., and ultra-sonic" was specifically prohibited. Id. at 3.02(3).

The Administrative Code further provided that: "The science of chiropractic is based on the premise that disease or abnormal function can be caused by abnormal nerve impulse transmission..., due to compression, traction, pressure or irritation upon nerves, as the result of bony segments, especially of the spine or contiguous structures, either deviating from juxtaposition and/or functioning in an abnormal manner so as to irritate nerves or their receptors." Id. at 3.01.

Through the enactment of this legislation, the legislature has recognized the practice of chiropractic as a separate and distinct health care discipline. In licensing chiropractors to examine into the cause of departure from complete health and by authorizing chiropractors to diagnose, treat or prevent disease, ... the legislature has recognized chiropractors as providers of health care. However, by limiting chiropractors to the use of chiropractic adjustments and the principles or techniques of chiropractic science in the diagnosis, treatment or prevention of disease while prohibiting the use of traditional medical tools, e.g., drugs or surgery, ... the legislature has recognized that the practice of chiropractic is distinct from the practice of medicine.

The testimony of Dr. John V. Whaley (Whaley), a chiropractor licensed to practice in Wisconsin, supports the distinct nature of chiropractic care. According to Whaley, a chiropractor does not treat or diagnose disease. Instead, a chiropractor's practice is limited to the analysis and correction of subluxation. The chiropractor's function is to locate the subluxation, if it exists, adjust it back to the correct position, and then allow the body to restore itself to normalcy. A medical doctor's practice, on the other hand, is completely opposite. The medical doctor is concerned with the diagnosis and treatment of the diseased area through the use of drugs and surgery or other techniques.

Although chiropractors are permitted to use some medical tools when analyzing and treating a patient, this overlap does not transform the practice of chiropractic into the practice of medicine. Because of this legislative recognition of chiropractors as a separate health care discipline, the underlying premise of Kuechler and its conclusion, that chiropractors are to be held to a medical standard, can no longer be followed.

Our conclusion that chiropractors should not be held to a medical standard is supported by an examination of the limited legislative authorization of chiropractors to diagnose and/or analyze and treat by chiropractic means. This authorization extends to individuals whose knowledge is limited to that provided by chiropractic training. Sec. 446.01(2), Stats. (1981–82); Wis. Admin. Code, sec. Chir 3.02(1). In light of the fact that chiropractic training is limited primarily to analysis and adjustments of the spine, the legislature, in granting chiropractors the authorization to analyze a patient's ailment, must be held to have determined that the judgment of whether to treat a patient would be made based upon chiropractic knowledge, not medical knowledge. In fact, because a chiropractor is prohibited from using certain medical diagnostic tools, a chiropractor could not analyze a patient's ailment based upon medical knowledge. Consistent with this, a chiropractor's decision to treat cannot be tested in accordance with medical knowledge; it must be tested in accordance with chiropractic knowledge.

We note that Kerkman's reference to Treptau v. Behrens Spa, Inc., 247 Wis. 438, 449–50, 20 N.W.2d 108 (1945), in support of the argument that Kuechler has not been abrogated, is erroneous. According to Kerkman, Treptau in 1945 cited Kuechler for the proposition that a chiropractor is to be held to that degree of care which is usually exercised by a recognized school of medicine. Although this case does cite Kuechler for this proposition, Treptau involved a chiropractor who had gone outside the practice authorized by his license and had, therefore, engaged in the practice of medicine. Because we are concerned in this case with conduct which is within the scope of a chiropractor's license (diagnosis and analysis of a patient), Treptau is inapplicable.

Having concluded that the chiropractic standard of care set out in Kuechler is no longer valid, we must establish a new standard of care for Wisconsin chiropractors. In determining this standard of care, the standards to which we have held other professions are instructive. In analyzing the quality of care required of physicians, we have held that a physician must "'exercise that degree of care and skill which is exercised by the average practitioner in the class to which he belongs, acting in the same or similar circumstances.'" Francois v. Mokrohisky, 67 Wis. 2d 196, 200, 226 N.W.2d 470 (1975). A dentist is required to "exercise that degree of care, diligence, judgment, or skill which dentists in good standing usually exercise … under like or similar circumstances, having regard to the advanced state of dental science at the time of discharging his legal duty to his patient." Lindloff v. Ross, 208 Wis. 482, 487, 243 N.W. 403 (1932). An attorney must exercise "'a reasonable degree of care and skill, and … possess to a reasonable extent the knowledge requisite to a proper performance of the duties of his profession, and, if injury results to the client as a proximate consequence of the lack of such knowledge or skill, or from the failure to exercise it, the client may recover damages to the extent of the injury sustained.'" Malone v. Gerth, 100 Wis. 166, 173, 75 N.W. 972 (1898); Helmbrecht v. St. Paul Insurance Co., 122 Wis. 2d 94, 111, 362 N.W.2d 118 (1985). In Helmbrecht the court noted that the trier of fact must determine what the alleged negligent attorney did and what a reasonable or prudent attorney would have done in the same circumstance. Id. at 112.

In each of these cases, the focus of the inquiry has been on whether the allegedly negligent professional failed to exercise that degree of care, diligence, judgment, or skill which is usually exercised by someone of the same school, under like or similar circumstances. See also Gordon v. Milwaukee County, 125 Wis. 2d 62, 69, 370 N.W.2d 803 (Ct. App. 1985) (county liable for failure to predict course of a mental patient's disease only if "county-employed psychiatrists who examine and diagnose persons alleged to be ill and dangerous fail to exercise that degree of care and skill which would be exercised by the average psychiatrist acting in the same or similar circumstances"). Other courts, in articulating a standard of care, have held that a chiropractor must "exercise the degree of care and skill ordinarily exercised by other chiropractors in a similar community." Boudreaux v. Panger, 490 So. 2d 1083, 1085 (La. 1986); Maxwell v. McCaffrey, 219 Va. 909, 913, 252 S.E.2d 342 (1979); See also Janssen v. Mulder, 232 Mich. 183, 190, 205 N.W. 159 (1925) (plaintiff must prove that chiropractor was negligent through the testimony of one engaged in treatment by similar methods to those employed by defendant).

We have previously recognized that a chiropractor is "authorized to treat the sick only to the extent authorized by their chiropractic license." Grayson, 5 Wis. 2d at 207. Consistent with this limitation and the standards which have been imposed on other professionals, we conclude that a chiropractor must exercise that degree of care, diligence, judgment, and skill which is exercised by a reasonable chiropractor under like or similar circumstances.

We further note that the standard of care adopted by the court of appeals in this case fails to recognize limitations imposed by the legislature upon chiropractors. In delineating the standard of care applicable to a chiropractor, the court of appeals held that a chiropractor is required to "(1) recognize a medical problem as contrasted with a chiropractic problem; (2) refrain from further chiropractic treatment when a reasonable chiropractor should be aware that the patient's condition is not amenable to chiropractic treatment and the continuation of the treatment may aggravate the condition; and (3) refer the patient to a medical doctor when a medical mode of treatment is indicated." Kerkman, 138 Wis. 2d at 144.

As previously noted, a chiropractor is limited by his or her license to practice within the scope of chiropractic knowledge and training. Consistent with this limitation, we hold that a chiropractor is required first to determine whether the patient presents a problem which is treatable through chiropractic means. If the patient has a problem which is treatable through chiropractic means, the chiropractor may provide chiropractic treatment to the patient. However, the chiropractic must refrain from further chiropractic treatment when a reasonable chiropractor should be aware that the patient's condition will not be responsive to further treatment. If the patient presents a problem which is outside the scope of chiropractic treatment, then the chiropractor must inform the patient that the problem presented is not within the chiropractor's license to treat. Having explained to the patient that the problem is not within the chiropractor's license to treat, the chiropractor does not have a duty to refer the patient to a medical doctor. Cf. Howe v. Smith, 203 Pa. Super. 212, 218, 199 A.2d 521 (1964) (although chiropractor has authority to diagnose, that authority is for the limited purpose of determining whether the particular treatment which may be legally rendered to a patient is proper treatment for the disease from which the patient is suffering; a chiropractor, therefore, does not have the authority to diagnose generally).

In holding that a chiropractor does not have a duty to refer, we recognize that a number of states have imposed such a requirement. See, e.g., Rosenberg by Rosenberg

v. Cahill, 99 N.J. 318, 333, 492 A.2d 371 (1985); Mostrom v. Pettibon, 25 Wash. App. 158, 163, 607 P.2d 864 (1980). However, because implicit in a requirement that a chiropractor refer a patient to a medical doctor is the imposition on the chiropractor to make a medical determination that the patient needs medical care, such a determination could not be made without employing medical knowledge. Because a chiropractor is not licensed to make such a determination, we hold that a chiropractor does not have a duty to refer a patient who is not treatable through chiropractic means to a medical doctor.

In summary, we hold that a chiropractor has a duty to (1) determine whether the patient presents a problem which is treatable through chiropractic means; (2) refrain from further chiropractic treatment when a reasonable chiropractor should be aware that the patient's condition will not be responsive to further treatment; and (3) if the ailment presented is outside the scope of chiropractic care, inform the patient that the ailment is not treatable through chiropractic means. In determining whether a chiropractor breaches these duties, the chiropractor is held to that degree of care, diligence, judgment, and skill which is exercised by a reasonable chiropractor under like or similar circumstances.

In the present case, the jury was instructed that Hintz was required to exercise the same degree of care and skill which is usually exercised by a recognized school of the medical profession. Under the rule announced today, that instruction is erroneous. We therefore remand the question of negligence to the circuit court for a new trial consistent with the standard of care articulated in this opinion.

Hintz has asked that this case be dismissed because the only competent evidence indicated that his actions were consistent with the care usually exercised by a chiropractor. Regardless of the accuracy of this assertion, we conclude that the proper remedy is a remand for a new trial. The Kerkmans initiated and pursued their claim in accordance with Kuechler v. Volgmann, supra. Having determined for the first time that the standard of care enunciated in Kuechler is no longer applicable, the parties are entitled to a new trial consistent with this opinion.

The court of appeals also addressed the question of the competency of nonchiropractic experts to testify regarding a breach of the chiropractic standard of care. The admission of expert testimony is largely a matter within the discretion of the circuit court. State v. Friedrich, 135 Wis. 2d 1, 15, 398 N.W.2d 763 (1987). In Wisconsin, the general rule is that expert testimony is admissible if it will assist the trier of fact to understand the evidence or to determine a fact in issue and if the person testifying is qualified in the field in which the testimony is being elicited. Sec. 907.02, Stats.; see Herman v. Milwaukee Children's Hospital, 121 Wis. 2d 531, 551, 361 N.W.2d 297 (Ct. App. 1984).

Thus, a chiropractor is qualified to testify regarding the practice of chiropractic and the corresponding standard of care. Green v. Rosenow, 63 Wis. 2d 463, 470, 217 N.W.2d 388 (1974). Moreover, one who is not licensed to practice chiropractic may testify regarding the standard of care for a chiropractor if qualified as an expert in the area in which testimony will be given.

We next address Hintz's argument that the jury's award of $241,000 for damages to Kerkman is excessive. The question on review is whether there exists any credible evidence which supports the jury's award. Coryell v. Conn, 88 Wis. 2d 310, 315, 276 N.W.2d 723 (1979). In determining whether any credible evidence exists to support the award, we must view the evidence in the light most favorable to the plaintiff. Id. at 317. There was testimony in this case which indicated that Kerkman had suffered a series of damages, including, but not limited to, considerable pain and suffering and permanent partial disability. Based upon the testimony in the record, we are satisfied that there is credible evidence to support the jury's award of $ 241,000 to Mr. Kerkman. Accordingly, we reverse that part of the decision of the court of appeals which remanded, with instructions, the question of Mr. Kerkman's damages.

In conclusion, we address Mrs. Kerkman's argument that the jury's award of no damages for loss of consortium should be reversed in the interest of justice. This court may reverse a judgment or order appealed from when it is necessary to accomplish the ends of justice. Sec. 751.06, Stats. Under sec. 751.06 and our prior cases, discretionary reversal is appropriate (1) whenever the real controversy has not been fully tried or (2) whenever it is probable that justice has for any reason miscarried. See, e.g., State v. Wyss, 124 Wis. 2d 681, 735, 370 N.W.2d 745 (1985); State v. Cuyler, 110 Wis. 2d 133, 142, 327 N.W.2d 662 (1983); Jones (George Michael) v. State, 70 Wis. 2d 41, 56, 233 N.W.2d 430 (1975). Our review of the record indicates that only a modest amount of evidence was presented regarding damages to Mrs. Kerkman. The jury evaluated this evidence and determined that no damages should be awarded. We are not convinced that the controversy has not been fully tried or that justice has miscarried. Accordingly, we reverse that part of the decision of the court of appeals which remanded, with instructions, the question of Mrs. Kerkman's damages.

BY THE COURT.—The decision of the court of appeals is affirmed in part, reversed in part, and the cause is remanded for a new trial on the question of negligence only.

* * *

Notes and Questions

1. Is the holding in *Kerkman*—that chiropractors are not held to a medical standard but instead a chiropractic standard—necessary? Otherwise, would not all defendant chiropractors be found negligent for failing to adhere to a medical standard? Or, are there situations in which a medical and chiropractic standard are one and the same?

2. *Kerkman* holds that a chiropractor has a duty to: (1) determine whether the patient presents a problem which is treatable through chiropractic means; (2) refrain from further chiropractic treatment when a reasonable chiropractor should be aware that the patient's condition will not be responsive to further treatment; and (3) if the ailment presented is outside the scope of chiropractic care, inform the patient that the ailment is not treatable through chiropractic means. *Kerkman*, 142 Wisc. 2d at 421–22. *Kerkman* stops short of imposing a duty on a chiropractor to transfer a patient to an allopathic physician, reasoning that, "implicit in a requirement that a chiropractor refer a patient to a medical doctor is the imposition on the chiropractor to make a medical determination that the patient needs medical care, such a determination could not be made without employing medical knowledge. Because a chiropractor is not licensed to make such a determination, we hold that a chiropractor does not have a duty to refer a patient who is not treatable through chiropractic means to a medical doctor." *Kerkman*, 142 Wisc. 2d at 421. Do you agree that a chiropractor can have a duty to recognize when a patient's ailment is outside the scope of chiropractic but not a corresponding duty to recognize that the patient needs medical care? Is the court drawing too fine of a line between recognizing the scope of chiropractic and not recognizing the scope of medicine?

3. *Majority Rule.* What is the majority rule? Do most jurisdictions hold chiropractors to a medical standard or a chiropractic standard? *See, e.g.,* MICHAEL H. COHEN, COMPLEMENTARY AND ALTERNATIVE MEDICINE: LEGAL BOUNDARIES AND REGULATORY PER-

spectives 64 (1998) (stating that, "... in general, a chiropractor is held to a chiropractic standard of care, a naturopath to the standard of care of the naturopathic profession, an acupuncturist to the same standard as other acupuncturists, and so on").

4. *Working Outside the Scope of Practice.* Even in a jurisdiction that follows the majority rule, when might a chiropractor be held to a medical standard? When he performs a spinal manipulation? Or, when he attempts to conduct a surgery that is outside the scope of chiropractic and within the scope of medicine? *See, e.g., Liability of Chiropractors and Other Drugless Practitioners for Medical Malpractice*, 77 A.L.R.4th 273 (2008) ("Where a drugless healer invades the scope of any field of practice outside his own..., such as that of a medical doctor, the courts have ruled that he will be judged by the standard of care applicable to a practitioner in the field which he has invaded ...").

5. *Expert Testimony. Kerkman* holds that "one who is not licensed to practice chiropractic may testify regarding the standard of care for a chiropractor if qualified as an expert in the area in which testimony will be given." *Kerkman*, 142 Wisc.2d at 423. Do you agree that a non-chiropractor should be able to testify regarding the standard of care applicable to chiropractors? *See generally* Susan M. Hobson, *The Standard of Admissibility of a Physician's Expert Testimony in a Chiropractic Malpractice Action*, 64 INDIANA L. J. 737 (1989).

6. *Relevant Scholarship.* For a more thorough discussion of the different standards of care that may apply or should be applied to CAM practitioners, *see* Christine C. Kung, *Defining a Standard of Care in the Practice of Acupuncture*, 31 AM. J. L. & M. 117 (2005); Michael H. Cohen & Mary C. Ruggie, *Integrating Complementary and Alternative Medical Therapies in Conventional Medical Settings: Legal Quandaries and Potential Policy Models*, 72 U. CIN. L. REV. 702 at §III(B)(1) (2003); MICHAEL H. COHEN, COMPLEMENTARY AND ALTERNATIVE MEDICINE: LEGAL BOUNDARIES AND REGULATORY PERSPECTIVES 56–72 (1998).

B. Statutes

Over the last thirty years, many state legislatures have codified the standards of care that apply to both conventional and CAM practitioners. Consider the following standard of care, set forth in the Iowa Acupuncture Practice Act, which applies to non-physicians who practice acupuncture in the State of Iowa:

> IOWA CODE § 148E.4. Standard of Care. A person licensed under this chapter shall be held to the same standard of care as a person licensed to practice medicine and surgery or osteopathic medicine and surgery.

* * *

Let us compare the Iowa standard for acupuncturists with the standards to which Louisiana and Nevada hold their chiropractors, respectively:

> LOUISIANA REVISED STATUTES § 9:2794.... A. In a malpractice action based on the negligence of a ... chiropractic physician ... the plaintiff shall have the burden of proving: (1) The degree of knowledge or skill possessed or the degree of care ordinarily exercised by ... chiropractic physicians licensed to practice in the state of Louisiana and actively practicing in a similar community or locale and under similar circumstances ...

* * *

Nevada Revised Statutes § 634.017. "Malpractice" defined. "Malpractice" means failure on the part of a chiropractor to exercise the degree of care, diligence and skill ordinarily exercised by chiropractors in good standing in the community in which he practices.

* * *

Let us further compare the single standards to which Louisiana and Nevada hold their chiropractors to the bi-level standard of care adopted by Iowa for its chiropractors. Under Iowa law, chiropractors are held to the standard of care of other chiropractors when performing neuromusculoskeletal adjustments by hand or instrument. Iowa Code § 151.8.2. However, if an Iowa chiropractor withdraws a patient's blood for diagnostic purposes, performs or utilizes laboratory tests, performs physical examinations, renders nutritional advice, or uses chiropractic physiotherapy procedures (collectively referred to as "additional procedures and practices"), the chiropractor will be held to the following standard of care:

Iowa Code § 151.8.3. Training in procedures used in practice.... 3. A chiropractor using the additional procedures and practices authorized by this chapter shall be held to the standard of care applicable to any other health care practitioner in this state.

* * *

Notes and Questions

1. *Iowa Standard of Care for Acupuncturists.* Why do you think the Iowa Legislature decided to hold its acupuncturists to the standard of allopathic and osteopathic physicians? Will this standard have any practical effect on the daily practices of acupuncturists? Or, do acupuncturists practice acupuncture, including the insertion of needles, in the same manner as conventional physicians? Does Iowa's standard for acupuncturists depart from the general rule that CAM practitioners are held to the standard of other practitioners of the same school of thought? *See, e.g.*, Liability of Chiropractors and Other Drugless Practitioners for Medical Malpractice, 77 A.L.R.4th 273 (2008) ("In malpractice actions against them, chiropractors and other drugless healers have been held to the standard of the use of the same degree of care ... as is ... used by prudent, skillful, and careful practitioners of the same school..., and not that of a medical doctor or specialist.").

2. *Iowa Standard of Care for Chiropractors.* Why do you think the Iowa Legislature decided to hold chiropractors to two different standards of care; that is: (1) the standard of other chiropractors when the chiropractor performs a neuromusculoskeletal adjustment; but (2) the standard of other health care practitioners when the chiropractor withdraws blood, utilizes routine laboratory tests, performs a physical examination, renders nutritional advice, or uses chiropractic physiotherapy procedures? What training do chiropractic students receive in chiropractic school? What is the scope of practice of a chiropractor in Iowa? *See* Iowa Code § 151.1. *See also* Liability of Chiropractors and Other Drugless Practitioners for Medical Malpractice, 77 A.L.R.4th 273 (2008) ("Where a drugless healer invades the scope of any field of practice outside his own..., such as that of a medical doctor, the courts have ruled that he will be judged by the standard of care applicable to a practitioner in the field which he has invaded ...").

* * *

C. Scope of Practice Statutes, Unprofessional Conduct Statutes, and Malpractice Standards of Care

When a state statute defines the scope of practice of a conventional or CAM practitioner, or identifies the activities that constitute 'unprofessional conduct' of a conventional or CAM practitioner for purposes of licensure revocation or state medical board disciplinary proceedings, may that statute be used to establish or support a standard of care in a private malpractice case?

Consider the following Arizona statute, reprinted in part below, which prohibits conventional physicians from ordering chelation therapy except in certain situations. If a physician licensed to practice medicine in Arizona orders chelation therapy for a patient, could the patient use the statute as evidence of the standard of care in a private malpractice case?

> ARIZONA STATUTES § 32-1401(27)(gg). "Unprofessional conduct" includes the following, whether occurring in this state or elsewhere: … Using chelation therapy in the treatment of arteriosclerosis or as any other form of therapy, with the exception of treatment of heavy metal poisoning, without: (i) Adequate informed patient consent[;] (ii) Conforming to generally accepted experimental criteria, including protocols, detailed records, periodic analysis of results and periodic review by a medical peer review committee[; and] (iii) Approval by the federal food and drug administration or its successor agency.

* * *

In *Wengel v. Herfert*, reprinted in part below, the Court of Appeals of Michigan examined a similar issue; that is, whether a Michigan law defining the scope of practice of chiropractors could be used to establish or to support the standard of care in a private malpractice case.

Wengel v. Herfert
Court of Appeals of Michigan
473 N.W.2d 741 (1991)

SHEPHERD, PRESIDING JUDGE.

In this chiropractic malpractice action, defendants R.C. Herfert, D.C., and Herfert Chiropractic Clinics (hereinafter referred to in the singular) appeal as of right a judgment entered in favor of plaintiff and the denial of their motion for judgment notwithstanding the verdict or a new trial. We reverse and remand for a new trial.

Plaintiff, who was suffering from diabetes, claimed that he sought treatment from defendant after reading one of defendant's "Life Line" publications and speaking to one of defendant's employees, both of which led him to believe chiropractic manipulation could help his diabetes. Plaintiff was treated by defendant three times a week for approximately 1 1/2 months in early 1984 after defendant diagnosed plaintiff as having three areas in his spine that needed correcting. Plaintiff claimed that while he suffered no back pain before being manipulated by defendant, he began experiencing severe low back pain as a result of that treatment. After becoming dissatisfied with defendant, plaintiff eventually sought treatment elsewhere. In his suit, plaintiff asserted in pertinent part that defendant's failure to properly diagnose and treat him aggravated a preexisting but asymptomatic condition in his back called spondylolisthesis. Plaintiff further alleged that defendant lured him into receiving chiropractic treatment by falsely representing that such treatment would cure his diabetes and that he relied upon defendant's misrepresentations to his detriment. A jury awarded plaintiff $250,000 in damages.

Defendant first claims that a new trial is necessary because the trial court allowed plaintiff's expert to criticize defendant for failing to do certain things defendant was not permitted to do by law and because of the trial court's failure to instruct the jury regarding provisions of the chiropractic act, MCL 333.16401 et seq.; MSA 14.15(16401) et seq. We agree.

The chiropractic act not only defines the practice of chiropractic but also limits the scope of such practice. It provides in pertinent part as follows:

(1) As used in this part:

* * *

(b) "Practice of chiropractic" means that discipline within the healing arts which deals with the nervous system and its relationship to the spinal column and its interrelationship with other body systems. Practice of chiropractic includes:

(i) Diagnosis, including spinal analysis, to determine the existence of spinal subluxations or misalignments that produce nerve interference, indicating the necessity for chiropractic care.

(ii) The adjustment of spinal subluxations or misalignments and related bones and tissues for the establishment of neural integrity utilizing the inherent recuperative powers of the body for restoration and maintenance of health.

(iii) The use of analytical instruments, nutritional advice, rehabilitative exercise and adjustment apparatus regulated by rules promulgated by the board pursuant to section 16423, and the use of x-ray machines in the examination of patients for the purpose of locating spinal subluxations or misaligned vertebrae of the human spine. The practice of chiropractic does not include the performance of incisive surgical procedures, the performance of an invasive procedure requiring instrumentation, or the dispensing or prescribing of drugs or medicine. [MCL 333.16401; MSA 14.15(16401).]

In the instant matter, plaintiff's expert voiced a number of criticisms of defendant's care and treatment of plaintiff. Included among these were defendant's failure to conduct a thorough physical examination of plaintiff to ascertain his overall health and to ensure there were no conditions that would contraindicate manipulation, as well as to rule out other causes of the purported back pain, and defendant's failure to use the x-rays taken to rule out conditions that might contraindicate manipulative therapy.

While the chiropractic act does not and should not be interpreted as setting forth a standard of care, it does set the parameters of the practice of chiropractic. Nowhere in the act is there language suggesting that chiropractors are licensed to conduct general physical examinations or laboratory tests or to diagnose, by x-ray or otherwise, anything other than spinal subluxations or misalignments. Both this Court and the Michigan Supreme Court have specifically so ruled. See Attorney General v. Beno, 124 Mich App 342; 335 NW2d 31 (1983), modified 422 Mich 293; 373 NW2d 544 (1985). The fact that the Court of Appeals decision in Beno may not have been binding precedent at the time defendant treated plaintiff, People v. Phillips, 416 Mich 63, 74–75; 330 NW2d 366 (1982), did not render the chiropractic act ineffective. A statute does not lie dormant until judicially interpreted. Defendant was bound by the statute at the time plaintiff was treated and cannot be held accountable for failing to do that which the act prohibited.

We further find that the trial court abused its discretion in declining to read the statute to the jury as part of the jury charge. When a party requests an instruction that is not covered by the standard jury instructions, the trial court may, at its discretion, give additional, concise, understandable, conversational, and nonargumentative instructions, provided they are applicable and accurately state the law. MCR 2.516(D)(4); Houston v. Grand Trunk W R Co., 159 Mich. App. 602, 608–609; 407 N.W.2d 52 (1987). The giving of supplemental instructions is to be determined by the trial court "not in the abstract or theoretical sense, but in the context of the 'personality' of the particular case on trial, and with due regard for the adversaries' theories of the case and of counsel's legitimate desire to structure jury argument around anticipated jury instruction." Jones v. Poretta, 428 Mich. 132, 146; 405 N.W.2d 863 (1987), quoting Johnson v. Corbet, 423 Mich. 304, 327; 377 N.W.2d 713 (1985).

Here, while defendant was permitted to utilize the chiropractic act's provisions in cross-examining plaintiff's expert, the act was not admitted into evidence. More importantly, the jury was never formally advised that the scope of defendant's practice was limited by law. Consequently, it was free to find defendant negligent for failing to do that which was not permitted by law. For this reason, the instruction setting forth the professional standard of care, while properly given, was not sufficient by itself to inform the jury of the law which limits the practice of chiropractic. Although a general verdict form was used in this case and we cannot determine the basis for the jury's verdict, we find the result might well have been different without the instructional error and, therefore, reverse. Body Rustproofing, Inc v. Michigan Bell Telephone Co, 149 Mich.App. 385, 392; 385 N.W.2d 797 (1986). On remand, the jury should be instructed regarding the scope of chiropractic as delimited by statute.

* * *

Reversed and remanded for a new trial.

* * *

II. Breach

Following the identification of the appropriate standard of care, the question becomes whether the defendant practitioner breached that standard. In the CAM context, plaintiffs have alleged a number of different types of breach, including negligent persuasion of the patient to forego conventional care in favor of an alternative therapy, negligent failure to refer the patient to a conventional physician, negligent failure to recognize that the patient's condition would not be amenable to an alternative therapy, negligent performance of a CAM procedure, and negligent failure to diagnose or misdiagnosis, just to name a few. Several case law examples are set forth below.

A. Foregoing Conventional Care

In *Charell v. Gonzalez*, reprinted in part below, a patient who had been diagnosed with uterine cancer sued her conventionally trained physician after he allegedly recommended that she undergo a nutritional protocol in lieu of conventional radiation and chemotherapy. On a motion to set aside the jury verdict, the Supreme Court of New York, New York

County, was asked to decide whether the defendant had deviated from "accepted medical standards" by persuading the patient to submit to his nutritional protocol. The Supreme Court of New York's opinion is set forth below, as well as the brief opinion of the Appellate Division.

Charell v. Gonzalez
Supreme Court of New York, New York County
173 Misc. 2d 227 (1997)

Edward H. Lehner, J.

Before me is a motion by defendant to set aside the jury verdict against him and a cross motion by plaintiff to vacate the jury finding that she impliedly assumed a risk of injury to herself when she agreed to undergo treatment by defendant.

In 1991, after being diagnosed with uterine cancer, plaintiff underwent a hysterectomy at Mt. Sinai Hospital, subsequent to which the physicians at that hospital recommended a course of radiation and chemotherapy. That protocol, considering plaintiff's condition, was variously described as "investigative" or "experimental", and was apparently recommended due to the fact that plaintiff had a high chance of recurrence because her cancer cells were found to be poorly differentiated.

Plaintiff then, in seeking a "second opinion", arranged an appointment with defendant in October 1991. She testified that he dissuaded her from having chemotherapy or radiation, and recommended treatment through his protocol of a special diet, including six coffee enemas a day. A tape of the conversation between the parties shows that he advised her not to "mess" with chemotherapy and stated that he had experienced a 75% success rate with persons in her condition. He also informed her that, through a hair test he had devised, he had determined that cancer cells remained in her body, which condition was undetected by the Mt. Sinai physicians. Plaintiff, who knew of defendant through attendance at one of his lectures and listening to his tapes, and who had witnessed the severe discomfort experienced by a relative who had undertaken chemotherapy and radiation, agreed to be treated by defendant and until June 1992 religiously followed his protocol. Plaintiff was encouraged to continue the treatment when defendant advised her that subsequent hair tests showed a reduction in the number of cancer cells in her body. She testified that she was never told by defendant that he was not an oncologist, nor that his protocol was experimental and not generally accepted in the medical community.

In June 1992, after experiencing back discomfort and failing vision, she discontinued treatment with defendant and returned to Mt. Sinai Hospital where it was determined that cancer cells had metastasized in her spine, which condition eventually caused her blindness and severe back problems.

In this action plaintiff asserted damage claims against defendant (i) in negligence for persuading her to forego traditional treatment and undertaking a nutritional protocol which she contends, by itself, was of no therapeutic value, and (ii) for lack of obtaining an informed consent to the treatment. In addition, she sought punitive damages.

At trial the jury unanimously determined: that the treatment provided by defendant was a departure from good and accepted medical practice, which departure was a proximate cause of injuries to plaintiff; that defendant did not provide plaintiff with appropriate information with respect to the risks of his treatment and the alternatives thereto, and that a reasonably prudent person in plaintiff's position would not have agreed to have the treatment if provided the appropriate information; that by accepting treatment by defendant, plaintiff did not expressly assume risk of injury to herself, but did impliedly assume such risk; that defendant was 51% responsible for plaintiff's injuries, while plaintiff was 49% responsible; that plaintiff was entitled to damages for pain and suffering sustained prior to verdict of $2,500,000 and $2,000,000 for future suffering, as well $125,000 for past loss of earnings and $75,000 for future loss of earnings; and finally that plaintiff was entitled to punitive damages. At the separate punitive damages aspect of the trial, the jury awarded plaintiff an additional $150,000.

Defendant argues that if the verdict is sustained he will not be able to practice and this will send a chill to all alternative medicine practitioners. He notes that in 1994 the State Legislature recognized the work of nonconventional physicians when in chapter 558 of the Laws of 1994 it amended Education Law 6527 by adding paragraph (e) to subdivision (4) to specifically provide that the law does not prevent a "physician's use of whatever medical care, conventional or non-conventional, which effectively treats human disease, pain, injury, deformity or physical condition", and that subdivision (1) of section 230 of the Public Health Law was amended to provide that no less than 2 of the 18 members of the Board for Professional Medical Conduct "shall be physicians who dedicate a significant portion of their practice to the use of non-conventional medical treatments".

During the course of the trial, a telecast of a two-hour lecture by one of the more famous practitioners of alternative medicine, Dr. Andrew Weil, was broadcast on public television, during which he indicated that the use of chemotherapy and radiation for the treatment of cancer will be a thing of the past. At the request of plaintiff's counsel, the court inquired whether any of the jurors had seen the telecast and, when it was indicated that none had seen the program, instructed them not to view its rebroadcast. In his 1995 "number one" bestseller, Spontaneous Healing, Dr. Weil wrote (at 268–276):

> "Current therapies for cancer, both conventional and alternative, are far from satisfactory. Conventional medicine has three main treatments: surgery, radiation, and chemotherapy, of which only the first makes sense...

> "Radiation and chemotherapy are crude treatments that will be obsolete before long... If you have cancer and are faced with a decision about whether to use conventional therapies, the question you must try to answer is this: Will the damage done to the cancer justify the damage done to the immune system?...

> "Cancer treatments abound in the world of alternative medicine, most of them much less toxic than radiation and chemotherapy, but none of them works reliably for large numbers of patients. Many of the therapies I have looked into appear to have induced remissions in some people; in many more they improve quality of life for a time, yet the cancers remain and continue to grow...

> "New and better cancer treatment is on the horizon in the form of immunotherapy, methods that will take advantage of natural healing mechanisms to recognize and destroy malignant cells without harming normal ones. In the meantime, a concerted effort to discover and study cases of spontaneous remission may help us understand that phenomenon and increase its incidence. To make wise decisions regarding the use of existing therapies for cancer, you must have reliable information about their benefits and risks."

In the May 12, 1997 issue of Time Magazine, which had a photograph of Dr. Weil on the cover with the subtitle: "Is it sound advice or snake oil?", a former editor of the New England Journal of Medicine is quoted as saying of Dr. Weil (at 75): "I resent well-educated people exploiting irrational elements in our culture, and that's what he's doing." The reporters in the article conclude (at 75): "The debate between alternative and mainstream medicine will not get settled anytime soon ... [What is not] clear—at least for now—is whether Weil and other alternative healers are selling real cures or ... just casting good spells."

While there may be a public debate as to the merits of certain practices of nonconventional physicians, there was no similar debate with respect to the evidence at this trial. The standard for proving negligence in a malpractice case is whether the treatment deviates from accepted medical standards (Jackson v. Presbyterian Hosp., 227 A.D.2d 236 [1st Dept. 1996]). There was no testimony on behalf of defendant on this issue. Moreover, it would seem that no practitioner of alternative medicine could prevail on such a question as the reference to the term "non-conventional" may well necessitate a finding that the doctor who practices such medicine deviates from "accepted" medical standards. This indeed creates a problem for such physicians which perhaps can only be solved by having the patient execute a comprehensive consent containing appropriate information as to the risks involved. In this connection, in Schneider v. Revici (817 F.2d 987 [2d Cir. 1987]), where although the court stated that "an informed decision to avoid surgery and conventional chemotherapy is within the patient's right", and there is "no reason why a patient should not be allowed to make an informed decision to go outside currently approved medical methods in search for an unconventional treatment", it declined to enforce the covenant not to sue executed by the patient, but said it was appropriate for the jury to determine whether the language of the form she signed and "testimony relating to specific consent informed by her awareness of the risk of refusing conventional treatment" amounted to an express assumption of risk that would totally bar recovery (at 995–996). In Boyle v. Revici (961 F.2d 1060 [2d Cir. 1992] [a case involving the same nonconventional physician as in Schneider, supra]), the court ruled that even without a written consent the jury should, based on the evidence, have been permitted to determine whether plaintiff "knowingly accepted all of the risks of a defendant's negligence" (at 1063), and thus expressly assumed the risk of injury to herself.

On the issue of proximate cause, while there was conflicting evidence, the jury was entitled to find, in accordance with the testimony of plaintiff's expert (Dr. Holland), that if plaintiff were not improperly dissuaded from undertaking conventional treatment the cancer probably would not have metastasized and she would not have had the recurrence and the resulting blindness and back problems. Plaintiff's experts also testified that the hair test employed by defendant to ascertain the presence of cancer was completely bogus, the treatment provided by him was of no value, and (in addition to being damaging in the sense that plaintiff was persuaded not to undergo conventional treatment) was harmful in that the nutrition provided aided the growth of the cancer cells.

Thus, the jury's findings on the questions of negligence and proximate cause cannot be said to be against the weight of the evidence or lacking a rational basis. The same can be said about its findings on the cause of action for lack of informed consent as there clearly was evidence to support the conclusion that defendant did not provide "appropriate information" with respect to the risks of, and the alternatives to, employing his protocol alone and not combining it with conventional treatment.

* * *

In the case at bar, plaintiff offered evidence to show that defendant's practice of prescribing nutrition as a cure was designed to enable companies in which he had a financial interest to sell product. While there was evidence offered by the defendant to the contrary, the jury was entitled to find that defendant's intent in dealing with plaintiff was motivated by greed and that he was reckless in his care of her. It should be noted that although, as aforesaid, there is pending controversy between the medical establishment and nonconventional practitioners, defendant failed to produce a single witness at trial who defended his treatment of plaintiff as medically sound, whereas plaintiff's experts clearly painted him as a charlatan. With only such evidence before it, I cannot say that the jury award on punitive damages was unsupported by the weight of the evidence. That the jury found that plaintiff had knowledge of the risks involved and thus impliedly assumed a risk of injury should not bar the jury from also awarding punitive damages based on conduct by a physician which it deemed reckless and improperly motivated.

In summary, both motions to set aside the verdict are denied and a judgment shall be entered in accordance with the jury verdict.

* * *

Charell v. Gonzalez
Supreme Court of New York, Appellate Division, First Department
251 A.D.2d 72 (1998)

OPINION

Judgment, Supreme Court, New York County (Edward Lehner, J.), entered August 7, 1997, upon a jury verdict apportioning liability for plaintiff's injuries 51% against defendant and 49% against plaintiff and awarding plaintiff damages in the amount of $2,500,000 for past pain and suffering, $2,000,000 for future pain and suffering, $125,000 for past loss of earnings, $75,000 for future loss of earnings, and punitive damages of $150,000, such awards being reduced pursuant to CPLR article 14-A and structured pursuant to CPLR article 50-A, and bringing up for review an order of the same court and Justice, entered on or about June 10, 1997, which denied defendant's motion to set aside the verdict and plaintiff's cross motion to set aside that portion of the verdict as found that she assumed a risk of injury to herself, and an order of the same court (Karla Moskowitz, J.), entered on or about October 17, 1996, which denied defendant's motion for summary judgment, unanimously modified, on the law and the facts, to vacate that portion of the judgment awarding plaintiff punitive damages, and otherwise affirmed, without costs.

In this action for medical malpractice and lack of informed consent in connection with plaintiff's decision to forgo conventional chemotherapy/radiation treatments for her cancer and instead follow defendant's alternative nutritional regimen, the jury found defendant 51% liable for plaintiff's injuries and plaintiff 49% liable for her injuries, based on its conclusion that the treatment provided by defendant was a departure from good and accepted medical practice, which departure was a proximate cause of plaintiff's injuries. The jury also premised its verdict upon the finding that defendant failed to provide plaintiff with appropriate information with respect to the risks of the treatment he offered and the alternatives thereto. It further found that a reasonably prudent person in plaintiff's position would not have agreed to the course of treatment offered by defendant if appropriately advised, but that, even without the benefit of proper advice, plaintiff, at least impliedly, assumed some of the risk of injury entailed by her election to undergo defendant's alternative therapy.

According due deference to the jury's determination, which was based upon its opportunity to observe and hear the witnesses, and weighing the conflicting testimony of the parties and their respective experts, it cannot be said that the evidence so preponderated in favor of defendant that the jury could not have reached its conclusion based upon any fair interpretation of the evidence (Arpino v. Jovin C. Lombardo, P. C., 215 A.D.2d 614, 615). We conclude, then, that the verdict with respect to liability was supported by sufficient evidence and was not against the weight of the evidence (Cohen v. Hallmark Cards, 45 N.Y.2d 493, 498–499; Nicastro v. Park, 113 A.D.2d 129). In this connection, we are of the view that, based upon the evidence that plaintiff refused the treatment plan recommended to her by conventional oncological specialists and elected instead to follow defendant's alternative protocol, the jury's finding that plaintiff impliedly accepted a substantial part of the risk entailed by the alternative protocol is sustainable, notwithstanding the jury's concurrent finding that defendant did not discharge his duty to advise plaintiff respecting the risks of pursuing the alternative protocol.

We modify only to the extent of vacating the award of punitive damages. Defendant's conduct was not so wantonly dishonest (Moskowitz v. Spitz, 243 A.D.2d 357), grossly indifferent to patient care (Pascazi v. Pelton, 210 A.D.2d 910), or so malicious and/or reckless (see, Camillo v. Geer, 185 A.D.2d 192) as to warrant such an award. We have considered the parties' remaining contentions for affirmative relief and find them to be without merit.

* * *

Notes and Questions

1. *Chilling Innovation?* What do you think of the policy argument made by Dr. Gonzalez in *Charell*; that is, "if the verdict is sustained [Dr. Gonzalez] will not be able to practice and this will send a chill to all alternative medicine practitioners." *Charell*, 173 Misc. 2d at 230. Is there any merit to Dr. Gonzalez's argument? Are scientific and medical discoveries always based on conventional methods of innovation? Asked another way, what scientific and medical discoveries have been made by individuals whose hypotheses were 'outside the box'?

2. *Standard of Care.* In the first *Charell* opinion, the Supreme Court of New York stated that, "The standard for proving negligence in a malpractice case is whether the treatment deviates from accepted medical standards . . ." *Charell*, 173 Misc.2d at 232. The Court then recognized that, "it would seem that no practitioner of alternative medicine could prevail on such a question as the reference to the term 'non-conventional' may well necessitate a finding that the doctor who practices such medicine deviates from 'accepted' medical standards. This indeed creates a problem for such physicians . . ." *Id*. Note that the defendant in *Charell* was a conventionally-trained allopathic physician who just happened to use CAM therapies in his private practice. If the defendant had not been an M.D., would the standard of care have been different? Further, is the Court not correct that, almost by definition, a conventionally-trained physician who uses an alternative therapy is deviating from 'accepted medical standards'? As such, could a conventionally-trained physician who shuns a conventional therapy in favor of an alternative therapy ever prove that he did not deviate from the standard of care?

3. *Relevant Scholarship.* The plaintiff in *Charell* alleged, among other things, that Dr. Gonzalez negligently persuaded the patient to forego conventional care in favor of an alternative nutritional protocol. For a thorough discussion of this particular allegation as well as other types of breach allegations made by plaintiffs in the CAM context, *see, e.g.*, Michael Cohen & David M. Eisenberg, *Potential Physician Malpractice Liability Associated with Complementary and Integrative Medical Therapies*, 136(8) Annals of Internal Medicine 596 (Apr. 16, 2002); David M. Studdert, *Medical Malpractice Implications of*

Alternative Medicine, 280(18) JAMA 1610 (Nov. 11, 1998); *Alternative and Complementary Medicine: Liability Risks for Physician*, Norcal Mutual Insurance Company (1999), *available at* http://www.norcalmutual.com/publications/ claimsrx/feb_99.pdf.

B. Failure to Refer

A second theory of CAM malpractice relates to a CAM practitioner's failure to refer the patient to a conventional physician.

Mostrom v. Pettibon
Court of Appeals of Washington
607 P.2d 864 (1980)

Soule, J.

Gordon Mostrom appeals from the Superior Court's award of summary judgment for defendants, practitioners of chiropractic medicine, in his action against them for malpractice. The issue is whether the court properly concluded the action as joined presented no genuine issues of fact to go to a jury. We hold that the case presents material issues of fact concerning viable theories of recovery, and we reverse.

The affidavits, depositions, and pleadings establish the following facts. In April of 1971, plaintiff was injured at work when struck in the back by a push cart. He stated he felt pain in his neck, back, and hips, radiating down his right leg. He visited Dr. Buel Sever, his family physician, for treatment on May 3, 1971. He had visited Dr. Sever in 1969 and in 1970 complaining of back pain, but no X rays were taken and plaintiff had recovered with heat treatments. Dr. Sever's records showed that when plaintiff came in on May 3, 1971,

> he felt like there was pain in his abdomen going through to his back and he said his muscles hurt all around from the abdomen through to his back and that he had some vomiting and appetite was kind of failing him.

He had no other complaints. Dr. Sever suspected an ulcer and ordered X rays, an upper gastrointestinal series, which was done the next day. The X rays showed a mild deformity of the duodenal cap, and Dr. Sever, diagnosing an "ulcer brewing," treated plaintiff with antacids and dietary instructions. Plaintiff's own recollection was that he saw Dr. Sever in May for back and leg pain due to the push cart accident, and that he got a heat treatment at that time.

In any event, on May 6, 1971, plaintiff saw Dr. Brian Long, a chiropractor associated with defendant Pettibon Clinic, complaining of lower back pain and weakness and numbness in the legs. After examining plaintiff and taking X rays, Dr. Long diagnosed subluxation (dislocation) of the spine which he deemed amenable to chiropractic treatment. The symptoms included restricted lateral flexions of the neck; restricted extension and rotation of the neck; restricted lumbar flexions, front and in both lateral directions; electrical shocks in the extremities produced by full backward extension of the neck; the subluxations visible in the X rays; and "advanced pathology of a chronic nature" visible in the X ray of the cervical spine. On May 7, 1971, Dr. Long commenced chiropractic treatment by means of an "adjustment" of the neck by application of pressure. Plaintiff returned for eight more "adjustments" of the neck or back in May, nine more in June, and two in early July. On July 6, Dr. Long took an X ray and pronounced the treatments successful, stating that plaintiff was free of pain.

On July 7, 1971, plaintiff was again injured at work when struck in the head by falling doors. He returned to Dr. Long on July 10 complaining of severe headaches, back pain, and more leg weakness and numbness. Dr. Long found "left spasms of the trapezius muscle; very restricted cervical motions; dull, constant pain exaggerated on extreme neck movements." He took more X rays and diagnosed worsened subluxation of the neck vertebrae, a narrowing of the space between C-3 and C-4, and C-5 and C-6, and some large hypertrophic changes, i.e., osteophytic spurring, on C-3, C-4, C-5, and C-6. Dr. Long continued chiropractic treatment, including neck "adjustments," several times between July 10 and 23. Meanwhile, plaintiff returned to Dr. Sever on July 12, 1971, complaining of pain in the right knee and difficulty in walking. He did not complain of any other pain or report any injuries. Dr. Sever observed swelling in the knee and diagnosed rheumatoid arthritis.

On July 26, plaintiff came to Dr. Long's office on crutches, walking with difficulty and experiencing severe lower back pain. His right leg was losing strength. His neck was resubluxated, and Dr. Long adjusted it. Dr. Long also stated that he recommended that plaintiff consult a neurologist or orthopedist in case spinal cord injury was involved. Plaintiff denied that Dr. Long so recommended. Nevertheless, plaintiff went to see Dr. George Race, an internal medicine specialist, on July 16. Dr. Race learned about the accidents at work in April and on July 7 and that plaintiff had been treated by Dr. Sever and the Pettibon Clinic. Dr. Race examined plaintiff, who was walking awkwardly and staggering, and tentatively diagnosed an ulcer, arthritis of the spine, and possible spinal cord injury. He referred him to a neurologist, Dr. George Delyanis, who first saw him on August 13. Meanwhile, plaintiff continued to visit Dr. Long for treatments on July 28 and 30 and August 2, 5, and 10.

Dr. Delyanis diagnosed cervical (neck) cord compression and ordered a myelogram. The myelogram showed an obstruction of the spinal cord at the neck vertebrae C-4 and C-5. Plaintiff's condition continued to deteriorate. Dr. W. Ben Blackett performed surgery on August 19 to remove the extruded disc material that was found to be compressing the spinal cord.

Following surgery plaintiff did not recover full use of his arms and legs and was classified as totally and permanently disabled for purposes of carrying on any sort of work or productive function. He sued Dr. Long and the Pettibon Clinic for malpractice, claiming that the chiropractor should have recognized that his symptoms indicated a medical problem, that he should have been referred promptly to a medical doctor, and that the chiropractic treatment delayed medical treatment and, in fact, aggravated his condition.

In reviewing the summary judgment for defendants, we are mindful of the rule that a motion for summary judgment is to be granted when, construing the evidence in the record in favor of the nonmoving party, no genuine issue of fact exists and the moving party is entitled to judgment as a matter of law. E.g., Morris v. McNicol, 83 Wn.2d 491, 494, 519 P.2d 7 (1974); Adamski v. Tacoma Gen. Hosp., 20 Wn. App. 98, 103, 579 P.2d 970 (1978). The trial court must deny a motion for summary judgment if the record shows any reasonable hypothesis which entitles the nonmoving party to relief. Adamski v. Tacoma Gen. Hosp., supra. CR 56(e) requires that affidavits submitted in support of or opposition to a motion for summary judgment set forth facts based upon personal knowledge admissible as evidence to which the affiant is competent to testify. However, evidence may be presented in affidavits by reference to other sworn statements in the record such as depositions and other affidavits. Meadows v. Grant's Auto Brokers, Inc., 71 Wn.2d 874, 878, 431 P.2d 216 (1967); Caldwell v. Yellow Cab Serv., Inc., 2 Wn. App. 588, 592, 469 P.2d 218 (1970).

Chiropractors and other drugless healers who are licensed providers of primary patient care owe a duty to exercise reasonable care in the diagnosis and treatment of their patients and a duty to inform them when nonmedical treatment has become useless or harmful and medical treatment should be sought. Kelly v. Carroll, 36 Wn.2d 482, 492, 497, 219 P.2d 79, cert. denied, 340 U.S. 892, 95 L. Ed. 646, 71 S. Ct. 208 (1950); Annot., 58 A.L.R.3d 590, 591 (1974); Annot., 19 A.L.R.2d 1191–92 (1951). In determining whether a chiropractor breaches these duties, he is held to the standard of care of a reasonable chiropractor in the same circumstances. Carney v. Lydon, 36 Wn.2d 878, 880, 220 P.2d 894 (1950); 19 A.L.R.2d at 1192. See generally Hayes v. Hulswit, 73 Wn.2d 796, 797, 440 P.2d 849 (1968).

The trial court found that the facts supported a finding of no negligence as a matter of law inasmuch as plaintiff saw Dr. Sever once in early May and again on July 12, 1971, and it could not be said, therefore, that defendant's chiropractic treatment prevented or delayed him from receiving medical treatment.

Although the court's conclusion may be correct as far as it goes, it ignores the other possible breach of a duty imposed on chiropractors, i.e., the duty to use reasonable care in the course of treatment. This duty has three related aspects pertinent to this case: (1) to diagnose a medical problem as contrasted with a chiropractic problem; (2) to refrain from further chiropractic treatment when a reasonable chiropractor should be aware that the patient's condition is not amenable to chiropractic treatment and that continuation of such treatment may aggravate the condition; (3) to refer the patient to a medical doctor when a medical mode of treatment is indicated. See Carney v. Lydon, supra; Kelly v. Carroll, supra; Salazar v. Ehmann, 505 P.2d 387 (Colo. App. 1972); Annot., 58 A.L.R.3d 590 (1974). A breach of duty, if it proximately caused plaintiff's permanent injury, could result in damages from the continued administration of chiropractic treatments, aside from any delay in obtaining medical treatments.

Chiropractic treatment is defined by statute as the treatment of subluxations of the spine by adjustment or manipulation of the vertebral column. RCW 18.25.005. See also State v. Wilson, 11 Wn. App. 916, 528 P.2d 279 (1974). It is clear that a chiropractor and other similar health care practitioners who depart from statutory limitations and practice medicine are liable for negligent treatment. E.g., Kelly v. Carroll, supra at 492; Faasch v. Karney, 145 Wash. 390, 260 P. 255 (1927). See also Ritter v. Sivils, 206 Ore. 410, 293 P.2d 211 (1956). Defendants suggest that because Dr. Long was treating spinal subluxations by means of adjustments, his method of treatment fell within the statute and he cannot be liable for any aggravation of plaintiff's injuries as a matter of law. This argument, however, ignores the fact that evidence of a drugless healer's treatment within the limits of his licensing limitations can still form the basis for liability if he has breached his duty to cease treatment or refrain from treating and refer the patient to a physician. See Wilcox v. Carroll, 127 Wash. 1, 219 P. 34 (1923); Salazar v. Ehmann, supra; Deward v. Whitney, 298 Mass. 41, 9 N.E.2d 369 (1937); Tschirhart v. Pethtel, 61 Mich. App. 581, 233 N.W.2d 93 (1975); Ison v. McFall, 55 Tenn. App. 326, 400 S.W.2d 243 (1964).

It becomes necessary for us, therefore, to examine the record before the trial court and determine if the affidavits, depositions, and medical records raise genuine issues of material fact whether the chiropractic treatments beginning on July 10 aggravated plaintiff's condition; whether Dr. Long should have realized they could aggravate that condition; and whether he should have declined to administer further treatments and directed plaintiff to see a physician. As noted, the requirements under CR 56(e) for supporting and opposing affidavits with reference to a motion for summary judgment are that they shall set forth such facts as would be admissible in evidence, and shall show affirmatively that the affiant is competent to testify to the matters stated therein. Sworn or certified copies of all papers or parts thereof referred to in an affidavit shall be attached thereto or served therewith. The court may permit affidavits to be supplemented or opposed by depositions, answers to interrogatories, or further affidavits. When a motion for summary judgment is made and supported as provided in this rule, an adverse party may not rest upon the mere allegations or denials of his pleading, but his response, by affidavits or as otherwise provided in this rule, must set forth specific facts showing that there is a genuine issue for trial. If he does not so respond, summary judgment, if appropriate, shall be entered against him. See also Peterick v. State, 22 Wn. App. 163, 180–81, 589 P.2d 250 (1977).

The motion for summary judgment was supported primarily by the affidavit and deposition of Dr. Long, in which he described at length his diagnosis and progression of treatment for Mr. Mostrom.

In opposition to the motion for summary judgment plaintiff submitted depositions of Drs. Blackett, Race, and Sever and three affidavits by a licensed chiropractor, Dr. Peter J. Modde. Dr. Modde did not see plaintiff personally. In his first two affidavits Dr. Modde listed the standard chiropractic diagnosis procedures, stated that he had reviewed the depositions of the plaintiff, the defendants and the medical doctors who had diagnosed or treated plaintiff, and concluded that the symptoms described in the record indicated a severe cervical injury which should have received immediate medical treatment; that the chiropractor did not engage in a "proper diagnostic workup" and should have refrained from spinal manipulations. Although Dr. Modde's description of standard chiropractic procedures in his first two affidavits is in acceptable form, the general references to the depositions and records are insufficient under CR 56(e) to refute a motion for summary judgment. They do not set forth specific facts showing a genuine issue for trial.

Dr. Modde's third affidavit stands on firmer ground, however. In it he quotes several excerpts from the Long affidavit regarding the symptoms Dr. Long encountered and the treatment he followed. Dr. Modde specifically indicates that the three X rays taken on July 10, 1971 were too limited, the narrowing of the cervical interspaces and the hypertrophic changes on the vertebrae indicated a "predisposition or weakness to further insult or injury," and that these facts before Dr. Long warranted a different diagnostic workup and a referral for neurological examination. This affidavit contains specific facts pertaining to the alleged breach of Dr. Long's duty to use proper diagnostic procedures in concluding whether the problem was chiropractic and not medical in nature, and if it was medical, to refrain from chiropractic treatment and refer the patient to a medical doctor. In addition, an affidavit may refer to another person's deposition and qualify as testimonial knowledge, as long as the affiant could testify in court about the content of the deposition. Meadows v. Grant's Auto Brokers, Inc., supra. Here, Dr. Modde could give expert testimony regarding the standard of care, i.e., proper diagnostic procedures for a chiropractor to follow, given plaintiff's symptoms, and what course of action was dictated by prevailing standards of professional care.

The deposition of W. Ben Blackett, M.D., is also important in deciding whether the trial court erred in granting a summary judgment to the defense. Dr. Delyanis, a neurologist in practice with Dr. Blackett, first referred Mr. Mostrom to him on August 18, 1971, due to the rapidly progressing weakness in plaintiff's arms and legs. Dr. Blackett examined plaintiff in the hospital, viewed the myelogram showing an obstruction in the spinal canal at the C-4 and C-5 level, and confirmed the findings and diagnosis of Dr. Delyanis.

Dr. Blackett was asked for his medical opinion, and concluded that Mr. Mostrom's disability was caused by a compression of his cervical cord by a central herniated disc—the material he surgically removed on August 19, 1979—and that the herniation probably began with the industrial accident on July 7 and was aggravated by the subsequent chiropractic manipulations. The defense contends Dr. Blackett's opinions should not be considered in connection with the motion for summary judgment because they are based, at least in part, on alleged hearsay—a medical history given by Mr. Mostrom and his wife to Dr. Delyanis and made known to Dr. Blackett prior to surgery only through a written summary prepared by Dr. Delyanis; because the opinions were also based on speculation as to what form of treatment Dr. Long had applied to Mr. Mostrom; and because the opinions do not reach the level of testimonial knowledge.

The record shows that Mr. Mostrom told Dr. Blackett he had undergone "neck snapping" by a chiropractor, which Dr. Blackett understood to mean manipulations of the neck. In his deposition Mr. Mostrom described a technique whereby the chiropractor "trips the hammer" on his neck. Moreover, at trial Dr. Delyanis obviously could be called to sponsor the admission into evidence of his written case history and findings on which Dr. Blackett relied to supplement his own examination prior to surgery. Dr. Blackett could then be asked if that were in fact the report he had reviewed. At that point in the trial, the foundation would be laid for Dr. Blackett to state his opinion on the original cause of the disc injury and its aggravation by chiropractic adjustments, based on the case history contained in the Delyanis report; the progressive symptoms stated therein and confirmed by his own examination; his own review of the myelogram; and the herniated disc he encountered in surgery. Dr. Blackett's statement of opinion would be probative of one of plaintiff's theories of liability, namely, that the chiropractor's treatments in July and early August were responsible for an advanced state of disability that surgery was not able to rectify at that late date.

The purpose of summary judgment is to avoid useless trials on formal issues which cannot be supported factually or, if factually supported, could not as a matter of law lead to a result favorable to the nonmoving party. Peterick v. State, supra at 179. This is not such a case. This is a case in which the proposed testimony for the plaintiff, as set forth in the affidavits and depositions of Drs. Modde, Blackett, plaintiff himself, and the other physicians involved, when construed against defendants' motion for summary judgment, do present issues of fact on material issues of defendants' duty, the applicable standard of care, and proximate cause of the injury. It is true the chiropractic treatments did not prevent plaintiff from visiting a physician while he was having them; but other theories of liability derived from the complaint include the allegation that Dr. Long misrepresented the back pain as a chiropractic and not a medical problem, which may have led plaintiff into thinking he had no reason to mention it to Dr. Sever on July 12; that Dr. Long should have recognized the problem as medical in nature, ceased his own treatments, and promptly referred plaintiff to a medical specialist; and that the continued chiropractic treatments in July and August aggravated plaintiff's injury. With the factual issues in the record concerning these theories of liability, a judgment precluding their presentation to a jury was inappropriate.

The judgment is reversed.

* * *

Mostrom v. Pettibon is not the only CAM malpractice case based on a negligent failure-to-refer theory. The short opinion in *Salazar v. Ehmann*, reprinted in part below, provides a second straightforward example of a failure-to-refer (as well as a failure-to-X-ray) claim.

Salazar v. Ehmann
Court of Appeals of Colorado
505 P.2d 387 (1972)

Smith, J.

Defendant, a chiropractor, appeals from the judgment entered upon a $35,000 verdict against him in a malpractice action. We affirm. Plaintiff alleged he had a fractured bone as well as a dislocated shoulder when he went to defendant for treatment. Defendant was charged with negligence in failing to take x-rays to perceive the condition and in failing to refer plaintiff to a medical doctor.

* * *

III.

Several of defendant's allegations of error concern instructions given by the trial court to the jury. We have examined all the instructions and have made a careful review of the record. We find the evidence in the record justifying the giving of the questions instructions and conclude that they are correct statements of the law.

The theory upon which the case was tried by both parties was one of failure to conform to the standards of chiropractic practice in the community, specifically, failure to take x-rays and failure to refer plaintiff to a medical doctor. Defendant's tendered instruction, which advised the jury that plaintiff could not recover solely because the treatment did not achieve the desired result, was not applicable to a material question of fact in controversy, and the refusal of such instruction was within the discretion of the court. See Marsh v. Cramer, 16 Colo. 331, 27 P. 169. We find no abuse of the trial court's discretion.

IV.

Defendant contends the court erred in not directing a verdict in his favor, because of the lack of evidence presented to establish defendant's failure to meet the standard of care required by law. This contention is without merit. Plaintiff called as a witness a licensed local chiropractor, who testified that in the locality in which the witness and defendant practiced, it was customary, in cases such as plaintiff's, to take x-rays, and, where a fracture was present, to refer the case to a medical doctor. Plaintiff also introduced a portion of the oath administered to chiropractors by the state licensing board requiring referral to medical doctors where the patient's problem extends beyond the limits of chiropractic practice. Defendant argues that the admission of this material was error because it was irrelevant and immaterial. This assertion is plainly without merit for, as defendant argues above, plaintiff's case depends on proof of violation of a standard of conduct, and the chiropractic oath must be considered as evidence having probative value upon the issue of that standard of conduct agreed to by all chiropractors in Colorado. See Rude v. MacCormac, 72 Colo. 221, 210 P. 844.

V.

Defendant asserts that the trial court erred in precluding that portion of defendant's cross-examination of a medical witness that would have shown that the witness referred plaintiff to an attorney upon finding that plaintiff had no resources with which to pay his medical expenses. The decision to exclude this purported "impeachment" testimony was within the discretion of the trial court, and there is no showing of an abuse of that discretion. Layton v. Purcell, 267 P.2d 547 (Okl.). See Mendoza v. Gomes, 143 Cal.App. 2d 172, 299 P.2d 707.

Finding defendant's assertions of error without merit, we affirm.

* * *

C. Not Amenable to CAM Care

A third common CAM malpractice allegation, similar to the failure-to-refer allegation, is that the defendant practitioner negligently failed to recognize that the patient's condition was not amenable to CAM care. In *Tschirhart v. Pethel*, reprinted in part below, the Court of Appeals of Michigan was asked to decide whether sufficient evidence was presented at trial regarding the defendant's negligence in failing to inform the plaintiff that his condition was not amenable to chiropractic treatment.

Tschirhart v. Pethtel
Court of Appeals of Michigan
233 N.W.2d 93 (1975)

Brennan, J.

In January of 1970, plaintiff, Leo Tschirhart, was experiencing some pain in his back so he sought the assistance of his family physician, Dr. Harold Podolsky. After several visits Dr. Podolsky informed plaintiff that he believed him to be suffering from arthritis and that a conservative plan of treatment was going to be followed. Pain medication and muscle relaxants were prescribed but plaintiff apparently obtained no relief. Plaintiff thereupon contacted defendant, a licensed chiropractor, to see if he could be of any help. Plaintiff had earlier received a brochure through the mail from defendant outlining the advantages of the chiropractic method of treatment and containing testimonials from certain of his prior patients, some of whom claimed to have had disc problems and arthritis satisfactorily treated by defendant. Plaintiff first saw defendant on March 6, 1970 and thereafter on a regular basis until May 29, 1970. Initially, defendant's treatment of plaintiff proceeded satisfactorily. Plaintiff testified that after three weeks of treatment he began to respond, with the pain he had been experiencing in his right arm, shoulder and shoulder blade diminishing. In early May, while still receiving treatment, plaintiff began to paint the breezeway on his house. At about this same time plaintiff began experiencing an increase in the amount of pain he was suffering. On May 29, 1970, plaintiff visited defendant complaining about the increased pain and stating that the pain was now in his left arm also. Although the precise manner in which defendant proceeded to handle plaintiff on this occasion is in dispute, it nevertheless appears that while plaintiff was on the table he experienced a "flash of light in his brain", a shock throughout his body and numbness all over. Plaintiff was thereupon taken to the hospital and subsequently underwent two surgical operations for a herniated disc.

On December 23, 1970, plaintiff instituted this action against defendant alleging malpractice, breach of contract, and fraud. Plaintiff's wife, Ruth Tschirhart, also brought an action against defendant for loss of consortium. Plaintiff subsequently filed two amended complaints refining the allegations contained in his first complaint. On the day trial began the trial judge dismissed the count alleging fraud and trial proceeded on the other two counts. Plaintiff presented no expert witnesses of his own, relying, instead, on the testimony of defendant to establish the requisite standard of care and a breach thereof. At the conclusion of all the proofs, the trial judge granted defendant's motion for a directed verdict. It is from this decision that plaintiff now appeals.

Plaintiff first contends that the trial court erred in granting defendant's motion for a directed verdict as to the count of malpractice. In reviewing such a claim this Court is required to view the facts, and all legitimate inferences therefrom, in the light most favorable to plaintiff. Heins v. Synkonis, 58 Mich App 119; 227 NW2d 247 (1975), Daniel v. McNamara, 10 Mich App 299; 159 NW2d 339 (1968).

On this appeal plaintiff claims that sufficient evidence of malpractice was presented to permit this issue to go to the jury. Plaintiff claims that the evidence presented at trial establishes the breach of four separate duties: (1) to determine whether plaintiff's condition was one he could treat; (2) to follow the appropriate chiropractic standards of care in treating plaintiff; (3) to warn plaintiff not to engage in certain activity; and (4) to warn plaintiff of the risks of treatment.

After reviewing the evidence presented in this case in the light most favorable to plaintiff, we find that sufficient evidence of malpractice was presented on the issue of whether defendant was negligent in failing to inform plaintiff that his condition was one which was not amenable to chiropractic treatment. With respect to the other alleged acts of malpractice, however, we find, as did the trial judge, that the evidence presented at trial was insufficient to allow the case to go to the jury.

When defendant first saw plaintiff he made several observations about plaintiff's condition, one of which was that there was the possibility of a herniated disc. At trial defendant testified that he performed a compression test to determine whether plaintiff did, in fact, have a herniated disc and that the results of this test were negative. Defendant further testified that he informed plaintiff that he did not have a herniated disc and also testified that he did not undertake to treat herniated discs. In his deposition, however, defendant stated that on several occasions, near the beginning of the adjustments, he suggested to plaintiff that he seek the assistance of a physician because he might have a herniated disc and that his initial tests showed weak disc material or a possible herniation. Plaintiff, on the other hand, testified that defendant never informed him that he should seek the advice of a physician with respect to the possibility of a herniated disc. While the facts in this regard are clearly in dispute, viewing them in the light most favorable to plaintiff, the jury could properly have found that defendant was aware of the fact that plaintiff had a possible herniated disc, a malady defendant stated he did not treat, and that he failed to inform plaintiff of this fact and refer him to a physician. Defendant's negligence in this respect, if proven to the satisfaction of the jury, would sustain plaintiff's charge of malpractice and entitle him to recover damages for any injuries which were proximately caused by such malpractice. Janssen v. Mulder, 232 Mich 183; 205 NW 159 (1925).

* * *

Affirmed in part; reversed in part. Remanded for a new trial.

* * *

D. Negligent Performance of a CAM Procedure

Perhaps the largest class of CAM malpractice cases involve allegations that a CAM practitioner negligently administered or performed a CAM therapy or procedure. In *Hinthorn v. Garrison*, for example, the Supreme Court of Kansas reviewed in 1921 the patient's allegation that the defendant chiropractor treated the patient "in a negligent and careless manner" when the chiropractor used excessive force with his thumb to adjust the patient's spine.

Hinthorn v. Garrison
Supreme Court of Kansas
108 Kan. 510 (1921)

West, J.

The plaintiff sued for damages alleged to have been caused by the defendant in giving a chiropractic treatment. The court sustained a demurrer to the plaintiff's evidence, from which ruling this appeal is taken. The petition alleged that on the 16th of May, 1917, the plaintiff as a patient was treated by the defendant in a careless and negligent manner by thrusting his thumb between the shoulder blades with such force and violence as to dislocate the plaintiff's ribs from the "spinal process," injuring the plaintiff and causing double curvature of the spine; that he failed to treat properly such injuries, by reason of which the plaintiff has double curvature of the spine and two ribs loosened from the "spinal process"; and that the injury will be permanent.

The answer so far as the alleged injury is concerned was a general denial.

The defendant's books show a charge for treatments from May 16 to 18, 1917, inclusive.

The plaintiff testified that he had been in the furniture business for something like twenty-five years. He suffered from grippe, and took treatments from the defendant. Prior to the 16th day of May, 1917, he never had any nervous trouble and never suffered with any back or spine trouble and the part of his back and spine about his shoulders had never been sore. He did not strike or injure himself in any way on that day. When he got out of the defendant's office on May 16 he was suffering intensely. His back and spine after that time continued sore and sensitive and as a result of the condition he had to guard against anything like heavy lifting or any pressure on the spine. In the way of trying to seek rest he had to steer clear of any pressure of any kind around the spine. To lie in comfort he had to be bolstered up at an angle of forty-five degrees, most of his sleep being obtained in a rocking chair. Before that time he had no difficulty in sleeping and since that date he has been unable to sleep except part of the night.

Doctor Williamson testified that he examined the plaintiff and in his opinion the condition was caused by some injury to his spine. Doctor Montgomery, a chiropractor, testified that when he examined the plaintiff he found him suffering with intense pain in his back about the region of his shoulder blades, and with insomnia. He found a contracted condition of all the muscles in that region and an impingement of the nerves about the sixth dorsal vertebra. He had an X-ray picture taken and from his examination of the picture he thought the trouble was double scoliosis. He testified that the mechanical method of chiropractic is the adjusting of the spinal column to its normal position with the hand:

> "The hand is used in various ways, we have the hold that is called the thumb hold. The bilateral hold is given by that way, the crossed-thumb hold is given that way, the hand movement is given that way ... We brace the thumb in that situation, cross thumbs your hands crossed and use flat-hand movement or pressure. The kind and amount of pressure is regulated by the skill of the physician knowing what he is about to do. That is the scientific part of it."

Doctor Hay testified among other things that from the X-ray picture he found the plaintiff's spine in an abnormal position, showing a slight double curvature.

> "The curvature was probably caused by force, it is either by some force or disease of the vertebrae; it may be caused by disease but it doesn't show any disease of the vertebrae."

The plaintiff insists that it was error to sustain a demurrer to his testimony, and that is the only point before us. The rule is thoroughly established in this state that before a demurrer can be sustained the evidence and all fair inferences to be drawn therefrom must fail to show or tend to show the plaintiff's right to recover. Any substantial evidence must be submitted to the jury for their consideration. (Mentze v. Rice, 102 Kan. 855, 172 P. 516; Dudas v. Railway Co., 105 Kan. 451, 185 P. 28; Reddy v. Graham, 106 Kan. 339, 187 P. 653.)

It is argued by counsel in his brief that the evidence fails to show that the plaintiff was treated on the 16th of May, but we think the testimony quite convincing that he was. Also, it is contended that the plaintiff must show that the muscles of his arm and shoulder were permanently impaired and he was rendered unable to sleep by the alleged treatment by the defendant. While he alleged permanent injury, proof of temporary injury would be sufficient for a recovery.

It is argued that plaintiff must prove that the defendant did not exercise ordinary skill as a chiropractor. This is correct, but the quoted part of the evidence taken by itself without any explanation tends to show that a chiropractor who treated a man entirely free from any trouble with his spine who thereafter suffered as the testimony shows the plaintiff did must have been unskillful or careless.

The judgment is reversed, and the cause is remanded with directions to overrule the demurrer to the plaintiff's evidence and for further proceedings in accordance herewith.

* * *

E. Failure to Diagnose; Incorrect Diagnosis

A final illustrative example of a CAM malpractice allegation involves the negligent failure to diagnose a patient or the incorrect diagnosis of a patient. In *Wilcox v. Carroll*, reprinted in part below, the defendant was a 'sanipractor physician' who was licensed in the State of Washington to use hydrotherapy, dietetics, electrotherapy, and psychotherapy but prohibited from using drugs or performing surgery. The plaintiff was the mother of an eight-year-old boy whom the plaintiff suspected had appendicitis. Although the plaintiff repeatedly expressed her concern to the defendant that her son had appendicitis, the defendant refused to make the diagnosis, relying on his belief that the appendix does not form as an organ until ten years of age. After the boy was transferred to the care of an allopathic physician, the allopathic physician diagnosed him with acute appendicitis and attempted an appendectomy, although 'at least a pint of pus shot up out of the abdominal cavity' upon surgical opening. The child died the morning after surgery and the plaintiff thereafter sued the sanipractor physician, alleging negligent diagnosis. The Supreme Court of Washington's decision follows.

Wilcox v. Carroll
Supreme Court of Washington
127 Wash. 1 (1923)

Holcomb, J.

In this action for damages against appellant on account of the death of a minor son of respondent, the amended complaint alleged that death was caused by the negligence of appellant, a drugless physician, in failing to properly diagnose the disease from which the child was suffering, and in failing to give the child proper treatment. A trial to the court and a jury resulted in a verdict and judgment in the sum of $2,500. A motion for a directed verdict had been timely made and denied, and motions were unsuccessfully made for judgment non obstante veredicto, and for a new trial.

Appealing, appellant strenuously contends that the trial court admitted such evidence and so submitted the case to the jury upon instructions that the jury were allowed to judge of appellant's capacity or incapacity to diagnose the case, and his negligence in treating the case, upon the testimony of physicians of other schools. Nine errors are relied upon for a reversal upon his theory of the case.

Appellant is what is called a sanipractor physician, not licensed as a full sanipractor, but licensed to use the methods of treating disease known as hydrotherapy, diatetics, electrotherapy, and psychotherapy. Such practitioners are not permitted to use drugs such as physicians of the regular schools use, nor to perform operations.

The case made by respondent to go to the jury was substantially as follows:

The eight-year-old son of respondent was taken ill on Wednesday, December 28, 1921, complaining of stomach ache. He was confined to his bed on the next day and on the 30th. On that day, he displayed such symptoms of appendicitis as to make the mother fearful that he was suffering from that disease, and that he should be put in the care of a physician. Accordingly, on the 30th, having faith in appellant as a drugless physician, she telephoned him, described the symptoms to him, and expressed the fear that the child had appendicitis. Appellant told her that the child could not possibly have appendicitis because the appendix did not form until a child was at least ten years of age. On that day she took the child to appellant's office, again explained the symptoms to him, with the statement that, if the child had appendicitis, she wanted an operation if appellant thought one necessary. She was again assured by appellant that the disease could not be appendicitis. She was also told by appellant that the child was suffering from either spinal meningitis or from infantile paralysis; and that, if a regular physician had been called on the case he would inject a serum into the spine of the child which would make him a cripple for life. He asked respondent if she desired him to give the child treatment, and because, as she said, she thought appellant could do as well as anyone if the child did not have appendicitis, she employed him to treat the child.

The next day, Saturday, appellant gave the child another treatment at his office, but did not express an opinion as to what disease the child was suffering from. On Sunday he again treated the child at his office, and then diagnosed the child's trouble as being inflammation of the spine and congestion of the bowels, and continued the same treatment he had been giving theretofore. He gave the child daily treatment until Friday, January 6, 1922. The treatments in general consisted of electric massage of the spine, alternate applications of hot and cold compresses to the abdomen and back, sitz baths and internal baths. The child was brought to appellant's office by automobile for each treatment.

From the first day appellant treated the child—that is, on Friday the 30th, until the following Wednesday—by direction of appellant, respondent gave the child no food. On the following Wednesday, she told appellant that the child asked for food and, she testified, appellant told her to give the child a little beef broth and a little diluted grape juice, which she said she gave according to directions that night and the next day.

It seems that the child grew worse, or at least grew no better under the treatment; and on Friday, January 6, respondent became so alarmed at the child's condition that she called appellant to her home. He went about 2:30 p.m., and gave the child a treatment there consisting of wrapping him in a wet sheet. After remaining a short time, he left, leaving instructions for the mother to call him at 5:30 p.m. The child's temperature dropped until it had become below normal—in fact about 94 degrees—when respondent became so alarmed that she telephoned appellant before the prescribed time, telling him of the temperature. Appellant then told her that there was something about the condition of the child that he did not understand; for her to take the child out of the wet sheet and call a regular physician, but not to let the physician know that appellant had been treating the child.

Respondent thereupon called Dr. R. E. Ahlquist, a regular physician and surgeon, who diagnosed the disease as acute appendicitis where the appendix had already bursted and peritonitis had set in. Dr. Ahlquist found the child in practically a dying condition when he was called in, but believed that the child would have more chances of surviving with an operation than without. He therefore operated on the child that night; and upon the abdomen being opened, at least a pint of pus shot up out of the abdominal cavity and the appendix was found to be ruptured and gangrenous. The child died the next morning.

There is a conflict in the evidence between respondent and appellant as to whether appellant requested respondent to bring the child about one mile to his office for treatment, and as to whether he informed respondent that it was dangerous and might prove fatal to bring the child from the home to his office for treatment because he was busy and could not make house visits. Respondent testified that appellant said nothing about it being dangerous to move the child, but did tell her she should bring the child to his office for treatment.

There is also a conflict in the testimony as to the responsibility for giving food to the child while it was under the treatment of appellant. Appellant testified that the food was given to the child by respondent contrary to his orders, while respondent testified as before stated.

It was admitted by experts of the same school of practice as appellant, testifying at the trial, that absolute or nearly absolute quiet is required by all schools of healing for patients suffering from appendicitis. It was also proven that food should not be given to one suffering from appendicitis. One of appellant's experts testified that all food should be taken away; that he would regard as negligence the giving of food to the child, which would probably result in death.

Appellant stated, and it is conceded, that the first proposition of law governing the case is that it is the law in this state that a physician cannot be held liable for damages for merely making a wrong diagnosis, and that there can be no liability until an improper treatment follows the wrong diagnosis. Appellant then contends that the facts in this case show, beyond dispute, that the treatment which was given by appellant was the correct treatment according to the school or class to which he belonged, whether the disease from which the child was suffering was appendicitis or was as diagnosed by the appellant.

Of course, it must be admitted that, when respondent employed appellant to doctor her child, she knew that he belonged to what is called the drugless school of healing, which would not operate. She cannot be heard to complain because an operation was not performed or advised by appellant. She cannot employ a doctor whom she knows will not operate and then recover damages because an operation was not performed.

But, as indicated by the above statement of the facts, there was more evidence of negligence to go to the jury than the matters covered by the above proposition. While it is true that there was a conflict of evidence as to which was responsible for the moving of the patient, and for the giving of food to the patient, yet there is evidence that it was appellant who was responsible, and the facts were for the jury. Since appellant's own experts stated that absolute, or nearly absolute, quiet should be prescribed for a patient suffering from appendicitis, and that the giving of food to such a patient was negligent, and probably would prove fatal, the jury believing these facts, the negligence of appellant was established.

It is true that a mere wrong diagnosis, unless followed by maltreatment, would not alone be sufficient to establish negligence as against a practitioner of medicine or healing. But when it became established that the child had been suffering for nine days from acute appendicitis, it then became established that the child suffered from a disease for which appellant gave wrongful treatment, if the evidence of respondent and her witnesses was believed, which the jury had a right to do.

The first error claimed by appellant involves this question to a certain extent—that is, that the court erred in permitting allopath doctors to testify as to their diagnosis of the disease, their operations, and various other matters in connection with their treatment of the case after they were employed, and also the methods which they would use to determine whether or not the patient did in fact have appendicitis.

According to the evidence of respondent, appellant, on January 6, surrendered or abandoned the case. Maternal affection and humanity both required that respondent employ some one else to treat the child in its then desperate condition. What they found was the result of their examination of the history of the case, and of their operation, which found a diseased appendix, and there could be no avoidance of introducing their evidence of what they found as to the condition of the child. The fact that they operated upon the child when appellant, in following the system of practice of the school of healing to which he belonged, would not operate, and what they found upon operating, cannot be held to prejudice appellant. The fact was established by the operation by the allopaths, as well as by their preliminary examination, if they were to be believed, that the child was suffering from a diseased appendix, and that it had so suffered for nine days. Appellant, who was admitted to practice under Laws of 1919, ch. 36, p. 65, §3, was required to satisfy the examiners that he was competent in the subject of symptomatology, which, of course, means about the same as diagnosis does to regular schools of medicine and healing. Undoubtedly, therefore, appellant had some skill required of him as to his ability to diagnose or determine diseases by symptoms. He and his experts contend that the treatment would have been the same whether the child was in fact suffering from spinal meningitis, infantile paralysis, or appendicitis, and that the treatment that he gave the child was the proper treatment for appendicitis, according to their system of healing; but they all admit that the symptoms of appendicitis are determined by the same methods by all schools of medicine or healing, except that the experts of the regular school testified that they usually gave blood tests for the purpose of counting the white corpuscles in the blood. If there was an excess of white corpuscles it indicated appendicitis. They made no such examination in the case of this boy, for the reason that his case was then very critical, and they knew that the case was a well developed case of appendicitis. All the other symptoms were present and it was unnecessary to make a leucocytic test. The fact that they testified that they usually did so in the earlier stages of appendicitis was of no harm to appellant. In fact, so far as the evidence shows to the contrary, those following the same system of healing as appellant may also use this same system of determining appendicitis in the early stages. Respondent did not call in expert witnesses as such to testify in the case. The physicians who testified were the physicians who examined the boy and performed the operation, and examined the appendix after the operation. All that these physicians called by appellant testified to as experts they did on cross-examination by appellant's counsel and on re-direct examination covering the matters brought out by cross-examination, by counsel for respondent.

Counsel for appellant are in error, however, when they insist that all the expert testimony as to the character of the treatment given by appellant was that it was proper treatment. Under the admissions of appellant and the testimony of his expert witnesses of the same school of medicine as himself, there is evidence of negligent diagnosis and negligent treatment on the part of appellant sufficient to take the case to the jury.

The above being true, appellant's motions for directed verdict, and for judgment non obstante veredicto were both properly denied.

What we have said above largely disposes of the contention of appellant as to the testimony of allopathic doctors who treated the boy after appellant had ceased to treat him and who performed the operation. They gave no opinion as to such, except that the operation should have been performed nine days before they received the patient. That testimony, however, was received without objection on the part of appellant, and appellant cannot now complain of it.

Questions arise over the instructions given by the court to the jury. Appellant concedes that instruction No. 8 correctly states the law, as follows:

> "You are instructed that in diagnosing the disease or ailment from which the patient was suffering, a physician is bound to use a degree of skill and learning which ordinarily characterizes the school or class of physicians to which he belongs, in the locality in which he practices, and if you find by a preponderance of the evidence that the defendant did not use that degree of skill and learning in this case, and as a result of such failure to use such degree of skill and learning wrongfully diagnosed the disease from which said child was suffering and then gave such child improper treatment for the disease from which he was suffering, then your verdict should be for the plaintiff."

Other instructions are complained of as inconsistent with the instruction just quoted, and confusing in their effect upon the jury, as follows:

> "No. 2. In order to entitle plaintiff to recovery herein, it must be established by a preponderance of the evidence in the case that the illness of said child was caused by appendicitis, that defendant negligently made an incorrect diagnosis or determination of the character of the illness of said child, and also that defendant negligently treated said child for an illness which he did not have, and failed to properly treat him for appendicitis and that as the direct result of said diagnosis and treatment the said child died. The burden of establishing said facts by a preponderance of the evidence is upon the plaintiff" etc.

> "No. 4. You are instructed that while persons who hold themselves out to the public as physicians are not required to possess the highest degree of knowledge and skill which the most learned in their profession may have acquired, yet they are bound to possess and exercise in their practice at least the average degree of knowledge and skill possessed and exercised by the members of their profession generally in the locality in which they practice.

> "No. 5. You are also instructed that if you find from the evidence that there is more than one branch or school of physicians and surgeons which apply or use different methods in the treatment of diseases, each school or branch is entitled to practice in its own way, and a practitioner in any such school or branch is only expected to follow the methods ordinarily followed by the school to which

he belongs, and the question of his skillfulness, carelessness or negligence is not to be governed by the beliefs or practices of any other school of physicians or surgeons.

"You are further instructed that if you find from the evidence that the defendant in this case used or employed the methods ordinarily followed by the school to which he belongs in preparing for the treatment, and in the treatment of the child of plaintiff that, in that event, defendant would not be guilty and your verdict should be for the defendant."

Appellant argues that in one instruction the jury are told that appellant must possess "the average degree of knowledge and skill possessed and exercised by members of their profession generally in the locality in which they practice"; and in another instruction, the knowledge and skill which appellant must possess is limited to the school to which he belongs.

The first instruction complained of, No. 2, merely states the general rule of negligence as to incorrect diagnosis and improper or negligent treatment. It is not necessarily limited to any particular school, for all schools alike are liable under the same rules of negligence.

No. 4, however, would have been more complete, technically, if there had been added at the conclusion of the instruction "of the school of healing of which they are members." No. 5 is very explicit and states the law perfectly. Unless the jury were misled by the inconsistency between the incompleteness of No. 4 and the positive directness of No. 5, the instruction should not be held fatally erroneous. No. 6 tells the jury that if they find from the evidence that the defendant made a wrong diagnosis of the condition and ailment he would not be liable unless such wrong diagnosis, if they find any such to have been made, was followed by improper treatment; and should they find from the evidence that the defendant did make a wrong diagnosis their verdict should be for the defendant unless they also found from the evidence that the defendant did not use ordinary care and skill in treating the child after making such wrong diagnosis. It was imperfect, standing alone, in that it did not conclude by saying "according to the school of practice to which he belonged." No. 7 is a general instruction defining "careless" and "negligent," as used in the instructions, and concludes to the effect that if the jury believe the defendant to have possessed all of the qualifications necessary to a competent and skillful physician, yet if it has been proven by a preponderance of the evidence that he was careless and negligent in his treatment of it, then the mere fact that he may have been competent and skillful constitutes no defense to the action.

We conclude, therefore, that instructions Nos. 2, 4, 5, 6, and 7, considered together with instruction No. 8, were not so deficient in not limiting the consideration of the jury in judging the skill and care of appellant in treating the child, to the school of practice to which he belonged, that the jury may have been impressed that they could judge of his care and skill by the tests required by other schools.

It is well settled that in such cases the test must be by the school of thought of which the alleged practitioner is a member. Ennis v. Banks, 95 Wash. 513, 164 P. 58; State v. Smith, 25 Idaho 541, 138 P. 1107; Force v. Gregory, 63 Conn. 167, 27 A. 1116, 22 L.R.A. 343; Nelson v. Harrington, 72 Wis. 591, 40 N.W. 228, 7 Am. St. 900, 1 L.R.A. 719; McGraw v. Kerr, 23 Colo. App. 163, 128 P. 870.

We consider that, upon the instructions as a whole, the case was fairly submitted to the jury upon that theory.

* * *

Finding no reversible error, the judgment stands affirmed.

* * *

Notes and Questions

1. *No Liability for Wrong Diagnosis?* In *Wilcox*, the Supreme Court of Washington stated that, "It is true that a mere wrong diagnosis, unless followed by maltreatment, would not alone be sufficient to establish negligence as against a practitioner of medicine or healing." 127 Wash. at *7. The Court implies that an incorrect diagnosis must be followed by improper treatment for negligence to occur. If a defendant practitioner makes a wrong diagnosis, however, and such wrong diagnosis delays the provision of necessary treatment, can the delay caused by the wrong diagnosis, even in the absence of improper treatment, result in a finding of negligence? Many "loss of chance" malpractice cases are based on a wrong diagnosis followed by a delay of conventional care. *See, e.g., Groover v. Johnston*, 2009 Ala. LEXIS 239 (2009) (failure to diagnose developmental delays); Sandra J. Smith & Ugo Colella, *Lost Chance Recovery and the Folly of Expanding Medical Malpractice Liability*, 27(3) Tort & Insurance Law J. 615 (Spring 1992).

2. *Local v. National Standard.* In Jury Instructions Numbers 4 and 8, the Supreme Court of Washington states that a defendant physician must use that degree of skill and learning that is used not only by other physicians in the same school as the defendant but also in the locality in which the defendant practices. Do courts still look to the standard within the defendant's local community? Or to a national standard? Or to a national standard with a resource-based component? *See, e.g., Hall v. Hilbun*, 466 So.2d 856 (Miss. 1985) ("the physician's non-delegable duty of care is this: given the circumstances of each patient, each physician has a duty to use his or her knowledge and therewith treat through maximum reasonable medical recovery, each patient, with such reasonable diligence, skill, competence, and prudence as are practiced by minimally competent physicians throughout the United States who have available to them the same general facilities, services, equipment, and options.").

3. *Two Schools of Thought.* In Jury Instruction Number 5, the Supreme Court of Washington states that, "if ... there is more than one branch or school of physicians and surgeons which apply or use different methods in the treatment of diseases, each school or branch is entitled to practice in its own way, and a practitioner in any such school or branch is only expected to follow the methods ordinarily followed by the school to which he belongs, and the question of his skillfulness, carelessness or negligence is not to be governed by the beliefs or practices of any other school of physicians or surgeons." This doctrine, known as the "two schools of thought" doctrine, has been adopted by some jurisdictions as an affirmative defense for practitioners whose treatments may be accepted by one school of thought, but not another. *See* Chapter 4, Section III(A), *infra*.

* * *

Plaintiffs do not always win negligent diagnosis and misdiagnoses cases. In *Sell v. Shore*, reprinted below, the Court of Appeals of Ohio was asked to decide whether a chiropractor who failed to diagnose the patient's prostate cancer could be liable for malpractice. While treating the patient, the chiropractor had ordered several rounds of blood and urine tests after the patient complained of back, neck, and shoulder pain, as well as unusual fatigue. The results of the first two rounds of tests came back normal, but when the third round of tests revealed possible abnormalities, the chiropractor quickly referred the patient to a hospital. Conventional physicians then diagnosed the plaintiff's prostate cancer, although the patient died shortly thereafter. The legal question became: If the patient's diagnosis of prostate cancer could only be confirmed by a biopsy, which the chiropractor was legally prohibited from conducting, and an expert medical witness testified at trial that he did not think that the patient's fatal outcome could have been avoided even with a correct diagnosis by the chiropractor, could the chiropractor be liable for malpractice based on a failure-to-diagnose theory?

Sell v. Shore
Court of Appeals of Ohio
1988 Ohio App. LEXIS 177 (1988)

Per Curiam.

This cause went to trial in the Court of Common Pleas of Clark County upon an amended complaint which alleges that the defendant, Dr. E. R. Shore, a chiropractor, was negligent in the treatment of the plaintiff, Lester D. Sell, and that such negligence was the proximate cause of permanent damage to him. On the third day of the trial, after the plaintiff had rested, the trial court sustained a motion of Dr. Shore for a directed verdict, and from the judgment thereupon entered, the plaintiff, Darlene Sell, has appealed to this court.

According to the evidence, Mr. Sell visited Dr. Shore for the first time on November 9, 1982, at which time he was experiencing soreness in the back and pain in his neck and shoulder. He also complained of unusual fatigue and indicated that he could have a kidney stone. Thereafter, Dr. Shore took a medical history, during which Mr. Sell represented that he did not have a family physician and that he had seen only chiropractors in recent years. At the time, Dr. Shore took Sell's blood pressure and a urine specimen, and Shore recommended that Mr. Sell should take a food supplement.

The urine specimen was analyzed in Shore's office and found to be normal, and at the trial, Dr. Shore testified that the purpose of such testing was to rule out possible causes for the pain that Mr. Sell was experiencing. On November 11, 1982, Sell returned to the office, at which time Dr. Shore performed manipulations on his back, and on November 15, 1982, during a subsequent visit, Dr. Shore took a blood and urine specimen from Mr. Sell to be analyzed at an area laboratory. These specimens were reported to be normal. Then, on November 23, 1982, Shore did another urine analysis at his office. This specimen was likewise found to be normal, but on December 12, 1982, a blood and urine specimen taken from Mr. Sell suggested an abnormality, whereupon Shore contacted Sell and advised him to go to the hospital for further examinations.

Thereafter, tests at Grandview Hospital in Dayton, Ohio revealed that Mr. Sell had prostate cancer, and he was transferred to University Hospital in Cincinnati, Ohio, where he lapsed into a coma. While at University Hospital, Mr. Sell had immediate surgery to withdraw poison from his failing kidneys, and tests indicated that his cancer had been metastasizing for about five years. In late December, cancer treatment was begun, and after a six-week stay at the hospital, Mr. Sell returned to his home. He died on September 18, 1983.

At the conclusion of the plaintiff's case, both sides moved for a directed verdict, and from the order sustaining the motion of the defendant, the plaintiff has perfected an appeal which is based upon two assignments of error, the first of which has been stated as follows:

"1. The trial court erred by directing a verdict for the defendant where in a malpractice case, the defendant-chiropractor testifies during cross-examination that he has the requisite skill, knowledge and background to diagnose cancer, performs blood tests and urinalyses for the express purpose of ruling out other pathologies such as cancer, with the resultant effect being that the patient is misled as to the chiropractor's ability and authority to make a purely medical diagnosis."

The underlying issue posed by both motions for a directed verdict was whether the evidence showed professional negligence on the part of Dr. Shore. In other words, did he exhibit an unreasonable lack of skill or fidelity in the performance of his professional and fiduciary duties. See, 67 Ohio Jur. 3d 8, Sections 1 and 18.

In this regard, the record discloses the testimony of two witnesses, Dr. Shore and Darlene Sell (Frakes), and additionally, the trial court admitted the deposition of Dr. Bruce Bracken, a physician with expertise in urological cancers, who treated Mr. Sell at University Hospital. Dr. Bracken testified that he had no knowledge of medical standards in the chiropractic community, and that he did not know anything about the treatment which Dr. Shore rendered to Lester Sell. However, he did indicate that the cancer was not subject to diagnosis from the blood and urine tests that were performed. He testified further that a rectal examination would have alerted a physician to an abnormality, but that only a biopsy would have confirmed the ultimate finding that Mr. Sell had prostate cancer. During his summary, Dr. Bracken expressed doubt that the "fatal outcome" of the illness would have been altered by a correct diagnosis on November 9, 1982, but he did conclude that some of the treatment and the duration of the stay in the hospital would have been "less likely" if the cancerous condition had been discovered a month earlier.

With regard for the fundamental principles which must be applied in ruling upon a motion for a directed verdict (O'Day v. Webb, 29 Ohio St. 2d 215), the plaintiff's most impressive evidence was presented through Mr. Sell's wife, Darlene, who testified that Dr. Shore told her, when she specifically asked him, that her husband did not have cancer. However, a misdiagnosis does not necessarily constitute negligence, and "when a patient selects a doctor of a recognized school, he thereby adopts the kind of treatment common to that school; and the care, skill and diligence with which he is treated must be tested by the evidence of those who are trained and skilled with reference to the kind of treatment adopted by the patient." Willett v. Rowekamp, 134 Ohio St. 285.

In the present case, the plaintiff did not present expert testimony as to the limitations upon the practice of chiropractic (R.C. 4734.09), and as heretofore indicated, Dr. Bracken testified that he was without expertise in such matters. Where fields of medicine overlap, a witness may qualify as an expert even though he does not practice the same specialty, but where no expert testimony is presented as to a certain field of practice, a plaintiff cannot, in the usual situation, make a prima facie case of malpractice. Bruni v. Tatsumi, 46 Ohio St. 2d 127. See also, Alexander v. Med. Center, 56 Ohio St. 2d 155; Willett v. Rowekamp, 134 Ohio St. 285.

Moreover, even if we were to assume that Dr. Shore exceeded the permissible scope of his specialty and should be held to a higher standard of care, as argued by the appellant, the record is nonetheless devoid of evidence that the alleged damages, as testified to by Dr. Bracken, were caused by anything that Dr. Shore did or failed to do. See, Ault v. Hall, 119 Ohio St. 422. In fact, Dr. Bracken commented that he would have been "surprised" if general practitioners of medicine would have done a rectal examination on Mr. Sell on November 9, 1982. In the absence of any expert evidence as to the care and skill required of a chiropractor, and after a careful examination of the evidence as a whole, the first assignment of error must be overruled.

The second assignment of error has been set forth by the appellant as follows:

> "2. The trial court erred in a malpractice action by requiring expert testimony from a member of the same specialty as the defendant physician wherein: other available evidence is sufficient to show the applicable standard of care, the treatment complained of is practiced in numerous fields and easily understood by layman, and where plaintiffs' expert would have aided the trier of fact regardless of his medical classification."

According to the record, the deposition of Dr. Bracken was admitted without objection and by stipulation of the parties on November 14, 1986, but Dr. Bracken admitted that he was not familiar with the standard of care, skill, and diligence required in the practice of chiropractic procedures. However, Dr. Bracken did testify from experiences in his own specialty that neither the blood test nor the urine analysis would have revealed the cancer of the prostate.

In argument, the appellant also suggests that some restrictions were placed upon the transcript of the testimony of Dr. Bracken, but on the contrary, the record discloses that it was his admitted lack of expertise as to the proper standard of care in the chiropractice [sic] profession rather than any restriction upon the evidence which left the void in the plaintiff's case.

The appellant also argues that the standard of care required of Dr. Shore was a matter of common knowledge and that expert testimony was not therefore necessary, but this contention appears to run counter to the direct testimony of Dr. Bracken. Likewise, such argument is refuted to a considerable extent by such cases as Bruni v. Tatsumi, 46 Ohio St. 2d 127, Alexander v. Med. Center, 56 Ohio St. 2d 155 and Willett v. Rowekamp, 134 Ohio St. 285. The second assignment of error is overruled.

Upon consideration of all of the evidence, and after construing such evidence most strongly in favor of the plaintiff, we are of the opinion that the trial court did not err in sustaining the defendant's motion for a directed verdict. Accordingly, the judgment of the Common Pleas Court will be affirmed.

Notes and Questions

1. *Incidence of CAM Malpractice.* Given the number of cases in this section, one might think that CAM malpractice claims constitute a large percentage of total medical malpractice claims. Is this the case? *See, e.g.*, Michael H. Cohen et al., *Emerging Credentialing Practices, Malpractice Liability Policies, and Guidelines Governing Complementary and Alternative Medical Practices and Dietary Supplement Recommendations*, 165 Archives Internal Medicine 289–295 (2005) ("CAM therapies also account for only approximately 5% of the total medical malpractice insurance market; to date, both the number of claims against CAM providers and the average indemnity paid per claim have been lower than claims against primary care physicians. However, this situation may change as integrative care expands.").

2. *Incidence of Chiropractic Malpractice.* Given the number of cases in this section in which chiropractors are named defendants, one might think that chiropractic malpractice cases constitute a large percentage of total CAM malpractice cases. Is this the case?

III. Causation

A. Causal Link

Like traditional medical malpractice cases, CAM malpractice cases not only require proof of duty and breach but also causation and damages. The causation element has proved difficult for some CAM plaintiffs. In both *Ireland v. Eckerly* and *White v. Jones*, reprinted in part below, patients sued their practitioners for malpractice following the administration of a CAM therapy. On appeal, the reviewing courts were asked to decide whether there was a causal link between the defendant's conduct and the patient's injuries.

Ireland v. Eckerly, M.D.
Court of Appeals of Minnesota
1989 Minn. App. LEXIS 13 (Unpublished Opinion) (1989)

Randall, J.

FACTS

On April 23, 1984, appellants Wayne and Bernadine Ireland brought an action against respondent Dr. Jean Eckerly for medical malpractice. Respondent told Bernadine Ireland (appellant) that she was a "good candidate" for chelation therapy because she had clogged arteries. Between September 1983 and January 1984, appellant received 16 chelation treatments at respondent's clinic.

On January 3, 1984, appellant had a chelation therapy session lasting approximately three hours. Later that evening, appellant lost consciousness and fell down the stairs in her home. She subsequently suffered two seizures and was hospitalized for ten days. The fall caused some permanent impairment to appellant's spine. Appellant sued, claiming the fall was directly caused by respondent's negligent medical treatment.

* * *

Appellants also claim the evidence does not support the jury's finding that respondent's negligence was not the direct cause of appellant's injuries. Appellants argue that as a direct result of taking the chelation treatment, appellant lost consciousness, fell down the stairs, and sustained permanent impairment to her spine.

DECISION

We affirm the trial court's order denying appellants' motion for judgment notwithstanding the verdict, or in the alternative, a new trial. This is a private medical malpractice case for personal injury. We will not expand the scope of the Minnesota consumer protection statutes to include individual medical services which only affect a specific patient.

Prescribing medical treatment to a patient requires that a physician exercise his or her professional judgment. Such judgment, when later found to be ineffective, cannot be susceptible to the consumer protection statutes. See Jenson v. Touche Ross & Co., 335 N.W.2d 720, 728 (Minn. 1983) (the consumer protection statutes are not intended to second-guess professional judgment). There is no evidence that respondent used fraud or deception in prescribing the chelation treatment to appellant; nor is there evidence on how respondent's conduct affects the public interest. The trial court properly found the deceptive trade practices and consumer fraud statutes do not apply to this case.

* * *

Lastly, we hold that the evidence supports the jury finding respondent's negligence not to be the direct cause of appellant's injuries. Appellants' expert testified that appellant's seizures were due to the chelation therapy because it lowered her calcium level, causing a particle of calcium emboli to lodge in a blood vessel. Respondent's expert testified there was no relation between the chelation treatment and appellant's seizures.

It is within the discretion of the jury to determine which conflicting medical testimony is more believable. If the record contains conflicting inferences in support of either party, depending largely upon the credibility of the witnesses and the reasonableness of their testimony, the jury's determination is binding upon a reviewing court. State v. Henry, 278 Minn. 344, 346, 154 N.W.2d 503, 505 (1967). We hold the jury finding of no causal link between the chelation therapy and appellant's fall and resulting injuries is supported by the evidence.

The trial court's order denying appellant's motion for judgment notwithstanding the verdict or a new trial was proper.

* * *

White v. Jones
Court of Civil Appeals of Alabama
717 So. 2d 413 (1998)

Monroe, J.

Minnie White sued Dr. R.M. Jones, a chiropractor, alleging that he had negligently treated her knee. The case proceeded to trial. After White had completed her case-in-chief, Jones moved for a directed verdict. After hearing the arguments of counsel, the trial court entered a directed verdict in favor of Jones, saying that White had not presented substantial evidence that Jones had committed malpractice. While appealed to the Alabama Supreme Court, which deflected the case to this court pursuant to § 12-2-7(6), Ala. Code 1975.

* * *

White testified that she first saw Dr. Jones on May 5, 1992, because of pain she had in her right shoulder and hip. She went in for follow-up visits on May 8 and May 13. White said that on the May 13 visit, as she got out of her car and stepped up onto the curb to go into Dr. Jones's office, she "caught a catch" in her knee. White said that she told Dr. Jones about the "catch" and that he examined her knee. She said that as he examined her knee, he "twisted" it, "just did one little twist."

White said that the next morning she could not put any weight on her knee. She went to her physician, who referred her to an orthopaedic surgeon, Dr. Warner Pinchback. She did not tell Dr. Pinchback that Dr. Jones had twisted her knee. Dr. Pinchback recommended physical therapy, but White's knee failed to improve and she eventually required arthroscopic surgery.

Dr. Jones testified that he did not treat White's knee at all. His office notes show that on the May 8 visit, White complained of a catch in her left leg. In his notes of May 13, there is no mention of any problem associated with her knee. Dr. Jones said that if White had complained of knee pain, he would have checked the knee's range of motion and would have checked for tenderness or soreness. He said a range-of-motion test would not require twisting.

White's attorney asked Dr. Jones whether, if White's version of the events was true, the treatment White alleged Dr. Jones gave would have constituted malpractice. Dr. Jones said that it would, but that he disagreed with White's version of the events.

Dr. Pinchback's deposition also was admitted into evidence. He testified that he first saw White on May 22, 1992. At that time, he said, she told him she had no history of trauma to the knee, but that her knee had gotten persistently worse. She told Dr. Pinchback that her knee had been bothering her for about a month. Dr. Pinchback eventually determined that White had a partial tear in the lateral meniscus of her left knee. He described the meniscus as a disc-shaped structure that acts as a shock absorber for the knee. He said such tears can be the result of age, persistent wear, or trauma such as "a forceful twisting type motion of the knee." Dr. Pinchback said that tears in the meniscus can result from pivoting, such as would occur when one abruptly changes directions while walking. He noted that White also had arthritis in her knee and that she showed a softness of the "gristle" in her knee, a condition that comes with age, he said.

No other witnesses testified. Although depositions had been taken from White's expert witness and from Dr. Jones's expert witness, White did not attempt to have either of those depositions admitted into evidence.

"In order to recover in a medical malpractice case, a plaintiff must prove by expert testimony that the physician breached the standard of care and by the breach proximately caused the plaintiff's injury." Hawkins v. Carroll, 676 So. 2d 338, 340 (Ala. Civ. App. 1996); University of Alabama Health Services v. Bush, 638 So. 2d 794, 798–99 (Ala. 1994). A "community" standard of care must be established by expert medical testimony. Hawkins, supra. "Community" has been held to mean the national medical community. Id.

White contends that Dr. Jones's testimony that, if White's version of the events was true then his action would have been malpractice, constitutes expert medical testimony that proves a community standard of care and a breach of that duty. We disagree. Nothing in that testimony establishes a community standard, and there is no evidence that Dr. Jones breached a community standard of care.

Dr. Jones did testify as to how he would have examined White's knee if she had complained to him about her knee. However, testimony as to how Dr. Jones would have handled the examination is insufficient to establish a community standard. See, e.g., Hawkins, supra, at 341.

Even if we were to determine that Dr. Jones's testimony established a community standard and that his treatment of White constituted a breach of that standard, there is no evidence that that treatment was the proximate cause of White's injury. "'To prove causation in a medical malpractice case, the plaintiff must prove, through expert medical testimony, that the alleged negligence probably caused, rather than only possibly caused, the plaintiff's injury.'" Id. (quoting Bush, supra, 638 So. 2d at 802). Even if White's version of what happened is true, there is no evidence that Dr. Jones's alleged treatment of White's knee probably caused her injury. Dr. Pinchback testified as to several possible causes of tears in the meniscus; he gave no testimony as to the probable cause of her injury. We note that on May 22, just over a week from the day she said Dr. Jones injured her knee, White told Dr. Pinchback that her knee had been hurting her for about a month. She also testified that she hurt her knee stepping onto the curb at Dr. Jones's office, and that is why she said he treated her knee in the first place. After reviewing the record, including the deposition of Dr. Pinchback, we agree with Dr. Jones that there is no evidence to suggest that his alleged treatment of White's knee probably caused her injury.

Because White failed to present substantial evidence of the elements required for her to prevail in her case, the trial court properly directed a verdict in favor of Dr. Jones.

* * *

The trial court properly directed a verdict in favor of Dr. Jones. The judgment based on that verdict is affirmed.

AFFIRMED.

* * *

Notes and Questions

1. *Malpractice v. Consumer Protection.* The *Ireland* opinion distinguishes consumer protection and medical malpractice cases. Can the same set of facts give rise to both a consumer protection complaint and a medical malpractice case? *See, e.g., Ambach v. French*, 216 P.3d 405 (Wash. 2009) (Washington Consumer Protection Act does not provide a remedy in medical malpractice cases).

2. *Actual Cause and Proximate Cause.* Once a plaintiff has shown that the defendant has breached an applicable standard of care, the plaintiff also must show that the defendant's action is both the cause in fact, or actual cause, of the injury, as well as the proximate cause of the injury. In the *White* opinion, does the Court of Civil Appeals of Alabama discuss both types of causation?

B. Expert Testimony Regarding Causation

Expert testimony may be required to establish a causal link between the defendant's conduct and the plaintiff's injuries. In Section I(A) of this Chapter, *supra*, the Supreme Court of Wisconsin in *Kerkman v. Hintz* considered whether an expert witness who had a different education and training than the defendant could be permitted testify as to the standard of care applicable to the defendant. In *Morgan v. Hill*, reprinted in part below, the Court of Appeals of Kentucky examined a second evidentiary question; that is, can an expert witness who has a different education and training than the defendant testify regarding whether the defendant's conduct caused the plaintiff's injuries?

Morgan v. Hill
Court of Appeals of Kentucky
663 S.W.2d 232 (1984)

Hayes, C. J.

The sole question to be considered in this appeal is whether the trial judge erred in granting directed verdicts in favor of the appellees. In our opinion, the trial judge improperly concluded that the evidence was not sufficient to submit the case to the jury, and accordingly, we reverse the judgment and remand this action for trial on the merits.

On February 5, 1979, appellant Michael Morgan injured his cervical spine while installing an electrical conduit. Despite the discomfort he was experiencing, he continued to work for about three weeks before seeking medical attention at the emergency room of the Bowling Green—Warren County Hospital where his condition was diagnosed as a "sprained back." Morgan returned to work, but later that afternoon he sought treatment from appellee James Hill, a chiropractor. Dr. Hill treated Morgan for approximately one month. On one occasion he was treated by Dr. Hill's associate, Dr. William Judge.

Morgan testified that during one of the chiropractic treatments rendered by Dr. Hill he experienced a sharp pain that radiated down his arm, a sensation that had not been present prior to the treatment. When Morgan's condition did not improve despite the ongoing chiropractic treatments, he consulted a neurosurgeon who diagnosed Morgan's condition as a "ruptured disc." A myelogram confirmed the diagnosis and ultimately a cervical laminectomy was performed.

Morgan and his wife instituted this action alleging that the chiropractic treatments he received caused his disc to rupture. A jury trial was conducted but the trial judge directed verdicts in favor of both Drs. Hill and Judge. The trial judge ruled that Dr. Judge's participation in the treatment program was so minimal that liability could not attach to him. With this ruling we agree and hold that it was proper to direct a verdict in favor of Dr. Judge.

A verdict was later directed in Dr. Hill's favor on the basis that appellants had failed to establish a causal connection between the injuries Michael Morgan sustained and the treatment rendered by Dr. Hill. The trial judge also ruled that appellants had failed to establish the standard of care by which the conduct of the chiropractors was to be judged.

Appellants argue that both elements, causation and standard of care, were adequately established by the testimony of Dr. Russell Rothrock, a neurosurgeon, the testimony of Michael and Gail Morgan, and the testimony of the defendant, Dr. James S. Hill.

We disagree with the trial judge's assessment as to when and how the injury to Morgan's disc occurred and believe that question was one for the jury to decide. Absent an adequate standard by which to judge the treatment received by Michael Morgan, the case should not have gone to a jury. At the close of the plaintiff's case, no such standard had been established, but at the close of all evidence this defect in the plaintiff's case was remedied by the evidence put on by the defendants. See Cassinelli v. Begley, Ky., 433 S.W.2d 651 (1968). The defendant testified that Morgan's condition called for "gentle" manipulations. Morgan testified that the manipulations that Dr. Hill performed on him were anything but "gentle." If the jury chooses to believe Morgan, then negligence has been established.

Certainly, a medical doctor can testify as to the cause of any injury, just as a chiropractor may so testify. A physician may not testify to the chiropractor's standard of care, however, because he does not have the appropriate training and experience to determine what constitutes chiropractic malpractice. Here, the neurosurgeon testified that it was his expert medical opinion to a reasonable medical certainty that the ruptured disc was caused by the manipulations. See Seaton v. Rosenberg, Ky., 573 S.W.2d 333 (1978); and Walden v. Jones, Ky., 439 S.W.2d 571 (1968). The record contains chiropractic testimony which established the standard of care, and the plaintiff Michael Morgan testified that the chiropractor treated him in such a way that the standard of care was not followed. We have causation from the neurosurgeon, standard of care from the defendants, and breach of the standard from the plaintiff. If a jury chooses to accept the testimony, then the defendant Dr. Hill may be held liable for malpractice.

The judgment of the Warren Circuit Court is affirmed as to Dr. Judge and reversed as to Dr. Hill and remanded for proceedings consistent with this opinion.

ALL CONCUR.

* * *

IV. Malpractice Defenses

Like traditional medical malpractice defendants, CAM malpractice defendants may try to plead and prove any one of several classic defenses to negligence, including contributory negligence, comparative negligence, assumption of risk, and immunity. CAM malpractice defendants also may argue that the plaintiff's lawsuit is barred by a statute of limitations.

A. Two Schools of Thought

One defense that may have special application to the CAM context is the 'two schools of thought' doctrine. According to the 'two schools of thought' doctrine, a health care practitioner has an absolute defense to a claim of negligence when it is determined that the prescribed treatment or procedure has been approved by one group of medical experts even though an alternate school of thought recommends another approach.

In *Jones v. Chidester*, reprinted in part below, the Supreme Court of Pennsylvania examined the 'two schools of thought' doctrine to determine when a defendant from a particular school of thought may qualify for the defense. Although *Jones* involved a defendant who was an allopathic physician, not a CAM practitioner, the opinion provides an excellent overview of the multiple approaches to the 'two schools of thought' doctrine and the approach taken by Pennsylvania. The opinion also lays the groundwork for the application of the doctrine to the CAM setting.

Jones v. Chidester
Supreme Court of Pennsylvania
531 Pa. 31 (1992)

OPINION OF THE COURT

Papadakos, J.

We granted review in this case in order to re-examine our test for the defense of the so-called "two schools" doctrine in a medical malpractice case arising in the context of a jury instruction. The necessity of our re-examination arises from the vacillation of the Superior Court and our Court in applying the appropriate standard.

A medical practitioner has an absolute defense to a claim of negligence when it is determined that the prescribed treatment or procedure has been approved by one group of medical experts even though an alternate school of thought recommends another approach, or it is agreed among experts that alternative treatments and practices are acceptable. The doctrine is applicable only where there is more than one method of accepted treatment or procedure. In specific terms, however, we are called upon in this case to decide once again whether a school of thought qualifies as such when it is advocated by a "considerable number" of medical experts or when it commands acceptance by "respective, reputable and reasonable" practitioners. The former test calls for a quantitative analysis, while the latter is premised on qualitative grounds.

The facts indicate that in November, 1979, Appellant, Billy Jones, underwent orthopedic surgery on his leg performed by Dr. John H. Chidester. In order to create a bloodless field for the surgery, the surgeon employed a tourniquet which was elevated and released at various intervals. Because of subsequent problems with the leg, the patient was referred to a neurosurgeon who determined that Jones had suffered nerve injury to the leg. Additional examinations by other doctors confirmed that the nerve injury had resulted in a condition known as "drop foot."

At trial in June, 1988, Jones complained, inter alia, that his nerve injury was the result of Dr. Chidester's use of the tourniquet. Both sides presented testimony by medical experts supporting their positions. Unsurprisingly, Dr. Chidester's experts told the court and jury that his technique was acceptable medically in this particular case, and the plaintiffs' experts insisted that it constituted unacceptable practice.

At the close of the evidence, the court gave the following instruction to the jury:

> A physician, then, is excused from an error of judgment only if he has used all of the skills and care required of him in the treatment of his patient and if he has obtained a complete and accurate factual basis upon which to base the exercise of his judgment.
>
> There is a vast difference between an error in judgment and negligence.
>
> Members of the jury, you have heard one of the plaintiff's (sic) experts testify to the procedure that would be employed during the course of an operation of this type, and I believe his name was Dr. Hyatt, and also you heard from a defense witness who testified as to the type of procedure to be used during this course of operation, and I believe that was the last witness.
>
> Ladies and gentlemen, I instruct you upon this additional principle of law known as the two schools of thought doctrine. This principle provides that it is improper for a jury to be required to decide which of two schools of thought as to proper procedure should have been followed in this case, when both schools have their respective and respected advocates and followers in the medical profession.
>
> In essence, then, a jury of lay persons is not to be put in a position of choosing one respected body of medical opinion over another when each has a reasonable following among the members of the medical community.
>
> Thus, under the two schools of thought doctrine, a physician in the position of Dr. Chidester will not be held liable to a plaintiff merely for exercising his judgment in applying the course of treatment supported by a reputable and respected body of medical experts, even if another body of medical experts' opinion would favor a different course of treatment. Those are the two schools of thought, and that is the two schools of thought doctrine. (R.R., pp. 18–20).

* * *

The jury returned a verdict in favor of Dr. Chidester and Jones filed a post-trial motion alleging that he was entitled to a new trial because the court's instruction to the jury on the two schools of thought doctrine was reversible error. At trial and on appeal, Jones argues that under Pennsylvania law, the test for the doctrine is "considerable number" rather than "reputable and respected" as the court had charged the jury.

We note at the outset of our analysis that there appears to be confusion and contradiction in the use of these standards — a confusion apparent even between the trial court's charge to the jury ("reputable and respected") and its subsequent opinion denying the post-trial motion ("considerable number"):

> Inasmuch as the two schools of thought doctrine applies only to a school of thought advocated by a "considerable number" of reputable and respected physicians, we thus found in light of the testimony of all of the foregoing witnesses (including Plaintiffs' own expert), that there are two schools of thought on the appropriate use of tourniquets during extremity surgery and that the school to which Dr. Chidester adhered during Plaintiff's operation is advocated by a considerable number of reputable doctors. (Slip opinion, pp. 6–7).

The initial modern case in this jurisdiction on the subject of the two schools of thought doctrine was Remley v. Plummer, 79 Pa. Superior Ct. 117 (1922). Relevant portions of that opinion are as follows:

> The question actually passed upon by the jury was not whether the defendants, in their handling of the case, had been guilty of negligence in not following a well-recognized and established mode of treatment, but rather, which of two methods, both having their respective advocates and followers of respectable authority, was the safer and better from a surgical standpoint. (Emphasis added.)

> * * *

> ... [A]nd where competent medical authority is divided, a physician will not be held responsible if in the exercise of his judgment he followed the course of treatment advocated by a considerable number of his professional brethren in good standing in his community. (Emphasis added).

> * * *

> Thus practitioners of a reputable school of medicine are not to be harassed by litigation and mulcted in damages because the course of treatment prescribed by that school differs from that adopted by another school: (citations omitted) ... As we said in Patten v. Wiggin, [51 Maine 594] supra, "The jury are not to judge by determining which school, in their judgment, is the best." "If the treatment is in accordance with a recognized system of surgery, it is not for the court or jury to undertake to determine whether that system is best, nor to decide questions of surgical science on which surgeons differ among themselves:" ...

> The testimony clearly showed a difference of medical opinion expressed by physicians and surgeons of unquestioned standing and reputation, and the defendants were not negligent for having adopted the view held by the majority of their brethren who testified.

Id., 79 Pa.Superior Ct. at 121–123 (citations omitted).

Our first review of the issue following Remley dropped all references to the "reputable and respected" test by grounding the decision on "considerable number" language alone:

> Where competent medical authority is divided, a physician will not be held responsible if in the exercise of his judgment he followed a course of treatment advocated by a considerable number of his professional brethren in good standing in his community.

Duckworth v. Bennett, 320 Pa. 47, 181 A. 558 (1935).

In Tobash v. Jones, 419 Pa. 205, 213 A.2d 588 (1965), our Court regressed from the Duckworth standard and returned to the Remley standard when it approved the jury instruction of the trial judge which stated:

> Now if you find that under that evidence there are two schools of belief, if you find that there is competent authority, although divided, competent medical authority, subscribed to by reputable and reasonable medical experts, and if you find that Dr. Jones followed one of those lines in performing this laminectomy and in excising that tissue from the spinal cord of Mr. Tobash, then you couldn't say he was negligent for following any of the recognized experts in the field.

In fact, the Tobash court totally ignored Duckworth and cited Remley with approval. 419 Pa. at 217, 213 A.2d at 592. Not until Brannan v. Lankenau Hospital, 490 Pa. 588, 417 A.2d 196 (1980), did we have occasion to return to the Duckworth rule:

> There is, of course, the longstanding rule that the jury may not decide which of "two methods, both having their respective advocates and followers of respectable authority, was the safer and better from the surgical standpoint." Tobash v. Jones, 419 Pa. 205, 217, 213 A.2d 588, 593 (1965), quoting Remley v. Plummer, 79 Pa. Super. 117 (1922).

In Duckworth v. Bennett, we stated the rule as:

> "Where competent medical authority is divided, a physician will not be held responsible if in the exercise of his judgment he followed a course of treatment advocated by a considerable number of his brethren in good standing in his community." 320 Pa. 47, 51, 181 A. 558, 559 (1935). Here, appellant's expert initially testified that he knew of no reason to await final diagnosis of esophageal perforation before administering antibiotics. Although on cross-examination the expert indicated that a "small respected body" of medical practitioners believed otherwise, this is a far cry from treatment approved by a considerable number of physicians. Indeed, the expert witness reaffirmed on cross-examination that "the great majority" of physicians would not apply the practice appellee doctors utilized here. Thus, we cannot agree with appellees that Dr. Thompson's testimony alone triggered the application of the Duckworth standard regarding "a course of treatment advocated by a considerable number of his brethren."

By contrast, with the exception of D'Angelis v. Zakuto, 383 Pa.Superior Ct. 65, 556 A.2d 431 (1989), (the doctrine applies only to a school of thought advocated by "a considerable number" of "reputable and respected physicians"), the Superior Court has held steadfastly to the "reputable, respected" standard. Tobash v. Jones, 419 Pa. 205, 213 A.2d 588 (1965) ("if you find that there is competent, although divided, competent medical authority, subscribed to by reputable, respectable and reasonable medical experts"); Furey v. Thomas Jefferson University Hospital, 325 Pa.Superior Ct. 212, 472 A.2d 1083 (1984) ("reputable, respected and reasonable medical experts"); Trent v. Trotman, 352 Pa.Superior Ct. 490, 508 A.2d 580 (1986) ("as long as that school of thought is reputable and respected by reasonable experts"); Morganstein v. House, 377 Pa.Superior Ct. 512, 547 A.2d 1180 (1988); Levine v. Rosen, 394 Pa.Superior Ct. 178, 575 A.2d 579 (1990); Sinclair by Sinclair v. Block, 406 Pa.Superior Ct. 540, 594 A.2d 750 (1991) (quoting Levine, supra, on "reputable, respectable and reasonable medical experts").

Other jurisdictions also appear to waffle between the two standards. In McHugh v. Audet, 72 F.Supp. 394 (M.D., Pa.1947), the "considerable number" test was held to be the test. Some years later, however, another federal court in Pennsylvania cited Remley for the proposition that the two schools of thought doctrine is applicable where one is advocated by "reputable, respectable and reasonable" experts. Harrigan v. United States, 408 F.Supp. 177 (E.D., Pa.1976). This result should be contrasted with the holding in Oneill v. Kiledjian, 511 F.2d 511, 513 (6th Cir., 1975), that the defense is available "when both alternatives have the support of a considerable body of competent medical opinion in the community." Oneill followed Gresham v. Ford, 192 Tenn. 310, 241 S.W.2d 408 (1951), which construed Duckworth and concluded in a quantitative fashion that an accepted alternative treatment is "one advocated by many of the doctors in good standing."

In Borja v. Phoenix General Hospital, Inc., 151 Ariz. 302, 727 P.2d 355 (1986), the court adopted Furey, supra, in holding that the doctrine requires only support by a "respectable minority." California has defined its standard as one where "a physician chooses one of alternative accepted methods of treatment, with which other physicians agree." Meier v. Ross General Hospital, 69 Cal.2d 420, 434, 71 Cal.Rptr. 903, 445 P.2d 519 (1968). Florida has adopted the "respectable minority" test in Schwab v. Tolley, Florida App., 345 So.2d 747 (1977), while Arkansas accepts the doctrine when any alternative "recognized method" is employed by the physician. Rickett v. Hayes, 256 Ark. 893, 511 S.W.2d 187 (1974). Louisiana courts have favored an "acceptable alternative treatment" test. Reid v. North Caddo Memorial Hospital, La.App., 528 So.2d 653 (1988). The most recent Connecticut decision exonerates a practitioner who employed a treatment which was "one of choice among competent physicians." Wasfi v. Chaddna, 218 Conn. 200, 588 A.2d 204 (1991).

In a similar vein, other states also have refused to adopt a quantitative test. Gruginski v. Lane, 177 Wash. 121, 30 P.2d 970 (1934) ("respectable minority"); Walkenhorst v. Kesler, 92 Utah 312, 67 P.2d 654 (1937) ("approval of at least a respectable portion of the profession"); Holton v. Burton, 197 Wis. 405, 222 N.W. 225 (1928) ("two accepted or recognized methods of treatment").

From this harvest of case law, we glean the following conclusions. First, the qualitative standard is the preferred choice of the Pennsylvania Supreme Court as well as most sister jurisdictions. Second, generally where courts, including our own, have applied Remley, there appears to be a blurring of distinctions between quantitative and qualitative standards. Third, in spite of this apparent blurring, our recent decision in Brannan seems to have drawn a bright line between the two tests, although the opinion itself employed the language of both tests. Last, it is obvious that the fork in the legal road, splitting off the law in the two directions enumerated herein, was provided by Remley itself because subsequent interpretations depended on which paragraph in Remley was adopted as the rule of the case.

It is incumbent upon us to settle this confusion.... The "two schools of thought doctrine" provides a complete defense to malpractice. It is therefore insufficient to show that there exists a "small minority" of physicians who agree with the defendant's questioned practice. Thus, the Superior Court's "reputable and respected by reasonable medical experts" test is improper. Rather, there must be a considerable number of physicians, recognized and respected in their field, sufficient to create another "school of thought."

Notwithstanding what appears to be conflicting interpretations, we find that both standards have been used appropriately by our precedents. We read Remley, Duckworth and, most recently, Brannan, to define a school of thought as a "considerable number of reputable and respected physicians." A school of thought should be adopted not only by "reputable and respected physicians" in order to insure quality but also by a "considerable number" of medical practitioners for the purpose of meeting general acceptance even if it does not rise to the level of a majority.

We, therefore, provide the following as a correct statement of the law:

> Where competent medical authority is divided, a physician will not be held responsible if in the exercise of his judgment he followed a course of treatment advocated by a considerable number of recognized and respected professionals in his given area of expertise.

In recognizing this doctrine, we do not attempt to place a numerical certainty on what constitutes a "considerable number." The burden of proving that there are two schools of thought falls to the defendant. The burden, however, should not prove burdensome. The proper use of expert witnesses should supply the answers. Once the expert states the factual reasons to support his claim that there is a considerable number of professionals who agree with the treatment employed by the defendant, there is sufficient evidence to warrant an instruction to the jury on the two "schools of thought." It then becomes a question for the jury to determine whether they believe that there are two legitimate schools of thought such that the defendant should be insulated from liability.

Reversed and remanded for a new trial consistent with this opinion.

* * *

Zappala, J., concurring.

While I join in the opinion, I vehemently disagree with the majority that the existence of two schools of medical thought may ever be a question of fact to be submitted to a jury. The majority states that, "It then becomes a question for the jury to determine whether they believe that there are two legitimate schools of thought such that the defendant should be insulated from liability." (Majority opinion at 41). It is the responsibility of the trial judge to determine in the first instance whether there are two schools of medical thought so that competent medical authority as to a course of treatment is divided. It is a question of law for the trial judge. It is not a question of fact. In all other respects, I agree with the majority's analysis of the two schools of medical thought doctrine.

* * *

Notes and Questions

1. *More than One Accepted Method.* The *Jones* opinion states that the 'two schools of thought' doctrine only applies "when there is more than one method of accepted treatment or procedure." *Jones*, 531 Pa. at 33. Are chiropractic adjustments considered a second method of 'accepted treatment' for lower back pain? Is acupuncture considered a second method of 'accepted treatment' for post-surgery nausea? Could a homeopathic remedy be considered a second method of 'accepted treatment' for a chronic disease? Could a homeopathic remedy be considered a second method of 'accepted treatment' for an acute condition, such as appendicitis or heart attack?

2. *When Is Enough Enough?* In jurisdictions that follow the simple quantitative "considerable number of experts" test, would chiropractic, acupuncture, naturopathy, homeopathy, and other CAM schools of thought be considered to have a sufficient number of like-minded experts?

3. *Who Is Sufficiently Reputable?* In jurisdictions that follow the simple qualitative "respective, reputable and reasonable practitioner" test, would chiropractic, acupuncture,

naturopathy, homeopathy and other CAM schools of thought be considered to be sufficiently respectable and reputable?

4. *The* Jones *Test.* In jurisdictions such as Pennsylvania that follow the rule in *Jones* and require a "considerable number of recognized and respected professionals in his given area of expertise," would chiropractic, acupuncture, naturopathy, homeopathy, and other CAM schools of thought be considered to have a sufficient number of recognized and respected professionals?

B. Assumption of the Risk

As illustrated in both of the following cases reprinted in part below, CAM malpractice defendants commonly raise assumption of the risk as a defense to negligence.

Schneider v. Revici
United States Court of Appeals for the Second Circuit
817 F.2d 987 (1987)

[The full text of this judicial opinion is available at p. 184, *infra*.]

* * *

C. Assumption of Risk

An examination of the complaint reveals that appellants sufficiently pleaded assumption of risk in their Third Affirmative Defense by broadly asserting Mrs. Schneider's "culpable conduct." Cf. Hoyt v. McCann, 88 A.D.2d 633, 450 N.Y.S.2d 231 (2d Dep't 1982) (assumption of risk is a form of "culpable conduct"); 1B Warren's N.Y. Negligence 2.02[3], at 1027 (rev. 2d ed. 1980). We therefore address the district court's ruling that assumption of risk was inapplicable to this case, and the court's subsequent failure to charge the jury on express assumption of risk.

In 1975, New York adopted a comparative negligence statute eliminating contributory negligence as a total bar to recovery. Prior to adoption of the statute a plaintiff was required to be free of any negligence contributing in the slightest degree to his injury, in order to recover. The plaintiff's own negligence was viewed as an intervening cause, between the defendant's negligent act and the plaintiff's injury, which prevented any recovery. Dowd v. New York, Ontario & W. Ry. Co., 170 N.Y. 459, 63 N.E. 541 (1902). See generally Arbegast v. Board of Educ., 65 N.Y.2d 161, 165, 480 N.E.2d 365, 368, 490 N.Y.S.2d 751, 754 (1985).

The doctrine of assumption of risk was also a defense to an action for the recovery of damages for personal injuries, prior to the adoption of the comparative negligence statute. Murphy v. Steeplechase Amusement Co., 250 N.Y. 479, 166 N.E. 173 (1929); Ruggerio v. Board of Educ., 31 A.D.2d 884, 298 N.Y.S.2d 149 (4th Dep't 1969), aff'd, 26 N.Y.2d 849, 258 N.E.2d 92, 309 N.Y.S.2d 596 (1970).

The doctrine of assumption of risk lies in the maxim, volenti non fit injuria. Based as it is upon the plaintiff's assent to endure a situation created by the negligence of the defendant, it relieves the defendant from performing a duty which might otherwise be owed to the plaintiff. McEvoy v. City of New York, 266 A.D. 445, 447, 42 N.Y.S.2d 746, 749 (2d Dep't 1943), aff'd, 292 N.Y. 654, 55 N.E.2d 517 (1944). While assumption of risk, like contributory negligence, barred recovery, it was predicated on a theory of contract rather than on a theory of culpable conduct: the plaintiff's agreement, either express or implied, to absolve the defendant from responsibility. Arbegast, 65 N.Y.2d at 165, 480 N.E.2d at 368, 490 N.Y.S.2d at 754. "Express" assumption of risk resulted from an advance agreement that the defendant need not use reasonable care for the plaintiff's benefit. "Implied" assumption of risk, on the other hand, was founded on plaintiff's unreasonable and voluntary consent to the risk of harm from defendant's conduct with full understanding of the possible harm. Id. at 169, 480 N.E.2d at 371, 490 N.Y.S.2d at 757; Restatement (Second) of Torts 496B, 496E.

In 1975, New York's Civil Practice Law and Rules were amended by the addition of a pure comparative negligence statute, Act of May 6, 1975, ch. 69, 1975 N.Y. Laws 94, applicable prospectively as follows:

> In any action to recover damages for personal injury, injury to property, or wrongful death, the culpable conduct attributable to the claimant or to the decedent, including contributory negligence or assumption of risk, shall not bar recovery, but the amount of damages otherwise recoverable shall be diminished in the proportion which the culpable conduct attributable to the claimant or decedent bears to the culpable conduct which caused the damages.

N.Y.Civ.Prac.L. & R. 1411 (McKinney 1976) (emphasis supplied). By including "assumption of risk" as culpable conduct of the plaintiff that would diminish damages proportionately, the plain language of N.Y.Civ.Prac.L. & R. 1411 seemingly abolished assumption of risk as a complete bar to recovery. However, while the common law distinguished between express and implied assumption of risk, neither section 1411 nor its legislative history defined the phrase or discussed the difference between express and implied assumption of risk.

In accord with the plain language of the statute and the legislative intent expressed in the Report to the 1975 Legislature by the Judicial Conference of the State of New York 21–22 (Feb. 1, 1975) reprinted in 1975 N.Y. Laws 1485 ("it is expected that the courts will treat assumption of risk as a form of culpable conduct under this article"), commentators assumed that under the new comparative negligence statute assumption of risk was no longer a total bar to recovery, but simply diminished the amount of damages recoverable. See 1B Warren's N.Y. Negligence 2.03, at 1028 (rev. 2d ed. 1980); N.Y.Civ.Prac.L. & R. 1411 practice commentary (McKinney 1976). However, the failure of the statute to define assumption of risk or to distinguish express from implied assumption of risk, and the different theoretical bases upon which assumption of risk and contributory negligence rest, suggested that express assumption of risk might not be subject to the comparative fault provisions of section 1411.

In 1985, the Court of Appeals of New York discussed section 1411 and its effect on the doctrine of express assumption of risk in Arbegast v. Board of Educ., 65 N.Y.2d 161, 480 N.E.2d 365, 490 N.Y.S.2d 751 (1985). The court held that express assumption of risk would provide a complete defense, while implied assumption of risk was subsumed by N.Y.Civ.Prac.L. & R. 1411:

> CPLR 1411 requires diminishment of damages in the case of an implied assumption of risk but, except as public policy proscribes an agreement limiting liability, does not foreclose a complete defense that by express consent of the injured party no duty exists and, therefore, no recovery may be had.

Arbegast, 65 N.Y.2d at 170, 480 N.E.2d at 371, 490 N.Y.S.2d at 757–58 (footnote omitted). In reaching this conclusion the court reasoned that prior to enactment of the pure comparative negligence statute, the law had recognized that contractual limitations of liability did not violate public policy "except as specific statutes imposed limitations upon such agreements or interdicted them entirely." Id. at 169–70, 480 N.E.2d at 371, 490 N.Y.S.2d at 757 (citations omitted).

In the case before us, appellees contend that it is against public policy for one expressly to assume the risk of medical malpractice and thereby dissolve the physician's duty to treat a patient according to medical community standards. We first note that the "public policy" referred to by the Arbegast court is defined solely by statute, id., and appellant points to no statute imposing limitations on such express agreements. Moreover, we see no reason why a patient should not be allowed to make an informed decision to go outside currently approved medical methods in search of an unconventional treatment. While a patient should be encouraged to exercise care for his own safety, we believe that an informed decision to avoid surgery and conventional chemotherapy is within the patient's right "to determine what shall be done with his own body," Schloendorff v. Society of the New York Hospital, 211 N.Y. 125, 129, 105 N.E. 92 (1914) (Cardozo, J.) (overruled on other grounds by Bing v. Thunig, 2 N.Y.2d 656, 143 N.E.2d 3, 163 N.Y.S.2d 3 (1957)). Finally, we note that in a recent post-Arbegast case, the Court of Appeals of New York applied the Arbegast distinction between express and implied assumption of risk to a medical malpractice action. In Resnick v. Gribetz, 66 N.Y.2d 729, 487 N.E.2d 908, 496 N.Y.S.2d 998 (1985), the defendant doctor contended that plaintiff's refusal to undergo a suggested biopsy amounted to an assumption of risk. The court, citing Arbegast, ruled that the trial court erred in charging the jury that assumption of risk would bar recovery when no evidence supported a finding of express, as opposed to implied, assumption of risk.

While we do not determine, in the case before us, whether Mrs. Schneider expressly assumed the risk of Dr. Revici's treatment, we hold that there existed sufficient evidence—in the language of the Consent for Medical Care form that she signed, and in testimony relating to specific consent informed by her awareness of the risk of refusing conventional treatment to undergo the Revici method—to allow the jury to consider express assumption of risk as an affirmative defense that would totally bar recovery. It was therefore error for the district court to deny the defendants' request for a jury charge on the issue, and we reverse and remand for that reason.

III. CONCLUSION

To summarize, we hold that the district court erred in refusing to charge the jury with the affirmative defense of express assumption of risk, and therefore reverse the judgment and remand the case to the district court for a new trial limited to the issue of assumption of risk.

* * *

Charell v. Gonzalez
Supreme Court of New York, New York County
173 Misc. 2d 227 (1997)

Edward H. Lehner, J.

[The full text of this judicial opinion is available at p. 179, *infra*.]

* * *

On the question of assumption of risk, the jury was asked both whether plaintiff expressly assumed the risk of injury to herself in agreeing to defendant's protocol (a finding of which would have exonerated defendant), and whether she impliedly assumed a risk of injury (a finding of which would, and did, bring into play the comparative fault provisions of CPLR article 14-A). (See, Arbegast v. Board of Educ., 65 NY2d 161 [1985]).

With respect to the jury determination that plaintiff "impliedly" assumed risk of injury to herself in agreeing to undergo the treatment, plaintiff's counsel states that the question thus posed is "whether or not plaintiff had knowledge and a full understanding of the risks of harm of defendant's proposed treatment from a source other than defendant himself" (plaintiff's mem of law, at 7). Counsel argues that she did not. However, the evidence showed that plaintiff was a well-educated person who, together with her husband and daughter, did a significant amount of investigation regarding the treatment being offered by defendant and hence became quite knowledgeable on the subject, and that she sought to avoid the suffering that accompanied the chemotherapy/radiation regimen that she had witnessed when a relative had undertaken that treatment. Thus, even though the jury found that defendant had not given appropriate information regarding the risks of his procedure and the available alternatives, it was within the province of the jury, based on the evidence, for it to also find that plaintiff independently obtained sufficient information about the treatment so as to conclude that there was an implied assumption of risk when she agreed to follow defendant's protocol. (See, Boyle v. Revici, supra; Schneider v. Revici, supra.)

* * *

Chapter Five

Informed Consent

I. Introduction

A. Early Foundations

During the last thirty years, Congress, state legislatures, and federal and state administrative agencies have developed a number of statutory and regulatory provisions that govern the doctrine, form, and process of informed consent to treatment. *See* Chapter 5, § 2(B), *infra*. The common law, however, provided the earliest legal recognition of a duty to obtain a patient's prior consent to medical or surgical treatment. In the 1914 decision in *Schloendorff v. Society of New York Hospital*, reprinted in part below, one of the threshold questions before the Court of Appeals of New York was whether damages could be imposed for a surgeon's failure to obtain a patient's informed consent prior to stomach surgery. Although a conventional surgeon, not an alternative health care practitioner, operated on Mrs. Schloendorff, the opinion provides a foundation for later applications of the doctrine of informed consent to cases involving complementary and alternative medicine.

Schloendorff v. The Society of New York Hospital
Court of Appeals of New York
211 N.Y. 125 (1914)

Cardozo, J.

In the year 1771, by royal charter of George III., the Society of the New York Hospital was organized for the care and healing of the sick.

* * *

To this hospital the plaintiff came in January, 1908. She was suffering from some disorder of the stomach. She asked the superintendent or one of his assistants what the charge would be and was told that it would be $7 a week. She became an inmate of the hospital, and after some weeks of treatment the house physician, Dr. Bartlett, discovered a lump, which proved to be a fibroid tumor. He consulted the visiting surgeon, Dr. Stimson, who advised an operation. The plaintiff's testimony is that the character of the lump could not, so the physicians informed her, be determined without an ether examination. She consented to such an examination, but notified Dr. Bartlett, as she says, that there must be no operation. She was taken at night from the medical to the surgical ward and prepared for an operation by a nurse. On the following day ether was administered, and while she was unconscious a tumor was removed. Her testimony is that this was done without her consent or knowledge. She is contradicted both by Dr. Stimson and by Dr. Bartlett, as well as by many of the attendant nurses. For the purpose of this appeal, however, since a verdict was directed in favor of the defendant, her narrative, even if improbable, must be taken as true. Following the operation, and, according to the testimony of her witnesses, because of it, gangrene developed in her left arm; some of her fingers had to be amputated; and her sufferings were intense. She now seeks to charge the hospital with liability for the wrong.

* * *

In the case at hand, the wrong complained of is not merely negligence. It is trespass. Every human being of adult years and sound mind has a right to determine what shall be done with his own body; and a surgeon who performs an operation without his patient's consent, commits an assault, for which he is liable in damages. (Pratt v. Davis, 224 Ill. 300; Mohr v. Williams, 95 Minn. 261.) This is true except in cases of emergency where the patient is unconscious and where it is necessary to operate before consent can be obtained. The fact that the wrong complained of here is trespass rather than negligence, distinguishes this case from most of the cases that have preceded it. In such circumstances the hospital's exemption from liability can hardly rest upon implied waiver. Relatively to this transaction, the plaintiff was a stranger. She had never consented to become a patient for any purpose other than an examination under ether. She had never waived the right to recover damages for any wrong resulting from this operation, for she had forbidden the operation.

* * *

… I do not think that anything said by the plaintiff to any of the defendant's nurses fairly gave notice to them that the purpose was to cut open the plaintiff's body without her consent. The visiting surgeon in charge of the case was one of the most eminent in the city of New York. The assistant physicians and surgeons were men of tested merit. The plaintiff was prepared for the operation at night. She said to the night nurse, according to her statement, that she was not going to be operated on, that she was merely going to be examined under the influence of ether, and the nurse professed to understand that this was so. "Every now and then I asked, 'Do you understand that I am not to be operated on?' 'Yes, I understand; ether examination.' 'But,' I asked, 'I understand that this preparation is for operation.' She said, 'It is just the same in ether examination as in operation—the same preparation.'" The nurse with whom this conversation is said to have occurred left the ward early in the morning, and the operation was performed in her absence the following afternoon. Was she to infer from the plaintiff's words that a distinguished surgeon intended to mutilate the plaintiff's body in defiance of the plaintiff's orders? Was it her duty, as a result of this talk, to report to the superintendent of the hospital that the ward was about to be utilized for the commission of an assault? I think that no such interpretation of the facts would have suggested itself to any reasonable mind. The preparation for an ether examination is to some extent the same as for an operation. The hour was midnight, and the plaintiff was nervous and excited. The nurse soothed her by acquiescing in the statement that an ether examination was all that was then intended. An ether examination was intended, and how soon the operation was to follow, if at all, the nurse had no means of knowing. Still less had she reason to suspect that it would follow against the plaintiff's orders. If, when the following afternoon came, the plaintiff persisted in being unwilling to submit to an operation, the presumption was that the distinguished surgeon in charge of the case would perform none. There may be cases where a patient ought not to be advised of a contemplated operation until shortly before the appointed hour. To discuss such a subject at midnight might cause needless and even harmful agitation. About such matters a nurse is not qualified to judge. She is drilled to habits of strict obedience. She is accustomed to rely unquestioningly upon the judgment of her superiors. No woman occupying such a position would reasonably infer from the plaintiff's words that it was the purpose of the surgeons to operate whether the plaintiff forbade it or not. I conclude, therefore, that the plaintiff's statements to the nurse on the night before the operation are insufficient to charge the hospital with notice of a contemplated wrong. I can conceive of cases where a patient's struggles or outcries in the effort to avoid an operation might be such as to give notice to the administrative staff that the surgeons were acting in disregard of their patient's commands. In such circumstances, it may well be that by permitting its facilities to be utilized for such a purpose without resistance or at least protest, the hospital would make itself a party to the trespass, and become liable as a joint tort feasor. (Sharp v. Erie R. R. Co., 184 N. Y. 100.) I do not find in this record the elements necessary to call that principle into play.

Still more clearly, the defendant is not chargeable with notice because of the plaintiff's statements to the physician who administered the gas and ether. She says she asked him whether an operation was to be performed, and that he told her he did not know; that his duty was to give the gas, and nothing more. She answered that she wished to tell some one that there must be no operation; that she had come merely for an ether examination, and he told her that if she had come only for examination, nothing else would be done. There is nothing in the record to suggest that he believed anything to the contrary. He took no part in the operation, and had no knowledge of it. After the gas was administered she was taken into another room. It does not appear, therefore, that this physician was a party to any wrong....

* * *

The judgment should be affirmed, with costs.

* * *

Note and Questions

1. *Available Causes of Action.* The Court of Appeals of New York stated in 1914 that the cause of action for a surgeon's failure to obtain informed consent should be assault. *Schloendorff*, 211 N.Y. at 129–30. Today, most jurisdictions classify failure to obtain informed consent claims as battery (if no consent was obtained) or negligence (if the physician technically obtained the patient's consent but failed to disclose a material risk to the patient and then such risk materialized). *See, e.g.*, Tex. Civ. Prac. & Rem. Code §74.101 ("In a suit against a physician or health care provider involving a health care liability claim that is based on the failure of the physician or health care provider to disclose or adequately disclose the risks and hazards involved in the medical care or surgical procedure rendered by the physician or health care provider, the only theory on which recovery may be obtained is that of negligence in failing to disclose the risks or hazards that could have influenced a reasonable person in making a decision to give or withhold consent."); *SpineCare Med. Group, Inc.*, 52 Cal. App. 4th 1285, 131 (1997) (quoting an earlier opinion of the California Supreme Court for the following principles: "The battery theory should be reserved for those circumstances when a doctor performs an operation to which the patient has not consented. When the patient gives permission to perform one type of treatment and the doctor performs another, the requisite element of deliberate intent to deviate from the consent given is present. However, when the patient consents to certain treatment and the doctor performs that treatment but an undisclosed inherent compli-

cation with a low probability occurs, no intentional deviation from the consent given appears; rather, the doctor in obtaining consent may have failed to meet his due care duty to disclose pertinent information."). What are the benefits to the plaintiff of grounding a cause of action for failure to obtain informed consent in battery? In negligence? Does the battery cause of action require proof of causation? Of damages? The use of expert testimony? Does the negligence cause of action require proof of specific or general intent? Which cause of action, battery or negligence, usually has a longer statute of limitations? Some of these questions are addressed in the *Canterbury v. Spence* case, presented immediately below.

B. The Patient Standard

Following *Schloendorff*'s recognition of a cause of action for failure to obtain a patient's informed consent prior to a proposed medical or surgical procedure, the courts were forced to address the required scope of disclosure. Should a physician have a duty to disclose information that a reasonably prudent physician in the same or similar circumstances would disclose? Or, should a physician have a duty to disclose information that a reasonably prudent patient in the same or similar circumstances would consider material in making a decision about whether to consent to the proposed medical or surgical procedure?

In *Canterbury v. Spence*, reprinted in part below, a surgeon allegedly failed to disclose to the patient certain risks of a proposed laminectomy. Although the defendant in *Canterbury* was a conventional surgeon, not an alternative health care practitioner, the opinion provides a wonderful overview of the development of the common law doctrine of informed consent to treatment as well as a few doctrinal exceptions. The opinion also examines the different informed consent disclosure standards, problems relating to causation, the burden of proof in informed consent cases, the need for expert testimony, and relevant statutes of limitation.

Canterbury v. Spence
The United States Court of Appeals for the District of Columbia Circuit
464 F.2d 772 (1972)

Spottswood W. Robinson, III, Circuit Judge:

This appeal is from a judgment entered in the District Court on verdicts directed for the two appellees at the conclusion of plaintiff-appellant Canterbury's case in chief. His action sought damages for personal injuries allegedly sustained as a result of an operation negligently performed by appellee Spence, a negligent failure by Dr. Spence to disclose a risk of serious disability inherent in the operation, and negligent post-operative care by appellee Washington Hospital Center. On close examination of the record, we find evidence which required submission of these issues to the jury. We accordingly reverse the judgment as to each appellee and remand the case to the District Court for a new trial.

I.

The record we review tells a depressing tale. A youth troubled only by back pain submitted to an operation without being informed of a risk of paralysis incidental thereto. A day after the operation he fell from his hospital bed after having been left without assistance while voiding. A few hours after the fall, the lower half of his body was paralyzed, and he had to be operated on again. Despite extensive medical care, he has never been what he was before. Instead of the back pain, even years later, he hobbled about on crutches, a victim of paralysis of the bowels and urinary incontinence. In a very real sense this lawsuit is an understandable search for reasons.

At the time of the events which gave rise to this litigation, appellant was nineteen years of age, a clerk-typist employed by the Federal Bureau of Investigation. In December, 1958, he began to experience severe pain between his shoulder blades. He consulted two general practitioners, but the medications they prescribed failed to eliminate the pain. Thereafter, appellant secured an appointment with Dr. Spence, who is a neurosurgeon....

* * *

Dr. Spence examined appellant in his office at some length but found nothing amiss. On Dr. Spence's advice appellant was x-rayed, but the films did not identify any abnormality. Dr. Spence then recommended that appellant undergo a myelogram—a procedure in which dye is injected into the spinal column and traced to find evidence of disease or other disorder—at the Washington Hospital Center.

Appellant entered the hospital on February 4, 1959. The myelogram revealed a "filling defect" in the region of the fourth thoracic vertebra. Since a myelogram often does no more than pinpoint the location of an aberration, surgery may be necessary to discover the cause. Dr. Spence told appellant that he would have to undergo a laminectomy—the excision of the posterior arch of the vertebra—to correct what he suspected was a ruptured disc. Appellant did not raise any objection to the proposed operation nor did he probe into its exact nature.

* * *

Appellant explained to Dr. Spence that his mother was a widow of slender financial means living in Cyclone, West Virginia, and that she could be reached through a neighbor's telephone. Appellant called his mother the day after the myelogram was performed and, failing to contact her, left Dr. Spence's telephone number with the neighbor. When Mrs. Canterbury returned the call, Dr. Spence told her that the surgery was occasioned by a suspected ruptured disc. Mrs. Canterbury then asked if the recommended operation was serious and Dr. Spence replied "not anymore than any other operation." He added that he knew Mrs. Canterbury was not well off and that her presence in Washington would not be necessary. The testimony is contradictory as to whether during the course of the conversation Mrs. Canterbury expressed her consent to the operation. Appellant himself apparently did not converse again with Dr. Spence prior to the operation.

Dr. Spence performed the laminectomy on February 11 ... at the Washington Hospital Center. Mrs. Canterbury traveled to Washington, arriving on that date but after the operation was over, and signed a consent form at the hospital. The laminectomy revealed several anomalies: a spinal cord that was swollen and unable to pulsate, an accumulation of large tortuous and dilated veins, and a complete absence of epidural fat which normally surrounds the spine. A thin hypodermic needle was inserted into the spinal cord to aspirate any cysts which might have been present, but no fluid emerged. In suturing the wound, Dr. Spence attempted to relieve the pressure on the spinal cord by enlarging the dura—the outer protective wall of the spinal cord—at the area of swelling.

* * *

For approximately the first day after the operation appellant recuperated normally, but then suffered a fall and an almost immediate setback. Since there is some conflict as to precisely when or why appellant fell, we reconstruct the events from the evidence most favorable to him. Dr. Spence left orders that appellant was to remain in bed during the process of voiding. These orders were changed to direct that voiding be done out of bed, and the jury could find that the change was made by hospital personnel. Just prior to the fall, appellant summoned a nurse and was given a receptacle for use in voiding, but was then left unattended. Appellant testified that during the course of the endeavor he slipped off the side of the bed, and that there was no one to assist him, or side rail to prevent the fall.

* * *

Several hours later, appellant began to complain that he could not move his legs and that he was having trouble breathing; paralysis seems to have been virtually total from the waist down. Dr. Spence was notified on the night of February 12, and he rushed to the hospital. Mrs. Canterbury signed another consent form and appellant was again taken into the operating room. The surgical wound was reopened and Dr. Spense [Ed.: sic] created a gusset to allow the spinal cord greater room in which to pulsate.

Appellant's control over his muscles improved somewhat after the second operation but he was unable to void properly. As a result of this condition, he came under the care of a urologist while still in the hospital. In April, following a cystoscopic examination, appellant was operated on for removal of bladder stones, and in May was released from the hospital. He reentered the hospital the following August for a 10-day period, apparently because of his urologic problems. For several years after his discharge he was under the care of several specialists, and at all times was under the care of a urologist. At the time of the trial in April, 1968, appellant required crutches to walk, still suffered from urinal incontinence and paralysis of the bowels, and wore a penile clamp.

In November, 1959 on Dr. Spence's recommendation, appellant was transferred by the F.B.I. to Miami where he could get more swimming and exercise. Appellant worked three years for the F.B.I. in Miami, Los Angeles and Houston, resigning finally in June, 1962. From then until the time of the trial, he held a number of jobs, but had constant trouble finding work because he needed to remain seated and close to a bathroom. The damages appellant claims include extensive pain and suffering, medical expenses, and loss of earnings.

II.

Appellant filed suit in the District Court on March 7, 1963, four years after the laminectomy and approximately two years after he attained his majority. The complaint stated several causes of action against each defendant. Against Dr. Spence it alleged, among other things, negligence in the performance of the laminectomy and failure to inform him beforehand of the risk involved. Against the hospital the complaint charged negligent postoperative care in permitting appellant to remain unattended after the laminectomy, in failing to provide a nurse or orderly to assist him at the time of his fall, and in failing to maintain a side rail on his bed. The answers denied the allegations of negligence and defended on the ground that the suit was barred by the statute of limitations.

Pretrial discovery—including depositions by appellant, his mother and Dr. Spence—continuances and other delays consumed five years. At trial, disposition of the threshold question whether the statute of limitations had run was held in abeyance until the relevant facts developed. Appellant introduced no evidence to show medical and hospital practices, if any, customarily pursued in regard to the critical aspects of the case, and only Dr. Spence, called as an adverse witness, testified on the issue of causality. Dr. Spence described the surgical procedures he utilized in the two operations and expressed his opinion that appellant's disabilities stemmed from his pre-operative condition as symptomatized by the swollen, non-pulsating spinal cord. He stated, however, that neither he nor any of the other physicians with whom he consulted was certain as to what that condition was, and he admitted that trauma can be a cause of paralysis. Dr. Spence further testified that even without trauma paralysis can be anticipated "somewhere in the nature of one percent" of the laminectomies performed, a risk he termed "a very slight possibility." He felt that communication of that risk to the patient is not good medical practice because it might deter patients from undergoing needed surgery and might produce adverse psychological reactions which could preclude the success of the operation.

At the close of appellant's case in chief, each defendant moved for a directed verdict and the trial judge granted both motions. The basis of the ruling, he explained, was that appellant had failed to produce any medical evidence indicating negligence on Dr. Spence's part in diagnosing appellant's malady or in performing the laminectomy; that there was no proof that Dr. Spence's treatment was responsible for appellant's disabilities; and that notwithstanding some evidence to show negligent post-operative care, an absence of medical testimony to show causality precluded submission of the case against the hospital to the jury. The judge did not allude specifically to the alleged breach of duty by Dr. Spence to divulge the possible consequences of the laminectomy.

We reverse. The testimony of appellant and his mother that Dr. Spence did not reveal the risk of paralysis from the laminectomy made out a prima facie case of violation of the physician's duty to disclose which Dr. Spence's explanation did not negate as a matter of law. There was also testimony from which the jury could have found that the laminectomy was negligently performed by Dr. Spence, and that appellant's fall was the consequence of negligence on the part of the hospital. The record, moreover, contains evidence of sufficient quantity and quality to tender jury issues as to whether and to what extent any such negligence was causally related to appellant's post-laminectomy condition. These considerations entitled appellant to a new trial.

Elucidation of our reasoning necessitates elaboration on a number of points. In Parts III and IV we explore the origins and rationale of the physician's duty to reasonably inform an ailing patient as to the treatment alternatives available and the risks incidental to them. In Part V we investigate the scope of the disclosure requirement and in Part VI the physician's privileges not to disclose. In Part VII we examine the role of causality, and in Part VIII the need for expert testimony in non-disclosure litigation.... [I]n Part X we apply the principles discussed to the case at bar.

* * *

III.

Suits charging failure by a physician adequately to disclose the risks and alternatives of proposed treatment are not innovations in American law. They date back a good half-century, and in the last decade they have multiplied rapidly. There is, nonetheless, disagreement among the courts and the commentators on many major questions, and there is no precedent of our own directly in point. For the tools enabling resolution of the issues on this appeal, we are forced to begin at first principles.

* * *

The root premise is the concept, fundamental in American jurisprudence, that "every human being of adult years and sound mind has a right to determine what shall be done with his own body...." True consent to what happens to one's self is the informed exercise of a choice, and that entails an opportunity to evaluate knowledgeably the options available and the risks attendant upon each. The average patient has little or no understanding of the medical arts, and ordinarily has only his physician to whom he can look for enlightenment with which to reach an intelligent decision. From these almost axiomatic considerations springs the need, and in turn the requirement, of a reasonable divulgence by physician to patient to make such a decision possible.

* * *

In duty-to-disclose cases, the focus of attention is more properly upon the nature and content of the physician's divulgence than the patient's understanding or consent. Adequate disclosure and informed consent are, of course, two sides of the same coin — the former a sine qua non of the latter. But the vital inquiry on duty to disclose relates to the physician's performance of an obligation, while one of the difficulties with analysis in terms of "informed consent" is its tendency to imply that what is decisive is the degree of the patient's comprehension. As we later emphasize, the physician discharges the duty when he makes a reasonable effort to convey sufficient information although the patient, without fault of the physician, may not fully grasp it. Even though the fact-finder may have occasion to draw an inference on the state of the patient's enlightenment, the fact-finding process on performance of the duty ultimately reaches back to what the physician actually said or failed to say. And while the factual conclusion on adequacy of the revelation will vary as between patients — as, for example, between a lay patient and a physician-patient — the fluctuations are attributable to the kind of divulgence which may be reasonable under the circumstances.

* * *

A physician is under a duty to treat his patient skillfully but proficiency in diagnosis and therapy is not the full measure of his responsibility. The cases demonstrate that the physician is under an obligation to communicate specific information to the patient when the exigencies of reasonable care call for it. Due care may require a physician perceiving symptoms of bodily abnormality to alert the patient to the condition. It may call upon the physician confronting an ailment which does not respond to his ministrations to inform the patient thereof. It may command the physician to instruct the patient as to any limitations to be presently observed for his own welfare, and as to any precautionary therapy he should seek in the future. It may oblige the physician to advise the patient of the need for or desirability of any alternative treatment promising greater benefit than that being pursued. Just as plainly, due care normally demands that the physician warn the patient of any risks to his well-being which contemplated therapy may involve.

* * *

The context in which the duty of risk-disclosure arises is invariably the occasion for decision as to whether a particular treatment procedure is to be undertaken. To the physician, whose training enables a self-satisfying evaluation, the answer may seem clear, but it is the prerogative of the patient, not the physician, to determine for himself the direction in which his interests seem to lie. To enable the patient to chart his course understandably, some familiarity with the therapeutic alternatives and their hazards becomes essential.

* * *

A reasonable revelation in these respects is not only a necessity but, as we see it, is as much a matter of the physician's duty. It is a duty to warn of the dangers lurking in the proposed treatment, and that is surely a facet of due care. It is, too, a duty to impart information which the patient has every right to expect. The patient's reliance upon the physician is a trust of the kind which traditionally has exacted obligations beyond those associated with armslength transactions. His dependence upon the physician for information affecting his well-being, in terms of contemplated treatment, is well-nigh abject. As earlier noted, long before the instant litigation arose, courts had recognized that the physician had the responsibility of satisfying the vital informational needs of the patient. More recently, we ourselves have found "in the fiducial qualities of [the physician-patient] relationship the physician's duty to reveal to the patient that which in his best interests it is important that he should know." We now find, as a part of the physician's overall obligation to the patient, a similar duty of reasonable disclosure of the choices with respect to proposed therapy and the dangers inherently and potentially involved.

This disclosure requirement, on analysis, reflects much more of a change in doctrinal emphasis than a substantive addition to malpractice law. It is well established that the physician must seek and secure his patient's consent before commencing an operation or other course of treatment. It is also clear that the consent, to be efficacious, must be free from imposition upon the patient. It is the settled rule that therapy not authorized by the patient may amount to a tort—a common law battery—by the physician. And it is evident that it is normally impossible to obtain a consent worthy of the name unless the physician first elucidates the options and the perils for the patient's edification. Thus the physician has long borne a duty, on pain of liability for unauthorized treatment, to make adequate disclosure to the patient. The evolution of the obligation to communicate for the patient's benefit as well as the physician's protection has hardly involved an extraordinary restructuring of the law.

IV.

Duty to disclose has gained recognition in a large number of American jurisdictions, but more largely on a different rationale. The majority of courts dealing with the problem have made the duty depend on whether it was the custom of physicians practicing in the community to make the particular disclosure to the patient. If so, the physician may be held liable for an unreasonable and injurious failure to divulge, but there can be no recovery unless the omission forsakes a practice prevalent in the profession. We agree that the physician's noncompliance with a professional custom to reveal, like any other departure from prevailing medical practice, may give rise to liability to the patient. We do not agree that the patient's cause of action is dependent upon the existence and nonperformance of a relevant professional tradition.

There are, in our view, formidable obstacles to acceptance of the notion that the physician's obligation to disclose is either germinated or limited by medical practice. To begin with, the reality of any discernible custom reflecting a professional consensus on communication of option and risk information to patients is open to serious doubt. We sense the danger that what in fact is no custom at all may be taken as an affirmative custom to maintain silence, and that physician-witnesses to the so-called custom may state merely their personal opinions as to what they or others would do under given conditions. We cannot gloss over the inconsistency between reliance on a general practice respecting divulgence and, on the other hand, realization that the myriad of variables among patients makes each case so different that its omission can rationally be justified only by the effect of its individual circumstances. Nor can we ignore the fact that to bind the disclosure obligation to medical usage is to arrogate the decision on revelation to the physician alone. Respect for the patient's right of self-determination on particular therapy demands a standard set by law for physicians rather than one which physicians may or may not impose upon themselves.

More fundamentally, the majority rule overlooks the graduation of reasonable-care demands in Anglo-American jurisprudence and the position of professional custom in the hierarchy. The caliber of the performance exacted by the reasonable-care standard varies between the professional and non-professional worlds, and so also the role of professional custom. "With but few exceptions," we recently declared, "society demands that everyone under a duty to use care observe minimally a general standard." "Familiarly expressed judicially," we added, "the yardstick is that degree of care which a reasonably prudent person would have exercised under the same or similar circumstances." "Beyond this," however, we emphasized, "the law requires those engaging in activities requiring unique knowledge and ability to give a performance commensurate with the undertaking." Thus physicians treating the sick must perform at higher levels than non-physicians in order to meet the reasonable care standard in its special application to physicians — "that degree of care and skill ordinarily exercised by the profession in [the physician's] own or similar localities." And practices adopted by the profession have indispensable value as evidence tending to establish just what that degree of care and skill is.

We have admonished, however, that "the special medical standards are but adaptions of the general standard to a group who are required to act as reasonable men possessing their medical talents presumably would." There is, by the same token, no basis for operation of the special medical standard where the physician's activity does not bring his medical knowledge and skills peculiarly into play. And where the challenge to the physician's conduct is not to be gauged by the special standard, it follows that medical custom cannot furnish the test of its propriety, whatever its relevance under the proper test may be. The decision to unveil the patient's condition and the chances as to remediation, as we shall see, is ofttimes a non-medical judgment and, if so, is a decision outside the ambit of the special standard. Where that is the situation, professional custom hardly furnishes the legal criterion for measuring the physician's responsibility to reasonably inform his patient of the options and the hazards as to treatment.

The majority rule, moreover, is at war with our prior holdings that a showing of medical practice, however probative, does not fix the standard governing recovery for medical malpractice. Prevailing medical practice, we have maintained, has evidentiary value in determinations as to what the specific criteria measuring challenged professional conduct are and whether they have been met, but does not itself define the standard. That has been our position in treatment cases, where the physician's performance is ordinarily to be adjudicated by the special medical standard of due care. We see no logic in a different rule for nondisclosure cases, where the governing standard is much more largely divorced from professional considerations. And surely in nondisclosure cases the factfinder is not invariably functioning in an area of such technical complexity that it must be bound to medical custom as an inexorable application of the community standard of reasonable care.

Thus we distinguished, for purposes of duty to disclose, the special and general-standard aspects of the physician-patient relationship. When medical judgment enters the picture and for that reason the special standard controls, prevailing medical practice must be given its just due. In all other instances, however, the general standard exacting ordinary care applies, and that standard is set by law. In sum, the physician's duty to disclose is governed by the same legal principles applicable to others in comparable situations, with modifications only to the extent that medical judgment enters the picture. We hold that the standard measuring performance of that duty by physicians, as by others, is conduct which is reasonable under the circumstances.

V.

Once the circumstances give rise to a duty on the physician's part to inform his patient, the next inquiry is the scope of the disclosure the physician is legally obliged to make. The courts have frequently confronted this problem but no uniform standard defining the adequacy of the divulgence emerges from the decisions. Some have said "full" disclosure, a norm we are unwilling to adopt literally. It seems obviously prohibitive and unrealistic to expect physicians to discuss with their patients every risk of proposed treatment—no matter how small or remote—and generally unnecessary from the patient's viewpoint as well. Indeed, the cases speaking in terms of "full" disclosure appear to envision something less than total disclosure, leaving unanswered the question of just how much.

The larger number of courts, as might be expected, have applied tests framed with reference to prevailing fashion within the medical profession. Some have measured the disclosure by "good medical practice," others by what a reasonable practitioner would have bared under the circumstances, and still others by what medical custom in the community would demand. We have explored this rather considerable body of law but are unprepared to follow it. The duty to disclose, we have reasoned, arises from phenomena apart from medical custom and practice. The latter, we think, should no more establish the scope of the duty than its existence. Any definition of scope in terms purely of a professional standard is at odds with the patient's prerogative to decide on projected therapy himself. That prerogative, we have said, is at the very foundation of the duty to disclose, and both the patient's right to know and the physician's correlative obligation to tell him are diluted to the extent that its compass is dictated by the medical profession.

In our view, the patient's right of self-decision shapes the boundaries of the duty to reveal. That right can be effectively exercised only if the patient possesses enough information to enable an intelligent choice. The scope of the physician's communications to the patient, then, must be measured by the patient's need, and that need is the information material to the decision. Thus the test for determining whether a particular peril must be divulged is its materiality to the patient's decision: all risks potentially affecting the decision must be unmasked. And to safeguard the patient's interest in achieving his own determination on treatment, the law must itself set the standard for adequate disclosure.

Optimally for the patient, exposure of a risk would be mandatory whenever the patient would deem it significant to his decision, either singly or in combination with other risks. Such a requirement, however, would summon the physician to second-guess the patient, whose ideas on materiality could hardly be known to the physician. That would make an undue demand upon medical practitioners, whose conduct, like that of others, is to be measured in terms of reasonableness. Consonantly with orthodox negligence doctrine, the physician's liability for nondisclosure is to be determined on the basis of foresight, not hindsight; no less than any other aspect of negligence, the issue on nondisclosure must be approached from the viewpoint of the reasonableness of the physician's divulgence in terms of what he knows or should know to be the patient's informational needs. If, but only if, the fact-finder can say that the physician's communication was unreasonably inadequate is an imposition of liability legally or morally justified.

Of necessity, the content of the disclosure rests in the first instance with the physician. Ordinarily it is only he who is in position to identify particular dangers; always he must make a judgment, in terms of materiality, as to whether and to what extent revelation to the patient is called for. He cannot know with complete exactitude what the patient would consider important to his decision, but on the basis of his medical training and experience he can sense how the average, reasonable patient expectably would react. Indeed, with knowledge of, or ability to learn, his patient's background and current condition, he is in a position superior to that of most others—attorneys, for example—who are called upon to make judgments on pain of liability in damages for unreasonable miscalculation.

From these considerations we derive the breadth of the disclosure of risks legally to be required. The scope of the standard is not subjective as to either the physician or the patient; it remains objective with due regard for the patient's informational needs and with suitable leeway for the physician's situation. In broad outline, we agree that "[a] risk is thus material when a reasonable person, in what the physician knows or should know to be the patient's position, would be likely to attach significance to the risk or cluster of risks in deciding whether or not to forego the proposed therapy."

The category of risks which the physician should communicate is, of course, no broader than the complement he could communicate. See Block v. McVay, 80 S.D. 469, 126 N.W.2d 808, 812 (1964). The duty to divulge may extend to any risk he actually knows, but he obviously cannot divulge any of which he may be unaware. Nondisclosure of an unknown risk does not, strictly speaking, present a problem in terms of the duty to disclose although it very well might pose problems in terms of the physician's duties to have known of it and to have acted accordingly. See Waltz & Scheuneman, Informed Consent to Therapy, 64 N.W.U.L.Rev. 628, 630–35 (1970). We have no occasion to explore problems of the latter type on this appeal.

The topics importantly demanding a communication of information are the inherent and potential hazards of the proposed treatment, the alternatives to that treatment, if any, and the results likely if the patient remains untreated. The factors contributing significance to the dangerousness of a medical technique are, of course, the incidence of injury and the degree of the harm threatened. A very small chance of death or serious disablement may well be significant; a potential disability which dramatically outweighs the potential benefit of the therapy or the detriments of the existing malady may summons discussion with the patient.

There is no bright line separating the significant from the insignificant; the answer in any case must abide a rule of reason. Some dangers—infection, for example—are inherent in any operation; there is no obligation to communicate those of which persons of average sophistication are aware. Even more clearly, the physician bears no responsibility for discussion of hazards the patient has already discovered, or those having no apparent materiality to patients' decision on therapy. The disclosure doctrine, like others marking lines between permissible and impermissible behavior in medical practice, is in essence a requirement of conduct prudent under the circumstances. Whenever nondisclosure of particular risk information is open to debate by reasonable-minded men, the issue is for the finder of the facts.

VI.

Two exceptions to the general rule of disclosure have been noted by the courts. Each is in the nature of a physician's privilege not to disclose, and the reasoning underlying them is appealing. Each, indeed, is but a recognition that, as important as is the patient's right to know, it is greatly outweighed by the magnitudinous circumstances giving rise to the privilege. The first comes into play when the patient is unconscious or otherwise incapable of consenting, and harm from a failure to treat is imminent and outweighs any harm threatened by the proposed treatment. When a genuine emergency of that sort arises, it is settled that the impracticality of conferring with the patient dispenses with need for it. Even in situations of that character the physician should, as current law requires, attempt to secure a relative's consent if possible. But if time is too short to accommodate discussion, obviously the physician should proceed with the treatment.

The second exception obtains when risk-disclosure poses such a threat of detriment to the patient as to become unfeasible or contraindicated from a medical point of view. It is recognized that patients occasionally become so ill or emotionally distraught on disclosure as to foreclose a rational decision, or complicate or hinder the treatment, or perhaps even pose psychological damage to the patient. Where that is so, the cases have generally held that the physician is armed with a privilege to keep the information from the patient, and we think it clear that portents of that type may justify the physician in action he deems medically warranted. The critical inquiry is whether the physician responded to a sound medical judgment that communication of the risk information would present a threat to the patient's well-being.

The physician's privilege to withhold information for therapeutic reasons must be carefully circumscribed, however, for otherwise it might devour the disclosure rule itself. The privilege does not accept the paternalistic notion that the physician may remain silent simply because divulgence might prompt the patient to forego therapy the physician feels the patient really needs. That attitude presumes instability or perversity for even the normal patient, and runs counter to the foundation principle that the patient should and ordinarily can make the choice for himself. Nor does the privilege contemplate operation save where the patient's reaction to risk information, as reasonable foreseen by the physician, is menacing. And even in a situation of that kind, disclosure to a close relative with a view to securing consent to the proposed treatment may be the only alternative open to the physician.

VII.

No more than breach of any other legal duty does nonfulfillment of the physician's obligation to disclose alone establish liability to the patient. An unrevealed risk that should have been made known must materialize, for otherwise the omission, however unpardonable, is legally without consequence. Occurrence of the risk must be harmful to the patient, for negligence unrelated to injury is nonactionable. And, as in malpractice actions generally, there must be a causal relationship between the physician's failure to adequately divulge and damage to the patient.

A causal connection exists when, but only when, disclosure of significant risks incidental to treatment would have resulted in a decision against it. The patient obviously has no complaint if he would have submitted to the therapy notwithstanding awareness that the risk was one of its perils. On the other hand, the very purpose of the disclosure rule is to protect the patient against consequences which, if known, he would have avoided by foregoing the treatment. The more difficult question is whether the factual issue on causality calls for an objective or a subjective determination.

It has been assumed that the issue is to be resolved according to whether the fact-finder believes the patient's testimony that he would not have agreed to the treatment if he had known of the danger which later ripened into injury. We think a technique which ties the factual conclusion on causation simply to the assessment of the patient's credibility is unsatisfactory. To be sure, the objective of risk-disclosure is preservation of the patient's interest in intelligent self-choice on proposed treatment, a matter the patient is free to decide for any reason that appeals to him. When, prior to commencement of therapy, the patient is sufficiently informed on risks and he exercises his choice, it may truly be said that he did exactly what he wanted to do. But when causality is explored at a postinjury trial with a professedly uninformed patient, the question whether he actually would have turned the treatment down if he had known the risks is purely hypothetical: "Viewed from the point at which he had to decide, would the patient have decided differently had he known something he did not know?" And the answer which the patient supplies hardly represents more than a guess, perhaps tinged by the circumstance that the uncommunicated hazard has in fact materialized.

In our view, this method of dealing with the issue on causation comes in second-best. It places the physician in jeopardy of the patient's hindsight and bitterness. It places the fact-finder in the position of deciding whether a speculative answer to a hypothetical question is to be credited. It calls for a subjective determination solely on testimony of a patient-witness shadowed by the occurrence of the undisclosed risk.

Better it is, we believe, to resolve the causality issue on an objective basis: in terms of what a prudent person in the patient's position would have decided if suitably informed of all perils bearing significance. If adequate disclosure could reasonably be expected to have caused that person to decline the treatment because of the revelation of the kind of risk or danger that resulted in harm, causation is shown, but otherwise not. The patient's testimony is relevant on that score of course but it would not threaten to dominate the findings. And since that testimony would probably be appraised congruently with the fact-finder's belief in its reasonableness, the case for a wholly objective standard for passing on causation is strengthened. Such a standard would in any event ease the fact-finding process and better assure the truth as its product.

VIII.

In the context of trial of a suit claiming inadequate disclosure of risk information by a physician, the patient has the burden of going forward with evidence tending to establish prima facie the essential elements of the cause of action, and ultimately the burden of proof—the risk of nonpersuasion—on those elements. These are normal impositions upon moving litigants, and no reason why they should not attach in nondisclosure cases is apparent. The burden of going forward with evidence pertaining to a privilege not to disclose, however, rests properly upon the physician. This is not only because the patient has made out a prima facie case before an issue on privilege is reached, but also because any evidence bearing on the privilege is usually in the hands of the physician alone. Requiring him to open the proof on privilege is consistent with judicial policy laying such a burden on the party who seeks shelter from an exception to a general rule and who is more likely to have possession of the facts.

As in much malpractice litigation, recovery in nondisclosure lawsuits has hinged upon the patient's ability to prove through expert testimony that the physician's performance departed from medical custom. This is not surprising since, as we have pointed out, the majority of American jurisdictions have limited the patient's right to know to whatever boon can be found in medical practice. We have already discussed our disagreement with the majority rationale. We now delineate our view on the need for expert testimony in nondisclosure cases.

There are obviously important roles for medical testimony in such cases, and some roles which only medical evidence can fill. Experts are ordinarily indispensable to identify and elucidate for the fact-finder the risks of therapy and the consequences of leaving existing maladies untreated. They are normally needed on issues as to the cause of any injury or disability suffered by the patient and, where privileges are asserted, as to the existence of any emergency claimed and the nature and seriousness of any impact upon the patient from risk-disclosure. Save for relative infrequent instances where questions of this type are resolvable wholly within the realm of ordinary human knowledge and experience, the need for the expert is clear.

The guiding consideration our decisions distill, however, is that medical facts are for medical experts and other facts are for any witnesses—expert or not—having sufficient knowledge and capacity to testify to them. It is evident that many of the issues typically involved in nondisclosure cases do not reside peculiarly within the medical domain. Lay witness testimony can competently establish a physician's failure to disclose particular risk information, the patient's lack of knowledge of the risk, and the adverse consequences following the treatment. Experts are unnecessary to a showing of the materiality of a risk to a patient's decision on treatment, or to the reasonably, expectable effect of risk disclosure on the decision. These conspicuous examples of permissible uses of nonexpert testimony illustrate the relative freedom of broad areas of the legal problem of risk nondisclosure from the demands for expert testimony that shackle plaintiffs' other types of medical malpractice litigation.

One of the chief obstacles facing plaintiffs in malpractice cases has been the difficulty, and all too frequently the apparent impossibility, of securing testimony from the medical profession. See, e.g., Washington Hosp. Center v. Butler, supra note 48, 127 U.S.App.D.C. at 386 n. 27, 384 F.2d at 338 n. 27; Brown v. Keaveny, supra note 16, 117 U.S.App.D.C. at 118, 326 F.2d at 661 (dissenting opinion); Huffman v. Lindquist, 37 Cal.2d 465, 234 P.2d 34, 46 (1951) (dissenting opinion); Comment, Informed Consent in Medical Malpractice, 55 Calif.L.Rev. 1396, 1405–06 (1967); Note, 75 Harv.L.Rev. 1445, 1447 (1962).

IX.

We now confront the question whether appellant's suit was barred, wholly or partly, by the statute of limitations. The statutory periods relevant to this inquiry are one year for battery actions and three years for those charging negligence. For one a minor when his cause of action accrues, they do not begin to run until he has attained his majority. Appellant was nineteen years old when the laminectomy and related events occurred, and he filed his complaint roughly two years after he reached twenty-one. Consequently, any claim in suit subject to the one-year limitation came too late.

Appellant's causes of action for the allegedly faulty laminectomy by Dr. Spence and allegedly careless post-operative care by the hospital present no problem. Quite obviously, each was grounded in negligence and so was governed by the three-year provision. The duty-to-disclose claim appellant asserted against Dr. Spence, however, draws another consideration into the picture. We have previously observed that an unauthorized operation constitutes a battery, and that an uninformed consent to an operation does not confer the necessary authority. If, therefore, appellant had at stake no more than a recovery of damages on account of a laminectomy intentionally done without intelligent permission, the statute would have interposed a bar.

It is evident, however, that appellant had much more at stake. His interest in bodily integrity commanded protection, not only against an intentional invasion by an unauthorized operation but also against a negligent invasion by his physician's dereliction of duty to adequately disclose. Appellant has asserted and litigated a violation of that duty throughout the case. That claim, like the others, was governed by the three-year period of limitation applicable to negligence actions and was unaffected by the fact that its alternative was barred by the one-year period pertaining to batteries.

X.

This brings us to the remaining question, common to all three causes of action: whether appellant's evidence was of such caliber as to require a submission to the jury. On the first, the evidence was clearly sufficient to raise an issue as to whether Dr. Spence's obligation to disclose information on risks was reasonably met or was excused by the surrounding circumstances. Appellant testified that Dr. Spence revealed to him nothing suggesting a hazard associated with the laminectomy. His mother testified that, in response to her specific inquiry, Dr. Spence informed her that the laminectomy was no more serious than any other operation. When, at trial, it developed from Dr. Spence's testimony that paralysis can be expected in one percent of laminectomies, it became the jury's responsibility to decide whether that peril was of sufficient magnitude to bring the disclosure duty into play. There was no emergency to frustrate an opportunity to disclose, and Dr. Spence's expressed opinion that disclosure would have been unwise did not foreclose a contrary conclusion by the jury. There was no evidence that appellant's emotional makeup was such that concealment of the risk of paralysis was medically sound. Even if disclosure to appellant himself might have bred ill consequences, no reason appears for the omission to communicate the information to his mother, particularly in view of his minority. The jury, not Dr. Spence, was the final arbiter of whether nondisclosure was reasonable under the circumstances.

* * *

Reversed and remanded for a new trial.

* * *

Notes and Questions

1. *Scope of Disclosure—Objective or Subjective?* After much discussion, did *Canterbury* finally adopt a patient or professional standard of disclosure? In either case, is the standard objective or subjective? Stated another way, would a jurisdiction following the patient standard require disclosure of what a reasonable patient would want to know in making a decision to undergo a proposed medical or surgical procedure? Or, would the actual disclosure be compared to what the patient herself would have wanted to know in making a decision to undergo a procedure? In a jurisdiction following the professional standard of disclosure, would a court require disclosure of what a reasonable physician in the same or similar circumstances would have disclosed? Or, would the actual disclosure be compared to what the defendant physician thought should have been disclosed? Many commentators assume that the patient standard of disclosure will be more favorable to plaintiffs, but is this always the case?

2. *Exceptions to the Duty to Disclose. Canterbury* identifies two exceptions to the duty to disclose. What are they? Have other jurisdictions, either by common law, statute, or regulation, adopted other exceptions? *See, e.g., Pauscher v. Iowa Methodist Med. Ctr.*, 408 N.W.2d 355 (Iowa 1987) (identifying five possible exceptions to the duty to disclose); O.C.G.A. § 31-9-6.1(e)(1)-(5) (Georgia statutory provision identifying five exceptions to the duty to disclose). Exceptions to the duty to disclose are state-specific. State law *always* should be consulted before a health care provider relies on the exception to the general rule of disclosure. *Compare Canterbury*, 464 F.2d at 788 (infection does not need to be disclosed as a risk of an operation under D.C. law because infection is inherent in any operation and there is no obligation to disclose those risks of which persons of average sophistication are aware) *with* 25 Tex. Admin. Code § 601.2 (Texas regulation requiring the disclosure of infection in several different contexts).

3. *Age of Consent.* Plaintiff Canterbury was nineteen years old at the time of his laminectomy procedure. The opinion examines the question of whether Canterbury's mother gave prior or subsequent consent to Canterbury's laminectomy. Is the question whether

Canterbury's mother consented to the procedure legally relevant to the question of whether Dr. Spence obtained consent to perform the procedure?

4. *Causation. Canterbury* notes that lawsuits based on failure to obtain informed consent are similar to malpractice actions in that both actions require a causal relationship between the physician's failure to do something (*i.e.*, inform the patient of the risks of treatment in a failure to obtain informed consent case or adhere to the appropriate clinical standard of care in a traditional malpractice case) and the damages suffered by the patient. Assuming that a physician fails to disclose a particular risk to a patient, when will the plaintiff be able to prove the causation element of the failure to obtain informed consent cause of action? Does the factual issue on causality call for an objective or subjective determination? If the standard is subjective, will not the patient always say that she would have refused to consent to the procedure if she had known of that particular risk? If the standard is objective, will risk-averse patients always be unsuccessful in informed consent litigation?

5. *Burden of Proof.* Who has the burden of proof in a lawsuit based on failure to obtain informed consent? Does the patient have the burden of proving that the physician did not obtain the patient's consent? Or, does the physician have the burden of proving that she did obtain the patient's consent? If the physician claims an exemption from the duty to obtain the patient's informed consent, who has the burden of proving such exemption? Although *Canterbury* establishes these burdens as a matter of common law, many state statutes and civil jury instructions clarify the allocation of burdens of proof. *See, e.g.*, Iowa Civil Jury Instruction 1600.10, Informed consent—Essentials For Recovery (providing that, "The plaintiff claims the defendant failed to obtain an informed consent from the plaintiff before performing (name of procedure or treatment). The plaintiff must prove all of the following propositions: (1) The existence of material information concerning the (name of procedure or treatment). (2) Material information concerning the (name of procedure or treatment) was unknown to the plaintiff.... (3) The defendant failed to disclose material information concerning the (name of procedure or treatment) to the plaintiff. (4) Disclosure of material information concerning the (name of procedure or treatment) would have led a reasonable patient in plaintiff's position to [reject the (treatment)] [choose a different course of treatment].... (5) The failure to obtain an informed consent was a proximate cause of plaintiff's damage. (6) The nature and amount of damage.... If the plaintiff has failed to prove any of these propositions, the plaintiff is not entitled to damages. If the plaintiff has proved all of these propositions, the plaintiff is entitled to damages in some amount...."). Many state statutes and civil jury instructions do not address or do not allocate the burden of proof with respect to a privilege not to disclose, however. *See, e.g., id.* §1600.11 (stating that, "The committee does not express any opinion as to how to instruct in these situations. The reasons are as follows ... Can these defenses be raised in a purely elective procedure? ... Who has the burden of pleading and proof on these issues?").

6. *Expert Testimony.* In a jurisdiction following the reasonable patient standard of disclosure, is expert testimony needed to clarify what a reasonable patient would have wanted to know in making a decision to undergo a medical or surgical procedure? In a jurisdiction following a reasonable professional standard of disclosure, is expert testimony needed to clarify what a reasonable physician would have disclosed to the patient?

7. *Statutes of Limitation.* In *Canterbury*, what was the statute of limitations for a battery cause of action? For negligence? Might the plaintiff's choice of a battery or negligence cause of action depend on how quickly the patient procured an attorney?

C. The Professional Standard

Although *Canterbury* adopted a reasonable patient standard of disclosure, other courts have adopted competing standards. Consider the standard of disclosure adopted by the Supreme Court of Indiana in 1992 in *Culbertson v. Mernitz*. The opinion, set in the context of conventional gynecological care, provides one final illustration of the development of the doctrine of informed consent in the conventional health care setting.

Culbertson v. Mernitz
Supreme Court of Indiana
602 N.E.2d 98 (1992)

Krahulik, J.

Roland B. Mernitz, M.D., (Appellee-Defendant) seeks transfer from the Court of Appeals' reversal of a summary judgment entered in his favor. Culbertson v. Mernitz (1992), Ind. App., 591 N.E.2d 1040. The issue squarely presented in this petition is whether expert medical testimony is required to establish the standard of care of health care providers on the issue of informed consent. Because this Court has not previously written on this subject, we accept transfer.

The facts of the case are as follows. Dr. Mernitz first saw Patty Jo Culbertson on March 28, 1988. Her chief complaint was that of uncontrollable leakage of urine and discharge from the vagina. After performing a physical examination, Dr. Mernitz determined that she was suffering from urinary stress incontinence due to a mild cystocele, which is a bulging of the bladder into the vagina. Additionally, he determined that she had cervicitis, which was causing the vaginal discharge. Thirdly, he found that she had multiple fibroid tumors of the uterus. His recommendation was that she should undergo a surgical procedure known as a MMK procedure in order to suspend the bladder and either a hysterectomy or cryosurgery to freeze the infected tip of the cervix. Dr. Mernitz contends that he advised her of the general risks of any surgery, viz. infection, bleeding, and death, and that, with respect to the bladder suspension, he explained to her the risk that the procedure could fail and the possibility that she would be unable to void. Additionally, with respect to the cryosurgery he contends he told her that she would have severe vaginal discharge for two weeks and a milder discharge for six weeks thereafter. Mrs. Culbertson, on the other hand, denies that any of these risks were explained to her. Both parties, however, agree that Dr. Mernitz did not advise her of a risk that the cervix could become adhered to the wall of the vagina.

Following this office visit, Mrs. Culbertson decided to proceed with the bladder suspension and cryosurgery. She was admitted to the hospital and underwent these procedures. Post-surgically, Mrs. Culbertson's cervix adhered to the wall of her vagina. Dr. Mernitz prescribed medication for this condition, but Mrs. Culbertson became dissatisfied with his care and saw another surgeon who eventually performed a total abdominal hysterectomy, bilateral salpingo-oophorectomy which involves the removal of both ovaries, and another bladder suspension.

Following this surgery, Mr. and Mrs. Culbertson filed a proposed complaint against Dr. Mernitz with the Indiana Department of Insurance in four counts. Count I alleged that the adherence of the cervix to the vagina was caused by negligent cautery of the cervix. Count II alleged that Dr. Mernitz failed to inform Mrs. Culbertson of the alternatives to surgery and the inherent risks and complications of surgery. Count III alleged that Dr. Mernitz refused to treat and abandoned Mrs. Culbertson. And Count IV alleged a claim for loss of consortium by Mr. Culbertson.

A medical review panel was convened and, after submission of evidence to it, issued its written opinion. On Count I the panel unanimously found that there was no evidence to support the allegation that the surgery had been negligently performed. Similarly, it found no evidence to support the allegation in Count III that Dr. Mernitz had abandoned Mrs. Culbertson. With respect to the informed consent issue alleged in Count II, the panel ruled:

> The Panel determines that [Dr. Mernitz] did not advise [Mrs. Culbertson] of the complication of cervical adhesion to the vagina; the Panel further determines that such non-disclosure does not constitute a failure to comply with the appropriate standard of care, as such complication is not considered a risk of such surgery requiring disclosure to the patient.

The Culbertsons filed their civil action in a complaint that mirrored the allegations of the proposed complaint. After answering this complaint, Dr. Mernitz moved for summary judgment relying on the expert opinion issued by the medical review panel. The Culbertsons did not file an affidavit or other evidence in opposition to the motion for summary judgment, but argued to the trial court that the "prudent patient" standard should be utilized in evaluating informed consent claims. The trial court entered summary judgment on all four counts. The Culbertsons appealed to the Court of Appeals on the informed consent issue and argued that expert medical testimony is not necessary to make a prima facie case of lack of informed consent because the "prudent patient" standard is the law in this State and such standard does not contemplate the necessity of expert medical testimony.

The Court of Appeals agreed with the Culbertsons that the trial court had erroneously entered summary judgment on Counts II and IV because an issue of fact remained as to whether the risk of cervical adhesion to the vagina was a "material risk". 591 N.E.2d at 1042. The court further held that that issue was a question for the jury which does not require expert testimony as to materiality, although expert testimony might be required to establish the existence and extent of the risk. Id. Judge Hoffman disagreed and filed a dissenting opinion in which he set forth his belief that a physician must disclose those risks which a reasonably prudent physician would disclose under the circumstances. Id. at 1043. He further reasoned that the situation in the instant case was clearly outside the realm of a layperson's comprehension, and that expert testimony was required to establish whether the disclosure was reasonable. He concluded that Culbertson's failure to present any expert testimony contrary to the panel's express findings on this issue made entry of summary judgment in favor of Dr. Mernitz proper. Because of the divergence of opinions in the Court of Appeals on this precise issue, we must determine the role, if any, played by expert medical opinion in resolving claims of medical malpractice premised upon a failure to obtain an informed consent.

The courts, historically, have established the standard of care required of physicians when treating patients. The law requires that a physician treating a patient possess and exercise that degree of skill and care ordinarily possessed and exercised by a physician treating such maladies in the same or similar locality. Worster v. Caylor (1953), 231 Ind. 625, 110 N.E.2d 337 (overruled on other grounds). In order for a lay jury to know whether a physician complied with the legally prescribed standard of care, expert testimony has generally been held to be required. Id., 231 Ind. at 630, 110 N.E.2d at 340. This requirement was premised on the logical belief that a non-physician could not know what a reasonably prudent physician would or would not have done under the circumstances of any given case. Therefore, an expert familiar with the practice of medicine needed to establish what a reasonably prudent physician would or would not have done in treating a patient in order to set before the jury a depiction of the reasonably prudent physician against which to judge the actions of the defendant physician. An exception was created in cases of *res ipsa loquitur* on the premise that in such cases a lay jury did not need guidance from a physician familiar with medical practice as to what was required of a reasonably prudent physician because the deficiency of practice "spoke for itself." Kranda v. Houser-Norburg Med. Corp. (1981), Ind. App., 419 N.E.2d 1024, 1042. This was the settled law of most American jurisdictions, including Indiana, prior to the early 1970s when two cases on the opposite coasts carved out an additional exception to the requirement of expert medical testimony in the area of "informed consent".

In Cobbs v. Grant (1972), 8 Cal.3d 229, 104 Cal. Rptr. 505, 502 P.2d 1, the California Supreme Court held that expert testimony is not required to establish a physician's duty to disclose risks of a proposed treatment. The premise of this opinion was that placing unlimited discretion in the medical community to determine what risks to disclose was irreconcilable with the basic right of a patient to make the ultimate informed decision regarding a course of treatment. The court reasoned that a physician is in the best position to appreciate the risks inherent in the proposed procedure, the risks inherent in deciding not to undergo the proposed procedure, as well as the chances of a successful outcome. The court held that once this information had been disclosed, however, the expert function of the physician had been performed and the decisional task of weighing the positive benefits of the proposed procedure against the negative possibilities inherent in the procedure passed solely and exclusively to the patient. Finally, the court opined that a jury is in the best position to determine whether the physician gave the patient the information needed by the patient to weigh the alternatives and make the ultimate decision of whether to proceed with the proposed treatment.

In the same year, the Court of Appeals for the District of Columbia decided Canterbury v. Spence (1972), 150 U.S. App. D.C. 263, 464 F.2d 772, cert. den. 409 U.S. 1064, 34 L. Ed. 2d 518, 93 S. Ct. 560. In Canterbury, the court also held that expert testimony was not required to establish a physician's duty to disclose risks of a proposed treatment. It reasoned that while an expert may be required to identify for the jury the risks of the proposed treatment and the risks of non-treatment, a jury did not need expert guidance on whether a particular risk was material to a patient's ultimate decision. The court held that "a risk is thus material when a reasonable person, in what the physician knows or should know to be the patient's position, would be likely to attach significance to the risk or cluster of risks in deciding whether or not to forego the proposed therapy." 404 F.2d at 787. With that as the standard of care in informed consent cases, the court concluded that a lay jury was in as good a position as a physician to determine whether the physician had informed the patient of the facts such a patient would "need to know" in order to arrive at a decision.

This view has been adopted in approximately ten jurisdictions, while the traditional view that expert medical testimony is necessary to inform the jury of what a reasonably prudent physician would disclose remains the law in approximately 25 jurisdictions. See Daniel E. Fields, Annotation, Necessity and Sufficiency of Expert Evidence to Establish Existence and Extent of Physician's Duty to Inform Patient of Risks of Proposed Treatment, 52 A.L.R.3d 1084 (1973 & Supp. 1991).

* * *

The Culbertsons urge that the Indiana Court of Appeals arguably adopted the "prudent patient" standard of care as discussed in Canterbury in the case of Spencer v. Christiansen (1990), Ind. App., 549 N.E.2d 1090. They are mistaken. The Spencer court, in a one paragraph review of the general law, stated that Indiana recognized the duty of a physician to "make a reasonable disclosure of material facts relevant to the decision which the patient is requested to make" and that, as a general rule, "expert medical testimony is required to establish the content of the 'reasonable disclosure'." Id. at 1091. The court, however, then continued and stated that "whether the required disclosure occurred and its adequacy is an issue of fact that does not require medical expertise; accordingly medical expert opinion on the jury issue is inappropriate." Id. As was recently recognized in Dickey v. Long (1992), Ind., 591 N.E.2d 1010, much of the language contained in Spencer was merely dicta because the specific holding in Spencer was that a medical review panel had not resolved a disputed fact and, consequently, the issue of whether that case required expert medical opinion was not decided. Spencer is not, therefore, support for the proposition advocated by the Culbertsons.

Finally, in Griffith v. Jones (1991), Ind. App., 577 N.E.2d 258, the Court of Appeals for the first time departed from its previous holdings and concluded that "the weight of authority supports the trial court's determination that the prudent patient standard of care in informed consent cases, as articulated in Canterbury, supra, has been adopted in Indiana." Id. at 264. Simply stated, our reading of the prior cases, as set forth above, does not support this statement and, to the contrary, leads us to conclude that expert medical testimony is necessary to establish whether a physician's disclosure of risks comports with what a reasonably prudent physician would have disclosed. Because the court in the case at issue here relied on its previous holding in Griffith to reverse the summary judgment entered in favor of Dr. Mernitz, it erred. We hold that pursuant to the precedent discussed above, the trial court properly entered summary judgment in favor of Dr. Mernitz.

Resolution of the issue of the necessity of expert medical testimony in informed consent cases depends on whether the issue is viewed through the eyes of the physician or the patient. When viewed through the eyes of the physician, it is easy to see that a physician should not be required to guess or speculate as to what a hypothetical "reasonably prudent patient" would "need to know" in order to make a determination. A physician should only be required to do that which he is trained to do, namely, conduct himself as a reasonably prudent physician in taking a history, performing a physical examination, ordering appropriate tests reaching a diagnosis, prescribing a course of treatment, and in discussing with the patient the medical facts of the proposed procedure, including the risks inherent in either accepting or rejecting the proposed course of treatment. From a physician's viewpoint, he should not be called upon to be a "mind reader" with the ability to peer into the brain of a prudent patient to determine what such patient "needs to know," but should simply be called upon to discuss medical facts and recommendations with the patient as a reasonably prudent physician would.

On the other hand, from the patient's viewpoint, the physician should be required to give the patient sufficient information to enable the patient to reasonably exercise the patient's right of self-decision in a knowledgeable manner. Viewed from this vantage point, the patient does not want the medical profession to determine in a paternalistic manner what the patient should or should not be told concerning the course of treatment. Thus, such a patient would view the reasonably prudent physician standard as destroying the patient's right of self-decision and, impliedly, placing such decision under the exclusive domain of the medical profession. While this viewpoint may or may not have been justified in 1972 when Canterbury, supra, and Cobbs, supra, were decided, a review of medical ethics standards of care in 1992 should assuage this fear.

The 1992 Code of Medical Ethics, as prepared by the Council on Ethical and Judicial Affairs of the American Medical Association, sets forth the medical profession's standard on informed consent. It reads as follows:

> The patient's right of self-decision can be effectively exercised only if the patient possesses enough information to enable an intelligent choice. The patient should make his own determination on treatment. The physician's obligation is to present the medical facts accurately to the patient or to the individual responsible for his care and to make recommendations for management in accordance with good medical practice. The physician has an ethical obligation to help the patient make choices from among the therapeutic alternatives consistent with good medical practice. Informed consent is a basic social policy for which exceptions are permitted (1) where the patient is unconscious or otherwise incapable of consenting and harm from failure to treat is imminent; or (2) when risk-disclosure poses such a serious psychological threat of detriment to the patient as to be medically contraindicated. Social policy does not accept the paternalistic view that the physician may remain silent because divulgence might prompt the patient to forego needed therapy. Rational, informed patients should not be expected to act uniformly, even under similar circumstances, in agreeing to or refusing treatment.

We recognize this statement as a reasonable statement on the issue of informed consent. There is no need to change Indiana law on this issue. We therefore hold that, except in those cases where deviation from the standard of care is a matter commonly known by lay persons, expert medical testimony is necessary to establish whether a physician has or has not complied with the standard of a reasonably prudent physician.

In the present case we cannot say that the risk of the adherence of the cervix to the vaginal wall is a matter commonly known to lay persons. Therefore, the Culbertsons needed to provide expert medical testimony to refute the unanimous opinion issued by the medical review panel in order to present a material issue of fact as to what a reasonably prudent physician would have discussed concerning this proposed surgery. Without the presentation of such expert medical opinion, the trial court could only conclude that there was no genuine issue of material fact and that summary judgment should be entered for Dr. Mernitz.

We affirm the entry of summary judgment in this case.

* * *

II. Informed Consent in the CAM Context

In the last section, we considered one early twentieth century case that addressed whether a physician has a legal duty to obtain a patient's informed consent prior to performing a medical or surgical procedure, as well as two later twentieth century cases that examined the scope of required disclosure. Let us now apply this doctrine of informed consent to cases involving CAM.

Three categories of informed consent cases have arisen in the CAM context. In the first category of cases, plaintiffs have sued CAM practitioners or conventionally-trained physicians who practice CAM for allegedly failing to disclose the risks associated with foregoing conventional medical care and submitting to one or more alternative therapies. In the second category of cases, plaintiffs have sued conventional physicians who practice conventional medicine for allegedly failing to disclose the option or availability of a complementary or alternative therapy. In the third category of cases, plaintiffs have sued CAM practitioners for allegedly failing to disclose one or more risks associated with a CAM therapy. Each category of cases will be discussed in turn.

A. Failure to Disclose Risks of Foregoing Conventional Medical Care

The following case, *Charell v. Gonzalez* (also seen in Chapter 4), is illustrative of the first category of cases in which plaintiffs have sued CAM practitioners or conventionally-trained physicians who practice CAM for allegedly failing to disclose the risks associated with foregoing conventional medical care and submitting to one or more alternative therapies.

The *Charell* opinion does not describe defendant Gonzalez's education and training, which was quite conventional. Dr. Gonzalez received his B.A. in English Literature, *magna cum laude*, from Brown University in 1970, completed additional premedical coursework with a 4.0 grade point average at Columbia University in 1979, received his M.D. at Cornell Medical College with Honors in Internal Medicine in 1983, completed an internship in Internal Medicine at Vanderbilt University in 1984, and completed a fellowship in Cancer Immunology with Robert A. Good, Ph.D., M.D., considered by many to be the father of Immunology, in 1986.

Between his undergraduate and medical studies, Dr. Gonzalez also served as a journalist and free-lance writer for Time, Inc., where he wrote many health-related stories, including an article entitled, "Why This Psychiatrist Switched" about a psychiatrist-turn-alternative practitioner. Dr. Gonzalez began researching nutritional approaches to cancer treatment while a medical student and completed an investigation of the enzyme therapy of cancer while an immunology fellow. Additional biographical information about Dr. Gonzalez is available at http://www.dr-gonzalez.com/about_us.htm.

Charell v. Gonzalez
Supreme Court of New York, New York County
173 Misc. 2d 227 (1997)

OPINION BY: Edward H. Lehner

Before me is a motion by defendant to set aside the jury verdict against him and a cross motion by plaintiff to vacate the jury finding that she impliedly assumed a risk of injury to herself when she agreed to undergo treatment by defendant.

In 1991, after being diagnosed with uterine cancer, plaintiff underwent a hysterectomy at Mt. Sinai Hospital, subsequent to which the physicians at that hospital recommended a course of radiation and chemotherapy. That protocol, considering plaintiff's condition, was variously described as "investigative" or "experimental", and was apparently recommended due to the fact that plaintiff had a high chance of recurrence because her cancer cells were found to be poorly differentiated.

Plaintiff then, in seeking a "second opinion", arranged an appointment with defendant in October 1991. She testified that he dissuaded her from having chemotherapy or radiation, and recommended treatment through his protocol of a special diet, including six coffee enemas a day. A tape of the conversation between the parties shows that he advised her not to "mess" with chemotherapy and stated that he had experienced a 75% success rate with persons in her condition. He also informed her that, through a hair test he had devised, he had determined that cancer cells remained in her body, which condition was undetected by the Mt. Sinai physicians. Plaintiff, who knew of defendant through attendance at one of his lectures and listening to his tapes, and who had witnessed the severe discomfort experienced by a relative who had undertaken chemotherapy and radiation, agreed to be treated by defendant and until June 1992 religiously followed his protocol. Plaintiff was encouraged to continue the treatment when defendant advised her that subsequent hair tests showed a reduction in the number of cancer cells in her body. She testified that she was never told by defendant that he was not an oncologist, nor that his protocol was experimental and not generally accepted in the medical community.

In June 1992, after experiencing back discomfort and failing vision, she discontinued treatment with defendant and returned to Mt. Sinai Hospital where it was determined that cancer cells had metastasized in her spine, which condition eventually caused her blindness and severe back problems.

In this action plaintiff asserted damage claims against defendant (i) in negligence for persuading her to forego traditional treatment and undertaking a nutritional protocol which she contends, by itself, was of no therapeutic value, and (ii) for lack of obtaining an informed consent to the treatment. In addition, she sought punitive damages.

At trial the jury unanimously determined: that the treatment provided by defendant was a departure from good and accepted medical practice, which departure was a proximate cause of injuries to plaintiff; that defendant did not provide plaintiff with appropriate information with respect to the risks of his treatment and the alternatives thereto, and that a reasonably prudent person in plaintiff's position would not have agreed to have the treatment if provided the appropriate information; that by accepting treatment by defendant, plaintiff did not expressly assume risk of injury to herself, but did impliedly assume such risk; that defendant was 51% responsible for plaintiff's injuries, while plaintiff was 49% responsible; that plaintiff was entitled to damages for pain and suffering sustained prior to verdict of $2,500,000 and $2,000,000 for future suffering, as well $125,000 for past loss of earnings and $75,000 for future loss of earnings; and finally that plaintiff was entitled to punitive damages. At the separate punitive damages aspect of the trial, the jury awarded plaintiff an additional $150,000.

Defendant argues that if the verdict is sustained he will not be able to practice and this will send a chill to all alternative medicine practitioners. He notes that in 1994 the State Legislature recognized the work of nonconventional physicians when in chapter 558 of the Laws of 1994 it amended Education Law 6527 by adding paragraph (e) to subdivision (4) to specifically provide that the law does not prevent a "physician's use of whatever medical care, conventional or non-conventional, which effectively treats human disease, pain, injury, deformity or physical condition", and that subdivision (1) of section 230 of the Public Health Law was amended to provide that no less than 2 of the 18 members of the Board for Professional Medical Conduct "shall be physicians who dedicate a significant portion of their practice to the use of non-conventional medical treatments".

During the course of the trial, a telecast of a two-hour lecture by one of the more famous practitioners of alternative medicine, Dr. Andrew Weil, was broadcast on public television, during which he indicated that the use of chemotherapy and radiation for the treatment of cancer will be a thing of the past. At the request of plaintiff's counsel, the court inquired whether any of the jurors had seen the telecast and, when it was indicated that none had seen the program, instructed them not to view its rebroadcast. In his 1995 "number one" bestseller, Spontaneous Healing, Dr. Weil wrote (at 268–276):

> "Current therapies for cancer, both conventional and alternative, are far from satisfactory. Conventional medicine has three main treatments: surgery, radiation, and chemotherapy, of which only the first makes sense ...

> "Radiation and chemotherapy are crude treatments that will be obsolete before long ... If you have cancer and are faced with a decision about whether to use conventional therapies, the question you must try to answer is this: Will the damage done to the cancer justify the damage done to the immune system? ...

> "Cancer treatments abound in the world of alternative medicine, most of them much less toxic than radiation and chemotherapy, but none of them works reliably for large numbers of patients. Many of the therapies I have looked into appear to have induced remissions in some people; in many more they improve quality of life for a time, yet the cancers remain and continue to grow ...

> "New and better cancer treatment is on the horizon in the form of immunotherapy, methods that will take advantage of natural healing mechanisms to recognize and destroy malignant cells without harming normal ones. In the meantime, a concerted effort to discover and study cases of spontaneous remission may help us understand that phenomenon and increase its incidence. To make wise decisions regarding the use of existing therapies for cancer, you must have reliable information about their benefits and risks."

In the May 12, 1997 issue of Time Magazine, which had a photograph of Dr. Weil on the cover with the subtitle: "Is it sound advice or snake oil?", a former editor of the New England Journal of Medicine is quoted as saying of Dr. Weil (at 75): "I resent well-educated people exploiting irrational elements in our culture, and that's what he's doing." The reporters in the article conclude (at 75): "The debate between alternative and mainstream medicine will not get settled anytime soon ... [What is not] clear—at least for now—is whether Weil and other alternative healers are selling real cures or ... just casting good spells."

While there may be a public debate as to the merits of certain practices of nonconventional physicians, there was no similar debate with respect to the evidence at this trial. The standard for proving negligence in a malpractice case is whether the treatment deviates from accepted medical standards (Jackson v. Presbyterian Hosp., 227 A.D.2d 236 [1st Dept. 1996]). There was no testimony on behalf of defendant on this issue. Moreover, it would seem that no practitioner of alternative medicine could prevail on such a question as the reference to the term "non-conventional" may well necessitate a finding that the doctor who practices such medicine deviates from "accepted" medical standards. This indeed creates a problem for such physicians which perhaps can only be solved by having the patient execute a comprehensive consent containing appropriate information as to the risks involved. In this connection, in Schneider v. Revici (817 F.2d 987 [2d Cir. 1987]), where although the court stated that "an informed decision to avoid surgery and conventional chemotherapy is within the patient's right", and there is "no reason why a patient should not be allowed to make an informed decision to go outside currently approved medical methods in search for an unconventional treatment", it declined to enforce the covenant not to sue executed by the patient, but said it was appropriate for the jury to determine whether the language of the form she signed and "testimony relating to specific consent informed by her awareness of the risk of refusing conventional treatment" amounted to an express assumption of risk that would totally bar recovery (at 995–996). In Boyle v. Revici (961 F.2d 1060 [2d Cir. 1992] [a case involving the same nonconventional physician as in Schneider, supra]), the court ruled that even without a written consent the jury should, based on the evidence, have been permitted to determine whether plaintiff "knowingly accepted all of the risks of a defendant's negligence" (at 1063), and thus expressly assumed the risk of injury to herself.

On the issue of proximate cause, while there was conflicting evidence, the jury was entitled to find, in accordance with the testimony of plaintiff's expert (Dr. Holland), that if plaintiff were not improperly dissuaded from undertaking conventional treatment the cancer probably would not have metastasized and she would not have had the recurrence and the resulting blindness and back problems. Plaintiff's experts also testified that the hair test employed by defendant to ascertain the presence of cancer was completely bogus, the treatment provided by him was of no value, and (in addition to being damaging in the sense that plaintiff was persuaded not to undergo conventional treatment) was harmful in that the nutrition provided aided the growth of the cancer cells.

Thus, the jury's findings on the questions of negligence and proximate cause cannot be said to be against the weight of the evidence or lacking a rational basis. The same can be said about its findings on the cause of action for lack of informed consent as there clearly was evidence to support the conclusion that defendant did not provide "appropriate information" with respect to the risks of, and the alternatives to, employing his protocol alone and not combining it with conventional treatment.

On the question of assumption of risk, the jury was asked both whether plaintiff expressly assumed the risk of injury to herself in agreeing to defendant's protocol (a finding of which would have exonerated defendant), and whether she impliedly assumed a risk of injury (a finding of which would, and did, bring into play the comparative fault provisions of CPLR article 14-A). (See, Arbegast v. Board of Educ., 65 N.Y.2d 161 [1985]).

With respect to the jury determination that plaintiff "impliedly" assumed risk of injury to herself in agreeing to undergo the treatment, plaintiff's counsel states that the question thus posed is "whether or not plaintiff had knowledge and a full understanding of the risks of harm of defendant's proposed treatment from a source other than defendant himself" (plaintiff's mem of law, at 7). Counsel argues that she did not. However, the evidence showed that plaintiff was a well-educated person who, together with her husband and daughter, did a significant amount of investigation regarding the treatment being offered by defendant and hence became quite knowledgeable on the subject, and that she sought to avoid the suffering that accompanied the chemotherapy/radiation regimen that she had witnessed when a relative had undertaken that treatment. Thus, even though the jury found that defendant had not given appropriate information regarding the risks of his procedure and the available alternatives, it was within the province of the jury, based on the evidence, for it to also find that plaintiff independently obtained sufficient information about the treatment so as to conclude that there was an implied assumption of risk when she agreed to follow defendant's protocol. (See, Boyle v. Revici, supra; Schneider v. Revici, supra.)

Pertaining to the award of punitive damages, such "damages have been allowed in cases where the wrong complained of is morally culpable, or is actuated by evil and reprehensible motives, not only to punish the defendant but to deter him, as well as others who might otherwise be so prompted, from indulging in similar conduct in the future" (Walker v. Sheldon, 10 N.Y.2d 401, 404 [1961]). In cases involving motions directed to a pleading or for summary judgment, it has been held that punitive damages may be awarded in a medical malpractice case (e.g., Graham v. Columbia-Presbyterian Med. Ctr., 185 A.D.2d 753, 754 [1st Dept. 1992] [conduct that is " 'intentional, malicious, outrageous, or otherwise aggravated beyond mere negligence' "may support an award of punitive damages]; Frenya v. Champlain Val. Physicians' Hosp. Med. Ctr., 133 A.D.2d 1000, 1000–1001 [3d Dept 1987] [an award of punitive damages requires a showing of "wrongful motive ... willful or intentional misdoing, or a reckless indifference equivalent to willful or intentional misdoing ... (and) in the case of a tort action, the defendant's conduct must be so flagrant as to transcend mere carelessness"]; Jones v. Hospital for Joint Diseases & Med. Ctr., 96 A.D.2d 498 [1st Dept. 1983]). However, I have not located any case (other than an assault by a physician) where a verdict for punitive damages in a medical malpractice case has been upheld on appeal. For a lower court decision, see Gersten v. Levin (150 Misc. 2d 594 [Sup. Ct., NY County 1991]).

In the case at bar, plaintiff offered evidence to show that defendant's practice of prescribing nutrition as a cure was designed to enable companies in which he had a financial interest to sell product. While there was evidence offered by the defendant to the contrary, the jury was entitled to find that defendant's intent in dealing with plaintiff was motivated by greed and that he was reckless in his care of her. It should be noted that although, as aforesaid, there is pending controversy between the medical establishment and nonconventional practitioners, defendant failed to produce a single witness at trial who defended his treatment of plaintiff as medically sound, whereas plaintiff's experts clearly painted him as a charlatan. With only such evidence before it, I cannot say that the jury award on punitive damages was unsupported by the weight of the evidence. That the jury found that plaintiff had knowledge of the risks involved and thus impliedly assumed a risk of injury should not bar the jury from also awarding punitive damages based on conduct by a physician which it deemed reckless and improperly motivated.

In summary, both motions to set aside the verdict are denied and a judgment shall be entered in accordance with the jury verdict.

* * *

Charell is not the only case in which a plaintiff has sued a CAM practitioner or a conventionally-trained physician who practices CAM for allegedly failing to disclose the risks associated with foregoing conventional medical care and submitting to one or more alternative therapies. In a second case, *Schneider v. Revici*, the plaintiffs sued a conventionally-trained physician for several causes of action, including fraud, medical malpractice, failure to obtain informed consent, and loss of consortium after the physician allegedly advised the patient to undergo alternative, non-invasive therapy for her breast cancer.

When the district court judge refused to charge the jury on an alleged covenant not to sue as well as the affirmative defense of express assumption of risk, the defendant appealed the district court's ruling to the United States Court of Appeals for the Second Circuit. The Second Circuit's opinion, reprinted in part below, focuses on the missing jury charges and does not specifically address the validity of the plaintiff's failure to obtain informed consent cause of action. However, the opinion is valuable for illustrating how a plaintiff who receives alternative therapy may sue for failure to obtain informed consent. The opinion also raises the question of whether a health care provider, conventional or unconventional, may legally embed within an informed consent to treatment form a covenant not to sue as well as the question of whether such covenant will be considered against public policy.

Schneider v. Revici
United States Court of Appeals for the Second Circuit
817 F.2d 987 (1987)

MINER, CIRCUIT JUDGE:

Emanuel Revici, M.D. and the Institute of Applied Biology, Inc. (the "Institute") appeal from a judgment entered in the United States District Court for the Southern District of New York (Motley, J.), in a diversity action arising from Dr. Revici's treatment of plaintiff Edith Schneider's breast cancer with unconventional, non-invasive cancer therapy, after she had been advised by numerous doctors to undergo a biopsy and had refused to do so. Edith Schneider and her husband asserted four claims against Dr. Revici and the Institute: (1) fraud, premised on Dr. Revici's alleged promise to cure Mrs. Schneider of breast cancer; (2) medical malpractice; (3) a claim for lack of informed consent under N.Y. Pub. Health Law 2805-d; and, (4) a derivative claim asserted by Mr. Schneider for loss of consortium. After the district judge refused to charge the jury on the affirmative defense of express assumption of risk, the jury returned a verdict for the plaintiffs on the medical malpractice claim, and a loss of consortium claim. It awarded Edith Schneider and her husband $1,000,000.00 and $50,000.00 respectively. Because the jury found that Mrs. Schneider was equally responsible, through her own culpable conduct, for the damages she suffered, the awards were halved to $500,000.00 and $25,000.00, pursuant to New York's comparative negligence statute, N.Y. Civ. Prac. L. & R. 1411.

On appeal, Dr. Revici and the Institute challenge the district court's refusal to charge with respect to an alleged covenant not to sue and express assumption of risk as affirmative defenses, either of which would serve as a total bar to recovery. Appellants also contend that numerous evidentiary rulings were erroneous. Because we hold that express assumption of risk was available as a total defense to this action under New York law, we reverse and remand this case for determination of that issue only.

I. BACKGROUND

In October 1981, Dr. Cocoziello discovered a lump in appellee Edith Schneider's right breast during her annual gynecological checkup. Dr. Cocoziello referred Mrs. Schneider to Drs. Snyder and Lichy, who performed a bilateral mammogram and compared the results to one taken in 1978. Dr. Lichy's report indicated the presence of a "one centimeter nodulation" in the right breast, and advised a biopsy, both in the report to Dr. Cocoziello and by telephone to Mrs. Schneider. Joint App. at 1229. Mrs. Schneider told Dr. Lichy that she did not want a biopsy and would seek a doctor who would treat her nonsurgically. Id. Dr. Cocoziello also urged Mrs. Schneider to have a biopsy and referred her to three general surgeons: Dr. Abessi, Dr. Addeo, and Dr. Volke. Mrs. Schneider was examined by Dr. Abessi and Dr. Volke, who both separately advised her to undergo a biopsy and possibly a partial mastectomy, depending upon the analysis of the biopsied tissue. She refused. Id. at 1241.

In November 1981, Mrs. Schneider consulted with Dr. Emanuel Revici, defendant-appellant herein, who is the President and Scientific Director of the Institute. Dr. Revici is a physician and researcher who treats cancer patients with "non-toxic," non-invasive methods that have not been adopted by the medical community. Mrs. Schneider had learned of Dr. Revici and his novel cancer therapy from a radio program. After Mrs. Schneider signed a detailed consent form,[1] Dr. Revici diagnosed cancer of the right breast and began treatment with selenium and dietary restrictions. While Mrs. Schneider claims that Dr. Revici never advised either a biopsy or surgery, Joint App. at 485, his records show that in February 1982, and on three later occasions, he recommended that she have the tumor surgically removed. Joint App. at 1104–05. After fourteen months of treatment, the tumor had increased in size, and cancer had spread to her lymph system and left breast. Mrs. Schneider finally underwent a bilateral mastectomy at Memorial Sloan-Kettering Hospital in January 1983, followed by sixteen months of conventional chemotherapy.

[1] Mrs. Schneider signed a consent form that reads as follows:

CONSENT FOR MEDICAL CARE

This is to certify that I the undersigned: I am presenting myself for diagnosis and treatment to be rendered by Dr. Emanuel Revici, 164 East 91st, New York, N.Y.

I fully understand that some of the treatment procedures and medications are still investigatory awaiting further research and submission for F.D.A. approval. I was made aware of the fact that the preparations used were thoroughly investigated for being non-toxic and effective in treatments of human patients. I voluntarily consent to the rendering of such care, diagnostic procedures, medical treatments, rehabilitative procedures.

I am aware that the practice of medicine is not an exact science and I acknowledge that no guaranties have been made to me as to the results of the treatment procedures and medications.

I acknowledge that this form has been explained to me and I certify that I understand its contents.

I therefore release Dr. Emanuel Revici from all liabilities to me, including all claims and complaints by me or by other members of my family. I am here because I wish to try the Revici methods and preparations for disease control.

I also agree to have my medical records used for research purposes and for publication in books, scientific journals, newspapers and magazines.

Joint App. at 1101.

Dr. Revici testified that Mrs. Schneider had told him that she had not seen other doctors and had not yet had a mammogram. He testified that because of this, he explained the consent form to her in great detail:

I showed the consent and we showed clearly when we discussed every point because I had [the] impression that Mrs. Schneider was not telling me the truth when she told me that she has cysts of the breast and that she didn't see any other doctor before me, and I knew that she lied. For this I explained to her in detail as a precaution, knowing that she was lying.

Joint App. at 849.

Mrs. Schneider brought this diversity action against Dr. Revici and the Institute for damages, alleging common law fraud, common law medical malpractice and lack of informed consent pursuant to N.Y. Pub. Health Law 2805-d. Mr. Schneider also sued for loss of consortium. On the eve of trial, defendants sought leave either to clarify their Third Affirmative Defense of "culpable conduct" or to amend their answer to include express assumption of risk as an affirmative defense. In a pre-trial order, dated November 11, 1985, the trial judge denied the motion, apparently on the grounds that express assumption of risk is unavailable as a defense to medical malpractice under New York law:

Defendant's request for application of the assumption of risk doctrine ... is denied. The law of medical malpractice and informed consent are well-established areas of jurisprudence in N.Y. State. This case will be tried in accordance with those well-established principles, including the doctrine of comparative negligence.

Joint App. at 85–86. The court denied a similar oral motion on the first day of trial and, at the end of trial, refused to charge the jury on express assumption of risk. Joint App. at 134–35, 97–98.

The jury returned a verdict for Mrs. Schneider solely on the medical malpractice claim, and awarded $1,000,000.00 and $50,000.00 to her and her husband respectively. The jury found, however, that Mrs. Schneider was 50% comparatively negligent, and both awards were thereby halved to $500,000.00 and $25,000.00. On this appeal, appellants contend that the district court erred by refusing to charge as affirmative defenses an alleged covenant not to sue and express assumption of risk, and also erred in certain evidentiary rulings. We hold that, under New York law, express assumption of risk is available as an affirmative defense to a medical malpractice action and if proved, would totally bar recovery by a plaintiff. Therefore we reverse and remand this case to the district court for a new trial of the issue of express assumption of risk.

II. DISCUSSION

* * *

B. Covenant Not to Sue

New York law recognizes the efficacy of a covenant not to sue in the context of medical treatment:

> Specifically, where a patient voluntarily agrees to undergo an experimental and inherently dangerous surgical procedure, the parties may covenant to exempt the physician from liability for those injuries which are found to be the consequences of the non-negligent, proper performance of the procedure.... That is to say, that an experimental procedure which, because of its inherent dangers, may ordinarily be in and of itself a departure from customary and accepted practice (and thus possibly actionable as malpractice) even if performed in a non-negligent manner, may be rendered unactionable by a covenant not to sue.

Colton v. New York Hospital, 98 Misc. 2d 957, 414 N.Y.S.2d 866, 876 (Sup. Ct. 1979), and cases there cited. However, New York requires that "a covenant not to sue ... must be strictly construed against the party asserting it. Moreover, its wording must be 'clear and unequivocal.'" Id. at 874 (citations omitted). The form signed by Mrs. Schneider lacks the precision required by New York law.

In the first place, the form was not labeled a covenant or agreement not to sue but was instead captioned "CONSENT FOR MEDICAL CARE." That caption would lead most patients to believe that they were signing a form only to acknowledge informed consent, rather than forgoing the right to bring suit. Second, the one paragraph of the consent form that bears on legal liability is not "clear and unequivocal." It states: "I therefore release Dr. Emanuel Revici from all liabilities to me, including all claims and complaints by me or by other members of my family." Though this language can be interpreted to mean that the patient is agreeing not to bring suit for any consequences that may arise in the future as a result of Dr. Revici's treatment, or as a result of forgoing traditional treatment, that interpretation is not compelled. To "release ... from all liabilities" can plausibly be understood only to relinquish claims currently existing, rather than to promise not to sue in the future on claims that may subsequently arise. The ambiguous language of the form prepared by Dr. Revici stands in sharp contrast to the unequivocal language of the form enforced in Colton, which left no room for doubt that the patient was knowledgeably agreeing not to sue the doctor for consequences of the procedure to be performed. The form in Colton included the words "COVENANT NOT TO SUE" in block capitals in the caption and the text, and made clear that it covered future claims that might arise. Id. at 870–71.

The district judge did not err in declining to submit the covenant not to sue issue to the jury.

C. Assumption of Risk

An examination of the complaint reveals that appellants sufficiently pleaded assumption of risk in their Third Affirmative Defense by broadly asserting Mrs. Schneider's "culpable conduct." Cf. Hoyt v. McCann, 88 A.D.2d 633, 450 N.Y.S.2d 231 (2d Dep't 1982) (assumption of risk is a form of "culpable conduct"); 1B Warren's N.Y. Negligence 2.02[3], at 1027 (rev. 2d ed. 1980). We therefore address the district court's ruling that assumption of risk was inapplicable to this case, and the court's subsequent failure to charge the jury on express assumption of risk.

In 1975, New York adopted a comparative negligence statute eliminating contributory negligence as a total bar to recovery. Prior to adoption of the statute a plaintiff was required to be free of any negligence contributing in the slightest degree to his injury, in order to recover. The plaintiff's own negligence was viewed as an intervening cause, between the defendant's negligent act and the plaintiff's injury, which prevented any recovery. Dowd v. New York, Ontario & W. Ry. Co., 170 N.Y. 459, 63 N.E. 541 (1902). See generally Arbegast v. Board of Educ., 65 N.Y.2d 161, 165, 480 N.E.2d 365, 368, 490 N.Y.S.2d 751, 754 (1985).

The doctrine of assumption of risk was also a defense to an action for the recovery of damages for personal injuries, prior to the adoption of the comparative negligence statute. Murphy v. Steeplechase Amusement Co., 250 N.Y. 479, 166 N.E. 173 (1929); Ruggerio v. Board of Educ., 31 A.D.2d 884, 298 N.Y.S.2d 149 (4th Dep't 1969), aff'd, 26 N.Y.2d 849, 258 N.E.2d 92, 309 N.Y.S.2d 596 (1970).

The doctrine of assumption of risk lies in the maxim, volenti non fit injuria. Based as it is upon the plaintiff's assent to endure a situation created by the negligence of the defendant, it relieves the defendant from performing a duty which might otherwise be owed to the plaintiff. McEvoy v. City of New York, 266 A.D. 445, 447, 42 N.Y.S.2d 746, 749 (2d Dep't 1943), aff'd, 292 N.Y. 654, 55 N.E.2d 517 (1944). While assumption of risk, like contributory negligence, barred recovery, it was predicated on a theory of contract rather than on a theory of culpable conduct: the plaintiff's agreement, either express or implied, to absolve the defendant from responsibility. Arbegast, 65 N.Y.2d at 165, 480 N.E.2d at 368, 490 N.Y.S.2d at 754. "Express" assumption of risk resulted from an advance agreement that the defendant need not use reasonable care for the plaintiff's benefit. "Implied" assumption of risk, on the other hand, was founded on plaintiff's unreasonable and voluntary consent to the risk of harm from defendant's conduct with full understanding of the possible harm. Id. at 169, 480 N.E.2d at 371, 490 N.Y.S.2d at 757; Restatement (Second) of Torts 496B, 496E.

In 1975, New York's Civil Practice Law and Rules were amended by the addition of a pure comparative negligence statute, Act of May 6, 1975, ch. 69, 1975 N.Y. Laws 94, applicable prospectively as follows:

> In any action to recover damages for personal injury, injury to property, or wrongful death, the culpable conduct attributable to the claimant or to the decedent, including contributory negligence or assumption of risk, shall not bar recovery, but the amount of damages otherwise recoverable shall be diminished in

the proportion which the culpable conduct attributable to the claimant or decedent bears to the culpable conduct which caused the damages.

N.Y.Civ.Prac.L. & R. 1411 (McKinney 1976) (emphasis supplied). By including "assumption of risk" as culpable conduct of the plaintiff that would diminish damages proportionately, the plain language of N.Y.Civ.Prac.L. & R. 1411 seemingly abolished assumption of risk as a complete bar to recovery. However, while the common law distinguished between express and implied assumption of risk, neither section 1411 nor its legislative history defined the phrase or discussed the difference between express and implied assumption of risk.

In accord with the plain language of the statute and the legislative intent expressed in the Report to the 1975 Legislature by the Judicial Conference of the State of New York 21–22 (Feb. 1, 1975) reprinted in 1975 N.Y. Laws 1485 ("it is expected that the courts will treat assumption of risk as a form of culpable conduct under this article"), commentators assumed that under the new comparative negligence statute assumption of risk was no longer a total bar to recovery, but simply diminished the amount of damages recoverable. See 1B Warren's N.Y. Negligence 2.03, at 1028 (rev. 2d ed. 1980); N.Y.Civ.Prac.L. & R. 1411 practice commentary (McKinney 1976). However, the failure of the statute to define assumption of risk or to distinguish express from implied assumption of risk, and the different theoretical bases upon which assumption of risk and contributory negligence rest, suggested that express assumption of risk might not be subject to the comparative fault provisions of section 1411.

In 1985, the Court of Appeals of New York discussed section 1411 and its effect on the doctrine of express assumption of risk in Arbegast v. Board of Educ., 65 N.Y.2d 161, 480 N.E.2d 365, 490 N.Y.S.2d 751 (1985). The court held that express assumption of risk would provide a complete defense, while implied assumption of risk was subsumed by N.Y.Civ.Prac.L. & R. 1411:

> CPLR 1411 requires diminishment of damages in the case of an implied assumption of risk but, except as public policy proscribes an agreement limiting liability, does not foreclose a complete defense that by express consent of the injured party no duty exists and, therefore, no recovery may be had.

Arbegast, 65 N.Y.2d at 170, 480 N.E.2d at 371, 490 N.Y.S.2d at 757–58 (footnote omitted). In reaching this conclusion the court reasoned that prior to enactment of the pure comparative negligence statute, the law had recognized that contractual limitations of liability did not violate public policy "except as specific statutes imposed limitations upon such agreements or interdicted them entirely." Id. at 169–70, 480 N.E.2d at 371, 490 N.Y.S.2d at 757 (citations omitted).

In the case before us, appellees contend that it is against public policy for one expressly to assume the risk of medical malpractice and thereby dissolve the physician's duty to treat a patient according to medical community standards. We first note that the "public policy" referred to by the Arbegast court is defined solely by statute, id., and appellant points to no statute imposing limitations on such express agreements. Moreover, we see no reason why a patient should not be allowed to make an informed decision to go outside currently approved medical methods in search of an unconventional treatment. While a patient should be encouraged to exercise care for his own safety, we believe that an informed decision to avoid surgery and conventional chemotherapy is within the patient's right "to determine what shall be done with his own body," Schloendorff v. Society of the New York Hospital, 211 N.Y. 125, 129, 105 N.E. 92 (1914) (Cardozo, J.) (overruled on other grounds by Bing v. Thunig, 2 N.Y.2d 656, 143 N.E.2d 3, 163 N.Y.S.2d 3 (1957)). Finally, we note that in a recent post-Arbegast case, the Court of Appeals of New York applied the Arbegast distinction between express and implied assumption of risk to a medical malpractice action. In Resnick v. Gribetz, 66 N.Y.2d 729, 487 N.E.2d 908, 496 N.Y.S.2d 998 (1985), the defendant doctor contended that plaintiff's refusal to undergo a suggested biopsy amounted to an assumption of risk. The court, citing Arbegast, ruled that the trial court erred in charging the jury that assumption of risk would bar recovery when no evidence supported a finding of express, as opposed to implied, assumption of risk.

While we do not determine, in the case before us, whether Mrs. Schneider expressly assumed the risk of Dr. Revici's treatment, we hold that there existed sufficient evidence—in the language of the Consent for Medical Care form that she signed, and in testimony relating to specific consent informed by her awareness of the risk of refusing conventional treatment to undergo the Revici method—to allow the jury to consider express assumption of risk as an affirmative defense that would totally bar recovery. It was therefore error for the district court to deny the defendants' request for a jury charge on the issue, and we reverse and remand for that reason.

III. CONCLUSION

To summarize, we hold that the district court erred in refusing to charge the jury with the affirmative defense of express assumption of risk, and therefore reverse the judgment and remand the case to the district court for a new trial limited to the issue of assumption of risk.

* * *

Notes and Questions

1. *Assumption of Risk*. In both *Charell* and *Schneider*, the courts discussed the defense of assumption of the risk. What is the difference between express and implied assumption of the risk? What are the elements of these defenses? Who has the burden of proof? Do courts consider the patient's intelligence and level of education when analyzing assumption of the risk defenses in the health care setting? *See, e.g., Charell*, 173 Misc.2d at 233.

2. *Sufficiency of Consent Form*. The opinion in Schneider states that the consent form signed by Edith Schneider was 'detailed' (*Schneider*, 817 F.2d at 989 & n.1), but does the form provide information about the specific therapies (selenium and dietary restrictions) to which Edith Schneider allegedly consented? Does the form disclose any specific risks associated with these therapies? Does the form disclose any alternatives to such therapies, including conventional cancer care? As such, does the form satisfy the required scope of disclosure, as discussed in *Canterbury* and *Culbertson* in Section I of this Chapter, *supra*?

3. *Covenants Not to Sue; Binding Arbitration Clauses*. In *Schneider*, the Second Circuit held that the district judge did not err in declining to submit the covenant not to sue issue to the jury. Although New York law allowed covenants that would exempt a physician from liability for those injuries found to be the consequences of the non-negligent, proper performance of a medical or surgical procedure, New York law also required such covenants to be "clear and unequivocal" and to be "strictly construed against the party asserting it." *Schneider*, 817 F.2d at 993. How would you re-write the covenant not to sue provision to improve its likelihood of being upheld? Would you recommend that the covenant not to sue language be separated from the informed consent to treatment language? Would you recommend that the covenant not to sue language be in a certain size

font, or require the review of the patient's attorney prior to signing? Although not discussed by *Schneider*, should binding arbitration clauses within informed consent to treatment forms or other documentation signed by the patient be upheld in the health care context? Or, should they be against public policy? *See, e.g.*, Tex. Civ. Prac. & Rem. Code § 74.451(a) ("No physician, professional association of physicians, or other health care provider shall request or require a patient or prospective patient to execute an agreement to arbitrate a health care liability claim unless the form of agreement delivered to the patient contains a written notice in 10-point boldface type clearly and conspicuously stating: 'UNDER TEXAS LAW, THIS AGREEMENT IS INVALID AND OF NO LEGAL EFFECT UNLESS IT IS ALSO SIGNED BY AN ATTORNEY OF YOUR OWN CHOOSING. THIS AGREEMENT CONTAINS A WAIVER OF IMPORTANT LEGAL RIGHTS, INCLUDING YOUR RIGHT TO A JURY. YOU SHOULD NOT SIGN THIS AGREEMENT WITHOUT FIRST CONSULTING WITH AN ATTORNEY.'").

B. Failure to Inform the Patient of the Availability of CAM Care

In the cases immediately above, the plaintiffs sued conventionally-trained physicians who practiced CAM for allegedly failing to disclose the risks associated with foregoing conventional medical care and submitting to one or more alternative therapies. Let us turn the table for a moment and consider a quite different argument; that is, the argument that a conventionally-trained physician who treated a patient with a conventional therapy failed to obtain the patient's informed consent because the physician did not inform the patient of the availability of a complementary or alternative therapy. In *Moore v. Baker*, the United States Court of Appeals for the Eleventh Circuit considered this argument under Georgia's informed consent statute.

Moore v. Baker
United States Court of Appeals for the Eleventh Circuit
989 F.2d 1129 (1993)

Morgan Senior Circuit Judge:

Appellant contends that her doctor violated Georgia's informed consent law by failing to advise her that ethylene diamine tetra acetic acid chelation (EDTA) therapy was available as an alternative to surgery. The district court granted summary judgment in favor of defendants/appellees on the ground that EDTA therapy is not a "generally recognized or accepted" alternative treatment for coronary surgery. We AFFIRM.

FACTUAL AND PROCEDURAL BACKGROUND

Appellant, Judith Moore, was suffering from a partial blockage of her left common carotid artery, which impeded the flow of oxygen to her brain and caused her to feel dizzy and tired. In April of 1989, she consulted with appellee Dr. Roy Baker, an employee of the Neurological Institute of Savannah, P.C. (NIS), about her symptoms. Dr. Baker diagnosed a blockage of her left carotid artery due to artherosclerotic plaque and recommended that she undergo a neurosurgical procedure known as a carotid endarterectomy to correct her medical problem.

Dr. Baker discussed the proposed procedure with Moore and advised her of the risks of undergoing the surgery. He did not advise her, however, of an alternative treatment known as EDTA therapy. Moore signed a written consent allowing Dr. Baker to perform the carotid endarterectomy on April 7, 1989. Following surgery, she appeared to recover well, but soon the hospital staff discovered that Moore was weak on one side. Dr. Baker reopened the operative wound and removed a blood clot that had formed in the artery. Although the clot was removed and the area repaired, Moore suffered permanent brain damage. As a result, Moore is permanently and severely disabled.

On April 8, 1991, the last day permitted by the statute of limitations, Moore filed a complaint alleging that Dr. Baker committed medical malpractice by failing to inform her of the availability of EDTA therapy as an alternative to surgery in violation of Georgia's informed consent law, O.C.G.A. 31-9-6.1 (1991). According to Moore's complaint, EDTA therapy is as effective as carotid endarterectomy in treating coronary blockages, but it does not entail those risks that accompany invasive surgery.

On August 6, 1991 Dr. Baker filed a motion for summary judgment on the issue of informed consent. On August 26, 1991, Moore moved to amend her complaint to assert allegations of negligence by Dr. Baker in the performance of the surgery and in his postoperative care of Moore. Originally, on September 3, 1991, the district court granted Moore's motion to amend her complaint. Shortly thereafter, the district court granted Dr. Baker's motion for summary judgment on the informed consent issue, finding that EDTA therapy is not a "generally recognized or accepted" alternative treatment for coronary surgery. One month later, the district court vacated its September 3rd order and denied Moore's motion to amend her complaint, thus terminating all of Moore's outstanding claims. Moore now appeals the denial of her motion to amend her complaint as well as the grant of summary judgment in favor of Dr. Baker and NIS.

* * *

II.

Moore also challenges the district court's grant of summary judgment on the issue of informed consent. Summary judgment is appropriate where the nonmovant fails to make a showing sufficient to establish the existence of an element essential to that party's case. Celotex Corp. v. Catrett, 477 U.S. 317, 322, 106 S. Ct. 2548, 2552, 91 L. Ed. 2d 265 (1986). The nonmoving party must demonstrate more than a mere scintilla of evidence; if the nonmoving party's evidence is "merely colorable, or is not significantly probative, summary judgment may be granted." HN4 Anderson v. Liberty Lobby, Inc., 477 U.S. 242, 249–52, 106 S. Ct. 2505, 2510–12, 91 L. Ed. 2d 202 (1986). Georgia's informed consent law requires physicians, before performing surgery, to inform their patients of the risks of surgery and of "the practical alternatives to such proposed surgical or diagnostic procedure which are generally recognized and accepted by reasonably prudent physicians." O.C.G.A. 31-9-6.1(a)(5) (1991). It is undisputed that Dr. Baker failed to inform Moore of EDTA therapy as an alternative treatment. Dr. Baker contends that he had no duty to inform Moore about EDTA therapy because it is not generally recognized and accepted among the medical community as an alternative treatment for Moore's condition.

The evidence overwhelmingly suggests that the mainstream medical community does not recognize or accept EDTA therapy as an alternative to a carotid endarterectomy in treating coronary blockages. In his supporting affidavit, Dr. Baker avers that during his medical education, he never received any instruction relating to EDTA therapy as an alternative to a carotid endarterectomy. A neurologist at the Medical College of Georgia confirmed that no one at the Medical College of Georgia teaches EDTA therapy or considers it a practical alternative to a carotid endarterectomy. The record also reflects that a number of professional associations have voiced their opposition to EDTA therapy in this context.[2] Opposition to EDTA therapy is based not only upon the lack of objective evidence that the treatment is effective, but also upon evidence that the treatment may be dangerous.

Dr. Baker has produced ample evidence to negate an essential element of Moore's claim, thus shifting the burden to Moore to make a showing sufficient to create a genuine issue of fact. See Adickes v. S.H. Kress & Co., 398 U.S. 144, 160, 90 S. Ct. 1598, 1609, 26 L. Ed. 2d 142 (1970). In response to Baker's motion for summary judgment, Moore has produced the affidavits of two doctors: David A. Steenblock, an osteopathic physician, and Murray R. Susser, M.D. In essence, the testimony of Drs. Steenblock and Susser suggests that they believe the medical profession should embrace EDTA therapy as a viable alternative to surgery. However, whether the medical profession should change its opposition to this treatment is not the issue before this court. Georgia's informed consent law does not require physicians to inform patients of all alternatives to surgery or even of all the alternatives that the medical profession should accept. The law requires disclosure only of those alternatives that are "generally recognized and accepted by reasonably prudent physicians." Dr. Steenblock's testimony seems to concede that Dr. Baker met this standard.[3] Dr. Susser, likewise, concedes that EDTA therapy is unpopular with surgeons and other members of the medical profession.

Moore has produced evidence that suggests that some physicians approve of EDTA chelation therapy. Dr. Baker, on the other hand, has produced overwhelming evidence tending to show that EDTA therapy is not generally recognized and accepted by reasonably prudent physicians as an alternative to surgery. Moore's evidence is insufficient to create a genuine issue of material fact on the issue of whether EDTA chelation therapy is generally accepted. Therefore, we hold that the district court was correct in granting summary judgment in favor of Dr. Baker and NIS.

For all of the foregoing reasons, we AFFIRM the judgment of the district court.

* * *

Notes and Questions

1. *The Informed Consent Statute at Issue in* Moore. The Georgia informed consent statute interpreted by the Eleventh Circuit in *Moore* is set forth below. Which subsection

---

[2]. The American Medical Association published a document in 1983 that concluded EDTA therapy was not established as an acceptable treatment for coronary or other arterial atherosclerosis. The American Heart Association does not recommend EDTA therapy for treatment of heart disease because the benefits have not been scientifically proven. The American Academy of Family Physicians agreed that EDTA therapy is not an established treatment for atherosclerosis vascular disease. Both the American College of Cardiology and the American College of Physicians, have opposed the therapy except on an experimental basis.

[3]. Q: Chelation therapy is not a conservative, standard or recognized treatment recognized by physicians who perform endarterectomies; is that a fair statement?

A: That's true.

Q: Would that be true as well with cardiologists, neurosurgeons and physicians who perform vascular surgery, and cardiologists?

A: As of this point in time, since the FDA hasn't approved its use for vascular disease, the great majority of physicians, including those you mentioned, would not advocate the use of chelation therapy for treatment of vascular disease.

(Dr. Steenblock depo., pp. 120–21.)

within O.C.G.A. §31-9-6.1(a) did the plaintiff rely on in an attempt to argue that the physician had a duty to disclose the availability of EDTA therapy as an alternative to surgery? Is there anything else that Moore could have done to improve his chances of creating a genuine issue of material fact on the issue of whether EDTA therapy is generally accepted?

> O.C.G.A. §31-9-6.1. Disclosure of certain information to persons undergoing certain surgical or diagnostic procedures ...
>
> (a) Except as otherwise provided in this Code section, any person who undergoes any surgical procedure under general anesthesia, spinal anesthesia, or major regional anesthesia or any person who undergoes an amniocentesis diagnostic procedure or a diagnostic procedure which involves the intravenous or intraductal injection of a contrast material must consent to such procedure and shall be informed in general terms of the following:
>
> > (1) A diagnosis of the patient's condition requiring such proposed surgical or diagnostic procedure;
> >
> > (2) The nature and purpose of such proposed surgical or diagnostic procedure;
> >
> > (3) The material risks generally recognized and accepted by reasonably prudent physicians of infection, allergic reaction, severe loss of blood, loss or loss of function of any limb or organ, paralysis or partial paralysis, paraplegia or quadriplegia, disfiguring scar, brain damage, cardiac arrest, or death involved in such proposed surgical or diagnostic procedure which, if disclosed to a reasonably prudent person in the patient's position, could reasonably be expected to cause such prudent person to decline such proposed surgical or diagnostic procedure on the basis of the material risk of injury that could result from such proposed surgical or diagnostic procedure;
> >
> > (4) The likelihood of success of such proposed surgical or diagnostic procedure;
> >
> > (5) The practical alternatives to such proposed surgical or diagnostic procedure which are generally recognized and accepted by reasonably prudent physicians; and
> >
> > (6) The prognosis of the patient's condition if such proposed surgical or diagnostic procedure is rejected....

2. *Other States' Informed Consent Statutes and Regulations.* The states have taken different approaches to the doctrine, form, and process of informed consent to treatment. The Texas Legislature, for example, directed the formation of the Texas Medical Disclosure Panel ("Panel"). Tex. Civ. Prac. & Rem. Code §74.102. The Panel, composed of six physicians and three attorneys, determines which risks and hazards related to medical care and surgical procedures must be disclosed by physicians and health care providers to their patients or their legal representatives and to establish the form and substance of such disclosure. *Id.* §74.102(a), (c); *id.* §74.103. The Panel is responsible for preparing a list of treatments and procedures ("List A") that require the disclosure of certain enumerated risks. *Id.* §74.103(b); Tex. Admin. Code §§601.1(b), 601.2. If such risks are disclosed, the physician or health care provider has a rebuttable presumption in her favor that informed consent has been obtained. Tex. Civ. Prac. & Rem. Code §74.106. The Panel also creates a list of treatments and procedures ("List B") that require no disclosure. Tex. Admin. Code §§601.1(c), 601.3. Are any complementary or alternative treatments included on List A or List B? If any CAM treatments are listed on List A, what risks need to be disclosed? Do the treatments and procedures listed in List B really have no risks?

3. *Required Forms.* Some states require physicians and other health care providers to use a particular state- or agency-created form when obtaining a patient's informed consent to a treatment or procedure. *See, e.g.,* TEX. ADMIN. CODE §601.4(a) ("The Texas Medical Disclosure Panel adopts the following form which shall be used by a physician or health care provider to inform a patient or person authorized to consent for the patient of the possible risks and hazards involved in the medical treatments and surgical procedures named in the form."). Does the phrase 'health care providers' in the Texas regulations apply to CAM practitioners? Do you think that most CAM practitioners in Texas and other states that have required forms know about these forms? Does it help that the required forms are referenced within regulations that otherwise only apply to allopathic and osteopathic physicians? Finally, does either the required form or List A, *supra* note 2, require conventional physicians to disclose to patients the availability of alternative treatments?

4. *Obtaining Informed Consent: Institutional or Individual Obligation?* Regardless of whether the duty to obtain a patient's informed consent is based in common law, statute, or regulation, do most states impose the duty to obtain informed consent on the health care institution or the individual practitioner? For example, if an acupuncturist or a chiropractor working within a hospital provides health care services to which the patient has not consented, who may be liable for failure to obtain informed consent? The hospital or the CAM practitioner? In most states, the duty to obtain informed consent is imposed on the individual practitioner. *See, e.g., Pauscher v. Iowa Methodist*, 408 N.W.2d 355, 362 (Iowa 1987) ("In Iowa as elsewhere a hospital does not practice medicine.... This court has not imposed on a hospital a duty to inform a patient of matters that lie at the heart of the doctor-patient relationship.... In similar situations other jurisdictions have held the responsibility of obtaining informed consent is the duty of the doctor and the hospital should not intervene."). *See also Pickle v. Curns*, 106 Ill. App. 3d 734, 739, 435 N.E.2d 877, 880–81, 62 Ill. Dec. 79 (1982) ("We do not recognize the existence of a duty on the part of the hospital administration to insure that each of its staff physicians will always perform his duty of due care to his patient."). But, who has the deeper pocket—the practitioner or the health care institution with which the CAM practitioner may be affiliated?

5. *Maintaining Informed Consent Documentation.* Notwithstanding the authorities referenced in the previous note, the federal Medicare Conditions of Participation as well as many state health care institution licensing laws require hospitals and other health care institutions to maintain within the medical record copies of informed consent documentation. *See, e.g.,* 42 C.F.R. §482.24(c)(2)(v) ("All [medical] records must document the following, as appropriate: ... Properly executed informed consent forms for procedures and treatments specified by the medical staff, or by Federal or State law if applicable, to require written patient consent."). Do these federal and state laws establish a private cause of action by a patient against the health care institution for failure to maintain such documentation? Or, does an institution that fails to maintain appropriate documentation risk loss of Medicare-participating provider status, Joint Commission accreditation, or state licensure?

6. *CAM Practitioner Attitudes Towards Informed Consent.* Lawyers, scientists, conventional physicians, and others remain intrigued regarding CAM practitioners' feelings towards and compliance with the doctrine of informed consent, which admittedly first developed in cases involving allopathic physicians. Indeed, one herbalist has been quoted as saying, "I don't want to see forms of informed consent because [if that] happens, insurance [companies] will squeeze the life out of herbal medicine." *See* Caspi et al., *Informed Consent in Complementary and Alternative Medicine*, ECAM Advanced

Print, April 17, 2009, at 1. One group of scientists that has investigated CAM practitioners' attitudes towards informed consent ("IC") and assessed whether standard of practice for IC exist found that, "Very few consistent standards, approaches, or attitudes were found with respect to the IC process in CAM across providers and modalities. That is, in addition to the paucity of standards in CAM itself, there existed no unique profession-based patterns either. Rather, CAM practitioners seem to represent their own opinions or preferences and not profession-based standards, perhaps because there are none." *Id.* at 3.

7. *Relevant Scholarship.* A number of scholars have recently examined the duty of conventionally-trained physicians to provide information about the availability of alternative therapies. *See, e.g.*, Ireh O. Iyioha, *Informed Choice in Alternative Medicine: Expanding the Doctrine Beyond Conventional Alternative Therapies*, 5(2) ICFAI JOURNAL OF HEALTHCARE LAW (2007) (analyzing the doctrine of informed choice in the light of the evolving paradigm of alternative medicine: "The primary focus of the paper goes beyond the possible expansion of the doctrine to accommodate safe and efficacious unconventional alternative therapies and extends to a determination of the criteria by which physicians are required to judge which alternative therapies are safe and effective."). *See also* Michael H. Cohen, *Legal and Risk Management Issues in Complementary and Alternative Medicine*, in COMPLEMENTARY AND ALTERNATIVE MEDICINE 167 (2007); Jeremy Sugarbaker, *Informed Consent, Shared Decision-Making, and Complementary and Alternative Medicine*, 31(2) J. L. MED & ETHICS 247 (2003); and Michael H. Cohen, *Informed Consent in Complementary and Alternative Medicine*, 161(19) ARCHIVES INTERNAL MEDICINE 2288 (2001).

* * *

C. Failure to Inform of the Risks of CAM Care

In a third category of cases, plaintiffs have sued CAM practitioners for allegedly failing to disclose one or more risks associated with a CAM therapy. Let us explore this type of claim using a problem.

Problem

Assume that a 25-year-old female patient visits a chiropractor in a medical office building owned by Integrative Hospital, a Medicare-participating hospital devoted to integrative health care. During the office visit, the patient complains of back pain, neck pain, and headaches. The chiropractor states, "I recommend a spinal manipulation. Some patients who undergo spinal manipulation experience local discomfort, headache, tiredness, and radiating discomfort." The patient responds, "Okay." The chiropractor performs the spinal manipulation. The patient goes home but two days later suffers a stroke and dies. At the patient's autopsy, the coroner discovers a vertebral arterial dissection, which is a dissection (*i.e.*, a flap-like tear) in the vertebral artery. Vertebral arterial dissections have been linked in the scientific literature to physical trauma, including spinal manipulations, and are a major cause of stroke in young people.

- What are the general risks associated with spinal manipulation? How likely are they to occur? How likely is the particular risk of vertebral arterial dissection? *See, e.g.*, Clare Stevinson & Edzard Ernst, *Risks Associated with Spinal Manipulation*, 112 AM J. MED. 566 (2002); Grace Brooke Huffman, *What Are the Risks of Spinal*

Manipulation? AM. FAMILY PHYSICIAN, October 15, 2002; Edzard Ernst, *Intangible Risks of Complementary and Alternative Medicine*, 19(8) J. Clinical Oncology 2365 (2001); Edzard Ernst, *Risks Associated with Complementary Therapies, in* Meyler's Side Effects of Drugs 1649–1681 (2000).

- Which, if any, of the risks of spinal manipulation did the chiropractor have a duty to disclose to the patient prior to performing the spinal manipulation? Would a reasonable patient have wanted to know the risk of vertebral arterial dissection before making a decision to consent to spinal manipulation? Would a reasonable chiropractor have disclosed the risk of vertebral arterial dissection? In either case, does it matter that the risk of vertebral arterial dissection, at its highest, is only one in 20,000 to one in 100,000? *See* Huffman, *supra.*

- Would a reasonable patient have refused to consent to a spinal manipulation if the patient was told of the risk of vertebral arterial dissection?

- Assume that the patient's next of kin would like to sue the chiropractor for failure to obtain informed consent. Which cause of action—assault, battery, or negligence—would a court most likely allow to survive a motion to dismiss?

- The chiropractor obtained the patient's oral consent to the spinal manipulation. Assume for the moment the consent was informed. Do most states require health care providers to obtain written consent? On a particular form? Or, may a patient's consent to a treatment or procedure be provided orally? How would the chiropractor prove the existence of the patient's oral consent?

- Finally, assume that the chiropractor does not carry malpractice insurance. Can the patient's next of kin sue the hospital with which the chiropractor is affiliated for failure to obtain informed consent? Will the cause of action against the hospital likely survive a motion to dismiss?

Chapter Six

Regulation of Dietary Supplements by the Food and Drug Administration

I. Introduction

The use of dietary supplements is one of the most popular categories of Complementary and Alternative Medicine. Use of these products increased over 300% between 1990 and 1997, with approximately half of Americans reporting that they regularly use nonprescription vitamins, minerals or other dietary supplements. One recent study demonstrated that 40% of Americans used a dietary supplement within the last week. Slone Survey, Patterns of Medication Use in the United States 11 (Slone Epidemiology Center at Boston University 2005).

Individuals use supplements for a variety of reasons, from general wellness to warding off a cold or assisting with weight loss. Yet, consumers are often surprised to learn that the Food & Drug Administration (FDA) is relatively uninvolved in the supplement industry. Many consumers assume that if a product is on the market it has been approved for sale by the FDA. The truth is that supplements are not subject to the same premarket approval process as drugs. The labeling standards are less restrictive for supplements than for either foods or drugs. That is not to say that supplements are entirely *un*regulated, as the media and even the NCCAM have sometimes claimed. These claims are a way of expressing displeasure with the low level of regulation, but supplements are less regulated. This chapter focuses on the extent to which the FDA is concerned with dietary supplements, particularly in the areas of labeling and safety.

The FDA comes under closer public and media scrutiny than other federal agencies because its decisions impact people's lives on a very personal level. As in previous chapters, we consider the countervailing interests of individual autonomy and government protection with respect to access to medical treatment. Where competing interests are so great, the topic is invariably controversial. Throughout this chapter, we consider the tensions on all sides: when it comes to dietary supplements, should the FDA do more? Less? Or something different altogether?

Top 10 Most Commonly Used Dietary Supplements

Multivitamin	26%
Vitamin E	10%
Vitamin C	9.1%
Calcium	8.7%
Ginseng	3.3%
Magnesium	3%
Ginkgo biloba	2.2%
Zinc	2.2%
Folic Acid	2.2%
Garlic	1.9%

D.W. Kaufman, J.P. Kelly, L. Rosenberg et al. Recent Patterns of Medication Use in the Ambulatory Adult Population of the United States: The Slone Survey. 287 JAMA 337 (2002).

II. Organization and Authority of the Food and Drug Administration

A. Overview

The FDA is a federal regulatory agency that is a component of the larger Department of Health and Human Services (DHHS). The Food Drug, and Cosmetic Act (FDCA) is the statutory authority under which Congress vested power to the Secretary of DHHS to administer the provisions of the Act. The Secretary then delegated most of that power to the Commissioner of the FDA, an individual who is appointed by the President and confirmed by the Senate. The actions of the Secretary, taken on behalf of the agency, are reviewable by the judiciary to ensure that they are neither arbitrary nor capricious and that they are in accordance with the power granted by the FDCA.

Before we look at how the FDA regulates dietary supplements, we begin with the basics of what the FDA is responsible for regulating and how it regulates the two largest categories: food and drugs.

The FDA is responsible for regulating:

- Foods (other than meat & poultry, which are regulated by the U.S. Department of Agriculture)
- Drugs
- Cosmetics
- Medical devices
- Biologics (*e.g.*, the nation's blood supply)
- Radiation-emitting products (*e.g.*, x-ray equipment and microwave ovens)
- Veterinary products, including pet foods
- Tobacco (as of the Family Smoking Prevention and Tobacco Control Act legislation passed in 2009)
- Dietary Supplements

The FDA is NOT responsible for regulating:

- Alcohol

- Most household items, such as child-resistant packaging and baby-toys
- Illegal drugs

The FDA's stated mission:

> The FDA is responsible for protecting the public health by assuring the safety, efficacy, and security of human and veterinary drugs, biological products, medical devices, our nation's food supply, cosmetics, and products that emit radiation. The FDA is also responsible for advancing the public health by helping to speed innovations that make medicines and foods more effective, safer, and more affordable; and helping the public get the accurate, science-based information they need to use medicines and foods to improve their health.

U.S. Food and Drug Administration, About FDA, What We Do, http://www.fda.gov/About FDA/WhatWeDo/default.htm.

The FDA carries out its mission and regulatory responsibilities through its headquarters in Washington, D.C., five regional offices, 24 district offices, and 144 resident posts throughout the country. The work of the FDA includes research, inspections, and development of guidance for the industries.

Notes and Questions

1. Does anything on the lists of products for which the FDA is and is not responsible surprise you? There has been recent scrutiny regarding the efficacy of having one agency, the FDA, oversee all the above listed products. Reform proposals include creating separate agencies to regulate food and drugs. One reason behind reform proposals is the underfunding of the FDA as an agency. Another reason for reform rumors is that the regulation of drugs and medical devices is vastly different from the regulation of food. Under the current system, the FDA must approve drugs, investigate adverse event reports, and handle a nation-wide food born illness outbreak, sometimes simultaneously. Should one agency be responsible for all of these areas? Even when it may delay the other processes it manages?

2. In the Food and Drug Administration Modernization Act of 1997 (FDAMA), Congress added the mission of the FDA to the original Act:

> MISSION — The Administration shall —
>
> (1) promote the public health by promptly and efficiently reviewing clinical research and taking appropriate action on the marketing of regulated products in a timely manner;
>
> (2) with respect to such products, protect the public health by assuring that [they are not adulterated or misbranded].

§ 403, 21 U.S.C. § 903.

Compare this language with the FDA's stated mission for itself. Despite Congress' ordering of "promotion" over "protection," the FDA maintains that its first priority is protection of the public health. Furthermore, the FDA takes on the responsibilities of public outreach.

B. Regulation of Food

While the FDCA provides the FDA jurisdiction over most foods in interstate commerce, it does not provide clarity about what exactly counts as food. Section 201(f) of the

FDCA defines "food" as "(1) articles used for food and drink for man or other animals, (2) chewing gum, and (3) articles used for components of any such article." This circular definition (while testimony to the power of the chewing gum lobbyists in 1906 when the first Food and Drug Law was passed) is hardly a model of clarity. In order to fulfill its public health responsibility and ensure that what is eaten is both wholesome and fairly represented to the public, the FDA construes the term "food" to include certain items not intended for consumption. The list is composed of, in part, food contact articles such as containers and cutting surfaces, and inedible green coffee beans. Meat and poultry products (including eggs) generally are regulated by the U.S. Department of Agriculture. However, the FDA has jurisdiction over game meats and seafood products.

Assuming that a product is defined as "food" and subject to FDA regulation, how does the agency perform its public health function? Generally, three avenues of agency action stand between the public and unsafe food. First, the FDA strives to ensure that food is processed in a sanitary, safe environment. The FDCA gives the FDA power to take action if food is "adulterated." Food may be adulterated if it contains poisonous substances, unavoidable contaminants, putrid or decomposed substances or is "otherwise unfit for food." Food is also adulterated "if it has been prepared, packed, or held under unsanitary conditions whereby it may have been contaminated with filth, or whereby it may have been rendered injurious to health." To prevent adulteration during the manufacturing process, the FDA adopted a set of Good Manufacturing Practices (GMP) which is now a condition of doing business in the industry. GMPs (adopted by regulation) require a broad range of precautions such as material inspection, employee training, storage and transportation standards and cleaning.

Second, the FDA exercises some safety controls by limiting access to the market. Prior to 1958 there were no premarket clearance requirements for food products. Rather, if the FDA believed a food to be unsafe, it had to exercise its authority to remove "adulterated" products from the market after the item was in use. In 1958, Food Additive Amendments were passed, which broadly defined the term "food additive" to include all products that may directly or indirectly affect or become a part of a food. These "additives" were presumed adulterated unless the additive was the subject of a premarket approval by the FDA.

But this premarket approval requirement, especially when compared to the process used to approve drugs, is defined by large exceptions. Food additives do not include substances "generally recognized as safe" (GRAS). They do not include pesticide chemical residues and, significantly for our purposes, food additives do not include dietary supplements. Finally, a number of substances were grandfathered in as part of the Food Additive Amendments. The most significant exception to the food additive approval requirement is the exception for GRAS. It is typically the company that is responsible for determining that the ingredient meets the GRAS standard. This standard is defined as a general recognition among qualified experts that the substance is reasonably certain to not be harmful under its intended conditions of use. This recognition can come through scientific procedures, or, for substances in use before 1958 when the Food Additive Amendments passed, through experience based on common use of food. If an added ingredient is GRAS, the company may add the item to a food product without notifying FDA.

Third, the FDCA forbids "misbranding" food. The FDA uses its statutory authority to prevent misbranding by regulating the labels and labeling of food products. A label is the display of written or graphic matter on the immediate container of the article. "Labeling" is defined to include all labels and other written, printed or graphic matter on any of its containers, wrappers, or accompanying articles.

1. Label Requirements

Today, FDA regulations govern almost every aspect of food labeling. The basic components of the food label are as follows:

1. An *identity statement*, which is the common or usual name of the food and should accurately identify the basic nature of the product.
2. *Net quantity of contents* statement which declares the weight, common measure or numerical account of the container.
3. The *responsibility statement*, which states the name, street address and zip code of the person that manufactures, packages, distributes the product.
4. The *ingredients statement*, which lists the products ingredients by their common or usual name, in descending order of prominence.
5. *Flavor labeling*, which describes the flavoring of the product, including any natural, artificial flavors or combination thereof.
6. *Nutrition labeling*, which must appear in a detailed "nutrition facts" format on the product.
7. A disclosure statement if any *nutrient content claim*s are made. Nutrient content claims disclose the level of a nutrient in a food and may be placed on labels only if they use the descriptive terms defined by FDA regulations. For example, if a food claims to be a "good source" of a vitamin, it must contain 10% or more of the daily value. Relative claims, which compare the level of nutrient preserving in a product to that of a reference product, may also be included if they meet uniform FDA standards.
8. The *country of origin*.

2. Label Options

In addition to the nutrient content claims described above, the FDA permits structure-function and health claims on food labels in limited circumstances. Structure-function claims, such as "calcium builds strong bones," can be made for conventional food only if the claims are derived from the "nutrient value" of the food. Health claims generally are permitted only in two circumstances:

1. If the FDA has promulgated a regulation, based on significant scientific agreement, approving the claim and setting forth the conditions under which it may be used. Otherwise, a health claim is considered "misbranding" and may subject the food to regulation as an unapproved drug.

2. If the health claim is the subject of "authoritative statement" of a scientific body of the United States government with official responsibility of public health protection or research such as the National Institute of Health, the Centers for Disease Control and Prevention or the National Academy of Sciences.

In response to court decisions, the FDA also established a review process which may permit "qualified health claims" which lack significant scientific agreement to sustain the claim but where the agency believes that potential deception can be eliminated through a disclaimer.

C. Regulation of Drugs

1. Definition

The FDCA defines a drug. The definition begins:

The term "drug" means

A) articles recognized in the official United States Pharmacopoeia, official Homeopathic Pharmacopoeia of the United States, or the official National Formulary;

B) articles "intended for use in the diagnosis, cure, mitigation, treatment, or prevention of disease";

C) articles (other than food) intended to affect the structure or any function of the body of man or other animals; and

D) articles intended for use as a component of any article specified in clause (A), (B), or (C).

§ 201 (g)(1), 21 U.S.C. § 321

Before a new prescription drug can be marketed it must have an approved "new drug application" from the FDA unless it is a generic drug, which is subject to an abbreviated new drug application.

2. Safety and Efficacy

Before the FDA approves a new drug at the end of the New Drug Application (NDA) process, the drug must be supported by substantial evidence that it will be safe and effective under the indicated conditions of use. Typically, "substantial evidence" means evidence from two well controlled clinical studies. As one can see from the description below, the process leading the NDA approval is lengthy, expensive and often futile.

After preclinical investigation, which usually involves identifying essential drugs through laboratory experimentation and animal testing, the new drug sponsor will turn to the testing of the potential drug in people. In order to do so, the sponsor must provide formal notification to the FDA. This notification is called an Investigational New Drug Application (IND). If the FDA does not object to the IND within 30 days, it becomes effective and clinical trials may begin. In general the IND provides an overall investigative plan for the drug as well as the credentials of the investigators, the investigative protocol, information on the proposed drug chemistry, and a summary of the previous human experience with the drug. Finally, the IND must contain a commitment to conduct clinical trials under the supervision of an institutional review board and to follow all applicable rules, including those pertaining to informed consent.

Typically, clinical trials are conducted in three phases. Phase I studies administer the drug to a small number of healthy people. One of the primary goals of Phase I research is to determine the pharmalogical action in humans and study any associated side effects as dosage increases. In some cases, sponsors may derive some early evidence on effectiveness as well.

Phase II studies involve more patients, often 100–200 patients who have the disease or the condition. Phase II trials begin to obtain evidence of the drug's effectiveness, as well as to explore further side effect issues and other risks.

Phase III clinical studies typically involve several thousand patients. They may take place at multiple locations and involve numerous investigators. These studies begin with notification to the FDA after the sponsor has gathered evidence that the drug may be effective from the Phases I and II studies. Phase III is the group of critical trials. They gather information that may meet the sponsor's obligation to provide substantial evidence of safety and efficacy necessary for FDA approval.

After the Phase III clinical trials are completed, depending upon the success of the trials, the sponsor may prepare and submit its NDA to the FDA. The NDA includes not only the clinical data obtained through the studies, but also a description of the proposed method by which the drug will be manufactured, processed and packed; a description of the drug product and drug substance; a list of applicable patents; and the drug's proposed labeling. FDCA provides that 180 days after the filing of the NDA, or an additional period agreed between the parties, the FDA must make its approval decision. In reality, the FDA is rarely in a position to reach a final decision on the NDA within the 180 day time frame and the review of the drug may stretch on much longer.

In determining whether there is substantial evidence that the drug will be "safe" and "effective" as part of its approval decision, the FDA recognizes that no drug is absolutely safe. In making its decision, the FDA weighs the new drug's demonstrated effectiveness against its risks to determine whether the benefits outweigh the risks. To do so, it considers the seriousness of the targeted disease, the adequacy of other remedies, and the side effects which came to life during the clinical studies.

FDA approval of an NDA does not end the agency's oversight. As part of its approval, the FDA may require additional clinical studies. These are typically referred to as "Phase IV" studies. These studies are designed to obtain additional safety and efficacy data, detected uses or abuses of the drug, or determine effectiveness for the labeled indications under conditions of wide spread usage *after* the drug is introduced to the market. In addition, the holder of an approved NDA must monitor "adverse drug experiences" and report certain adverse reactions to the FDA.

3. Over the Counter Drugs

Over-the-counter (OTC) drugs, which are available without prescription, are also overseen by the FDA, although in a different matter than prescription drugs. Generally, OTC drugs have the following characteristics:

- their benefits outweigh their risks;
- the potential for misuse and abuse is low;
- consumers can use them for self diagnosed conditions;
- they can be adequately labeled; and
- health practitioners are not needed for the safe and effective use of these drugs.

Most medicinal products used in OTC drugs have been marketed for many years prior to the laws that required proof of safety and efficacy. As a result, they are not "new drugs." However, the FDA has a program for evaluating the ingredients in each type of OTC drug as part of the agency's OTC Drug Review Program. This program establishes drug monographs, which are a kind of "recipe book" covering acceptable ingredients, doses, formulations, labeling, and testing, for each class of products. If an OTC drug conforms to a monograph, it may be marketed without FDA pre-approval. If, however, the sponsor proposes that a new ingredient enter the over counter market place for the first time, that product must go through the new drug application process.

III. Regulation of Dietary Supplements

A. Is It a Drug or a Food?

Prior to the enactment of the Dietary Supplement Health and Education Act (DSHEA) (pronounced *da-shay*) in 1994, the FDCA provided only two categories under which dietary supplements could be regulated: foods or drugs. Generally, dietary supplements were regulated as foods and had to meet the GRAS standard for safety. Labels for dietary supplements also had to follow the standards set for food labeling, meaning that health claims could push a dietary supplement into the drug category. As you read the excerpt of the following case, consider the approach the court takes to dietary supplements.

United States v. Nutrition Service, Inc.
U.S. District Court, Western District of Pennsylvania
227 F. Supp. 375 (1964)

* * *

OPINION

On May 15, 1950, in compliance with Pennsylvania law requiring certification of those doing business under a Fictitious Name, [the defendant] certified that he was the person owning and interested in the business..., that the business was the 'research, development, and manufacture of biologically processed foods'.

* * *

The business was noted primarily, if not exclusively, for its production and promotion of Mucorhicin. This product results from the use of wheat basically with salt and yeast by fermentation, molding and aging. A liquid is eventually obtained, bottled and dispensed as Mucorhicin.

* * *

During these past years, much varied printed matter was distributed throughout the United States designating Mucorhicin for use by persons suffering with diseases and particularly cancer, and more particularly terminal cases of cancer. The distribution became widespread and many testimonials of its benefits for relief from disease were forthcoming. The defendants attempted to get aid from the American Cancer Society and from the Government but were never successful.

In October 1963, a corporation, Nutrition Service, Inc., was formed [by the defendant to replace the initial business] and the various recipients of the printed matter were told to destroy these because of the creation of the corporation.

The plaintiff contends that Mucorhicin is a drug. The defendants' primary defense is that it is not a drug but rather a food product. They say in their Memorandum of Law at page 1:

'The action of the plaintiff in the within matter is predicated upon the proposition that the subject material 'Mucorhicin' is a 'drug', whereas, it is the contention of the corporate defendant and the individual defendants connected therewith, that the subject matter is not a 'drug', but is and was at the time of institution of this suit, a food product of biologically processed whole wheat grain and is sold and distributed for special dietary purposes through licensed members of the healing arts for special dietary uses.'

Is this product identified by the name 'Mucorhicin' a drug or a food product?

* * *

From all of the evidence preliminarily presented in this case, I am unable to find that Mucorhicin is a food. I have weighed and re-weighed the evidence in this case and the balance remains overwhelmingly convincing that Mucorhicin was dispensed and used in the treatment, cure, prevention and mitigation of disease.

* * *

For the defendants, only Dr. Wilson, its medical director, testified; and if any proof were needed to support the plaintiff's case, he added much which convinced me that Mucorhicin was being used for the cure, treatment, mitigation and prevention of disease.

He talked only of disease and cure. He indicated that 5,000 patients in the United States and in seven other countries were on record as having been treated, cured and remedied by Mucorhicin. Of these many cases, he chose the two of the boy and the woman cancer patients as examples.

He spoke as a doctor. He spoke of diseases and he spoke of cures for these diseases by the administering of Mucorhicin. After the hearing had closed, I was able to properly examine the exhibits and here was more of the same proof going back through the many years—disease and Mucorhicin coming to the aid, treatment, prevention and mitigation of disease.

* * *

Certain evidence was presented by the plaintiff that the defendants here claimed for Mucorhicin antibiotic qualities by reason of a relationship with penicillin. The defendants countered this by their claim that Mucorhicin contained a strain of penicillium and that the many strains of penicillium in themselves are factually a part of many foods, as for instance in the case of such food as roquefort and camembert cheese. While in fact it may be true that mold growth exists naturally in certain foods and that such foods are sold regularly there is essentially this difference, that such foods are sold only as foods and not for treatment, mitigation and prevention of disease. If cheese were to be sold by any processor for the cure, treatment, mitigation and prevention of disease under the classification of food, within the provisions of the Food and Drug Act, it would be necessarily a drug.

* * *

The fact that the defendants have and are maintaining that Mucorhicin was and is a food and that they even registered with the State and County in 1950 as showing that they were researching in food does not help the defendants here. The real test is how was this product being sold? If as a food, was it for the furnishing of energy and body building? Or was it being sold for the treatment and mitigation of disease? The answer is presented all through the evidence that treatment, cure, mitigation and prevention of disease was the purpose for which Mucorhicin was sold by the defendants and bought (and very frequently prescribed) by the purchasers. No matter how loud and long one may declaim that black is white, black is nevertheless black. The same is true here. Designating Mucorhicin as a food supplement and recommending its merits in curbing death gripping diseases does not make it a food under the provisions of the Food and Drug Act.

Notes and Questions

1. What regulatory hurdles likely motivated the owners of Mucorhicin to label it as "food" rather than a "drug"?

2. Other purported food products that the FDA sought to regulate as drugs pre-"Dietary Supplement Health and Education Act of 1994" (DSHEA) include dietary supplements consisting of evening primrose oil and black currant oil (BCO), both of which the FDA challenged as unapproved food additives. See FDA, Import Alert No. 66-04 for Evening Primrose (Feb. 12. 1985); United States v. 29 Cartons of * * * An Article of Food, Etc., 987 F.2d 33 (1st Cir. 1993). Industry frustration with the FDA's stance on dietary supplements, particularly the agency's challenges to BCO, fueled the push for regulatory change. See Cassandra A. Saltis, Between a Rock and a Hard Place: FDA's Regulation of Dietary Ingredients in Dietary Supplements, 2 J. Food L. & Pol'y 11 (2006).

B. The Dietary Supplement Health and Education Act of 1994 (DSHEA)

The FDA's periodic attempts to regulate dietary supplements either as drugs (which would drive products from the marketplace without premarket approval) or as traditional foods (by evaluating the safety of all new ingredients used in dietary supplements, as the agency does with foods) brought concerns both from the growing supplement industry as well as from consumers who sought access to existing dietary supplements which had not been tested for safety. In 1994, Congress stepped into the fray. It sought to give consumers access to dietary supplements, while providing more information (though labeling guidelines) about the products.

In DSHEA, Congress amended provisions of the FDCA to address specifically how dietary supplements should be treated under the law. It began by formally defining dietary supplements and then setting up a regulatory structure specifically for these products. In general, dietary supplements would be regulated similarly to foods, which eliminated the threat of FDA's premarket approval authority for drugs. DSHEA also provided that the FDA's premarket safety evaluations of new food ingredients would not apply to the dietary ingredients used in supplements. The combination of these provisions provided for less oversight of these products than either drugs or traditional foods. It placed the FDA in a decidedly more reactive regulatory role with regard to dietary supplements.

1. Definition

Section 201(ff) of the FDCA defines dietary supplement as follows:

[A] product (other than tobacco) intended to supplement the diet that bears or contains one of more of the following dietary ingredients:

- a vitamin;

- a mineral;
- an herb or other botanical;
- an amino acid;
- a dietary substance for use by man to supplement the diet by increasing total dietary intake; or
- a concentrate, metabolite, constituent, extract, or combination of any ingredient described above.

§ 201 (ff), 21 U.S.C. § 321.

The statute also states that dietary supplements must be labeled as such and must not be represented for use as a conventional food or as a sole item of a meal or the diet.

The effect of this amendment is that dietary supplements are still treated like food products under the law, but they are a unique type of food with separate standards for safety and labeling.

2. Safety Standards
a. The Statute

Section 402 of the FDCA states that a food is adulterated if—

(f)(1) It is a dietary supplement or contains a dietary ingredient that—

(A) presents a significant or unreasonable risk of illness or injury under

(i) conditions of use recommended or suggested in labeling, or

(ii) if no conditions of use are suggested or recommended in the labeling, under ordinary conditions of use

§ 402, 21 U.S.C. § 342.

* * *

In any proceeding under this subparagraph, the United States shall bear the burden of proof on each element to show that a dietary supplement is adulterated ...

Under this amendment, dietary supplement manufacturers (unlike manufacturers of drugs and complex medical devices) make the determination that a product is sufficiently safe to be put on the market. The FDA then has the burden of proving otherwise in order to remove that product from the market. The following section on the ban on Ephedra describes the first time the FDA blocked the sale of a dietary supplement under the authority of DSHEA.

b. The Ban on Ephedra: Enforcement of the Limited Power

Ephedrine alkaloids are naturally occurring substances found in many plant species. They act similarly to amphetamines in their stimulation of the heart and nervous system. These botanicals have long been used for medicinal purposes and recently became popular for use in dietary supplements to promote weight loss, increase energy, and enhance athletic performance.

Although products containing ephedra accounted for only one percent of dietary supplement sales, it is estimated that just before the ban was enacted they accounted for more than sixty percent of the serious side effects reported to the CDC in association with dietary supplements. Various adverse events began to be reported to the FDA in the 1990s. The reported side effects included stroke, heart palpitations, tremors, and insomnia. Ephedra has also been linked by some to the deaths of Minnesota Vikings football player Korey Stringer in 2001 and Baltimore Orioles pitcher Steve Belcher in 2003. Both men died suddenly while training with their teams.

After the initial reports to the FDA in the 1990s, the agency began its own investigation of the supplement. After the investigation, the FDA recognized a need to address the issue of ephedra and proposed regulations in 1997. Because of the exception that supplement manufactures do not have to report the scientific data on their supplements, the evidence used in the study was limited to medical literature and a Food Advisory Committee opinion. The investigation continued into the new millennium. Finally, in 2004, the FDA banned the use of all levels of ephedra because of its "unreasonable risk of illness or injury."

> 21 C.F.R. § 119.1
>
> Dietary supplements containing ephedrine alkaloids present an unreasonable risk of illness or injury under conditions of use recommended or suggested in the labeling, or if no conditions of use are recommended or suggested in the labeling, under ordinary conditions of use. Therefore, dietary supplements containing ephedrine alkaloids are adulterated under section 402(f)(1)(A) of the Federal Food, Drug, and Cosmetic Act.
>
> Dietary Supplements Containing Ephedrine Alkaloids, 69 Fed. Reg. 6853, (February 11, 2004).

Nutraceutical Corporation v. Von Eschenbach
Tenth Circuit Court of Appeals
459 F.3d 1033 (2006)

Eagan, District Judge.

Defendants-appellants, Andrew von Eschenbach, M.D., Acting Commissioner of the U.S. Food and Drug Administration, the United States Food and Drug Administration ("FDA" or "the agency"), Michael O. Leavitt, Secretary of the Department of Health and Human Services, the Department of Health and Human Services, and the United States, appeal from a judgment of the district court denying their motion for summary judgment and granting the cross-motion of plaintiffs-appellees for summary judgment. [Citation omitted]. Plaintiffs-appellees, Nutraceutical Corporation and its wholly-owned subsidiary, Solaray Corporation (collectively, "Nutraceutical"), manufacture and sell Ephedra, a product containing ephedrine-alkaloid dietary supplements ("EDS"). In 2004, the FDA issued a regulation which banned all EDS sales in the United States market. Nutraceutical brought this action challenging the regulation as unlawful. The district court agreed with Nutraceutical. Our jurisdiction arises under 28 U.S.C. § 1291, and we reverse.

Background

In its published decision, the district court determined that the risk-benefit analysis employed by the FDA to support an EDS ban was contrary to the intent of Congress and that the FDA had failed to prove by a preponderance of the evidence that EDS pose an unreasonable risk of illness or injury at 10 milligrams ("mg") or less a day. It accordingly entered summary judgment in favor of Nutraceutical, enjoined the FDA from enforcing its proscription against Nutraceutical for the sale of products with a recommended daily dosage of 10 mg or less of EDS, and remanded to the FDA for new rule-making.

* * *

Discussion

* * *

In this case, we must determine whether Congress unambiguously manifested its intent to restrict the FDA from weighing benefits when determining the risk posed by a dietary supplement. The district court was correct to proceed under *Chevron* step one in deciding the question of whether the FDA properly used a risk-benefit analysis in determining whether EDS pose an "unreasonable risk." [Citation omitted.] We nevertheless reverse the district court after finding that Congress unambiguously required the FDA to conduct a risk-benefit analysis under DSHEA.

In 1994, Congress enacted DSHEA to clarify that dietary supplements, absent declarations promoting the supplements as drugs, would be regulated in a manner similar to food products. Accordingly, in the interest of public health, Congress imposed a duty on the FDA to keep adulterated dietary supplements off the market. 108 Stat. at 4326 (instructing the FDA to "take swift action against [dietary supplements] that are unsafe or adulterated."). DSHEA classifies a dietary supplement as adulterated if it "presents a significant or unreasonable risk of illness or injury." [Citation omitted.] The FDA understood "[t]he plain meaning of 'unreasonable'... [to] connote [ ] comparison of the risks and benefits of the product." We agree. The plain language of the statute directs the FDA to restrict distribution of dietary supplements which pose any risk that is unreasonable in light of its potential benefits. [Citation omitted.]

Congress enacted DSHEA in an effort to improve public access to dietary supplements based on the belief that there may be a positive relationship between dietary supplement use, reduced health-care expenses, and disease prevention. *See Pharmanex,* 221 F.3d at 1158–59 ("It is true that DSHEA was enacted to alleviate the regulatory burdens on the dietary supplement industry, allowing consumers greater access to safe dietary supplements in order to promote greater wellness among the American population.") (citation omitted). The FDCA should not be read too restrictively but in manner consistent with the statute's overriding purpose to protect public health. Accordingly, DSHEA should receive a liberal construction where the FDA has taken remedial steps in response to a perceived public health problem.

According to the district court, by injecting a risk-benefit analysis, the FDA required Nutraceutical to make a showing of the benefits of its product. However, at no time has the FDA required manufacturers of EDS to provide data on the benefits of their products. Rather, the FDA has assumed its responsibility of gathering data, soliciting comments, and conducting the risk-benefit analysis.[5] Congress expressly placed the burden

---

5. The district court compared the language of DSHEA to the statutory language governing medical devices and drugs and concluded that, unlike manufacturers of medical devices and drugs, manufacturers of dietary supplements do not need to prove effectiveness prior to taking their product to market. 364 F.Supp.2d at 1318 ("A brief look at the legislative history of the DSHEA indicates that Congress generally intended to harmonize the treatment of dietary supplements with that of foods when it added the dietary supplement subsection to the food adulteration provision."). The district court is correct. However, the district court confused effectiveness with safety. The FDA did not ban EDS

of proof on the government to determine whether a dietary supplement is adulterated. Accordingly, EDS were allowed to enter the market without findings of safety or effectiveness. The FDA did not impose a premarket requirement for the sale of EDS. * * * Based on the record, we disagree with the district court and find that the FDA did not shift the burden of proof to manufacturers. The risk-benefit analysis is conducted by, and at the expense of, the agency. Despite Nutraceutical's characterization of the process, the agency did not "require proof of a substantial benefit to counterbalance risk as a condition precedent to lawful sale of EDS." The burden remains on the agency to show that risks associated with a dietary supplement outweigh benefits and are, therefore, unreasonable. Thus, a risk-benefit analysis does not undermine congressional intent by improperly shifting the burden of proof onto manufacturers of dietary supplements.

* * *

The majority of data in the administrative record suggests that EDS pose an unreasonable threat to the public's health. The FDA:

> looked at the seriousness of the risks and the quality and persuasiveness of the totality of the evidence to support the presence of those risks. [It] then weighed the risks against the importance of the benefits and the quality and persuasiveness of the totality of the evidence to support the existence of those benefits ... giv[ing] more weight to benefits that improve health outcomes, especially in the long term, than to benefits that are temporary or rely on subjective measures such as feeling or looking better.

69 Fed.Reg. at 6799.

The agency expressed that it would not deem EDS adulterated based on "risks that are insignificant and reasonable in light of the benefits from the supplement...." [Citation omitted.] The evidence in the administrative record was sufficiently probative to demonstrate by a preponderance of the evidence that EDS at any dose level pose an unreasonable risk. The greater weight of the evidence supports the FDA's ban on EDS, thus satisfying the agency's burden.

The FDA's extensive research identified the dose level at which ephedrine alkaloids present unreasonable risk of illness or injury to be so minuscule that no amount of EDS is reasonably safe. The FDA reasonably concluded that there is no recommended dose of EDS that does not present an unreasonable risk. The FDA was not arbitrary or capricious in its Final Rule; the FDA met its statutory burden of justifying a total ban of EDS by a preponderance of the evidence.

We find that the FDA correctly followed the congressional directive to analyze the risks and benefits of EDS in determining that there is no dosage level of EDS acceptable for the market. Summary judgment for plaintiffs was therefore improper, and summary judgment for defendants should have been entered. Accordingly, the district court's decision is reversed, and we remand for entry of judgment in favor of defendants. As noted above, Nutraceutical's Motion to Correct Oral Argument Record is granted.

REVERSED AND REMANDED.

---

for failing to deliver promised health gains or for ineffectiveness; the FDA banned EDS because they were determined to be unsafe.

Notes and Questions

1. In its risk-benefit ephedrine analysis, the FDA reviewed both the peer-reviewed literature and the adverse events reports. These identified short and long term risks, including increased blood pressure and heart rate. It did so after receiving thousands of reports of adverse events, including a number of deaths. At the time, unlike with drugs, dietary supplement manufacturers were not required to report adverse events. As a result, while the FDA was successful in 2004 in banning ephedra, the ban became effective 10 years after the agency issued its first advisory.

Congress amended DSHEA after the ephedra ban to require dietary supplement companies that receive a serious adverse event report to submit information about the event to FDA beginning in December 2007. Serious adverse events include not only death, but inpatient hospitalization, birth defects, life-threatening experiences and medical interventions necessary to prevent these outcomes. Moderate events (such as headaches) are not required to be reported, although companies may do so. Health care practitioners and patients can voluntarily make adverse event reports about supplements to FDA as well.

In the period following the effective date of mandatory adverse reporting, the number of all dietary supplements adverse events reported to FDA tripled. From January through October 2008, 948 adverse event reports came to FDA, as compared with 298 during the same time the previous year. Despite the increase in reports, it appears that the reported events are only the tip of the iceberg. In 2008, FDA estimated that the number of total adverse events related to dietary supplements per year (including mild, moderate and serious event) is over 50,000.

2. In addition to the unreasonable risk standard used in the ephedra case, a dietary supplement may also be considered adulterated if it contains an undeclared active pharmaceutical ingredient (API). Dietary supplements which contain active ingredients of FDA-approved prescription drugs can no longer be categorized as dietary supplements. The adulteration of supplements with such ingredients may be unintentional, but may also be an intentional effort to increase the potency or effect of the supplement. Either way, the adulteration is a health hazard for consumers who are unaware of the presence of a prescription drug ingredient in the supplement. *See* Elizabeth Miller, *Drugged Dietary Supplements, Update: Food and Drug Law, Regulation, and Education*, 6 (Nov.–Dec. 2008).

3. Unlike the United States, Canada, Germany and France regulate herbal medicines as drugs. They require premarket approval. In both Germany and France, the manufacturer bears the burden of proving quality, safety and effectiveness. In Germany, an abridged approval process is available for products with a "history of traditional use." What would be the benefits — and drawbacks — to the regulatory approach in these countries?

4. While Congress passed DSHEA in part to increase the availability of dietary supplements, some critics believe the relatively unregulated status permits unsafe products to easily find their way to unsuspecting consumers. Consider the following concern as set forth by Peter J. Cohen.

> The government's obligation to assure the general welfare of its citizens through adequate public health measures provides justification for the current regulatory scheme mandated by the FD&C Act as applied to pharmaceuticals. These regulations are designed to ensure that the public has access to drugs that are safe, pure, and effective. A balancing of the burdens and benefits imposed by

regulating pharmaceuticals provides clear warrant for their continued enforcement. If we accept the rationale for strong regulation of pharmaceuticals, it is difficult to reject the thesis that the same standards should be applied to dietary supplements, which are similar to drugs in everything but statutorily-assigned name. Therefore, DSHEA should be repealed and the FD&C Act returned to its 1994 status. The first step will be revising the current definition of "drug." Although the biologic effects of vitamins and minerals in "normal" doses do not depend on whether they are ingested as food or "pills" (and are therefore of minimal concern), they may exert significant and sometimes pathologic biologic effects when ingested in amounts far greater than normal daily requirements. "Mega" doses of vitamins comprise a significant portion of the compounds produced by the nutritional supplement industry. The vast majority of products sold as dietary supplements by this industry are "drugs" in everything but statute in that they have significant physiologic, pharmacologic, and sometimes even pathologic properties. It follows that supplements and drugs should be subject to an identical regulatory scheme, regardless of whether the manufacturer intends or denies intending that these products can be used to treat disease.

Peter J. Cohen, *Science, Politics, and the Regulation of Dietary Supplements: It's Time to Repeal DSHEA*, 31 AM. J.L. & MED. 175 (2005). *See generally* Cary Elizabeth Zuk, *Herbal Remedies Are Not Dietary Supplements: A Proposal For Regulatory Reform*, 11 HASTINGS WOMEN'S L.J. 29 (2000); Iona N. Kaiser, *Dietary Supplements: Can the Law Control the Hype?*, 37 HOUS. L. REV. 1249 (2000).

Problem

Trumark Incorporated manufactures a dietary supplement which it promotes as "Energy for Men." "Energy for Men" is advertised as an "all natural" product which will "enhance sexual performance." One online advertisement states that it is a "natural alternative to treatments for erectile dysfunction." In response to a complaint by a competitor, the FDA conducted a chemical analysis of the product and found that it contained undeclared chemicals which were similar to the active ingredients used in an FDA-approved prescription drug product. While there is concern expressed by some physicians that "Energy for Men" may interact with prescription drugs (particularly those drugs which treat high blood pressure, high cholesterol or heart disease), there have been no reports of any adverse effects associated with the product.

What advice would you give in the following situations:

- To the FDA, which is considering what, if any, steps to take with regard to this dietary supplement.
- To a naturopath who regularly suggests use of this supplement to male patients. (The naturopath has had two patients complain of head aches after using "Energy for Men," but that is the only side effect she has encountered.)
- To the manufacturer of "Energy for Men."

3. Labeling

Both dietary supplement manufacturers and consumers must be able to understand the labeling requirements set out in DSHEA. Manufactures should understand the requirements when they seek to promote their products. Consumers, on the other hand, must properly understand the requirements when they seek aids to help them manage their health. To aid consumers, the FDA requires a Supplement Facts box similar to that required for conventional foods on dietary supplement packaging. The precise format of the box is set out in FDA regulations. It should include a statement of identity, ingredient statement, nutrition information, information on the manufacturer, packer or distributor, and an accurate statement of the quantity of the contents.

Labels and other promotional materials cannot, however, claim that an item can treat or cure a disease. That is the province of drugs, which require premarket approval. Supplements can make the following claims in prescribed circumstances:

- *Health claims* (such as "25 grams of soy protein a day, as part of a diet low in saturated fat and cholesterol, may reduce the risk of heart disease. 1 capsule provides X grams of soy protein.")

  These claims, which describe a relationship between the supplement and a disease or health-related condition, generally require FDA approval by regulation. Before authorizing these health claims, the FDA will conduct a careful review of the scientific literature. This evidence is usually brought to the agency's attention as a result of the submission of a health claim petition. The FDA then uses a "significant scientific agreement" standard to determine whether the health claim is well established. For conventional foods, two other mechanisms for approving health claims for foods are 1) claims based on authoritative statements from a scientific body of the U.S. Government or the National Academy of Sciences; and 2) qualified health claims where the weight of the scientific evidence does not reach the standard of significant scientific agreement, but which are allowed with an appropriate disclaimer. With regard to the former mechanism, Congress did not include dietary supplements in the provisions for health claims based on authoritative statements. As a result, this avenue to health claims is not available. The later set of "qualified" health claims was provided for as a result of the *Pearson v. Shalala* case set out below.

- *Nutrient Content Claims* (which can be express ("low sodium") or implied ("healthy"))

  These claims describe the level of a nutrient or dietary substance in the product, using terms such as "high," "free" or "good source." These claims can only be made (with a few exceptions) for nutrients or substances that have an established daily value. Moreover, there must be either an "authoritative statement," like those discussed above, supporting the claim or a FDA regulation specifying the criteria that a supplement must meet in order to use the claim. Percentage claims may be used as well.

- *Structure-Function Claims* ("helps promote digestion")

  These claims are statements that describe how a product affects the normal functions or general well being of the body. "Calcium builds strong bones" and "fiber maintains bowel regularity" are examples which describe general well-being from consumption of the supplement. Structure-function claims can be made with more regulatory ease in that they do not require an FDA regulation or scientific "authoritative statement." Rather, the manufacturer must notify FDA of any structure-function claims no later than 30 days after the product is first marketed. And while the manufacturer is responsible for ensuring the accuracy and truthfulness of the claim (i.e. they must be substantiated), this substantiation need not be shared with FDA when the notice is provided.

The following case illustrates how courts have interpreted the pre-approval requirement for health claims. Following the case is a recent example of FDA approval for a "qualified" health claim.

Pearson v. Donna E. Shalala, Secretary, United States Department of Health and Human Services

United States Court of Appeals for the District of Columbia
164 F.3d 650 (1999)

Silberman, Circuit Judge:

Marketers of dietary supplements must, before including on their labels a claim characterizing the relationship of the supplement to a disease or health-related condition, submit the claim to the Food and Drug Administration for preapproval. The FDA authorizes a claim only if it finds "significant scientific agreement" among experts that the claim is supported by the available evidence. Appellants failed to persuade the FDA to authorize four such claims and sought relief in the district court, where their various constitutional and statutory challenges were rejected. We reverse.

Dietary supplement marketers Durk Pearson and Sandy Shaw, presumably hoping to bolster sales by increasing the allure of their supplements' labels, asked the FDA to authorize four separate health claims ... Each of appellants' four claims links the consumption of a particular supplement to the reduction in risk of a particular disease:

> (1) "Consumption of antioxidant vitamins may reduce the risk of certain kinds of cancers."
>
> (2) "Consumption of fiber may reduce the risk of colorectal cancer."
>
> (3) "Consumption of omega-3 fatty acids may reduce the risk of coronary heart disease."
>
> (4) ".8 mg of folic acid in a dietary supplement is more effective in reducing the risk of neural tube defects than a lower amount in foods in common form."

* * *

Although there is apparently some definitional overlap between drugs and dietary supplements under the statute, it creates a safe harbor from designation as a "drug" for certain dietary supplements whose labels or labeling[1] advertise a beneficial relationship to a disease or health-related condition: If the FDA authorizes a label claim under 21 U.S.C.A. § 343(r), the product is not considered a drug under 21 U.S.C.A. § 321(g)(1). The FDA authorizes a claim only

> when it determines, based on the totality of publicly available scientific evidence (including evidence from well-designed studies conducted in a manner which is consistent with generally recognized scientific procedures and principles), that there is significant scientific agreement among experts qualified by scientific training and experience to evaluate such claims, that the claim is supported by such evidence.

21 C.F.R. § 101.14(c) (1998).

---

1. "Label" is defined as "a display of written, printed, or graphic matter upon the immediate container of any article." 21 U.S.C. § 321(k) (1994). "Labeling" is defined as "all labels and other written, printed, or graphic matter (1) upon any article or any of its containers or wrappers, or (2) accompanying such article." Id. § 321(m).

* * *

Appellants raise a host of challenges to the agency's action. But the most important are that their First Amendment rights have been impaired and that under the Administrative Procedure Act the FDA was obliged, at some point, to articulate a standard a good deal more concrete than the undefined "significant scientific agreement." Normally we would discuss the non-constitutional argument first, particularly because we believe it has merit. We invert the normal order here to discuss first appellants' most powerful constitutional claim, that the government has violated the First Amendment by declining to employ a less draconian method—the use of disclaimers—to serve the government's interests, because the requested remedy stands apart from appellants' request under the APA that the FDA flesh out its standards. That is to say, even if "significant scientific agreement" were given a more concrete meaning, appellants might be entitled to make health claims that do not meet that standard—with proper disclaimers.

* * *

It is undisputed that FDA's restrictions on appellants' health claims are evaluated under the commercial speech doctrine. It seems also undisputed that the FDA has unequivocally rejected the notion of requiring disclaimers to cure "misleading" health claims for dietary supplements... The government makes two alternative arguments in response to appellants' claim that it is unconstitutional for the government to refuse to entertain a disclaimer requirement for the proposed health claims: first, that health claims lacking "significant scientific agreement" are *inherently* misleading and thus entirely outside the protection of the First Amendment; and second, that even if the claims are only potentially misleading, under *Central Hudson Gas & Elec. Corp. v. Public Serv. Comm'n of New York*, [citation omitted] the government is not obliged to consider requiring disclaimers in lieu of an outright ban on all claims that lack significant scientific agreement.

If such health claims could be thought inherently misleading, that would be the end of the inquiry. Truthful advertising related to lawful activities is entitled to the protections of the First Amendment. But when the particular content or method of the advertising suggests that it is inherently misleading or when experience has proved that in fact such advertising is subject to abuse, the States may impose appropriate restrictions. [Inherently m]isleading advertising may be prohibited entirely. But the States may not place an absolute prohibition on... potentially misleading information... if the information also may be presented in a way that is not deceptive.

As best we understand the government, its first argument runs along the following lines: that health claims lacking "significant scientific agreement" are inherently misleading because they have such an awesome impact on consumers as to make it virtually impossible for them to exercise any judgment at the point of sale. It would be as if the consumers were asked to buy something while hypnotized, and therefore they are bound to be misled. We think this contention is almost frivolous * * * We reject it. But the government's alternative argument is more substantial. It is asserted that health claims on dietary supplements should be thought at least potentially misleading because the consumer would have difficulty in independently verifying these claims. We are told, in addition, that consumers might actually assume that the government has approved such claims.

Under *Central Hudson*, we are obliged to evaluate a government scheme to regulate potentially misleading commercial speech by applying a three-part test. First, we ask whether the asserted government interest is substantial. [Citation omitted.] The FDA advanced two general concerns: protection of public health and prevention of consumer fraud. The Supreme Court has said "there is no question that [the government's] interest in ensuring the accuracy of commercial information in the marketplace is substantial," and that government has a substantial interest in "promoting the health, safety, and welfare of its citizens." [Citation omitted.] At this level of generality, therefore, a substantial governmental interest is undeniable.

The more significant questions under *Central Hudson* are the next two factors: "whether the regulation *directly* advances the governmental interest asserted," and whether the fit between the government's ends and the means chosen to accomplish those ends "is not necessarily perfect, but reasonable.[5] We think that the government's regulatory approach encounters difficulty with both factors.

It is important to recognize that the government does not assert that appellants' dietary supplements in any fashion threaten consumer's health and safety.[6] The government simply asserts its "common sense judgment" that the health of consumers is advanced directly by barring any health claims not approved by the FDA. Because it is not claimed that the product is harmful, the government's underlying—if unarticulated—premise must be that consumers have a limited amount of either attention or dollars that could be devoted to pursuing health through nutrition, and therefore products that are not indisputably health enhancing should be discouraged as threatening to crowd out more worthy expenditures. We are rather dubious that this simplistic view of human nature or market behavior is sound, but, in any event, it surely cannot be said that this notion—which the government does not even dare openly to set forth—is a *direct* pursuit of consumer health; it would seem a rather indirect route, to say the least. [Citations omitted.]

On the other hand, the government would appear to advance directly its interest in protecting against consumer *fraud* through its regulatory scheme. If it can be assumed—and we think it can—that some health claims on dietary supplements will mislead consumers, it cannot be denied that requiring FDA pre-approval and setting the standard extremely, perhaps even impossibly, high will surely prevent any confusion among consumers. We also recognize that the government's interest in preventing consumer fraud/confusion may well take on added importance in the context of a product, such as dietary supplements, that can affect the public's health.

The difficulty with the government's consumer fraud justification comes at the final *Central Hudson* factor: Is there a "reasonable" fit between the government's goals and the means chosen to advance those goals? The government insists that it is never obliged to utilize the disclaimer approach, because the commercial speech doctrine does not embody a preference for disclosure over outright suppression. Our understanding of the doctrine is otherwise.

* * *

Our rejection of the government's position that there is no general First Amendment preference for disclosure over suppression, of course, does not determine that any supposed weaknesses in the claims at issue can be remedied by disclaimers and thus does not answer whether the sub-regulations, 21 C.F.R. § 101.71(a), (c), (e); id. § 101-79(c)(2)(i)(G), are valid. The FDA deemed the first three claims-(1) "Consumption of antioxidant vitamins may reduce the risk of certain kinds of cancers," (2) "Consumption of fiber may re-

---

5. The Supreme Court in turn reversed, explaining that *Central Hudson* does not impose a "least restrictive means" requirement, but only mandates a "reasonable" fit between means and ends.
6. Drugs, on the other hand, appear to be in an entirely different category—the potential harm presumably is much greater.

duce the risk of colorectal cancer," and (3) "Consumption of omega-3 fatty acids may reduce the risk of coronary heart disease"—to lack significant scientific agreement because existing research had examined only the relationship between consumption of *foods* containing these components and the risk of these diseases. The FDA logically determined that the specific effect of the *component* of the food constituting the dietary supplement could not be determined with certainty. (The FDA has approved similar health claims on *foods* containing these components. *See, e.g.,* 21 C.F.R. § 101.79 (folate-neural tube defects).) But certainly this concern could be accommodated, in the first claim for example, by adding a prominent disclaimer to the label along the following lines: "The evidence is inconclusive because existing studies have been performed with *foods* containing antioxidant vitamins, and the effect of those foods on reducing the risk of cancer may result from other components in those foods." A similar disclaimer would be equally effective for the latter two claims.

* * *

The government's general concern that, given the extensiveness of government regulation of the *sale* of drugs, consumers might assume that a claim on a supplement's label is approved by the government, suggests an obvious answer: The agency could require the label to state that "The FDA does not approve this claim."

* * *

We do not presume to draft precise disclaimers for each of appellants' four claims; we leave that task to the agency in the first instance. Nor do we rule out the possibility that where evidence in support of a claim is outweighed by evidence against the claim, the FDA could deem it incurable by a disclaimer and ban it outright.[10] For example, if the weight of the evidence were against the hypothetical claim that "Consumption of Vitamin E reduces the risk of Alzheimer's disease," the agency might reasonably determine that adding a disclaimer such as "The FDA has determined that *no* evidence supports this claim" would not suffice to mitigate the claim's misleadingness. [Citation omitted.] Finally, while we are skeptical that the government could demonstrate with empirical evidence that disclaimers similar to the ones we suggested above would bewilder consumers and fail to correct for deceptiveness, we do not rule out that possibility.

* * *

Summary Regarding Qualified Health Claims: B Vitamins & Vascular Disease

Docket No. 99P-3029
05/15/2002 clarification letter
11/28/2000 enforcement discretion letter

Claim Statement

As part of a well-balanced diet that is low in saturated fat and cholesterol, Folic Acid, Vitamin B6 and Vitamin B12 may reduce the risk of vascular disease. FDA evaluated the above claim and found that, while it is known that diets low in saturated fat and choles-

---

10. Similarly, we see no problem with the FDA imposing an outright ban on a claim where evidence in support of the claim is qualitatively weaker than evidence against the claim—for example, where the claim rests on only one or two old studies.

terol reduce the risk of heart disease and other vascular diseases, the evidence in support of the above claim is inconclusive.

Eligible Foods

Dietary supplements containing vitamin B6, B12, and/or folic acid

Factors

The disclaimer (i.e., FDA evaluated the above claim ...) must be immediately adjacent to and directly beneath the first claim (i.e., As part of a well-balanced diet ...) with no intervening material that separates the claim from the disclaimer, and the second sentence must be in the same size, type face and contrast as the first sentence.

Products that contain more than 100 percent of the Daily Value (DV) of folic acid (400 micrograms), when labeled for use by adults and children 4 or more years of age, must identify the safe upper limit of daily intake with respect to the DV. The folic acid safe upper limit of daily intake value of 1,000 micrograms (1 mg) may be included in parentheses.

The claim meets all 21 CFR 101.14 general health claim requirements, *except* for: (1) the requirement that the claim meet the significant scientific agreement standard and be made in accordance with an authorizing regulation, and (2) the requirement that the claim specify the daily dietary intake necessary to achieve the claimed effect. The claim may not suggest a level of vitamins B6, B12, and/or folic acid as being useful in achieving the claimed effect.

Dietary supplements containing folic acid must meet the United States Pharmacopeia (USP) standards for disintegration and dissolution, except that if there are no applicable USP standards, the folate in the dietary supplement shall be shown to be bioavailable under the conditions of use stated on the product label.

U.S. Food and Drug Administration, Qualified Health Claims Subject to Enforcement Discretion

Notes and Questions

1. Despite FDA resistance to qualified health claims as set out in *Pearson v. Shalala* and demonstrated in the early years following the case (See *Whitaker v. Thompson*, 248 F. Supp. 2d 1 (D.D.C. 2002)), the agency has left the heavy lifting on enforcement of the substantiation requirement for structure/function claims to the Federal Trade Commission. *See In the Matter of Goen Technologies Corp et al.*, F.T.C. File No. 042 3127 (2006); *In the Matter of Nutramax Laboratories, Inc.*, 138 F.T.C. 380 (2004). Private lawsuits, actions by the Center for Science in the Public Interest, and state attorney general investigations also serve to fill the FDA's enforcement void. *See* Elizabeth B. Fawell, Miguel H. Del Toro, *Substantiation Still Matters: The Importance of Science Behind Functional Food Claims*, 6 FDLI UPDATE Nov./Dec. 2008 at 15–17 (2008).

2. Additional examples of qualified health claims now approved by the FDA are as follows:

Claim Statement for Colon/Rectal Cancer: "Some evidence suggests that calcium supplements may reduce the risk of colon/rectal cancer, however, FDA has determined that this evidence is limited and not conclusive."

Claim Statement for Recurrent Colon Polyps: "Very limited and preliminary evidence suggests that calcium supplements may reduce the risk of colon/rectal polyps. FDA concludes that there is little scientific evidence to support this claim."

Do you think these types of qualified claims are what the Court of Appeals had in mind in *Pearson v. Shalala*?

IV. Rethinking the Regulation of Dietary Supplements

The United States regulates dietary supplements less restrictedly than either conventional food or drugs. Not so in Canada, Germany and France. And not in the manner that best protects the public health, note numerous commentators. Cohen, 31 Am. J.L. & Med. at 210. *See generally* Zuk, 11 Hastings Women's L.J. 29; and Kaiser, 37 Hous. L. Rev. 1249. Review the Executive Summary of the 2009 Government Accountability Office (GAO)'s examination of FDA oversight of Dietary Supplements and consider whether there should be more, less or simply different regulation. Or would following the GAO's recommendations address any regulatory voids?

Dietary Supplements: FDA Should Take Further Actions to Improve Oversight and Consumer Understanding
Summary of Findings and Recommendations of GAO
Gov't Accountability Office, 09-250 (January 29, 2009)

Summary: Dietary supplements and foods with added dietary ingredients, such as vitamins and herbs, constitute multibillion dollar industries. Past reports on the Food and Drug Administration's (FDA) regulation of these produces raised concerns about product safety and the availability of reliable information. Since then, FDA published draft guidance on requirements for reporting adverse events—which are harmful effects or illnesses—and Current Good Manufacturing Practice regulations for dietary supplements. GAO was asked to examine FDA's (1) actions to respond to the new serious adverse event reporting requirements, (2) ability to identify and act on concerns about the safety of dietary supplements, (3) ability to identify and act on concerns about the safety of foods with added dietary ingredients, and (4) actions to ensure that consumers have useful information about the safety and efficacy of supplements.

FDA has made several changes in response to the new serious adverse event reporting requirements and has subsequently received an increased number of reports. For example, FDA has modified its data system, issued draft guidance, and conducted outreach to industry. Since mandatory reporting went into effect on December 22, 2007, FDA has seen a threefold increase in the number of all adverse event reports received by the agency compared with the previous year. For example, from January through October 2008, FDA received 948 adverse event reports—596 of which were mandatory reports submitted by industry—compared with 298 received over the same time period in 2007. Although FDA has received a greater number of reports since the requirements went into effect, underreporting reminds a concern, and the agency has further actions planned to facilitate adverse event reporting. FDA has taken some steps to identify and act upon safety concerns related to dietary supplements; however several factors limit the agency's ability to detect concerns and remove products from the market. For example, FDA has limited information on the number and location of dietary supplement firms, the types of products currently available in the marketplace, and information about moderate and mild adverse events reported to industry. Additionally, FDA dedicates relatively few resources to oversight activities, such as providing guidance to industry regarding notification requirements for products containing new dietary ingredients. Also, once FDA has identified a safety concern, the agency's ability to remove a product from the market is hindered by a lack of mandatory recall authority and the difficult process of demonstrating significant or unreasonable risk for specific ingredients. Although FDA has taken some actions when foods contain unsafe dietary ingredients, certain factors may allow potentially unsafe products to reach consumers. FDA may not know when a company has made an unsupported or incorrect determination about whether an added dietary ingredient in a product is generally recognized as safe until after the product becomes available to consumers because companies are not required to notify FDA of their self-determinations. In addition, the boundary between dietary supplements and conventional foods containing dietary ingredients is not always clear, and some food products could be marketed as dietary supplements to circumvent the safety standard required for food additives. FDA has taken limited steps to educate consumers about dietary supplements, and studies and experts indicate that consumer understanding is lacking. While FDA has conducted some outreach, these initiatives have reached a relatively small proportion of dietary supplement consumers. Additionally, surveys and experts indicate that consumers are not well-informed about the safety and efficacy of dietary supplements and have difficulty interpreting labels on these products. Without a clear understanding of the safety, efficacy, and labeling of dietary supplements, consumers may be exposed to greater health risks associated with the uninformed use of these products.

Recommendation: To enhance FDA's oversight of dietary supplements and foods with added dietary ingredients, and to improve the information available to FDA for identifying safety concerns and better enable FDA to meet its responsibility to protect the public health, the Secretary of the Department of Health and Human Services should direct the Commissioner of FDA to request authority to require dietary supplement companies to (1) identify themselves as a dietary supplement company as part of the existing registration requirements and update this information annually, (2) provide a list of all dietary supplement products they sell and a copy of the labels and update this information annually, and (3) report all adverse events related to dietary supplements.

Recommendation: To enhance FDA's oversight of dietary supplements and foods with added dietary ingredients, and to better enable FDA to meet its responsibility to regulate dietary supplements that contain new dietary ingredients, the Secretary of the Department of Health and Human Services should direct the Commissioner of FDA to issue guidance to clarify when an ingredient is considered a new dietary ingredient, the evidence needed to document the safety of new dietary ingredients, and appropriate methods for establishing ingredient identity.

Recommendation: To enhance FDA's oversight of dietary supplements and foods with added dietary ingredients, and to help ensure that companies follow the appropriate laws and regulations and to renew a recommendation we made in July 2000, the Secretary of the Department of Health and Human Services should direct the Commissioner of FDA to provide to industry to clarify when an ingredient products should be marketed as either dietary supplements or conventional foods formulated with added dietary ingredients.

Recommendation: To enhance FDA's oversight of dietary supplements and foods with added dietary ingredients, and to improve consumer understanding about dietary supplements and better leverage existing resources, we recommend that the Secretary of the Department of Health and Human Services should direct the Commissioner of FDA to coordinate with stakeholder groups involved in consumer outreach to (1) identify additional mechanisms—such as the recent WebMD partnership—for educating consumers about the safety, efficacy, and labeling of dietary supplements; (2) implement these mechanisms; and (3) assess their effectiveness.

Chapter Seven

Antitrust

I. Introduction

A. Overview

Federal and state antitrust laws apply to almost all industries, including the traditional and alternative health care industries. Consider the breadth of the mission of the Department of Justice's Antitrust Division, as described in the following overview:

Department of Justice, Antitrust Division, Overview
http://www.usdoj.gov/atr/overview.html

For over six decades, the mission of the Antitrust Division has been to promote and protect the competitive process—and the American economy—through the enforcement of the antitrust laws. The antitrust laws apply to virtually all industries and to every level of business, including manufacturing, transportation, distribution, and marketing. They prohibit a variety of practices that restrain trade, such as price-fixing conspiracies, corporate mergers likely to reduce the competitive vigor of particular markets, and predatory acts designed to achieve or maintain monopoly power.

The Division prosecutes serious and willful violations of the antitrust laws by filing criminal suits that can lead to large fines and jail sentences. Where criminal prosecution is not appropriate, the Division institutes a civil action seeking a court order forbidding future violations of the law and requiring steps to remedy the anti-competitive effects of past violations. Many of the Division's accomplishments on these fronts were made possible by an unprecedented level of cooperation and coordination with foreign antitrust enforcement agencies and with state attorneys general.

The Division is also committed to ensuring that its essential efforts to preserve competition for the benefit of businesses and consumers do not impose unnecessary costs on American businesses and consumers.

* * *

The historic goal of the antitrust laws is to protect economic freedom and opportunity by promoting competition in the marketplace. Competition in a free market benefits American consumers through lower prices, better quality and greater choice. Competition provides businesses the opportunity to compete on price and quality, in an open market and on a level playing field, unhampered by anticompetitive restraints. Competition also tests and hardens American companies at home, the better to succeed abroad.

* * *

B. Federal and State Antitrust Authorities

At the federal level, the three main antitrust authorities include the Sherman Act, codified at 15 U.S.C. §§ 1–7, the Clayton Act, codified at 15 U.S.C. §§ 12–27, and the Federal Trade Commission (FTC) Act, codified at 15 U.S.C. § 41 et seq.

Section 1 of the Sherman Act, which is designed to prohibit contracts, combinations, and conspiracies in restraint of trade, provides: "Every contract, combination in the form of trust or otherwise, or conspiracy, in restraint of trade or commerce among the several States, or with foreign nations, is declared to be illegal. Every person who shall make any contract or engage in any combination or conspiracy hereby declared to be illegal shall be deemed guilty of a felony, and, on conviction thereof, shall be punished by fine not exceeding $100,000,000 if a corporation, or, if any other person, $1,000,000, or by imprisonment not exceeding 10 years, or by both said punishments, in the discretion of the court." 15 U.S.C. § 1.

Section 2 of the Sherman Act, which is designed to prohibit monopolies and attempted monopolies, provides: "Every person who shall monopolize, or attempt to monopolize, or combine or conspire with any other person or persons, to monopolize any part of the trade or commerce among the several States, or with foreign nations, shall be deemed guilty of a felony, and, on conviction thereof, shall be punished by fine not exceeding $100,000,000 if a corporation, or, if any other person, $1,000,000, or by imprisonment not exceeding 10 years, or by both said punishments, in the discretion of the court." 15 U.S.C. § 2.

Section 2 of the Clayton Act, which is designed to prohibit price discrimination between different purchasers if such a discrimination substantially lessens competition or tends to create a monopoly in any line of commerce, provides: "It shall be unlawful for any person engaged in commerce, in the course of such commerce, either directly or indirectly, to discriminate in price between different purchasers of commodities of like grade and quality, where either or any of the purchases involved in such discrimination are in commerce, where such commodities are sold for use, consumption, or resale within the United States or any Territory thereof or the District of Columbia or any insular possession or other place under the jurisdiction of the United States, and where the effect of such discrimination may be substantially to lessen competition or tend to create a monopoly in any line of commerce, or to injure, destroy, or prevent competition with any person who either grants or knowingly receives the benefit of such discrimination, or with customers of either of them ..." 15 U.S.C. § 13(a).

Section 3 of the Clayton Act is designed to prevent sales based on exclusive dealings (*i.e.*, sales on the condition that the buyer or lessee not deal with the competitors of the seller or lessor) and sales based on tying (*i.e.*, sales in which the buyer also purchases another different product), but only when these acts substantially lessen competition. Section 3 of the Clayton Act provides: "It shall be unlawful for any person engaged in commerce, in the course of such commerce, to lease or make a sale or contract for sale of goods, wares, merchandise, machinery, supplies, or other commodities, whether patented or unpatented, for use, consumption, or resale within the United States or any Territory thereof or the District of Columbia or any insular possession or other place under the jurisdiction of the United States, or fix a price charged therefor, or discount from, or rebate upon, such price, on the condition, agreement, or understanding that the lessee or purchaser thereof shall not use or deal in the goods, wares, merchandise, machinery, supplies, or other commodities of a competitor or competitors of the lessor or seller, where the effect of such lease, sale, or contract for sale or such condition, agreement, or understanding may be to substantially lessen competition or tend to create a monopoly in any line of commerce." 15 U.S.C. § 14.

Section 7 of the Clayton Act, which is designed to prohibit mergers and acquisitions that have the effect of substantially limiting competition or tend to create a monopoly, provides: "No person engaged in commerce or in any activity affecting commerce shall acquire, directly or indirectly, the whole or any part of the stock or other share capital and no person subject to the jurisdiction of the Federal Trade Commission shall acquire the whole or any part of the assets of another person engaged also in commerce or in any activity affecting commerce, where in any line of commerce or in any activity affecting commerce in any section of the country, the effect of such acquisition may be substantially to lessen competition, or to tend to create a monopoly.... No person shall acquire, directly or indirectly, the whole or any part of the stock or other share capital and no person subject to the jurisdiction of the Federal Trade Commission shall acquire the whole or any part of the assets of one or more persons engaged in commerce or in any activity affecting commerce, where in any line of commerce or in any activity affecting commerce in any section of the country, the effect of such acquisition, of such stocks or assets, or of the use of such stock by the voting or granting of proxies or otherwise, may be substantially to lessen competition, or to tend to create a monopoly." 15 U.S.C. § 18.

Section 8 of the Clayton Act prohibits certain persons from serving as a director of two or more competing corporations: "No person shall, at the same time, serve as a director or officer in any two corporations (other than banks, banking associations, and trust companies) that are — (A) engaged in whole or in part in commerce; and (B) by virtue of their business and location of operation, competitors, so that the elimination of competition by agreement between them would constitute a violation of any of the antitrust laws; if each of the corporations has capital, surplus, and undivided profits aggregating more than $10,000,000 as adjusted pursuant to paragraph (5) of this subsection." 15 U.S.C. § 19(a)(1).

Finally, Section 5 of the FTC Act declares unlawful "[u]nfair methods of competition in or affecting commerce, and unfair or deceptive acts or practices in or affecting commerce." 15 U.S.C. § 45(a)(1).

Federal antitrust laws are enforced through three different methods. First, the Antitrust Division of the Department of Justice (DOJ) can bring civil and criminal enforcement actions, including fines of up to $350,000 and sentences up to three years in federal prison for each offense by an individual and up to $10 million for each offense by a corporation. *See* 15 U.S.C. § 3 ("Every person who shall make any such contract or engage in any such combination or conspiracy, shall be deemed guilty of a felony, and, on conviction thereof, shall be punished by fine not exceeding $10,000,000 if a corporation, or, if any other person, $350,000, or by imprisonment not exceeding three years, or both said punishments, in the discretion of the court.").

Second, the Federal Trade Commission can bring civil enforcement actions. Third, private parties can sue for damages, including treble damages and injunctive relief. *See* 15 U.S.C. § 15 ("Except as provided in subsection (b) of this section, any person who shall be injured in his business or property by reason of anything forbidden in the antitrust laws may sue therefor in any district court of the United States in the district in which the defendant resides or is found or has an agent, without respect to the amount in controversy, and shall recover threefold the damages by him sustained, and the cost of suit, including a reasonable attorney's fee ..."); *id.* § 16 ("Any person, firm, corporation, or association shall be entitled to sue for and have injunctive relief, in any court of the United States having jurisdiction over the parties, against threatened loss or damage by a violation of the antitrust laws ...").

Many states also have antitrust laws that are similar to federal antitrust law. The Iowa Competition Law, for example, is construed to complement federal antitrust law. IOWA CODE § 553.2. Like Section 1 of the Sherman Act, the Iowa Competition Law prohibits contracts, combinations, and conspiracies in restraint of trade. *Id.* § 553.4 ("A contract, combination, or conspiracy between two or more persons shall not restrain or monopolize trade or commerce in a relevant market."). Like Section 2 of the Sherman Act, the Iowa Competition Law prohibits monopolies and attempted monopolies. *Id.* § 553.5 ("A person shall not attempt to establish or establish, maintain, or use a monopoly of trade or commerce in a relevant market for the purpose of excluding competition or of controlling, fixing, or maintaining prices."). Enforcement of the Iowa Competition Law may be through the Iowa Attorney General with respect to civil and criminal penalties, or through private lawsuits in which injured parties seek actual and exemplary damages, inunctions, and/or attorneys fees. *See id.* § 553.7 (Iowa Attorney General enforcement); § 553.12 (private lawsuits), § 553.12 (civil penalties), and § 553.13 (criminal penalties).

C. Antitrust Defenses

Several statutory and common law antitrust defenses exist. Under the well-known Noerr-Pennington doctrine, private entities are immune from antitrust liability for attempts to influence the passage or enforcement of laws, even if the laws for which they advocate have anticompetitive effects. The Noerr-Pennington doctrine is grounded in the First Amendment's protection of political speech and the recognition that antitrust laws may not be appropriate for the political arena. *See, e.g., Eastern Railroad Presidents Conference v. Noerr Motor Freight, Inc.*, 365 U.S. 127 (1961); *United Mine Workers v. Pennington*, 381 U.S. 657 (1965); and *California Motor Transport Co. v. Trucking Unlimited*, 404 U.S. 508 (1972).

Under the federal Health Care Quality Improvement Act (HCQIA), professional review bodies, including hospital peer review committees, that take certain professional review actions in accordance with certain standards designed to ensure a physician procedural due process are immune from non-civil rights liability under federal and state laws, including federal and state antitrust law. 42 U.S.C. § 11111.

The federal McCarran-Ferguson Act provides that federal antitrust laws will not apply to the 'business of insurance' if the particular insurance activities are regulated by state law. 15 U.S.C. § 1011. The McCarran-Ferguson Act does not, however, exempt insurance companies from having to comply with federal and state antitrust authorities.

The state action doctrine, also referred to as the Parker Doctrine, permits state governments and certain private actors to show that a state regulatory scheme precludes antitrust liability. *See, e.g., Parker v. Brown*, 317 U.S. 341 (1943).

Finally, many state antitrust laws also exempt certain activities from state antitrust enforcement. *See, e.g.,* IOWA CODE § 553.6.

* * *

D. A Policy Argument

In Sections II and III of this Chapter, several judicial opinions are presented to illustrate how the courts have applied antitrust law to the activities of both traditional and alternative health care practitioners, professional associations, hospitals, and insurance companies. Scholars also use antitrust law, however, to make policy arguments. Consider the following article, in which the author argues that antitrust law should be applied to prohibit: (1) states from permitting only physicians and nurse-midwives, but not non-nurse traditional midwives, to attend labor and deliveries in the out-of-hospital setting; and (2) hospitals from requiring one or more physicians to supervise a nurse-midwife's hospital-based practice. According to the author, health care consumers would benefit from increased competition in the arena of prenatal, maternity, and labor and delivery services.

Caitlin Slessor, *The Right to Choose in Childbirth: Regulation of Midwifery in Iowa*
8 J. Gender Race & Just. 511 (2004–05)

In the summer of 2003, Iowa Methodist Hospital in Des Moines, Iowa, fired four nurse-midwives from its obstetrical staff, triggering a series of unfortunate events. First, four highly qualified women who met all the requirements set out by the state of Iowa for the practice of midwifery lost their jobs. Second, women for whom the midwives cared had their prenatal care interrupted for reasons beyond their control. Finally, other women in the Des Moines area who may become pregnant in the future have significantly fewer choices for possible birthing attendants. Iowa lawmakers should view these events as unacceptable.

Unfortunately, the current statutory scheme in Iowa is applied with hostility toward individuals who want to practice midwifery, as the Des Moines example shows. Three main problems exist in the application of the laws in Iowa. First, the current laws require that all midwives be Certified Nurse Midwives (CNMs), a profession which requires the practitioner to first become a registered nurse. The result unequivocally excludes qualified women from practicing who have become proficient at midwifery through other means, such as apprenticeships.

Second, even when CNMs have the necessary credentials, Iowa law requires an overseeing physician for each CNM. The supervising physicians often pay higher malpractice premiums when they agree to supervise a midwife and are often afraid of increased liability. This has led some physicians to simply refuse such responsibility, thereby reducing the number of CNMs practicing in Iowa. Physicians have no incentive to provide supervision for midwives, but the denial of supervision may be in violation of antitrust laws. Such blatant denial of a woman's choice is unacceptable.

Third, the State of Iowa's ban on direct-entry midwives is a further restriction of the choices available to women in the state. Iowa is in the minority of states that have an outright ban on the practice of midwifery by any direct-entry midwives. Direct-entry midwives provide yet another option for pregnant women. Direct-entry midwives are midwives who learn their trade through apprenticeship and alternative training schools rather than through a four-year RN program. When properly regulated, the direct-entry midwifery scheme is an appropriate avenue for low-risk pregnancies and can provide women with a model of care they may not otherwise be able to receive. In addition, direct-entry midwives often use alternative health options such as herbology, reflexology, and aromatherapy and are often more willing to attend home-births or other non-hospital birth settings. This is important because it diversifies women's choices.

* * *

C. Adverse Effects of the Application of Current Statutes and Regulations

In August of 2003, four midwives were fired from Des Moines hospitals because the doctors in charge of supervising them no longer wanted the legal burden. This reduced the number of midwives practicing in Des Moines by one-third and further limited Des Moines women's choices. One of the disturbing aspects of this situation is that Iowa Health physician group, the group that controls Iowa Methodist Hospital where the midwives were employed, imposes even more stringent requirements on its midwives than the law requires. In order to practice at Des Moines Methodist, for example, CNMs must have two over-seeing physicians and have a completely independent status. Since finding a doctor who is willing to oversee a midwife is so difficult, this requirement works to deny both a choice in maternal care for Iowa's women and a job to qualified CNMs who cannot acquire the necessary backup.

D. Antitrust Issues

The story about the nurse-midwives from Des Moines Methodist shows both sides of the problem when state law requires CNMs to have supervising physicians. This affects two groups of people. First, it affects the individuals who have been trained as midwives but now cannot practice their trade because hospitals keep them out. Second, it affects pregnant women whose choices of childbirth attendants are now restricted. The first problem—effects of restrictions on the practitioners themselves—is arguably a violation of federal antitrust laws. Keeping midwives out of hospitals for anti-competition reasons should constitute a violation of the law and should result in prosecution. But the law is not being enforced, as evidenced by the situation in Des Moines.

The Sherman Act governs antitrust law. The applicable section is Section 1, which prohibits conspiracies or contracts, which are in restraint of trade. Physicians may violate Section 1 of the Sherman Act when they actively conspire to exclude midwives from their practices. Thus far, such arguments have only had minor success, but groups supporting midwives are seeking to change this.

In a hearing in front of the Department of Justice and the Federal Trade Commission, Lynne Loeffler, from the American College of Nurse Midwives, testified about various practices hospitals and physicians employ that constitute a restraint on the trade of midwives. Among the violations were "physicians conspiring to refuse to provide consultative or collaborative services that may be necessary in order for nurse midwives to qualify for or maintain hospital privileges." This is exactly the type of violation that occurred in Des Moines when Des Moines Methodist Hospital fired four nurse midwives from its staff. Loeffler testified that hospital boards of directors pass the responsibility for credentialing the midwives on to the staff doctors, but the doctors have no reason to do so because midwives are in direct competition with them.

Loeffler emphasized that by restricting the practice of nurse midwives, much more is at stake than if a single doctor loses her privileges in a given area. Rather than just reducing the available number of professionals by disallowing nurse midwives to practice, hospitals remove an entire type of health care provider. This reduction in choice of provider type poses a much more serious risk to the consumers who benefit from healthy competition between different service providers. Midwives must have a physician who is willing to supervise them. Unlike most entrepreneurs, they cannot simply open up an office wherever they please. To keep healthy competition in place, the antitrust laws of this country and of the State of Iowa need to be enforced in cases such as that of the Des Moines midwives. The Sherman Act has been found to apply to healthcare institutions and should be enforced, especially in egregious situations such as that in Des Moines.

The argument has already achieved limited success. In *Sweeney v. Athens Regional Medical Center*, a nurse-midwife sued a group of physicians in a hospital for circumstances similar to that in Iowa. The group of doctors was denied summary judgment. Although the case later settled, this is an example of midwives beginning to fight back.

Until Iowa realizes that allowing CNMs to be independent practitioners who do not need a supervising physician is the best way to regulate CNMs, the state needs to make certain that antitrust laws are properly enforced. Without such action, individuals who meet all the other requirements necessary to practice as a CNM will be illegally denied their livelihood. This is a violation of federal antitrust law....

* * *

Notes

1. The federal government has issued several documents that examine the application of antitrust law in the health care context. *See, e.g.*, Federal Trade Commission & Department of Justice, Improving Health Care: A Dose of Competition (2004); Department of Justice & Federal Trade Commission Statements of Antitrust Enforcement Policy in Health Care (1996). The Federal Trade Commission (FTC) also maintains a Web site that provides information about several hundred antitrust actions taken by the FTC in the health care market. *See* Federal Trade Commission, Competition in the Health Care Marketplace, *available at* http://www.ftc.gov/bc/healthcare/ antitrust/index.htm. Finally, the Department of Justice provides online access to its recent enforcement actions as well as a number of health care case summaries, business review letter summaries, and health care competition public hearings. *See* Department of Justice, Health Care Antitrust Division, Public Documents, *available a*t http://www.usdoj.gov/atr/public/health_care/health_care.htm.

2. The application of antitrust law in the health care context also has captured the attention of several prominent health law professors and other scholars who write in the areas of health law, health care finance, and antitrust law. *See, e.g.*, Barak D. Richman, *Antitrust and Nonprofit Hospital Mergers: A Return to Basics*, 156 U. PENN. L. REV. 121 (2007); Kristin Madison, *Hospital Mergers in an Era of Quality Improvement*, 7 HOUS. J. HEALTH L. & POL'Y 265 (2007); Peter J. Hammer, *Competition and Quality as Dynamic Processes in the Balkans of American Health Care*, J. HEALTH POL. POL'Y & L. 473 (2006); Sara Rosenbaum, *A Dose of Reality: Assessing the Federal Trade Commission/Department of Justice Report in an Uninsured, Underserved, and Vulnerable Population Context*, 31 J. HEALTH POL. POL'Y & L. 657 (2006); Thomas L. Greaney, *Antitrust and Hospital Mergers: Does the Nonprofit Form Affect Competitive Substance*, 31 J. HEALTH POL. POL'Y & L. 511 (2006); Thomas L. Greaney, *Chicago's Procrustean Bed: Applying Antitrust Law in Health Care*, 71 ANTITRUST L.J. 857 (2004); Thomas B. Leary, *The Antitrust Implications of "Clinical Integration:" An Analysis of the FTC Staff's Advisory Opinion in MedSouth*, 47 ST. LOUIS U.

L.J. 227 (2003); Peter J. Hammer & William M. Sage, *Antitrust, Health Care Quality, and the Courts*, 102 COLUM. L. REV. 545 (2002); William S. Brewbaker III, *Physician Unions and the Future of Competition in the Health Care Sector*, 33 U.C. DAVIS L. REV. 545 (2000); THOMAS RICE, THE ECONOMICS OF HEALTH CARE RECONSIDERED (1998).

II. Applying Antitrust Law

A. An Antitrust Victory

Perhaps the most well-known case involving antitrust allegations by CAM practitioners against allopathic physicians and their professional associations is *Wilk v. American Medical Association*, 719 F.2d 207 (7th Cir. 1983), *remanded*, 671 F. Supp. 1465 (N.D. Ill. 1987), *affirmed*, 895 F.2d 352 (7th Cir. 1990), *writ denied*, 496 U.S. 927 (1990). The trilogy of *Wilk* opinions nicely illustrate the anticompetitive conduct, including group boycott and conspiracy activities, that may be complained of by CAM practitioners, as well as several legal issues relating to the reasonableness of restraints of trade, the sufficiency of claimed antitrust injuries, the differences between 'per se' and 'rule of reason' analyses, the appropriateness of damages and injunction as antitrust remedies, and possible defenses, including the 'patient care defense.'

In the original *Wilk* lawsuit, four plaintiff chiropractors named several allopathic physicians and professional medical associations as defendants, including the American Medical Association (AMA), American Hospital Association (AHA), American College of Surgeons (ACS), American College of Physicians (ACP), American College of Radiology (ACR), American Academy of Orthopaedic Surgeons (AAOS), Illinois State Medical Society (ISMS), and the former Joint Commission on Accreditation of Hospitals (JCAH). The excerpt below contains a discussion of only the plaintiffs' claims against the AMA.

Wilk v. American Medical Association
Northern District of Illinois
671 F. Supp 1465 (1987)

SUSAN GETZENDANNER, DISTRICT JUDGE.

* * *

I. *The First Trial and the Wilk Decision*

The plaintiffs, Chester A. Wilk, James W. Bryden, Patricia B. Arthur, and Michael D. Pedigo, are licensed chiropractors. In a complaint filed in 1976, plaintiffs charged the defendants with violating Sections 1 and 2 of the Sherman Act, 15 U.S.C. Sections 1 and 2. Section 1 of the Sherman Act declares illegal every contract, combination or conspiracy in restraint of trade or commerce. Section 2 prescribes penalties for every person who shall monopolize, or attempt to monopolize, or combine or conspire with any other person or persons, to monopolize any part of the trade or commerce.

* * *

At the first trial, the plaintiffs' principal claim was that the defendants engaged in a conspiracy to eliminate the chiropractic profession by refusing to deal with the plaintiffs and other chiropractors. Plaintiffs claimed that the boycott was accomplished through the use of Principle 3 of the AMA's Principles of Medical Ethics ("AMA's Principles") which prohibited medical physicians from associating professionally with unscientific practitioners. Principle 3 provided as follows:

> A physician should practice a method of healing founded on a scientific basis; and he should not voluntarily professionally associate with anyone who violates this principle.

It was the plaintiffs' contention that the AMA used Principle 3 to achieve a boycott of chiropractors by first calling chiropractors "unscientific practitioners," and then advising AMA members and other medical societies that it was unethical for medical physicians to associate with chiropractors. The other defendants, plaintiffs claimed, joined the boycott and the result was a conspiracy in restraint of trade in violation of Section 1 of the Sherman Act. The jury returned a verdict for the defendants and against the plaintiffs. That judgment was reversed on appeal and the case was remanded.

* * *

Shortly before the scheduled trial before this court, the plaintiffs waived their claim for damages and sought only injunctive relief. This turned the case from a jury to a bench trial, and it shifted the focus of the case from the past to the present in order to determine whether the plaintiffs were entitled to injunctive relief under Section 16 of the Clayton Act.

II. *Summary of This Court's Rulings*

In view of the length of this opinion, I shall summarize my principal findings. The AMA and its officials, including Dr. Sammons, instituted a boycott of chiropractors in the mid-1960s by informing AMA members that chiropractors were unscientific practitioners and that it was unethical for a medical physician to associate with chiropractors. The purpose of the boycott was to contain and eliminate the chiropractic profession. This conduct constituted a conspiracy among the AMA and its members and an unreasonable restraint of trade in violation of Section 1 of the Sherman Act.

The AMA sought to spread the boycott to other medical societies. Other groups agreed to participate in the boycott by agreeing to induce their members to forego any form of professional, research, or educational association with chiropractors. The defendants which knowingly joined in the conspiracy were ACR (which has now been dismissed from the case) and AAOS. None of the defendants established the patient care defense. The plaintiffs are entitled to injunctive relief against the AMA, but not against AAOS or Dr. Sammons. The actions of the other defendants, JCAH and ACP, were taken independently of the AMA boycott and these defendants did not join the conspiracy. Accordingly, defendants JCAH, ACP, AAOS and Dr. Sammons are dismissed.

The plaintiffs' Section 2 claim was limited to the defendants' alleged conspiracy to monopolize the hospital health care market through restrictive hospital accreditation standards promulgated by JCAH. In view of the court's finding that JCAH did not join the conspiracy, the Section 2 claim is dismissed.

* * *

IV. *Liability of the Defendants*

A. *American Medical Association ("AMA")* ...

1. *Boycott Activities*

In the early 1960s the AMA became concerned that medical physicians were cooperating with chiropractors. In 1963, the AMA hired as its general counsel the author of the Iowa Medical Society's plan to contain chiropractic in Iowa. As early as September 1963, the AMA's objective was the complete elimination of the chiropractic profession. In November of 1963, the AMA authorized the formation of the Committee on Quackery under the AMA's Department of Investigation.

In 1964, the Committee's primary goal was to contain and eliminate chiropractic. Throughout the 1960s and early 1970s, H. Doyl Taylor, the chairman of the Department of Investigation, repeatedly described the Committee's prime mission to be the containment and elimination of chiropractic as a recognized health care service. I found his video deposition denials, and his explanation that at all times he and the Committee only meant to eliminate chiropractic as a health hazard, incredible and unworthy of belief. Mr. Taylor believed that chiropractic was based on a "single cause-single cure" theory of disease and that given this baseless foundation, the entire profession should be swept away.

The Committee worked aggressively to achieve its goals in several areas. It conducted nationwide conferences on chiropractic; prepared and distributed numerous publications critical of chiropractic; assisted others in the preparation and distribution of anti-chiropractic literature; regularly communicated with medical boards and associations, warning that professional association between medical physicians and chiropractors was unethical; and attempted to discourage colleges, universities, and faculty members from cooperating with chiropractic schools.

* * *

In 1966, the AMA adopted an anti-chiropractic resolution. This resolution, recommended by the AMA Board of Trustees and adopted by the House of Delegates, called chiropractic an unscientific cult. This label implicitly invoked Principle 3 of the AMA's Principles which made it unethical for a physician to associate with an unscientific practitioner. In 1967, the AMA Judicial Council 3 issued an opinion under Principle 3 specifically holding that it was unethical for a physician to associate professionally with chiropractors. "Associating professionally" would include making referrals of patients to chiropractors, accepting referrals from chiropractors, providing diagnostic, laboratory, or radiology services for chiropractors, teaching chiropractors, or practicing together in any form. This opinion was published in the 1969 Opinions and Reports of the Judicial Council of the AMA ("1969 Opinions") which was widely circulated to members of the AMA. The opinion on chiropractic was also sent by the AMA to 56 medical specialty boards and associations.

The AMA and the Committee on Quackery used the anti-chiropractic policy statement as a tool—what the Committee called a "necessary tool"—to spread the boycott to other medical groups. The Committee's efforts were successful. Other groups, including some of the defendants, specifically adopted or approved the policy statement on the ethical prohibition against association with chiropractors. In 1971, the Committee made a report of its activities to the AMA Board of Trustees and described the policy statement as follows:

> This was the necessary tool with which your Committee has been able to widen the base of its chiropractic campaign. With it, other health-related groups were asked and did adopt the AMA policy statement or individually-phrased versions of it. These, in turn led to even wider acceptance of the AMA position.

* * *

> The hoped-for effect of this widened base of support was and is to minimize the chiropractic argument that the campaign is simply one of economics, dictated and manipulated by the AMA.

The memorandum further stated:

The Committee has not submitted such a report [earlier] because it believes that to make public some of its activities would have been and continues to be unwise. Thus this report is intended only for the information of the Board of Trustees.

Principle 3 was widely viewed as proscribing association with chiropractors. The three defendants who issued the Status Report on Chiropractic Lawsuits in 1978 acknowledged in that Report that Principle 3 pro-scribed association with chiropractors. Any reasonable medical physician who read Principle 3 and either the AMA policy statement or any AMA reference to chiropractors as unscientific practitioners, would conclude that it was unethical for medical physicians to associate with a chiropractor.

In 1973, the AMA drafted Standard X, which incorporated the unscientific practitioners' ethics bar into the JCAH hospital accrediting standards. The AMA urged JCAH to adopt Standard X, and JCAH complied. Keeping chiropractors out of hospitals was one of the goals of the boycott. When chiropractic was included under Medicare in 1973, the AMA became concerned that this would open the way for chiropractors to be on hospital staffs. Doyl Taylor caused the Office of General Counsel of the AMA to publish an article entitled "The Right and Duty of Hospitals to Exclude Chiropractors" in the Journal of the American Medical Association. This was intended to offer advice to hospital trustees across the country. It also told every hospital attorney that JCAH accreditation might be lost if hospitals dealt with chiropractors.

* * *

The Committee on Quackery disbanded in December of 1974. By this time, chiropractic had achieved licensing in all fifty states, chiropractic services had become reimbursable through Medicare, Medicaid, and virtually every private health insurance plan, and the chiropractic educational system had been given official sanction by the United States Office of Education. Nevertheless, the Committee pronounced itself a success. The AMA believed that chiropractic would have achieved greater growth if it success. The AMA believed that chiropractic would have achieved greater growth if it had not been for the Committee's activities. In May of 1975 the AMA Department of Investigation was disbanded and Doyl Taylor left the employ of the AMA.

This lawsuit was filed in 1976. In that year, the Judicial Council suspended distribution of the 1971 Opinions which contained the anti-chiropractic policy. Later that year the AMA Judicial Council adopted Opinion 3.50 and in March of 1977 Opinions 3.60, 3.70, and 3.71 were adopted. Under these opinions, a medical physician could refer a patient to a "limited licensed practitioner" for diagnostic or other health care services. Although there was no express reference to chiropractors, chiropractors would fall within the definition of "limited licensed practitioners." Next, a medical physician could choose to accept or decline patients sent to her or him by a licensed practitioner or by a layman. Finally, a medical physician could engage in any teaching permitted by law for which she or he is qualified. However, the relaxation of the right to refer patients was not without qualification. Opinion 3.60 specifically required that a medical physician should not refer a patient unless she or he is confident that the services provided on referral will be performed in accordance with accepted scientific standards. In addition, Opinion 3.01 provided that it is "wrong to engage in or aid and abet any treatment which has no scientific basis and is dangerous." Distribution of the revised opinions began in May of 1977. Principle 3 was still in effect.

In July of 1979, the AMA House of Delegates adopted Report UU. Report UU was the AMA's new policy statement on chiropractic. It was a very begrudging change of position.

Although it is now hailed by the AMA lawyers and Dr. Alan R. Nelson, present Chairman of AMA's Board of Trustees, as a recognition by the AMA of the growth and development of chiropractic as a valid health care service, the Report does not convey that change of heart. First, Report UU states that the AMA knows of no scientific evidence to support spinal manipulation and adjustment as appropriate treatment for such diseases as cancer, diabetes, and infections. It does not declare support for that which the AMA seemingly now approves—chiropractic manipulation for musculoskeletal problems. Next the Report condemns the single cause of disease theory and states that "chiropractors disagree on the extent to which they accept or reject traditional chiropractic doctrine." The Report does not state that the two major chiropractic associations had rejected the doctrine in 1969. But the Report continues:

> Describing chiropractic as an "unscientific cult" does not, however, necessarily mean that everything a chiropractor may do when acting within the scope of his or her license granted by the state is without therapeutic value, nor does it mean that all chiropractors should be equated with cultists. It is better to call attention to the limitations of chiropractic in the treatment of particular ailments than to label chiropractic an "unscientific cult."

The Report then reaffirms that a physician should at all times practice a method of healing founded on a scientific basis. This again directly tied into Principle 3 which prohibited association with unscientific practitioners. Although the Report ends by stating that a medical physician may refer a patient to a limited licensed practitioner permitted by law to furnish such services, there is no particular reference to chiropractors. Report UU was obviously written by lawyers in an effort to bring the AMA into compliance with the antitrust laws, and not a bold change of position designed to reverse the attitudes of the AMA members formed, at least in part, by the then eleven-year old boycott.

In December of 1978, the AMA House of Delegates adopted Resolution 14 which provided that medical physicians "continue to exercise the duty to expose unscientific practices and practitioners while supporting and protecting the freedom of individuals to choose among physicians, other licensed practitioners or religious healers as part of the American tradition." It is hard to tell the purpose of this resolution, other than to suggest a similarity between chiropractors and Elmer Gantry, but it once again keyed into Principle 3 which condemned association with unscientific practitioners.

In 1980 the AMA adopted a completely revised version of the principles of medical ethics. Principle 3 finally was eliminated. The new principles provided that a medical physician "shall be free to choose whom to serve, with whom to associate, and the environment in which to provide medical services." The revised principles theoretically do allow association with chiropractors but there is no explicit reference to chiropractors in the new code.

The revised code received a fair amount of publicity in the medical and private press in 1980. The revision was interpreted as changing the AMA's position on chiropractic in response to various pressures, including the legal climate. And yet, two years later, when Dr. Daniel T. Cloud, who was then finishing his term as president of the AMA, was asked in a formal interview whether the 1980 ethics code changed the position of doctors with regard to chiropractors—"Was there a change?"—he stated, "No." This fairly bizarre answer (considering the nature of the publicity the ethics revision received) today is explained by the AMA's lawyers as a technically accurate answer since, they assert, the change in position was accomplished in 1977 and 1979. Yet today the AMA relies on the revision of the ethical standards in 1980 as part of its change in position on chiropractic. The lawyers' argument is not persuasive. In 1982 the president of the AMA appears to be announcing that the AMA has not changed its position on chiropractic.

The AMA settled three chiropractic lawsuits in 1978, 1980 and 1986 by stipulating and agreeing that under its current opinions of the Judicial Council a medical physician may, without fear of discipline or sanction by the AMA, refer a patient to a duly licensed chiropractor when he believes that referral may benefit the patient. The AMA confirmed that a physician may teach at a chiropractic college or seminar and that a physician may choose to accept or decline patients sent to him by a chiropractor. The only settlement entered into prior to the end of the boycott was in 1978, and that settlement did not effectuate a termination of the boycott since Principle 3 was still in effect.

In 1983 the AMA participated in the revision of the JCAH accreditation standards for hospitals. The revision process started in 1982 with recommendations from the JCAH staff and the JCAH Standard-Survey Procedures Committee that each hospital, through its governing body, be permitted to decide for itself, under applicable state law, which licensed health care providers would be allowed hospital privileges and membership on the medical staff. The AMA initially supported this approach but it was severely criticized by its members and other medical societies which wanted to ensure medical and osteopathic physician control of the medical staff and patient care in hospitals. As a result of this criticism, the AMA changed its position and supported revisions which would ensure such control. In February of 1983, the AMA voted to recommend revised standards that would require the medical staff of each hospital to have an "executive committee," the majority of which had to be medical or osteopathic physicians. The executive committee would make recommendations to the hospital's governing body for its approval of credentialing, membership on the medical staff, hospital privileges delineations, and structure of the medical staff. Any dispute between the medical staff and the governing body of the hospital would have to be resolved jointly by them. In late 1983, JCAH adopted the new standards which included the mandatory, medical physician dominated executive committee concept.

The plaintiffs rely heavily on the 1983 accreditation standards to show that the conspiracy was ongoing. This issue is discussed generally in the section of this opinion dealing with JCAH, and, in short, I have rejected the argument. What is noteworthy with respect to the AMA, however, is that although it believed that the standards originally proposed by the JCAH Standards-Survey Procedures Committee were more in tune with the existing antitrust "legal climate," it was unable to sustain its position when faced with substantial criticism of its members and other medical groups.

Through the date of the trial, the AMA continued to respond to requests for information on chiropractic which it received from AMA members and others by sending out anti-chiropractic literature. The old boycott language has been eliminated, but the AMA has not had anything positive to say about chiropractic. It was not until mid-way through the trial of this case that the AMA announced that chiropractic has improved and that at least some forms of chiropractic treatment and joint adjustments are scientific. The membership has never been informed of this position.

The plaintiffs argue that the AMA boycott began in 1966 and continued until 1983 when the JCAH accreditation standards were revised. The AMA argues that Report UU and the 1977 opinions constituted a change in the AMA's policy on chiropractors and that any conspiracy ended in 1977 or before. I reject both positions. The discussion of the 1983 revision of the JCAH standards is continued in the section of this opinion dealing with JCAH. Regarding the AHA's argument, Report UU and the 1977 opinions were clearly inadequate to end the boycott, and probably deliberately so. This is well demonstrated by the American College of Physicians' analysis of the 1977 revisions of the opinions. In a 1978 report to its members, the ACP stated:

> In 1977, as noted above, a revision of the Judicial Council interpretations of the AMA Principles of Medical Ethics appeared. The explicit language of 1966 was absent; there was no reference to chiropractic per se. In many places, the language used was unclear and ambiguous.
>
> Paragraph 1, Section 3.50, of the 1977 Judicial Council Opinions and Reports does, however, remain forthright:
>
> "A physician should not use unscientific methods of treatment, nor should he voluntarily associate professionally with anyone who does. It is wrong to engage in, or to aid and abet in treatment which has no scientific basis and is dangerous, is calculated to deceive the patient by giving him false hope, or which may cause the patient to delay in seeking proper care until his condition becomes irreversible."

This interpretation supports the court's view that the 1977 opinions were ambiguous and that the use of the key phrase "unscientific methods" continued to signal the existence of the boycott. I also find that the settlement agreements in other chiropractic litigation that occurred prior to 1980 did not end the boycott since Principle 3 was still in effect and the AMA had never publicly stated that its policy on chiropractic (calling chiropractic "un-scientific") was wrong. I conclude that the AMA and its members engaged in a group boycott or conspiracy against chiropractors from 1966 to 1980, when Principle 3 was finally eliminated.

* * *

2. *Unreasonable Restraint of Trade*

The next question is whether the boycott or conspiracy constituted an unreasonable restraint of trade under Section 1 of the Sherman Act. To answer this question, I have undertaken a rule of reason analysis.

The relevant market was the provision of health care services to the American public on a nation-wide basis, particularly for the treatment of musculoskeletal problems. As noted by the Court of Appeals, some medical physicians (such as orthopedic surgeons, internists, and general practitioners) are in direct competition with chiropractors in this market. Medical physicians and chiropractors are interchangeable for the same purposes. Consumers seek both medical physicians and chiropractors for the same complaints, principally back pain and other neuromusculoskeletal problems, and both groups render services for the treatment of those complaints. Competition between medical physicians and chiropractors was recognized by Dr. Joseph A. Sabatier, a member of the Committee on Quackery and a former defendant in this case, as early as 1964. At one point, Dr. Sabatier stated, "it would be well to get across that the doctor of chiropractic is stealing [the young medical physician's] money."

The AMA's intent is clearly relevant to the rule of reason analysis. The boycott was intended to contain and eliminate the entire profession of chiropractic. Whether or not the elimination of competition per se was consciously intended, that was the natural result of an intent to destroy a competitor. The AMA's market power is also relevant. Members of the AMA constitute a substantial force in the provision of health care services in the United States. They constitute a majority of medical physicians, and a much greater portion of fees paid to medical physicians in the United States is paid to AMA members.

Given the substantial market power of AMA members and the specific intent of the AMA, a substantial adverse effect on competition is evident.... Despite the fact that the number of chiropractic schools, the number of chiropractors, and the number of patient visits to chiropractors grew during the boycott, I accept the Committee on Quackery's admissions that the boycott was successful. These admissions were not mere puffery. The success of the boycott is shown in part by the adverse reaction of various medical societies to the AMA's modification of its anti-chiropractic policy in 1977 and the AMA's settlement of some chiropractic lawsuits in the late '70s and early '80s. Many medical physicians individually criticized the AMA for ameliorating its policy. This shows substantial support for the boycott. It was also clear to me from the testimony, particularly of the older medical physicians, that medical physicians acted in conformity with Principle 3. A principle of medical ethics is inherently a forceful mandater of conduct. No honest professional wants to risk the stigma of being labeled unethical. As the Court of Appeals noted, the fact that the AMA never sanctioned or disciplined a member for violation of Principle 3 is not controlling. Enforcement was not necessary to obtain compliance with the boycott.

* * *

The anti-competitive effects of the boycott were generally conceded by the defendants' expert, William J. Lynk of Lexecon Inc. Some of the anti-competitive effects acknowledged by Mr. Lynk include the following: it is anti-competitive and it raises costs to interfere with the consumer's free choice to take the product of his liking; it is anti-competitive to prevent medical physicians from referring patients to a chiropractor; it is anti-competitive to impose higher costs on chiropractors by forcing them to pay for their own x-ray equipment rather than obtaining x-rays from hospital radiology departments or radiologists in private practice; and it is anti-competitive to prevent chiropractors from improving their education in a professional setting by pre-venting medical physicians from teaching or lecturing to chiropractors. Mr. Lynk agreed that in an economic sense a boycott such as the one described by plaintiffs raises the costs of chiropractic services and creates inefficiencies and economic dislocations. Obviously, Mr. Lynk did not concede the existence of the boycott but agreed that these would be anti-competitive effects that would flow from such a boycott. I have also considered the fact that, as conceded by Mr. Lynk, there are substantial barriers to the entry of new chiropractors into the field, such as substantial education requirements. These barriers increase the likelihood that the boycott had a substantial adverse effect on competition.

The Court of Appeals in *Wilk*, which reviewed substantially the same boycott evidence, concluded:

> Through such mechanisms, individual physicians were discouraged from cooperating with chiropractors in: patient treatment, because referrals were inhibited by defendants' activities; research; and educational activities, such as sharing clinical experience and research results. Chiropractors were denied access to the hospital facilities they considered necessary to practice their professions. Medical doctors were discouraged from aiding chiropractors in interpreting electrocardiograms. Requests by individual plaintiffs to use laboratory and X-ray facilities were not granted; requests for hospital in-patient privileges were similarly denied. Referrals from medical doctors were reduced. Public demand for chiropractic services was negatively affected.

719 F.2d at 214.

The defendants argue that all of this evidence is not enough—that the plaintiffs must specifically prove an impact on price and output. The cases do not support that position.

As Professor Areeda recently noted in his article "The Rule of Reason—a Catechism on Competition," 55 Antitrust Law Journal, 571 (1986), the Supreme Court has held that the purpose of the inquiry into market definition and market power is to determine whether an arrangement has the potential for genuine adverse effects on competition. If there is actual proof of adverse effects, then the plaintiffs need not prove market definition and market power. The Supreme Court in Federal Trade Commission v. Indiana Federation of Dentists, 476 U.S. 447, 106 S. Ct. 2009, 2019, 90 L. Ed. 2d 445 (1986), stated that "the inquiry into market power is but a surrogate for detrimental effects."

The AMA relies on Mr. Lynk's conclusion that the boycott had pro-competitive effects that would have outweighed the anti-competitive effects. Mr. Lynk's theory is that the boycott constituted nonverbal communication which informed consumers about the differences between medical physicians and chiropractors, and that this had a pro-competitive effect. I reject this opinion as speculative. Mr. Lynk neither conducted nor read any studies regarding the efficacy of such nonverbal communications. Id. He neither conducted nor read any surveys of consumer opinion to determine whether consumers were confused about the differences between medical physicians and chiropractors. I saw no evidence of any such confusion during the trial. Mr. Lynk's opinion does not accord with common sense. A nationwide conspiracy intended by its participants to contain and eliminate a licensed profession cannot be justified on the basis of Mr. Lynk's personal opinion that it was pro-competitive, nonverbal communication to consumers.

3. *Antitrust Injury*

Having determined that the effect of Principle 3 and the implementing conduct has been to unreasonably restrict competition rather than to promote it, I now consider whether the plaintiffs have shown injury of the kind the antitrust laws were designed to prevent.

The plaintiffs principally rely on the testimony of Dr. Miron Stano, their economic expert. Dr. Stano compared the income of chiropractors, podiatrists, and optometrists over the relevant period of time and concluded that the income of chiropractors was lower than that of the other, comparable limited licensed practitioners. He viewed this as consistent with the boycott theory. He also noted a jump in chiropractors' income during the period 1978 to 1980 and he concluded that the jump was consistent with the acknowledged lessening of the boycott by the AMA during that period.

The defendants' economic expert, Mr. Lynk, faulted the data relied upon by Dr. Stano, but he agreed that if he were to compare chiropractors' income to comparable groups, he would also include podiatrists and optometrists, as well as other groups, but he would seek further explanations for the differences between the groups' incomes. Mr. Lynk further criticized the "jump" analysis done by Dr. Stano due to the fact that Dr. Stano relied on income projections from the Bureau of Labor Statistics ("BLS"). Defendants argued that BLS statistics are a poor source to begin with, and that reliance on such statistics further was not justified because in 1980 BLS began to note that it obtained its income projections for chiropractors from the American Chiropractors Association, thus signaling a change in the data collection methodology used by the BLS. This revelation caused the recalling of Dr. Stano, the introduction of a new defense expert, Mr. Robert Topel, a labor economist from the University of Chicago, and a new deposition of Dr. Stano. Mr. Topel's testimony cast further doubt on the BLS data used by Dr. Stano. However, the cross examination of Mr. Lynk demonstrated to my satisfaction that the data used by Dr. Stano were reasonable. Several of the critical numbers had some independent verification. I have also considered Mr. Topel's criticism but find that the data collection procedures used by the BLS during the relevant time remained consistent enough to be useful in this case.

I do not rely on Dr. Stano's evidence in isolation. I understand that the data are not the best that could be used for such studies, but the best data, suggested by Mr. Topel, do not exist. What lends support to Dr. Stano's result is the very strong evidence of a pervasive, nation-wide, effective conspiracy which by its very nature would have affected the demand curve for chiropractic services and adversely affected income of chiropractors. Again, defendants' economist, Mr. Lynk, agreed that such a conspiracy would shift the demand curve for chiropractic services.

The plaintiffs also established injury to reputation suffered by chiropractors. Both economic experts believed that injury to reputation would constitute an anti-competitive effect of the boycott. See Weiss v. York Hospital, 745 F.2d 786, 806–07 (3rd Cir. 1984), cert. denied, 470 U.S. 1060, 84 L. Ed. 2d 836, 105 S. Ct. 1777 (1985) (policy denying staff privileges to osteopaths likely to injure their professional reputations). In addition to labeling all chiropractors as unscientific cultists and depriving chiropractors of association with medical physicians, injury to reputation was assured by the AMA's name-calling practice. For example, in 1973, Dr. Sabatier, an AMA official, described chiropractors as rabid dogs and killers. Such statements were made in furtherance of the conspiracy and obviously injure reputations.

* * *

5. *Patient Care Defense*

I now consider whether the AMA has established the *Wilk* patient care defense. The first element is whether the AMA and its members genuinely entertained a concern for scientific method in the care of patients. I have some questions about the genuineness of the AMA's concern for scientific method based on the fact that when the AMA adopted changes in its chiropractic policy between 1977 and 1980, it apparently did so without deciding whether chiropractic was scientific. That shows disregard for scientific method in patient care. Nevertheless, I conclude that the AMA has established this element. At the time it was attacking chiropractic as unscientific, it was attacking other unscientific methods of treatment of disease, for example the Krebiozen treatment of cancer. The existence of medical standards or guidelines against unscientific practice is common. Other medical societies have long had such prohibitions and the chiropractors themselves have a similar ethical guideline. So I conclude that the AMA has established the first element of genuine concern.

The next element is whether the concern for scientific method in patient care is objectively reasonable. In connection with this element of the patient care defense, the parties have devoted a substantial amount of effort in attempting to prove that chiropractic was either good or bad, efficacious or deleterious, quackery or science. At the time the Committee on Quackery was operating, there was a lot of material available to the Committee that supported its belief that all chiropractic was unscientific and deleterious. In fact, there was a substantial amount of evidence on which the Committee reasonably could conclude that chiropractic was based on the single cause of disease theory, despite some contrary evidence that the theory had been disavowed by modern practitioners.

There also was some evidence before the Committee that chiropractic was effective—more effective than the medical profession in treating certain kinds of problems such as workmen's back injuries. The Committee on Quackery was also aware that some medical physicians believed chiropractic to be effective and that chiropractors were better trained to deal with musculoskeletal problems than most medical physicians. The Committee did not follow up on any of these studies or opinions. Basically the Committee members were doctors who, because of their firm belief that chiropractic had to be stopped and eliminated, volunteered for service on the Committee. Dr. David B. Stevens, who testified during the trial, was one of these dedicated individuals who devoted a substantial amount of time to his committee work. But it was very clear that he and other committee members did not have minds open to pro-chiropractic arguments or evidence.

* * *

Most defense witnesses agreed that some chiropractic treatment is therapeutic—although certainly no one involved in this case, including the plaintiffs, believes that chiropractic treatment should be used for the treatment of diseases such as cancer, diabetes, heart disease, high blood pressure, and infections. It is hard to pinpoint when the changes in chiropractic testified to by AMA witnesses occurred, but it is likely that they occurred while the boycott was still in effect. Thus the AMA's own evidence suggests that at some point during the boycott there was no longer an objectively reasonable concern that would support a boycott of the entire chiropractic profession.

The plaintiffs clearly want more from the court. They want a judicial pronouncement that chiropractic is a valid, efficacious, even scientific health care service.... I believe that the answer to that question can only be provided by a well designed, controlled, scientific study such as the one urged by the United States Congress' Office of Technology Assessment in its review of the New Zealand Report. In 1980, the AMA House of Delegates urged that such a study be done. No such study has ever been done. In the absence of such a study, the court is left to decide the issue on the basis of largely anecdotal evidence. I decline to pronounce chiropractic valid or invalid on anecdotal evidence....

* * *

The plaintiffs, however, point out that the anecdotal evidence in the record favors chiropractors. The patients who testified were helped by chiropractors and not by medical physicians. Dr. Per Freitag, a medical physician who associates with chiropractors, has observed that patients in one hospital who receive chiropractic treatment are released sooner than patients in another hospital in which he is on staff which does not allow chiropractors. Dr. John McMillan Mennell, M.D. testified in favor of chiropractic. Even the defendants' economic witness, Mr. Lynk, assumed that chiropractors outperformed medical physicians in the treatment of certain conditions and he believed that was a reasonable assumption.

The defendants have offered some evidence as to the unscientific nature of chiropractic. The study of how the five original named plaintiffs diagnosed and actually treated patients with common symptoms was particularly impressive This study demonstrated that the plaintiffs do not use common methods in treating common symptoms and that the treatment of patients appears to be undertaken on an ad hoc rather than on a scientific basis. And there was evidence of the use of cranial adjustments to cure cerebral palsy and other equally alarming practices by some chiropractors.

I do not minimize the negative evidence. But most of the defense witnesses, surprisingly, appeared to be testifying for the plaintiffs. Taking into account all of the evidence, I conclude only that the AMA has failed to meet its burden on the issue of whether its concern for the scientific method in support of the boycott of the entire chiropractic profession was objectively reasonable throughout the entire period of the boycott. This finding is not and should not be construed as a judicial endorsement of chiropractic.

The next element of the patient care defense is whether the AMA's concern about scientific method has been the dominant motivating factor in the defendants' promulgation of Principle 3 in the conduct undertaken and intended to implement Principle 3.

The AMA has carried its burden on this issue. While there is some evidence that the Committee on Quackery and the AMA were motivated by economic concerns—there are too many references in the record to chiropractors as competitors to ignore—I am persuaded that the dominant factor was patient care and the AMA's subjective belief that chiropractic was not in the best interests of patients.

The final question is whether this concern for scientific method in patient care could have been adequately satisfied in a manner less restrictive of competition. It would be a difficult task to persuade a court that a boycott and conspiracy designed to contain and eliminate a profession that was licensed in all fifty states at the time the Committee on Quackery disbanded was the only way to satisfy the AMA's concern for the use of scientific method in patient care. The AMA presented no evidence that a public education approach or any other less restrictive approach was beyond the ability or resources of the AMA or had been tried and failed. The AMA obviously was not successful in defeating the licensing of chiropractic on a state by state basis, but that failure does not mean that they had to resort to the highly restrictive means of the boycott. The AMA and other medical societies have managed to change America's health-related conduct by what appears to be good public relations work and there has been no proof that a similar campaign would not have been at least as effective as the boycott in educating consumers about chiropractic and the AMA's concern for scientific method.

Based on these findings, I conclude that the AMA has failed to carry its burden of persuasion on the patient care defense.

* * *

ORDER

Based on the findings of fact and conclusions of law set forth in this opinion, the case is dismissed against defendants JCAH, ACP, AAOS, and Dr. Sammons, and an injunction shall issue against defendant AMA. The ACR has recently settled with plaintiffs and is dismissed.

It is so ordered.

* * *

Notes

1. On appeal, the United States Court of Appeals for the Seventh Circuit affirmed the Northern District of Illinois' opinion in the *Wilk* case. 895 F.2d 352 (7th Cir. 1990), *writ denied*, 496 U.S. 927 (1990).

2. In addition to chiropractors, the AMA also has had difficult relationships with homeopaths. Even after the AMA opened its doors to homeopaths in 1911, the AMA's Dr. J.N. McCormack stated, "We must admit that we have never fought the homeopath on matters of principle. We fought them because they came into our community and got the business." EDWARD SHALTS, THE AMERICAN INSTITUTE OF HOMEOPATHY HANDBOOK FOR PARENTS 12–13 (2005).

B. An Antitrust Loss

Although the plaintiffs in the *Wilk* case were able to prove both an unreasonable restraint of trade and injuries that the antitrust laws were designed to prevent, not all CAM plaintiffs have been as successful. In *Solla v. Aetna Health Plans of New York, Inc.*, 14 F. Supp. 2d 252 (E.D.N.Y. 1998), *aff'd mem.*, 182 F.3d 901 (2d Cir. 1999), the plaintiff chiropractors filed a lawsuit claiming violations of Section 1 of the Sherman Act and its New York counterpart based on allegations that the defendant health maintenance organizations (HMOs) excluded the chiropractors from providing health care services to HMO enrollees in the five counties of New York City, as well as Nassau and Suffolk Counties on Long Island. Unlike the *Wilk* case, where the legally distinct defendants were capable of conspiring, the *Solla* case illustrates the application of the "intra-enterprise conspiracy doctrine," which provides that officers, agents and employees of a single entity are legally incapable of conspiring for purposes of federal antitrust law.

Solla v. Aetna Health Plans of New York, Inc.
Eastern District of New York
14 F. Supp. 2d 252 (1998)

Gershon, District Judge:

Plaintiffs, three chiropractors licensed to practice in New York, bring this antitrust action pursuant to the Sherman Act, 15 U.S.C. § 1, and its New York counterpart, the Donnelly Act, N.Y. Gen. Bus. Law § 340(1), alleging that defendants, twelve Health Maintenance Organizations ("HMOs") licensed to operate in New York, engaged in unlawful conspiracies and combinations to exclude chiropractors from providing health care services to HMO enrollees. All defendants seek summary judgment pursuant to Rule 56 of the Federal Rules of Civil Procedure dismissing plaintiffs' Fourth Amended Complaint. Plaintiffs seek leave to file a Fifth Amended Complaint.

Facts

Unless otherwise indicated, the following facts are undisputed. Plaintiffs are three chiropractors, licensed to practice in New York pursuant to N.Y. Educ. L. § 6554, who maintain their businesses in Suffolk County, NY.... By statute, the practice of chiropractic is defined as:

> detecting and correcting by manual or mechanical means structural imbalance, distortion, or subluxations in the human body for the purpose of removing nerve interference and the effects thereof, where such interference is the result of or related to distortion, misalignment or subluxation of or in the vertebral column.

N.Y. Educ. L. § 6551(1).

* * *

Defendants are twelve HMOs licensed to operate in New York pursuant to Article 44 of New York Public Health Law. N.Y. Pub. Health L. §§ 4400, et. seq. Two of the defendants, Health Insurance Plan of Greater New York, Inc. ("HIP") and Managed Health, Inc. ("Managed Health"), operate group-model HMOs. This means that they contract with groups of physicians in the localities they serve to provide health care services to their enrollees. HIP contracts with six main constituent groups, and Managed Health contracts predominantly with Community Health Program of Queens-Nassau ("CHP"). The remaining defendants—Sanus Health Plan of Greater New York, Inc., now known as NYLCare Health Plans of New York, Inc. ("NYLCare"), CIGNA Healthplan of New York, Inc. ("CIGNA"), Empire Blue Cross and Blue Shield ("Empire"), Travelers Health Network of New York, Inc., ("THN of NY"), Oxford Health Plans (New York), Inc. ("Oxford"), ChoiceCare Long Island, Inc, now known as VYTRA

Healthcare ("VYTRA"), Aetna Health Plans of New York, Inc. ("AHPNY"), U.S. Healthcare, Inc. ("U.S. Healthcare"), The Prudential Health Care Plan of New York, Inc. ("Prucare"), MetLife HealthCare Network of New York, Inc. ("MetLife") — operate independent practice association ("IPA") model HMOs. As IPA-model HMOs, they contract directly with independent physicians or practice groups for the provision of health care services to their members.

Under New York law, each HMO is required to provide comprehensive health services to its enrollees. N.Y. Pub. Health L. §4403(1)(a). The HMOs are also obligated to provide each HMO enrollee with a primary care practitioner ("PCP"). 10 N.Y.C.R.R. §98.13(b). A PCP is "a physician or other licensed provider who supervises, coordinates and provides initial and basic care to enrollees and maintains continuity of care for enrollees." 10 N.Y.C.R.R. §98.2(t). With regard to referrals, the HMO or the PCP on behalf of the HMO is responsible for the "identification and selection of an appropriate provider of care in each individual instance where ser-vices are determined to be necessary for the enrollee." 10 N.Y.C.R.R. §98.13(c).

Defendants offer varying levels of coverage for chiropractic services. Five defendants, AHPNY, THN of NY, CIGNA, MetLife and Prucare, offer chiropractic coverage as part of their basic plan. Three defendants, NYLCare, U.S. Healthcare and Empire offer chiropractic-related services through an optional rider to employers who desire additional coverage. And four defendants, HIP, Managed Health, Oxford and VYTRA, do not offer chiropractic coverage at all.

The Complaint

This action arises out of the alleged exclusion of chiropractic doctors from providing health care services to HMO enrollees in the five counties of New York City, and Nassau and Suffolk counties on Long Island. The plaintiffs complain that, even where chiropractors are the most cost-effective providers of treatment for "mechanical-structural disorders of the back and neck," HMOs have failed to "authorize" chiropractors as providers for their enrollees.

The Fourth Amended Complaint makes three claims under the Sherman Act and under New York's Donnelly Act. One claim is that "in each and every one of the HMOs, two or more persons in power—whose identities are well known within each said HMO ... have formed one or more conspiracies [to] boycott ... chiropractic doctors." The intra-HMO conspiracies are alleged to set policies for the coverage levels of chiropractic care that "withhold[] treatment options from patients and ... promulgate restrictions on chiropractic services." It is also alleged that, within each intra-HMO conspiracy, "MDs [are] agreeing among themselves to under-refer enrollees to chiropractic doctors in order to bolster over-all MD income." According to the complaint, each of the conspirators within each HMO "is excessively driven by objectives that are disparate from those of the HMO — by an impermissible personal stake" in the outcome. A second claim is that the failure of each HMO to "authorize" chiropractors in such situations renders each HMO "by itself" a "combination in restraint of trade." A third claim alleges the existence of an inter-HMO conspiracy in which "representatives of some or all of the HMOs have conspired with each other to tolerate the aforesaid intra-HMO conspiracies."

* * *

Intra-HMO Conspiracies

Under Section 1 of the Sherman Act, "every contract, combination in the form of trust or other-wise, or conspiracy, in restraint of trade or commerce among the several States ...

is declared to be illegal." 15 U.S.C. § 1. To establish a claim under Section 1, plain-tiffs must first demonstrate "some form of concerted action between at least two legally distinct economic entities" and then demonstrate that the agreement constituted an unreasonable restraint of trade. Capital Imaging, 996 F.2d at 541. Defendants seek summary judgment on the ground that plaintiffs cannot establish a genuine issue of material fact as to the existence of concerted action.

A showing of concerted action requires "evidence that tends to exclude the possibility that [the alleged conspirators] were acting independently." Monsanto Co. v. Spray-Rite Serv. Corp., 465 U.S. 752, 764, 79 L. Ed. 2d 775, 104 S. Ct. 1464 (1984). That is, plaintiffs must demonstrate that there was "a conscious commitment to a common scheme designed to achieve an unlawful objective." Id. (quotations omitted).

The requirement of concerted action between separate entities means that "wholly unilateral" conduct is not actionable under Section 1. Copperweld Corp. v. Independence Tube Corp., 467 U.S. 752, 768, 104 S. Ct. 2731, 81 L. Ed. 2d 628 (1984) (citation omitted). Also, officers, agents or employees of a single entity are legally incapable of conspiring together for purposes of Section 1. Id. at 771. In discussing the "intra-enterprise conspiracy doctrine" the Supreme Court explained:

> It is perfectly plain that an internal "agreement" to implement a single, unitary firm's policies does not raise the antitrust dangers that § 1 was designed to police. The officers of a single firm are not separate actors pursuing separate economic interests, so agreements among them do not suddenly bring together economic power that was previously pursuing divergent goals.... For these reasons, officers or employees of the same firm do not provide the plurality of actors imperative for a § 1 conspiracy.

Id. at 769.

An exception to the intra-enterprise conspiracy doctrine applies to individuals within a single entity when they are pursuing economic interests separate from the entity. Capital Imaging, 996 F.2d at 544–45. These individuals, whose personal economic interests are furthered by the objectives of the alleged conspiracy, are legally capable of conspiring for purposes of Section 1. Id. In Capital Imaging, the Court of Appeals found that member physicians of an independent practice association that contracted with an HMO to provide medical services for HMO patients were legally capable of conspiring with one another to deny a competing group of radiologists access to HMO patients. Id. at 544. These physicians had the requisite personal interest in the outcome of the conspiracy because they "were not staff physicians employed by the HMO on a salaried basis, that is, they were not agents of the HMO. Instead, these health care professionals were independent practitioners with separate economic interests." Id.

According to plaintiffs, there are intra-HMO conspiracies operating within each defendant to accomplish two objectives. First, they contend that there are intra-HMO conspiracies to establish coverage policies that exclude or restrict chiropractic services. Second, they assert that there are intra-HMO conspiracies, consisting of primary care practitioners ("PCPs") conspiring with each other, to under-refer HMO enrollees to chiropractors.... Defendants contend that plaintiffs have failed to demonstrate any evidence of intra-HMO conspiracies of either variety.

* * *

As "wholly unilateral" conduct is not actionable under Section 1, Copperweld, 467 U.S. at 768, plaintiffs' claim of intra-HMO conspiracies to establish coverage policies that exclude or restrict chiropractic services fails absent a showing that the alleged policymakers had a personal stake in the outcome of their policy decisions. Plaintiffs, however, have offered no explanation of how policymakers at any of the defendant HMOs could personally benefit from making policy decisions to restrict chiropractic options. Moreover, plaintiffs' claim is unsupported by any evidence of a conspiracy. Plaintiffs have not identified any individuals who made any decisions regarding coverage policies on chiropractic services, nor demonstrated that any of those individuals conspired with one another. For this reason as well, plaintiffs' claim of intra-HMO conspiracies to establish coverage policies fails. See Maric v. St. Agnes Hospital Corp., 65 F.3d 310, 313 (2d Cir. 1995).

Plaintiffs seek to bring their claim of intra-HMO conspiracies to under-refer HMO patients to chiropractors within the exception to the Copperweld doctrine by arguing that the PCPs had personal interests in the outcome of the alleged conspiracy. But they have offered no evidence in support of the exception. Plaintiffs have not explained how a PCP might profit personally from referring an HMO patient needing treatment for a mechanical-structural disorder of the back or neck, for example, to a medical doctor rather than to a chiropractor. In contrast, in Capital Imaging, the physicians of an independent practice association were capable of conspiring for purposes of Section 1 because, as they were in direct competition with other groups of physicians, they had a direct personal stake in denying a group of radiologists access to their HMO patients. 996 F.2d at 544. Here, plaintiffs have not explained how, using referrals to other doctors, the PCPs have a personal interest in the outcome. Plaintiffs do not demonstrate, for example, that the PCPs agreed to refer HMO patients to one another in order to boost their personal incomes. Since there has been no showing that the PCPs had a personal interest in the intra-HMO conspiracies, the PCPs are incapable of conspiring for the purpose of under-referring patients to chiropractors.

Even if it were shown that the PCPs had personal interests in the outcome of the alleged conspiracy, plaintiffs have nevertheless failed to explain how those personal interests differ from the interests of their respective HMOs. A recent decision of another district court, facing the same issue in a case brought by other chiropractors, concluded that the interests of the PCPs did not diverge from those of the HMOs. Day v. Fallon Community Health Plan, 917 F. Supp. 72 (D.Mass. 1996). The Fallon court persuasively reasoned:

> If the conspirators have agreed to under-refer enrollees to chiropractors, they either 1) over-refer enrollees to medical doctors to compensate for such under-referrals, or 2) simply under-refer to chiropractors, without a corresponding increase in referrals to medical doctors. Under the first alternative, the total number of referrals remains the same, the conspirators do not increase their income and the alleged divergent financial incentive of the conspirators to under-refer enrollees to chiropractors does not exist. Under the second alternative, the total number of referrals decreases and both the conspirators and the HMOs increase their income under the alleged incentive system. The financial interests of the conspirators, in the latter case, do not diverge from those of the HMOs. In neither event, does the plaintiffs' allegation of divergent interests between the conspirators and their HMOs make any sense.

Id. at 77–78. In sum, the personal interests of the PCPs do not diverge from the interests of the HMOs; the PCPs are therefore legally incapable of conspiring for the purpose of under-referring HMO patients to chiropractors.

Finally, even if the PCPs within each HMO had the capacity to conspire to under-refer, plaintiffs failed to produce any evidence that they actually did conspire with each other.

In Capital Imaging, the court explained the plaintiffs' burden to show an antitrust conspiracy at the summary judgment stage:

> The mere opportunity to conspire does not by itself support the inference that such an illegal combination actually occurred. A plaintiff must prove that the defendants illegally conspired.... This means that a plaintiff—to withstand defendants' summary judgment motion—must present evidence that casts doubt on inferences of independent (not combined) action or proper conduct by defendants.

996 F.2d at 545 (citations omitted).

Plaintiffs have failed to identify a single PCP from any HMO who actually conspired with another PCP to under-refer HMO enrollees to chiropractors. Plaintiffs instead ask the court to infer a conspiracy, relying on the defendants' concession, for purposes of this motion, regarding the cost-effectiveness of chiropractic care. Their contention is that, as chiropractors are more cost-effective for the work they do than medical doctors, each referral to a medical doctor necessarily constitutes an under-referral. And as "cost-effectiveness is to be expected in HMOs," plaintiffs argue that the existence of under-referrals alone "bears witness to concerted action." Pl. Br. at 27. Plaintiffs' argument that all referrals to medical doctors represent under-referrals—even if true—would nevertheless be insufficient to "cast doubt on inferences of independent (not combined) action or proper conduct by defendants." Capital Imaging, 996 F.2d at 545. "In the context of antitrust litigation the range of inferences that may be drawn from ambiguous evidence is limited; the non-moving party must set forth facts that tend to preclude an inference of permissible conduct." Id. at 542. Plaintiffs' showing fails to establish a conspiracy because they have offered nothing to suggest that the referral decisions, even if they were all under-referrals, were motivated by impermissible conduct, as opposed to independent action of the PCPs.

Intra-HMO Combinations

Plaintiffs allege that each HMO defendant is "by itself ... a combination in restraint of trade." Plaintiffs suggest that there is a distinction between combination and conspiracy for purposes of a Section 1 claim and that there is no concerted action requirement for an illegal "combination." There is, however, no support for this suggestion. The "contract, combination or conspiracy" language of Section 1 encompasses a single concept meaning "concerted action." See, e.g., Orson, Inc. v. Miramax Film Corp., 79 F.3d 1358, 1366 (3d Cir. 1996) ("For a section 1 claim under the Sherman Act, a plaintiff must prove concerted action, a collective reference to the 'contract ... combination, or conspiracy.'") (citations omitted); Todorov v. DCH Healthcare Authority, 921 F.2d 1438, 1455 (11th Cir. 1991) ("The terms 'contract, combination ... or conspiracy' are used interchangeably to describe the requisite agreement between two or more persons to restrain trade."). This Circuit has used the terms interchangeably. See, e.g., Capital Imaging, 996 F.2d at 545 ("The mere opportunity to conspire does not by itself support the inference that such an illegal combination actually occurred."). Therefore, plaintiffs' claim must be evaluated within the traditional framework for Section 1 claims.

Since "wholly unilateral" conduct is not proscribed by Section 1, Copperweld, 467 U.S. at 768, an HMO "by itself" cannot constitute an illegal combination unless plaintiffs demonstrate that individuals within the HMO with personal interests in the outcome of the alleged conspiracy have conspired with one another. Capital Imaging, 996 F.2d at 544–45. As shown above, plaintiffs are unable to make this showing.

Inter-HMO Conspiracies

Plaintiffs' third claim is entirely derivative of the 12 intra-HMO conspiracies alleged in the first and second claims. The complaint alleges that "representatives of some or all of the HMOs have conspired with each other to tolerate the ... intra-HMO conspiracies." Since plaintiffs have failed to demonstrate the existence of any intra-HMO conspiracies, there cannot be any inter-HMO conspiracies tolerating them.

* * *

Conclusion

Defendants' motion for summary judgment is granted.... The Clerk of Court is directed to enter judgment dismissing the complaint.

SO ORDERED.

* * *

Notes

1. To establish a claim under Section 1 of the Sherman Act, a plaintiff must demonstrate some form of concerted action between at least two legally distinct economic entities and that the action between or among the defendants constituted an unreasonable restraint of trade. *See, e.g., Solla*, 14 F. Supp.2d at 256. A showing of concerted action requires evidence that tends to exclude the possibility that the alleged conspirators acted independently. *Id.* Unilateral conduct, the opposite of concerted action, is governed by Section 2 of the Sherman Act and is unlawful only when it threatens actual monopolization.

2. As a general rule, a corporation such as a hospital or health insurance company is considered legally incapable of conspiring with its employees or agents because these individuals are not considered separate economic actors pursuing separate economic interests. *See, e.g., Copperweld Corp. v. Independence Tube Corp.*, 467 U.S. 752, 769 (1984). One exception to this general rule is the 'personal stake' exception. If an employee has a personal economic interest that extends beyond the desire to enhance the corporation's welfare, the employee and employer may be seen as separate entities capable of conspiring with each other. *See, e.g., Oltz v. St. Peter's Community Hosp.*, 861 F.2d 1440 (9th Cir. 1988). Courts seldom apply the 'personal stake' exception unless direct, financial evidence of separate interests exists.

Problem

Assume that an orthopedic surgeon, Dr. Phil, sits on the Board of Directors of a local hospital and participates in quarterly Board of Director discussions and decisions, including discussions and decisions regarding the expansion of existing services, including the hospital's Orthopedic Service, as well as development of new specialties, allied health services, and ancillary services, including podiatric, chiropractic, and physical therapy services. Further assume that Dr. Phil also has medical staff membership and clinical privileges at the hospital and is the Chief of the hospital's Orthopedics Service.

- Do the decisions that Dr. Phil makes as a member of the Board of Directors affect his own ability to compete for the provision of services to patients with musculoskeletal conditions?

- When might Dr. Phil's actions be considered one with, or unilateral to, the hospital?
- Are there any circumstances in which Dr. Phil could be viewed as a separate legal entity capable of conspiring with the hospital?

III. Antitrust Allegations in Other Contexts

A. Denials of Clinical Privileges

Antitrust allegations arise not only in the context of professional association rules that restrict physicians from associating with alternative practitioners and HMO activities that may lessen the ability of or prohibit alternative practitioners from caring for HMO enrollees, but also in the context of medical staff bylaws and rules and regulations that restrict medical staff membership and clinical privileges to individuals with certain credentials. In the following case, two osteopathic physicians sued a national hospital chain after they were denied clinical privileges at a hospital in Hilton Head Island, South Carolina. At issue was the anticompetitive effect of a medical staff bylaw provision that limited clinical privileges to those individuals who were certified by or eligible for certification by the American Board of Medical Specialties, which certifies allopathic physicians, but not the American Osteopathic Association (AOA), which certifies osteopathic physicians. The opinion provides a nice discussion of the 'rule of reason' analysis used in many antitrust cases as well as the difficult task of defining relevant product and geographic markets. For example, in an antitrust lawsuit filed against Hilton Head Regional Medical Center based on alleged anticompetitive conduct in the context of orthopedic services, is the relevant geographic market just the town of Hilton Head Island? Or, is it the entire county of Beaufort, South Carolina?

Welchlin v. Tenet Healthcare Corporation
United States District of South Carolina
366 F. Supp. 2d 338 (2005)

Patrick Michael Duffy, District Judge.

* * *

This matter is before the court upon Defendants' Motion for Summary Judgment. For the reasons set forth herein, Defendants' motion is denied.

BACKGROUND

Plaintiffs, two osteopathic physicians, on behalf of themselves and all others similarly situated, ... sued the various Defendants here claiming they were denied privileges to practice at the Hilton Head Regional Medical Center ("the Medical Center"). More specifically, Plaintiffs allege that the Defendants conspired to limit or prevent osteopathic practitioners from practicing at the Medical Center by adopting a bylaw that required physicians seeking hospital privileges to be certified or eligible for certification by a board recognized by the American Board of Medical Specialties ("ABMS"). [Ed.: In order to obtain staff privileges, the bylaw required: "Current certification and/or re-certification, without restriction, by the appropriate medical specialty board(s) recognized by the American Board of Medical Specialties, applicable to these Practitioner's Clinical Privileges, or to be eligible at the time of application for such certification and/or recertification and to obtain such certification or recertification within five years of eligibility."] Osteopathic physicians such as the Plaintiffs are certified by boards recognized by the American Osteopathic Association (AOA), not the ABMS. Plaintiffs suggest that the effect of the bylaw is to prevent osteopathic physicians with "true osteopathic" education and training, or those osteopaths who receive their education and training at osteopathic medical schools and facilities, from obtaining privileges at the Medical Center. Further, Plaintiffs contend that Defendants have limited their ability to retain new patients. (Sec. Am. Comp. ¶ 26).

Plaintiffs applied for appointment to the Medical Center's staff in January of 2002, and their applications were returned the next month. Shortly thereafter, Plaintiffs resubmitted their applications. In October of 2002, Defendant Dennis Brans, CEO of the Medical Center, sent a letter to Plaintiffs informing them that their applications were returned because of the bylaw requirement that they be certified or eligible for certification by an ABMS-recognized board. Defendants contend that they offered Plaintiffs a chance to prove that their certifications were equivalent to ABMS-recognized board certifications, but that Plaintiffs have failed to submit adequate evidence of substantial equivalence in support of their applications. Defendants suggest that instead of presenting this evidence, Plaintiffs instigated the present lawsuit, alleging the following claims: (1) violation of the Sherman Antitrust Act, 15 U.S.C. §1 (Count One); (2) violation of the South Carolina Antitrust Act (Count Two) (3) tortious interference with contractual relationships (Count Three); (4) violation of the South Carolina Unfair Trade Practices Act (Count Four); and (5) civil conspiracy. Plaintiffs contend, on the other hand, that they have submitted overwhelming evidence of the equivalence of DOs and MDs which Defendants have failed to consider. (Pl. Supp. Mem. at 4–16; Sec. Am. Comp. ¶ 26).

Defendants filed an earlier motion to dismiss or for summary judgment, which this court granted in part on July 1, 2004. The court dismissed Plaintiff's claim for civil conspiracy, but denied Defendants' motion on all other causes of action.... Thus, four causes of action remain—Plaintiffs' state and federal antitrust claims (Counts One and Two), tortious interference with contractual relationships (Count Three), and violation of the South Carolina Unfair Trade Practices Act (Count Four). Defendants raise new arguments in support of summary judgment on each of these remaining claims.

* * *

Analysis

The court begins by considering whether Defendants are entitled to summary judgment on Plaintiffs' antitrust claims, and then considers Defendants' remaining arguments on Plaintiffs' state law claims.

* * *

Under federal antitrust law, the Sherman Act is violated only by agreements which unreasonably restrain trade. See generally Standard Oil of N.J. v. United States, 221 U.S. 1, 55 L. Ed. 619, 31 S. Ct. 502 (1911). To assess the reasonableness of a restraint on trade, courts have taken one of two approaches. The first method—the so-called per se analysis—involves certain kinds of agreements whose effect on competition is so egregious that they can be deemed to be unreasonable without proof of anti-competitive effect. See, e.g., NYNEX Corp. v. Discon, Inc., 525 U.S. 128, 133, 142 L. Ed. 2d 510, 119 S. Ct. 493 (1998). "An agreement of such a kind is unlawful per se." Id. (citing United States v. Socony-Vacuum Oil Co., 310 U.S. 150, 84 L. Ed. 1129, 60 S. Ct. 811 (1940)); see also

National Soc. of Prof. Engineers v. United States, 435 U.S. 679, 692, 55 L. Ed. 2d 637, 98 S. Ct. 1355 (1978) ("In the first category are agreements whose nature and necessary effect are so plainly anticompetitive that no elaborate study of the industry is needed to establish their illegality—they are 'illegal per se.'"). The second category of antitrust violation involves agreements which are not deemed to be per se violations of the antitrust laws. Such agreements are evaluated under a "rule of reason" analysis, weighing the pro-competitive and anti-competitive effects of the agreement in question. See generally Chicago Bd. of Trader. United States, 246 U.S. 231, 62 L. Ed. 683, 38 S. Ct. 242 (1918).

* * *

2. Application of the Rule of Reason to the Matter *Sub Judice*

Under a rule of reason analysis, "the reasonableness of a restraint is evaluated based on its impact on competition as a whole within the relevant market." Oksanen, 945 F.2d at 708; see also Continental T. V., Inc. v. GTE Sylvania, Inc., 433 U.S. 36, 49, 53 L. Ed. 2d 568, 97 S. Ct. 2549 (1997) (holding that rule of reason analysis requires "the factfinder [to weigh] all of the circumstances of the case in deciding whether a restrictive practice should be prohibited as imposing an unreasonable restraint on competition."). This evaluation requires a showing of "anticompetitive effect" resulting from the agreement in restraint of trade. "To have an anticompetitive effect, conduct must harm the competitive process and thereby harm consumers." Dickson v. Microsoft Corp., 309 F.3d 193, 206 (4th Cir. 2002) (internal quotations omitted). "Harm to one or many competitors will not suffice." Id. "The [Sherman Act] directs itself not against conduct which is competitive, even severely so, but against conduct which unfairly tends to destroy competition itself." Id. (internal quotation marks omitted). Under controlling Fourth Circuit precedent, "an inquiry into the lawfulness of the restraint begins by identifying the ways in which a challenged restraint might possibly impair competition." Id., citing 7 Areeda & Hovenkamp P 1503a, at 372. After this threshold inquiry, the court must proceed "to determine whether that harm is not only possible but likely and significant," which entails an "examination of market circumstances," including market power and share. Id.; see also Oksanen, 945 F.2d at 709 ("Under the rule of reason, Oksanen bears the burden of proving that the actions of the defendants have unreasonably restrained trade. To meet this burden, Oksanen must prove what market he contends was restrained and that the defendants played a significant role in the relevant market. Absent this market power, any restraint on trade created by the defendants' actions is unlikely to implicate section one.").

Defendants do not appear to dispute that the restraint alleged by Plaintiffs could conceivably restrain competition. Instead, Defendants contend that Plaintiffs have failed to offer evidence that could allow a reasonable jury to conclude that Defendants have market power. (Def. Mem. at 16). As Defendants note, defining the relevant market is essential to Plaintiffs' antitrust claims, as the definition of the relevant market is a prerequisite to determining whether Defendants possess market power. The relevant market generally can be defined as the "framework within which the competitive impact of conduct is assessed." Julian O. Von Kalinowski, Antitrust Laws and Trade Regulation § 24.01 [1] (2002). For purposes of antitrust analysis, a relevant market consists of (1) a product market, and (2) a geographic market. The relevant product market identifies the products that compete with each other as defined by "the reasonable interchangeability of use or the cross-elasticity of demand between the product itself and substitutes for it." Brown Shoe Co. v. United States, 370 U.S. 294, 325, 8 L. Ed. 2d 510, 82 S. Ct. 1502 (1962). The relevant geographic market is defined as "the area in which buyers or sellers of the product effectively compete," Consul, Ltd. v. Transco Energy Co., 805 F.2d 490, 495 (4th Cir. 1986), and the area "to which their customers could practically turn for alternative sources of such products." M & M Med. Supplies & Serv. v. Pleasant Valley Hosp., 981 F.2d 160, 170 (4th Cir. 1992).

Numerous courts have recognized that defining specific product and geographic markets is a complicated task requiring the consideration of detailed economic information. See, e.g., Cogan v. Harford Memorial Hosp., 843 F.Supp. 1013, 1020 (D.Md. 1994) ("To allow a jury to make a finding as to the geographic market, [the plaintiff] must provide the Court with expert testimony on this highly technical economic question."); Victus, Ltd. v. Collezione Europa U.S.A., Inc., 26 F.Supp.2d 772, 786 (M.D.N.C. 1998) (noting that defining relevant product markets is a "difficult economic question"). Here, the parties agree that the relevant product market is the market for orthopedic surgery. Definition of the appropriate geographic market, however, is thoroughly disputed by the parties. In essence, the dispute is whether the relevant geographic market is solely the town of Hilton Head Island, as Plaintiffs contend, or, as Defendants suggest, the entirety of Beaufort County. See Pl. Opp. at 18 ("[The] market area is not the entire county. Rather, it is more narrowly, and accurately defined as, essentially, Hilton Head Island."). Moreover, the parties dispute whether the unique features of Hilton Head Island as a tourist destination for some 2.5 million visitors annually impacts the definition of the geographic market, or Defendants' market power.

As Plaintiffs argue, "definition of the relevant geographic market ... is a question of fact to be determined in the context of each case in acknowledgment of the commercial realities of the industry under consideration." See Lansdale v. Philadelphia Electric Co., 692 F.2d 307, 311 (3d Cir. 1982); see also Oahu Gas Serv., Inc. v. Pac. Resources Inc., 838 F.2d 360, 363 (9th Cir. 1988) ("Our previous decisions establish that both market definition and market power are essentially questions of fact."); Weiss, 745 F.2d at 825 ("Market definition is a question of fact."); Precision Piping & Instruments, Inc. v. E.I. Dupont deNemours and Co., 707 F.Supp. 225, 230 (S.D.W.Va. 1989) (denying summary judgment when "the jury might reasonably find the identified product market to be an appropriate one under the facts in this case. Furthermore, the Plaintiff's identification of a range of geographic markets is sufficient to place that question before the jury...."). Here, given the factual disputes surrounding the correct geographical market, including any unique features of Hilton Head Island that may be relevant to this inquiry, the court finds that summary judgment is inappropriate....

* * *

3. Evidence of a Conspiracy

Defendants next argue that Plaintiffs' claims fail because Plaintiffs have failed to proffer sufficient evidence that Defendants conspired to restrain trade. To establish a §1 violation, a plaintiff must show: "(1) a contract, combination, or conspiracy, (2) that imposed an unreasonable restraint of trade." Dickson, 309 F.3d at 202. A plaintiff can offer direct or circumstantial evidence to prove concerted action. Monsanto Co. v. Spray-Rite Serv. Corp., 465 U.S. 752, 79 L. Ed. 2d 775, 104 S. Ct. 1464 (1984). "Direct evidence is extremely rare in antitrust cases and is usually referred to as the 'smoking gun.'" American Chiropractic Assoc. Inc. v. Trigon Healthcare, 367 F.3d 212, 227 (4th Cir. 2004), quoting InterVest, Inc. v. Bloomberg, L.P., 340 F.3d 144, 159 (3d Cir. 2003). "The antitrust plaintiff, when faced with a summary judgment motion, must merely offer significant probative evidence to support its case." Trident Neuro-Imaging Laboratory v. Blue Cross Blue Shield of South Carolina, 568 F.Supp. 1474, 1478 (D.S.C. 1983). "If reasonable inferences drawn from all of the evidence—which must be viewed in the light most favorable to the plaintiff—indicate the existence of a conspiracy, the plaintiff has introduced a sufficient basis for proceeding to trial." Id. Nonetheless, the Supreme Court has instructed that when there is evidence of conduct that is consistent with both legitimate competition and an illegal conspiracy, courts may not infer that an illegal conspiracy has occurred without other evidence. See Matsushita Elec. Indus. Co. v. Zenith Radio Corp., 475 U.S. 574, 588, 89 L. Ed. 2d 538, 106 S. Ct. 1348 (1986).

Plaintiffs here do not purport to have direct evidence of concerted action, but instead, argue that abundant circumstantial evidence of a conspiracy to restrain trade exists. This court has studied the allegations made by Plaintiffs, and concludes that there is sufficient evidence from which to draw reasonable inferences of the existence of a conspiracy for purposes of surviving summary judgment. First, as Plaintiffs note, Defendants have maintained, throughout this litigation, that the ABMS bylaw requirement was adopted in 1974 when the hospital first commenced operations and has remained as simply a relic of that early enactment. One of the founding physicians testified that the ABMS bylaw requirement was modeled upon a bylaw from a hospital where he held privileges prior to joining the staff at Hilton Head in an effort to increase the quality of medical care, and that the bylaw operated from "Day One" when the hospital opened. (LamotteDep. at 14, 16). However, after further discovery, it appears that the ABMS bylaw requirement was not adopted until 1990, ... and has been revisited on numerous occasions since Plaintiffs' recent applications for privileges. (Pl. Supp. Mem. at 4).

* * *

Second, Plaintiffs point to evidence that a proposed amendment to the bylaw requirement was considered within the last few years. According to Plaintiffs, Defendants have attempted to obfuscate this fact by insisting, untruthfully, that the bylaw requirement has been in existence since the hospital's inception. The proposed amendment would have allowed the Board to waive the ABMS requirement for "an active Medical Staff member upon recommendation by the Medical Executive Committee and in the Board's sole discretion without right to appeal." Dr. Kenneth Kunze, the Regional Chief Medical Officer of Tenet Healthcare and former medical director of the Hilton Head Hospital first affirmed by affidavit that the proposed amendment was "developed during the mid-to-late 1980s to address circumstances involving a particular member of the Medical Staff ... [who] was an M.D., not a D.O." (Kunze Aff. ¶ 5). Moreover, Kunze averred "without reservation or qualification, that the proposed amendment had nothing to do with the eligibility of osteopaths or membership on the Hilton Head Medical Staff." Id. at ¶ 6. Later, however, Kunze reneged this testimony, and now affirms that the bylaw provision was contemplated, and ultimately rejected, in the last several years in reference to allowing an osteopath to remain on the Medical Staff. (Kunze Dep. at 60–61). According to Plaintiffs, this demonstrates that the members of the Medical Staff have actively considered, and attempted to prevent, osteopathic membership on the medical staff in recent history, as opposed to simply keeping a remnant bylaw on the books since the inception of the hospital as Defendants suggest. At this stage of the litigation, and without additional evidence, the court cannot say that no reasonable jury could conclude that the medical staff member defendants' rejected this bylaw as part of concerted action to restrain competition from osteopaths, as their motivations are simply not clear upon the present record.

Next, Plaintiffs cite actions of the Board of Governors following their applications as evidence of concerted action to restrain trade. After Plaintiffs applied for privileges, the Executive Committee of the Board of Governors held a meeting, and noted in its Minutes that it "would like to initiate a requirement that Doctors of Osteopathy must be American Board certified." (Venable Dep., Ex. 1). This item was to be voted on at the

General Staff meeting. While Defendants attempt to explain this reference as "somewhat cryptic" and "a transcription mistake[,]" see Def. Reply at 19, the court believes that genuine issues of material fact exist as to whether, as Plaintiffs suggest, the Board of Governors and medical staff conceitedly took this action to strengthen their position that no osteopaths would be able to obtain staff membership in an attempt to eliminate competition. Moreover, Plaintiffs have produced evidence that, over the years, several allopathic physicians without ABMS certification have been allowed medical staff membership. (Honts Dep. at 68; Kunze Dep. at 81–85). According to Plaintiffs, the presence of other allopathic physicians without ABMS board certification on the medical staff is circumstantial evidence of the implicit conspiracy by members of the medical staff to favor allopaths over osteopaths.

* * *

In short, while Defendants attempt to explain how each of these acts cannot possibly establish conspiratorial conduct to any rational juror, in the court's opinion, genuine issues of material factual dispute exist. The court cannot conclude that, as a matter of law, no rational juror could believe that any of the aforementioned acts were conspiratorial actions taken to prevent competition from osteopaths. Because the court is not to weigh the evidence before it and must view all evidence in Plaintiffs' favor, summary judgment is inappropriate.

* * *

4. Antitrust Injury

Defendants' final argument with respect to the federal antitrust claims is that Plaintiffs have not proven a sufficient antitrust injury to withstand summary judgment. Antitrust injury is an injury from unlawful acts that results in reduced output or higher prices for consumers. Cont'l Airlines, Inc. v. United Airlines, Inc., 277 F.3d 499 at 516. "[A] plaintiff cannot demonstrate the unreasonableness of a restraint merely by showing that it caused him an economic injury." Oksanen, 945 F.2d at 708. In considering whether an antitrust injury exists, "the reasonableness of a restraint is evaluate based on its impact on competition as a whole within the relevant market." Id.

Here, while Defendants argue that summary judgment is appropriate because Plaintiffs' have failed to establish an antitrust injury, the court disagrees for several reasons. First and foremost, as discussed above, the factual disputes surrounding the relevant market render it impossible for this court to determine the effect of any restraint on competition within that market. Secondly, at the summary judgment stage, Plaintiffs are entitled to all reasonable inferences from the evidence presented, and need only establish a genuine issue of material fact with regard to the existence of antitrust injury. See R. C. Bigelow, Inc. v. Unilever N. V., 867 F.2d 102, 107–11 (2d Cir. 1989). Plaintiffs have proffered a report prepared by a consultant demonstrating that Plaintiffs were charging less for some services than other orthopedic practices in the area, leading the court to believe that, should Plaintiffs be able to prove their allegations of a conspiracy to restrain osteopaths from entering the relevant market, a cognizable antitrust injury could exist. Moreover, if it is ultimately proven that Defendants refused to refer patients to Plaintiffs as part of their unlawful conspiracy, this could similarly establish that consumers and competition were harmed by Defendants' alleged practices by facing artificially high practices or depriving consumers of fair choice among providers of medical services. See, e.g., FTC v. Indiana Federation of Dentists, 476 U.S. 447, 459, 90 L. Ed. 2d 445, 106 S. Ct. 2009 (1986).

* * *

CONCLUSION

It is therefore ORDERED, for the foregoing reasons, that Defendants' Motion for Summary Judgment is hereby DENIED.

AND IT IS SO ORDERED.

* * *

Notes and Problems

1. The federal Health Care Quality Improvement Act (HCQIA) immunizes professional review bodies that take professional review actions in accordance with certain standards from federal and state non-civil rights claims, including antitrust claims. 42 U.S.C. § 11111. Is an action taken by a hospital based on medical staff member's or applicant's board certification considered a professional review action? *See id.* § 11151.

2. Assume that a hospital that allows chiropractors, osteopaths, and other CAM practitioners to serve on its medical staff is considering taking an adverse professional review action against a particular CAM practitioner due to his professional incompetence. In order to shield itself from future antitrust liability, what process should the hospital follow in deciding whether to take the adverse professional review action? What procedural rights should be given to the physician? Does the hospital have any reporting obligations? Does the answer to any of these questions depend on whether the practitioner is an allopathic or osteopathic physician on the one hand, or a non-M.D. or D.O. practitioner on the other? *See* 42 U.S.C. §§ 11111, 11112, 11133, and 11134; 42 C.F.R. §§ 60.3, 60.4, 60.5; and 42 U.S.C. § 1396r-2.

B. Denial or Cancellation of Malpractice Insurance

Antitrust allegations also can arise when an insurance company refuses to provide malpractice insurance to a CAM practitioner or when an allopathic physician is stripped of malpractice insurance due to the physician's association with a CAM practitioner. In the case below, an obstetrician lost his malpractice insurance when his physician-owned insurance carrier learned of the obstetrician's intention to join two nurse-midwives in practice. The legal question becomes: When competing physicians join together to sell malpractice insurance, are they operating as a single entity pursuing a unified interest or as independent actors essential to the existence of a conspiracy?

Nurse Midwifery Associates v. Hibbett
United States Court of Appeals for the Sixth Circuit
918 F.2d 605 (1990)

ALAN E. NORRIS, CIRCUIT JUDGE.

This case involves two appeals arising out of an antitrust action brought by two nurse midwives, the obstetrician with whom they had affiliated, and three of their clients, against three Nashville hospitals, certain members of the medical staffs from two of the hospitals, another practicing obstetrician in Nashville, and a physician-controlled insurance company. Plaintiffs alleged that these defendants had engaged in several conspiracies to restrain trade, in violation of section 1 of the Sherman Antitrust

Act, 15 U.S.C. § 1. Plaintiffs now appeal the district court's decision awarding summary judgment to defendants with respect to all but one of the alleged conspiracies. 689 F. Supp. 799. Two of the hospitals also bring an interlocutory appeal, contending that the district court erred in denying summary judgment with respect to the alleged conspiracy between the two hospitals. For the reasons stated, we affirm in part and reverse in part.

* * *

Plaintiffs Susan Sizemore and Victoria Henderson are certified nurse midwives who formed Nurse Midwifery Associates ("NMA") in order to provide nurse midwifery service in the private sector of the Nashville, Tennessee area. NMA entered into an agreement with plaintiff Dr. Darrell Martin, a practicing obstetrician, under which NMA would operate as an independent practice, and Dr. Martin and his associates would provide medical supervision and services.

* * *

D. State Volunteer Mutual Insurance Company and Dr. Hibbett

State Volunteer Mutual Insurance Company ("SVMIC") is a nonprofit mutual insurance company, owned and operated by its physician policyholders. The policyholders elect the Board of Directors and participate on SVMIC's committees. SVMIC insures almost eighty percent of all physicians in Tennessee, and is organized under the auspices of the Tennessee Medical Association ("TMA"). Plaintiffs allege that the TMA has long been opposed to the expanded use of nurse midwives.

SVMIC learned in June of 1980 that Dr. Martin would be leaving his practice group and would be associated with NMA. SVMIC's underwriter wrote to Dr. Martin seeking clarification of his relationship with NMA and asking for "any other pertinent information which will help us to determine our exposure as your malpractice carrier."

On July 31, 1980, Dr. Hibbett, a member of the SVMIC Board of Directors and a member of the SVMIC Claims Review Committee, had a conversation with an obstetrical nurse at Baptist Hospital concerning SVMIC's upcoming meeting to consider whether to continue to insure Dr. Martin in light of his affiliation with NMA. During the conversation, Dr. Hibbett told the nurse something to the effect of "we're going to get Dr. Martin's insurance," and that "we would set nurse midwifery back twenty years." An obstetrician who practiced at Baptist Hospital also recalls a similar conversation with Dr. Hibbett.

The Underwriting Committee of SVMIC concluded that Dr. Martin's relationship with nurse midwives increased the underwriting risks to SVMIC to an unacceptable level, and adopted a motion to cancel his insurance. It also named an ad hoc subcommittee, composed of two Nashville physicians, SVMIC's outside counsel and staff to determine whether its assessment of the risks posed by coverage of Dr. Martin was justified. The committee concluded that the underwriting risks posed by Dr. Martin were in fact unacceptable.

On October 29, 1980, the recommendation of the Underwriting Committee to cancel Dr. Martin's coverage came before the Board of Directors. There was no discussion concerning competition from the midwives or any other competitive considerations. However, the board only reviewed the Consulting Agreement between NMA and Dr. Martin; it did not review the medical protocol which described in detail the medical supervision Dr. Martin would exercise over NMA's practice. The board, including Dr. Hibbett, voted unanimously not to renew Dr. Martin's coverage.

Dr. Martin requested a hearing before the Underwriting Committee and, at the meeting, presented information concerning his arrangement with NMA. The committee determined that it had made the correct decision in recommending that the insurance be terminated, and advised Dr. Martin of his right to appeal the decision to the Board of Directors. He did not appeal.

Henderson and Sizemore were unable to secure the services of another supervising physician and discontinued their nurse midwifery practice.

* * *

B. Conspiracy among Members of SVMIC

One of the means the defendant physicians allegedly used to prevent a qualified obstetrician from cooperating with nurse midwives was for Dr. Hibbett and physician members of SVMIC to cancel Dr. Martin's malpractice insurance because of his contract with nurse midwives.

On this claim, the district court granted summary judgment in favor of defendant SVMIC, holding that SVMIC must be viewed as a single entity when it decided to terminate Dr. Martin's coverage. In doing so, the court reversed the position it had previously taken in denying SVMIC's motion to dismiss. See Nurse Midwifery Assocs. v. Hibbett, 549 F. Supp. 1185 (M.D. Tenn. 1982). In that earlier decision, the district court thought that

> the existence of concerted action by a single corporation such as SVMIC is not, as a matter of law, precluded. Because SVMIC is owned and operated exclusively by its physician policyholders, who have elected a Board of Directors also dominated by physicians, and is closely affiliated with the Tennessee Medical Association, SVMIC may be considered capable of concerted action.... Indeed, in view of the member control of SVMIC, SVMIC may be considered the agent of its physician policyholders. Id. at 1190 (citations omitted).

But, in reversing itself, the district court pointed to Arizona v. Maricopa County Medical Soc'y, 457 U.S. 332, 73 L. Ed. 2d 48, 102 S. Ct. 2466 (1982). In that case, the Supreme Court held that an agreement among competing physicians which set, by majority vote, maximum fees that they would accept as full payment for services provided for patients insured by approved insurers was per se unlawful under section 1 as a horizontal price-fixing conspiracy. In distinguishing the "foundations" set up by the physicians to administer the agreement from other entities to which it had not applied the per se rule, the Supreme Court utilized the language relied upon by the district court:

> Each of the foundations is composed of individual practitioners who compete with one another for patients. Neither the foundations nor the doctors sell insurance, and they derive no profits from the sale of health insurance policies. The members of the foundations sell medical services. Their combination in the form of the foundation does not permit them to sell any different product. Their combination has merely permitted them to sell their services to certain customers at fixed prices and arguably to affect the prevailing market price of medical care.

> The foundations are not analogous to partnerships or other joint arrangements in which persons who would otherwise be competitors pool their capital and share the risks of loss as well as the opportunities for profit. In such joint ventures, the partnership is regarded as a single firm competing with other sellers in the market. The agreement under attack is an agreement among hundreds of competing doctors concerning the price at which each will offer his own services

to a substantial number of consumers. It is true that some are surgeons, some anesthesiologists, and some psychiatrists, but the doctors do not sell a package of three kinds of services. If a clinic offered complete medical coverage for a flat fee, the cooperating doctors would have the type of partnership arrangement in which a price-fixing agreement among the doctors ... would be perfectly proper. But the fee agreements disclosed by the record in this case are among independent competing entrepreneurs. They fit squarely into the horizontal price-fixing mold.

Id. at 356–57.

On its face, this language would appear to support the district court's apparent conclusion that, when the competing physicians joined together to sell malpractice insurance—a product different from the medical services over which they normally competed among themselves and with other providers—they operated as a single entity pursuing a complete unity of interest, rather than as the independent actors essential to the existence of a conspiracy. That reasoning would be persuasive if the selling of the different product had triggered a complaint that the defendants were restraining competition among sellers of malpractice insurance. But, here, plaintiffs allege that the anti-competitive effect of defendants' conduct is in the same area in which the physicians combining to form SVMIC usually compete—providing medical services. If these allegations are true, then the defendants' conduct cannot be characterized as that of former competitors operating a joint venture which competes in the market with other sellers of malpractice insurance. Instead, it will be the conduct of physicians who retain their identity as individuals who compete among themselves and with plaintiffs in providing maternity care services and combine to unreasonably restrain competition in that field by denying malpractice insurance coverage to a competing maternity care provider.

Accordingly, the language quoted from Maricopa does not compel the conclusion arrived at by the district court that, as a matter of law, "SMVIC [sic] must be viewed as a single entity." Since SVMIC and its members were theoretically capable of conspiring, the question remains upon remand whether physicians who had previously pursued their own interests separately, in this instance combined to unlawfully restrain competition among providers of maternity care.

* * *

For the reasons stated, we reverse the grant of summary judgment to defendants SVMIC and Dr. Hibbett to the extent that it disposed of plaintiffs' claim that Dr. Hibbett and other principals at SVMIC conspired in violation of the Act, and remand that claim pursuant to Section III(B) of this opinion.... In all other respects, the decision of the district court is affirmed, and this cause is remanded to the district court for further proceedings consistent with this opinion.

C. Reimbursement Caps and Disparities in Reimbursement Rates

Reimbursement caps and other disparities in reimbursement rates for professional health care services also may give rise to antitrust allegations, especially when the reimbursement caps or lower reimbursement rates are applied to CAM services. In the following case, the plaintiff chiropractors and chiropractic associations argued that a number of actions taken by the defendant health insurance company, including the adoption of a clinical practice guideline relating to the treatment of low back pain and the imposition of a reimbursement cap on spinal manipulations, violated federal antitrust law.

American Chiropractic Association v. Trigon Healthcare, Inc.
United States District Court for the Western District of Virginia
258 F. Supp. 2d 461 (2003)

JAMES P. JONES, DISTRICT JUDGE.

American Chiropractic Association, Inc., Virginia Chiropractic Association, Inc., and certain individual doctors and patients of chiropractic medicine filed this action against health insurer Trigon Healthcare, Inc., and affiliated companies ("Trigon") claiming anticompetitive activities harmful to chiropractic medicine. Following discovery, Trigon has moved for summary judgment For the reasons set forth in this opinion, I find that there are no genuine issues of material fact remaining for trial and that Trigon is entitled to judgment in its favor.

* * *

Chiropractic is a recognized branch of the healing arts, and chiropractic treatment is widely utilized by consumers of medical services, mainly for neuromusculoskeletal disorders such as back pain, neck pain, and headaches. Such disorders affect a large proportion of the American adult population.... Trigon is a health care insurer that does business as Trigon Blue Cross Blue Shield and was formerly known as Blue Cross and Blue Shield of Virginia.... Until 1991 Trigon was a not-for-profit entity, but thereafter became a for-profit, publically owned corporation, in the business of offering individual and group healthcare plans to its subscribers. It is currently "the largest managed healthcare company in Virginia." ...

* * *

The core claim made in this case is that Trigon has intentionally prevented or discouraged its subscribers from utilizing chiropractic at the behest of physicians. In the plaintiffs' words, the purpose of this conspiracy was "to prevent the transfer of insurance dollars from medical doctors to chiropractors." ... More specifically, the plaintiff's contend that Trigon's anticompetitive conduct included the issuance of a clinical practice guideline on the treatment of low back pain; the continuation of a $500 reimbursement cap on spinal manipulations; the reduction in the payment rate for services other than spinal manipulations; the "leveling" of payments for manipulations of multiple regions of the spine; suggesting to competing providers—osteopaths and physical therapists—ways to avoid payment limitations; and negotiation with medical doctors rather than chiropractors over reimbursement terms. The legal foundations for the plaintiffs' claims are the anticonspiracy provisions of the Sherman Act, 15 U.S.C.A. §1 (West 1997) (Count I), the Virginia Civil Conspiracy Act, Va. Code Ann. §§ 18.2-499, -500 (Michie 1996) (Count V), and the common law (Count VII); the antimonopolization provision of the Sherman Act, 15 U.S.C.A. §2 (West 1997) (Count II); tortious interference with business expectancies (Count IV); and breach of contract (Count VI).... The court has jurisdiction pursuant to 28 U.S.C.A. §§ 1331, 1337(a), and 1367(a) (West 1993 & Supp. 2002).

* * *

Following extensive discovery, Trigon has moved for summary judgment. The issues have been briefed and argued and the motion is ripe for decision.

* * *

At bottom, the plaintiffs' conspiracy argument makes no economic sense. Trigon, as a profit-seeking corporation, had no economic motive to prevent referrals to chiropractors. In fact, the uncontradicted evidence in the record is that from 1996 to 2001 the number of chiropractors in Trigon's Participating Provider ("PAR") and Preferred Provider Organization ("PPO") networks nearly doubled (from 1095 to 1934), ... the number of Trigon insureds receiving chiropractic manipulations nearly trebled (from 26,275 to 74,477), ... and chiropractors' share of Trigon's total payments to professional providers increased by fourteen percent. Trigon's profit-maximizing interest was to allow its members to obtain needed medical care while paying medical providers the lowest possible cost. If, as the plaintiffs' believe, chiropractic treatments are cheaper and more effective than certain competing medical remedies (such as drug therapies), it was clearly economically advantageous to Trigon to encourage, rather than discourage, the utilization of chiropractic. Moreover, to the extent potential subscribers desired chiropractic care, it was in Trigon's competitive interest to provide access to that treatment. The fact that Trigon did not increase the use of chiropractic treatment as much as the plaintiffs' desire is not evidence of conspiracy....

* * *

In addition, the specific alleged anticompetitive conduct complained of by the plaintiffs does not support the existence of an unlawful conspiracy.

For example, the plaintiffs rely heavily on Trigon's adoption of a clinical practice guideline in 1996 as proof of a conspiracy. This guideline, entitled "Managing Low Back Problems in Adults," was drafted by Trigon employees and considered (but not revised) by the Managed Care Advisory Panel. Trigon contends that its guideline, which was distributed to all of its providers including chiropractors, was merely a simplified version of a clinical guideline published by a federal agency in 1994.... The plaintiffs point to the opinion of their expert, Scott Haldeman, that the Trigon guideline is "inconsistent" and "in conflict" with the federal guideline, mainly because while the Trigon guideline recommends "manipulation" as a treatment option, it omits the federal definition of manipulation. The expert believes that the federal definition favors the type of manipulation given by chiropractors over other providers.... Even assuming that this opinion is credible — and I find it very thin — it is insufficient circumstantial proof of a conspiracy. It is clear that Trigon's guideline follows the federal guideline in a highly abbreviated form. The uncontested evidence is that since Trigon's guideline was issued in 1996, no chiropractor provider ever complained to Trigon about the omission of the definition of manipulation or anything else about it. Moreover, since it was issued, use of chiropractic treatment by Trigon subscribers has substantially increased.

The plaintiffs also complain that the continuation by Trigon in its health care plans of a maximum annual payment allowance of $500 for "spinal manipulations and other manual medical interventions" ... is evidence of a conspiracy with medical doctors and their organizations. Again, however, this fact supports the proposition that Trigon acted in its own self interest to limit its costs. The evidence shows that Trigon's payment and coverage policies were based on its understandable goal of obtaining professional services at the lowest possible cost the market would bear.

* * *

Trigon was not alone in its utilization of mechanisms for limiting the expense of chiropractic services. The summary judgment record shows that caps on chiropractic payments were used by ninety-four percent of selected large national private insurers, ... and that other healthcare insurers in Virginia have practices comparable to Trigon's.... There is no question but that the intent of these methods was to limit the quantity of chiropractic care. But that is not proof that Trigon (or other insurers) conspired with the medical profession to this end....

* * *

The plaintiffs submitted evidence that Trigon "suggested" to osteopaths and physical therapists ways to "get around" the limitations on manipulation reimbursement and that since those professions are "closely associated with" medical doctors, these efforts show evidence of the charged conspiracy.... Trigon denies any such suggestions; in any event, the record is clear that Trigon never changed its procedures to benefit osteopaths or physical therapists. I do not find these allegations sufficient to produce a triable issue of fact as to the existence of an anticompetitive conspiracy.

* * *

Finally, the plaintiffs contend that there is evidence that Trigon negotiated with the Medical Society of Virginia, representing medical doctors, over reimbursement terms, but did not similarly negotiate with chiropractors. However, I agree with the defendants that the evidence shows only that Trigon was willing to listen to suggestions by this physician group. Of course, there is no evidence in the record that Trigon ever discussed with the Medical Society of Virginia, or any other professional association, any policies harmful to chiropractic providers.

* * *

The plaintiffs allege in Count II that Trigon has attempted to monopolize the market for the treatment of neuromusculoskeletal disorders in violation of section 2 of the Sherman Act. They also allege that Trigon has conspired with BCBSA and medical doctors to monopolize this market. The plaintiffs' conspiracy to monopolize claim under section 2 of the Sherman Act fails for the same reason that the plaintiffs' section 1 claim fails—there is no evidence of a conspiracy between Trigon and any other persons.

The attempt to monopolize claim also is defective. This claim has four essential elements: (1) a specific intent to monopolize; (2) a relevant market; (3) predatory or anticompetitive acts; and (4) a dangerous probability of success in achieving monopolization. See Advanced Health-Care Servs., Inc., 910 F.2d at 147. The short answer to this claim is that Trigon and chiropractors do not compete in the same market. See White v. Rockingham Radiologists, Ltd., 820 F.2d 98, 104 (4th Cir. 1987) ("One who does not compete in a product market or conspire with a competitor cannot be held liable as a monopolist in that market.").

* * *

For the foregoing reasons, I will grant the defendants' Motion for Summary Judgment and enter final judgment on their behalf. A separate judgment consistent with this opinion is being entered herewith.

* * *

D. CAM Practitioners as Antitrust Defendants

In the majority of antitrust cases set in the health care context, the defendants are conventional allopathic physicians, conventional hospitals and health systems, conventional medical associations, and/or insurance companies that provide insurance to conventional practitioners. CAM practitioners and their professional associations also have been accused of engaging in anticompetitive conduct, however. In the following complaint, the Federal Trade Commission (FTC) alleged that the Connecticut Chiropractic Association (CCA), the Connecticut Chiropractic Council (CCC), and Robert L. Hirtle, CCA's legal counsel, conspired through a campaign of meetings and other communications to encourage and facilitate a collective refusal to deal with American Specialty Health (ASH). According to the FTC, the purpose and effect of the boycott was to prevent ASH from providing its cost-saving chiropractic benefits administration program in Connecticut. In a press release issued by the FTC, it referred to the boycott as a "naked boycott among competitors" and stated that the boycott was "a clear per se violation of the antitrust laws." Federal Trade Commission, FTC Challenges Illegal Boycott of Health Plan by Connecticut Chiropractors: Chiropractors Must Modify Behavior to Protect Competition (March 5, 2008), *available at* http://www.ftc.gov/opa/2008/03/chiro.shtm.

In the Matter of
The Connecticut Chiropractic Association,
The Connecticut Chiropractic Council, and
Robert L. Hirtle, Esq.
United States of America Federal Trade Commission

COMPLAINT

Pursuant to the provisions of the Federal Trade Commission Act, as amended, 15 U.S.C. §41 et seq., and by virtue of the authority vested in it by said Act, the Federal Trade Commission ("Commission"), having reason to believe that the Connecticut Chiropractic Association ("CCA"), the Connecticut Chiropractic Council ("CCC"), and Robert L. Hirtle, Esq., hereinafter sometimes collectively referred to as "Respondents," have violated Section 5 of the Federal Trade Commission Act, 15 U.S.C. §45, and it appearing to the Commission that a proceeding by it in respect thereof would be in the public interest, hereby issues this Complaint stating its charges in that respect as follows:

NATURE OF THE CASE

1. This matter concerns a series of agreements among competing chiropractors to boycott American Specialty Health ("ASH") to preclude ASH from administering a chiropractic cost-savings benefits administration program on behalf of payors offering coverage for health care services in the State of Connecticut. The chiropractors engaged in this conduct with and through their respective trade associations, CCA and CCC, CCA's legal counsel, Robert L. Hirtle, Esq., and through activities undertaken collectively among CCA, CCC, Mr. Hirtle, and other licensed chiropractors in the State of Connecticut.

2. The Respondents' illegal conduct had the purpose and effect of unreasonably restraining prices and other forms of competition among hundreds of otherwise independent chiropractors in the State of Connecticut.

RESPONDENTS

3. CCA is a not-for-profit corporation, organized, existing, and doing business under and by virtue of the laws of the State of Connecticut, with its office and principal address at 2257 Silas Deane Highway, Rocky Hill, Connecticut 06067. CCA is a voluntary trade association whose membership consists of approximately 375 chiropractors licensed to practice chiropractic in the State of Connecticut.

4. CCC is a not-for-profit corporation, organized, existing, and doing business under and by virtue of the laws of the State of Connecticut, with its office and principal address located at 8 Tyler Avenue, Branford, Connecticut 06405. CCC is a voluntary trade association whose membership consists of approximately 150 chiropractors licensed to practice chiropractic in the State of Connecticut.

5. Mr. Hirtle was legal counsel for CCA at all times relevant herein. His principal address is 185 Asylum Street, Hartford, Connecticut 06103.

JURISDICTION

6. CCA is organized for the purpose, among others, of serving the interests of its members. CCA exists and operates, and at all times relevant to this Complaint has existed and operated, in substantial part for the pecuniary benefit of its members.

7. CCC is organized for the purpose, among others, of serving the interests of its members. CCC exists and operates, and at all times relevant to this Complaint has existed and operated, in substantial part for the pecuniary benefit of its members.

8. At all times relevant to this Complaint CCA chiropractors and CCC chiropractors have been engaged in the business of providing chiropractic services for a fee. Except to the extent competition has been restrained as alleged herein:

> a. CCA chiropractors have been and are in competition with other CCA chiropractors for the provision of chiropractic services in areas throughout the State of Connecticut;
>
> b. CCC chiropractors have been and are in competition with other CCC chiropractors for the provision of chiropractic services in areas throughout the State of Connecticut; and
>
> c. CCA chiropractors and CCC chiropractors have been and are in competition with each other, and with other chiropractors, for the provision of chiropractic services in areas throughout the State of Connecticut.

9. All Respondents are "persons" or "corporations" within the meaning of Section 4 of the Federal Trade Commission Act, as amended, 15 U.S.C. § 44.

10. The general business practices of Respondents, including the acts and practices alleged herein, affect the interstate movement of patients, the interstate purchase of supplies and products, and the interstate flow of funds, and are in or affect "commerce" as defined in the Federal Trade Commission Act, as amended, 15 U.S.C. § 44.

OVERVIEW OF CHIROPRACTOR CONTRACTING WITH PAYORS

11. Individual chiropractors and chiropractic group practices contract with payors of health care services and benefits, including insurance companies, managed care organizations, health care benefits organizations, and others, to establish the terms and conditions, including price terms, under which the chiropractors will render their professional chiropractic services to the payors' enrollees. Chiropractors and chiropractic group practices entering into such contracts often agree to accept lower compensation from payors in order to obtain access to additional patients made available by the payors' relationship with the covered individuals. These contracts may reduce payors' costs and enable them to lower the price of insurance or of providing health benefits, thereby resulting in lower health care costs for covered individuals.

12. Absent anticompetitive agreements among them, otherwise competing chiropractors and chiropractic group practices unilaterally decide whether to enter into contracts with payors to provide services to individuals covered by a payor's programs, and

what prices and other terms they will accept as payment for their services pursuant to such contracts.

ASH CHIROPRACTIC COST-SAVINGS PROGRAM

13. ASH is a health care benefits organization that offers a chiropractic cost-savings benefits administration program to payors nationwide, including payors in the State of Connecticut. The purpose of the program is to improve the efficiency, increase the quality, and reduce the cost of providing chiropractic care to the payors' enrollees.

14. Under the program, payors delegate the management of chiropractic services and benefits for their enrollees to ASH. ASH contracts with chiropractors to provide chiropractic services to the payors' enrollees under the cost-savings program. In addition to its chiropractor network, ASH administers chiropractic benefits, including utilization management, credentialing, claims processing, and other management services, for payors under the program.

ANTICOMPETITIVE CONDUCT

15. CCA acted in conspiracy with its members, CCC acted in conspiracy with its members, and CCA, CCC, and their members acted in conspiracy with each other. Through their joint agreements, CCA, CCC, and their respective members, restrained competition by, among other things, collectively agreeing to boycott ASH. The purpose and effect of the boycott was to prevent ASH from providing its cost-savings chiropractic benefits administration program to Anthem Blue Cross and Blue Shield of Connecticut ("Anthem"), CIGNA HealthCare ("CIGNA"), Empire Blue Cross Blue Shield ("Empire"), and other payors.

16. Mr. Hirtle acted to restrain competition by, among other things, encouraging, facilitating, and implementing agreements, among competing CCA and CCC chiropractors, and other chiropractors licensed in the State of Connecticut, to boycott ASH to prevent ASH from providing its chiropractic cost-savings program to Anthem, CIGNA, Empire, and other payors.

17. In furtherance of the combinations and agreements, CCA, CCC, and Mr. Hirtle engaged in a campaign through meetings and other communications to encourage and assist chiropractors in the State of Connecticut to boycott ASH. CCA and CCC urged their respective members and other chiropractors licensed in the State of Connecticut to "take a stand and resign" from ASH. The communications conveyed the message, "united we stand, divided we fall."

18. During these meetings and through other communications, CCA and CCC chiropractors discussed with each other their dissatisfaction with ASH's price terms and utilization management requirements for chiropractic services. The chiropractors repeatedly incited each other to unite in their fight to defeat the ASH program through communications that included the following:

a. "We all need to unite on this issue."

b. "We must band together."

c. "Get [ASH] out of this state!"

CCA AND CCC CHIROPRACTORS COLLECTIVELY AGREE TO OPT OUT OF ASH'S CHIROPRACTIC NETWORK FOR ANTHEM

19. Anthem entered into an arrangement with ASH in early 2006 under which ASH agreed to provide a chiropractic provider network and administer chiropractic benefits for Anthem enrollees.

20. The arrangement required ASH to contract with a minimum of 80 percent of the chiropractors who were members of Anthem's existing chiropractic provider network to ensure adequate coverage of chiropractic services for Anthem enrollees in the State of Connecticut. ASH's existing chiropractic network included approximately 40 percent of the chiropractors in Anthem's chiropractic network. Therefore, ASH needed to contract with an additional 40 percent of the chiropractors in Anthem's network.

21. On July 28, 2006, ASH notified chiropractors that the arrangement with Anthem was effective November 1, 2006. ASH also provided applications and contracting materials to the chiropractors. The chiropractors who already were members of ASH's network had the opportunity to "opt out" of the ASH network for Anthem.

22. In response, CCA, CCC, and Mr. Hirtle organized monthly meetings starting in August, 2006, for all licensed chiropractors in the State of Connecticut to discuss their concerns regarding the ASH program and provide instructions on how to opt out of the ASH program.

23. CCA and CCC distributed a model opt-out letter to the chiropractors to notify ASH that the chiropractors elected not to participate in the ASH chiropractic network for Anthem. CCA and CCC also instructed the chiropractors to send copies of the signed opt-out letters to Mr. Hirtle. The chiropractors sent opt-out letters to ASH using the model CCA and CCC had provided to them.

24. Mr. Hirtle regularly circulated written updates to the chiropractors informing them of how many chiropractors had opted out of the ASH network. He also advised them on how many more chiropractors needed to opt out to ensure that ASH would not meet the minimum number of chiropractors required to have a sufficient network under the ASH/Anthem arrangement.

25. Mr. Hirtle also encouraged the chiropractors to refuse to participate in the ASH/Anthem program. Throughout the fall of 2006, he told them:

   a. "There need to be 60 more resignations to cripple the ASH provider list."

   b. "We need 50 more to destroy the panel."

   c. "A little more effort and we will be there."

   d. "The list is now 18 [chiropractors]. 5 Counties out 100%. A great victory for Chiropractic!"

   e. "It would be nice to get 100% out in Hartford and New Haven Counties tomorrow."

26. During this time, CCA and CCC conveyed the concerns of their members regarding the ASH fee schedule and utilization management requirements to ASH. In September 2006, CCA and CCC informed ASH that the chiropractors were "grateful that everyone at ASH [was] critically re-thinking things such as the fee schedule." Faced with numerous opt-outs and concerns about the program, ASH sent a revised offer to the chiropractors with an increase in the fee schedule on September 19, 2006.

27. Dissatisfied with ASH's revised offer, CCA, CCC, and Mr. Hirtle continued their efforts to persuade the chiropractors not to contract with ASH or, if they were currently members of ASH's existing network, to opt out of ASH's network for Anthem. In response, the chiropractors continued sending their opt-out letters to ASH to reject the revised offer.

28. As a consequence of the boycott, all but four chiropractors opted out of ASH's chiropractic network for Anthem, and the network had no chiropractors in seven out of the

eight counties in the State of Connecticut. The boycott succeeded in defeating the ASH network and forcing Anthem and ASH to cancel their arrangement as of December 1, 2006.

CCA AND CCC CHIROPRACTORS COLLECTIVELY TERMINATE THEIR PARTICIPATION FROM ASH'S PROGRAM FOR CIGNA ENROLLEES

29. ASH entered into an agreement with CIGNA in 2000 to provide a chiropractic provider network and administer chiropractic benefits for CIGNA enrollees in the State of Connecticut.

30. During the time CCA chiropractors and CCC chiropractors were opting out of the ASH chiropractic program for Anthem, they also collectively decided to terminate their existing relationship with the ASH chiropractic program for CIGNA.

31. Communications among the chiropractors included the warning that "[o]pting out of ASH/Anthem but staying with ASH/CIGNA sends a message of weakness and furthermore strengthens their position in our state. By not resigning completely we have to continue opting out of every new plan they try to pass.... Just Resign!!"

32. CCA and CCC echoed this rallying cry for action through their communications with the chiropractors. CCC told the chiropractors, "There is no option except for ASH to get out of Connecticut. No more negotiations. No more new contracts."

33. Following these communications, the chiropractors sent letters to ASH terminating their participation in the ASH program for CIGNA.

34. In November 2006, Mr. Hirtle announced that the chiropractors had "voted overwhelmingly" to terminate their participation in the ASH program for CIGNA.

35. The terminations forced CIGNA to develop its own chiropractic network to continue to provide adequate chiropractic coverage to its enrollees.

CCA AND CCC CHIROPRACTORS CONSPIRE TO BOYCOTT EMPIRE

36. ASH manages chiropractic benefits for Empire enrollees in the State of New York. Empire also has enrollees who reside in Connecticut, but obtain health coverage from their employers in New York. ASH attempted to contract with chiropractors in Connecticut to provide chiropractic services to Empire enrollees residing in Connecticut.

37. At a meeting in December 2006, CCA and CCC chiropractors discussed ASH's offer to provide services to Empire enrollees. CCA and CCC advised their members that if they did not want to participate in the ASH program for Empire, they should send a letter to ASH declining the offer and provide a copy of the letter to Mr. Hirtle. Following the meeting, many CCA and CCC members sent opt-out letters to Empire.

38. In January 2007, CCA informed all chiropractors in Connecticut that an insufficient number of chiropractors agreed to join ASH's chiropractic network for Empire enrollees residing in Connecticut. The collective conduct of the chiropractors forced ASH to abandon its efforts to contract with chiropractors in Connecticut.

RESPONDENTS' CONDUCT IS NOT LEGALLY JUSTIFIED

39. Respondents have not identified any reason for the agreement among CCA and CCC chiropractors to boycott ASH, and Mr. Hirtle's activities to encourage, facilitate, and help implement the boycott, other than to prevent ASH from managing chiropractic benefits on behalf of payors and their enrollees in Connecticut.

40. Neither CCA nor CCC has undertaken any programs or activities that create any integration among their members in the delivery of chiropractic services. Members do not

share any financial risk in providing chiropractic services, do not collaborate in a program to monitor and modify clinical practice patterns of their members to control costs and ensure quality, or otherwise integrate their delivery of care to patients.

41. Respondents' conduct described above has not been, and is not, reasonably related to any efficiency-enhancing integration among the chiropractor members of CCA and CCC, or between CCA and CCC and their respective members.

ANTICOMPETITIVE EFFECTS

42. Respondents' actions described in paragraphs 15 through 41 of this Complaint have had the effect of restraining trade unreasonably and hindering competition in the provision of chiropractic services in areas throughout the State of Connecticut in the following ways, among others:

   a. unreasonably restraining price and other forms of competition among chiropractors;

   b. increasing costs for chiropractic care;

   c. depriving payors and individual consumers access to chiropractic services cost-savings programs; and

   d. depriving payors and individual consumers of the benefits of competition among chiropractors.

43. The combination, conspiracy, acts, and practices described above constitute unfair methods of competition in violation of Section 5 of the Federal Trade Commission Act, as amended, 15 U.S.C. §45. Such combination, conspiracy, acts, and practices, or the effects thereof, are continuing and will continue or recur in the absence of the relief herein requested.

WHEREFORE, THE PREMISES CONSIDERED, the Federal Trade Commission on this fourteenth day of April, 2008, issues its Complaint against Respondents Connecticut Chiropractic Association, Connecticut Chiropractic Council, and Robert L. Hirtle, Esq.

Chapter Eight

Innovations in CAM Regulation

The growing use and acceptance of Complementary and Alternative Medicine brings legislators, health professionals and your textbook authors back to the issue: the extent to which CAM providers should be regulated in the United States, or whether they should be regulated at all. Traditionally, there are three broad categories of professional regulation: mandatory licensure, title licensure (sometimes referred to as "certification") and registration. With mandatory licensure, only those who are licensed may engage in the protected activity. Violators potentially face both civil and criminal penalties. Title licensure allows the licensee to use a professional title to describe their qualifications, while their unlicensed counterparts cannot. Registration requires providers to register their professional information and qualifications with the state.

Licensure is the most sought after, and fought over, of the three types of statuses. Because of the history of the medical profession in the United States of America, (which was described in Chapter Two) in the past, decisions regarding the regulation of CAM providers were often left to CAM's historical nemesis: medical doctors. Times are changing.

Throughout their history, CAM professions took—or were forced to take—two very different tracks of government regulation. The first group generally fell into the "if you can't beat them, join them" category. These practitioners sought, and were awarded, separate licensure or a lesser credential such as registration. However, the licenses limited the professionals' scopes of practice. Chiropractors are an early example of this group of practitioners who sought, and were awarded, licensure. Doulas, in certain states such as Minnesota, are another group that sought licensure. Now, in Minnesota, a doula may be included on the state licensure list if he or she is nationally certified and successfully completes a background check.

A second track followed the opposite approach. These practitioners continued to practice outside explicit government regulations. Various reasons may help explain the desire to stay free of government interference. Some practitioners believed that their therapies were not "the practice of medicine." Other practitioners expressed an abhorrence of government interference. Still others were unable to gain consensus upon the educational or experience requirements necessary to gain entry to the professions. In many states, lay midwives were an example of practitioners who practice outside the regulatory process. Most practiced in the shadows. But others openly advertised, almost daring State Medical Boards and district attorneys to seek injunctions based upon the unlicensed practice of medicine.

Over the past 20 years, as the country witnessed a surge in CAM usage, we also saw a surge in activities on both these fronts. On one hand, the first group grew to include additional CAM professions who sought licensure. On the other hand, the second group pursued legislation to protect their deregulatory approach. They combined with patients to advocate for passage of "Health Freedom Acts" to restrain heath licensing boards' actions against CAM providers.

In this Chapter we examine several state initiatives to alter the traditional regulatory structure of CAM providers. First, we consider different examples of "medical freedom" statutes which have been adopted by over 30 states in one form or another. Second, we review the decision by two states, Rhode Island and Minnesota, to create offices to govern unlicensed CAM practitioners. We end by returning to the question of how—if at all—CAM providers should be regulated.

I. Medical Freedom Acts

In response to cases like *Guess* and *Rogers*, addressed in Chapter Two, industry-wide calls for greater "medical freedom" resulted in legislative action in the late 1980s and early 1990s. Of course, what constitutes a "health freedom" law is open to interpretation. Some view the Minnesota and Rhode Island laws which spell out conduct that would subject an unlicensed CAM practitioner to discipline as "Medical Freedom" laws. Many consider laws that protect licensed physicians practicing CAM as "Medical Freedom" legislation, while others view this physician-centered focus as an anathema. The variation in opinions is reflected by the discrepancy in laws.

While consumer groups and some CAM providers sought broad new laws insulating *all* CAM providers from prosecution by state licensing boards, the resulting laws were much narrower. Most sought to curb state medical boards from imposing discipline solely on the basis of offering a CAM modality. Consider the following excerpts from laws loosely known as "medical freedom" or "health freedom" statutes:

North Carolina
N.C. Gen. Stat. Ann. § 90-14(a)(6).

> [...] The Board [of Medical Practice] shall not revoke the license of or deny a license to a person solely because of that person's practice of a therapy that is experimental, nontraditional, or that departs from acceptable and prevailing medical practices unless, by competent evidence, the Board can establish that the treatment has a safety risk greater than the prevailing treatment or that the treatment is generally not effective.

Alaska
Alaska Stat. § 08.64.326(a)(8)(A).

> The [Board of Medical Practice] may impose a sanction if the board finds after a hearing that a licensee ... has demonstrated
>
> A. professional incompetence, gross negligence, or repeated negligent conduct; the board may not base a finding of professional incompetence solely on the basis that a licensee's practice is unconventional or experimental in the absence of demonstrable physical harm to a patient.

Oklahoma
59 Okl. Stat. Ann. § 492(F)

> Nothing in the Oklahoma Allopathic Medical and Surgical Licensure and Supervision Act shall prohibit services rendered by any person not licensed by the Board and practicing any nonallopathic healing practice.

59 Okl. Stat. Ann. §509.1(D)(2)

> The [Board of Medical Licensure and Supervision] shall not revoke the license of a person otherwise qualified to practice allopathic medicine within the meaning of the [medical practice act] solely because the person's practice or a therapy is experimental or nontraditional.

Georgia
Ga. Code Ann. §43-34-38

> (b) Notwithstanding any other provision of law, and except as provided in subsection (c) of this Code section, an individual shall have the right to be treated for any illness or disease which is potentially life threatening or chronically disabling by a person licensed to practice medicine under this article with any experimental or nonconventional medical treatment that such individual desires ... if such person licensed to practice medicine under this article has personally examined such individual and agrees to treat such individual.
>
> (c) A person licensed to practice medicine under this article may provide any medical treatment to an individual described in subsection (b) of this Code section if:
>
> (1) There is no reasonable basis to conclude that the medical treatment itself, when administered as directed, poses an unreasonable and significant risk of danger to such individual; and
>
> (2) The person licensed to practice medicine under this article has provided the patient [with a written disclosure and oral explanation of the material risks and experimental nature and obtained patient's written acknowledgement thereof].

Notes and Questions

1. If one of these statutes had been in effect, would the outcomes have been any different for Doctors Guess and Atkins? What about Dr. Ames? Reread these cases from Chapter Two on pp. 42 and 47. Return to the problem on p. 79 involving Dr. Miller. Would your analysis change if any of these three "Medical Freedom" laws were in place?

2. New York's Medical Freedom Act, which took effect in 1994, struck a different approach. While the ultimate goals of its "Medical Freedom" Act (to protect the rights of patients to choose CAM and the ability of physicians to offer it) were similar to other states, New York sought to achieve them by including CAM physicians on the medical board which oversees the physician discipline process. The law provides that:

> "The board of professional medical conduct shall consist of not fewer than eighteen physicians licensed in the state for at least five years, two of whom shall be doctors of osteopathy, not fewer than two of whom shall be physicians who dedicate a significant portion of their practice to the use of non-conventional medical treatments..."

N.Y. Pub. Health Law §230(1).

CAM advocates (and a number of licensed physicians whose CAM practices were challenged in disciplinary proceedings) relied on statements of the sponsors of New York's medical freedom act to interpret this mandate to require that a board committee hearing the case of a CAM provider include a non-conventional physician. However, New York courts have rejected this reading of the law. Consider the following case.

Gonzalez v. New York State Dept. of Health
New York Supreme Court Appellate Division
232 A.D.2d 886 (1996)

Spain, Justice.

Proceeding pursuant to CPLR article 78 (initiated in this court pursuant to Public Health Law § 230-c [5]) to review a determination of respondent Administrative Review Board for Professional Medical Conduct which, *inter alia*, placed petitioner on probation and ordered him to participate in the State-sponsored Physician Prescribed Education Program.

In August 1993, petitioner, a physician who specializes in the area of nutritional therapy and who typically treats patients with advanced and incurable cancer, was charged by the Office of Professional Medical Conduct (hereinafter OPMC) with 15 specifications of misconduct including, *inter alia*, gross negligence, gross incompetence, negligence on more than one occasion, incompetence on more than one occasion and failing to maintain adequate records. The charges stemmed from petitioner's treatment of six incurable cancer patients (hereinafter patients A through F) who had either (1) exhausted conventional treatment options, or (2) rejected the only conventional treatment options remaining.

Thereafter, a Hearing Committee consisting of three members of respondent State Board for Professional Medical Conduct (hereinafter the Board) found that petitioner was negligent and incompetent on more than one occasion by reason of failing to correctly interpret the signs and symptoms of disease progression in all six patients and by reason of his failure to (1) perform appropriate assessments with respect to the different stages of the disease in patients A and B, (2) perform adequate neurological evaluations for patients B and C, (3) perform an adequate physical examination for patient D, (4) obtain adequate laboratory or radiological evaluations for patients B, C, D and F, (5) perform sufficient follow-up monitoring for patient E, and (6) perform sufficiently frequent follow-up evaluations for patient A. Petitioner was also found to have failed to maintain accurate records with regard to patients A, D and F.

The Hearing Committee ordered the suspension of petitioner's license to practice medicine for three years, but stayed the suspension subject to petitioner's compliance with certain probationary conditions, including (1) supervision by OPMC, (2) completion of a certified retraining program, and (3) completion of 200 hours of community service in a hospice program. In addition, petitioner was ordered to pay a $15,000 fine. Both OPMC and petitioner sought review by respondent Administrative Review Board for Professional Medical Conduct (hereinafter the ARB), which sustained the Hearing Committee's findings regarding the charges. The ARB, while rejecting OPMC's request for revocation of petitioner's license as too harsh, sustained the Hearing Committee's order of community service and retraining in oncology, but modified the terms of the retraining requirement such that petitioner was directed to undergo an evaluation and submit to retraining in a Physician Prescribed Education Program; additionally, it overruled the imposition of the $15,000 fine. The ARB also denied petitioner's request for a new hearing pursuant to the Alternative Medical Practice Act. Petitioner commenced this CPLR article 78 proceeding seeking, *inter alia*, annulment of the ARB's determination or, in the alternative, remittal for a new hearing.

Initially, we reject petitioner's assertion that the Alternative Medical Practice Act mandates that he is entitled to a new hearing before a Hearing Committee which consists of at least one nonconventional physician. The Alternative Medical Practice Act * * * requires that at least two of the physicians on the Board be "physicians who dedicate a significant portion of their practice to the use of non-conventional medical treatments" * * * [T]he legislation does not guarantee petitioner, as a nonconventional physician, that a nonconventional physician will be on the Hearing Committee which determines his case. Rather, Public Health Law §230(1), as amended, simply requires that the Board, consisting of at least 18 physicians and seven lay members, contain at least two nonconventional physicians among its many members.

Petitioner further asserts that the Board's determination should be annulled because the charges reflect a bias against alternative medicine and because his professional conduct was assessed according to the standards to which conventional practitioners are held, which are inconsistent or irrelevant to his therapy, especially in light of the fact that his patients fully consented to such nonconventional therapy. In our view petitioner's assertions are without merit. Both the Hearing Committee and the Board recognized that alternative medicine involves a different treatment regime, but held him to the same standard of care to which all physicians in New York are held. Without questioning the merits of petitioner's therapeutic protocol, the Board noted that:

> * * * physicians must still possess the same basic scientific knowledge of the nature of disease and the disease process. That knowledge is a standard to which all physicians are held. That standard and other basic standards, in areas such as record keeping and informed patient consent, do not vary based on the treatment regimes. In the treatment of all the patients in this case, [petitioner] demonstrated that he lacked the basic understanding of the disease from which all the patients were suffering.

Notably, "it is well settled that a patient's consent to or even insistence upon a certain treatment does not relieve a physician from the obligation of treating the patient with the usual standard of care." [Citations omitted.] Furthermore, petitioner has failed to present any persuasive evidence to support his assertion of bias [citation omitted].

* * *

Notes and Questions

1. Few cases have resulted from passage of "Medical Freedom Acts," although whether that is good news for their proponents is a matter of debate. In "Medical Freedom Legislation: Illusory Progress?" Michael Cohen writes the following:

> Legal definitions can be thorny, and the regulatory language of the various medical freedom acts does not necessarily reflect a complete evolution from prosecution to protection. It may be difficult to recommend satisfactory regulatory solutions to this problem at present, given that the language of regulation still reflects the conceptual separation of health care so prevalent in the medical literature — that of conventional versus "other than." (e.g., alternative).

Michael H. Cohen, *Medical Freedom Legislation: Illusory Progress?*, 12 ALTERNATIVE COMPLEMENTARY THERAPIES, 97–101 (Apr. 2006).

Despite these misgivings, as Michael Ruggio and Lauren DeSantis point out, "passage of a [Medical Freedom Act] can send a clear signal to state courts that a distinct standard of care is required for determining liability for physicians practicing non-conventional medicine." Michael Ruggio & Lauren DeSantis, *Then, Complementary and Alternative Medicine: Longstanding Legal Obstacles to Cutting Edge Treatment*, 2 J. HEALTH & LIFE SCI. L. 137, 159 (July 2009).

2. One result of the proliferation of efforts to pass "Medical Freedom" laws was the reaction of the Federation of State Medical Boards (FSMB). In 2002, the FSMB adopted *Model Guidelines for the Use of Complementary and Alternative Therapies in Medical Practice*. Against the back drop of "Medical Freedom" acts and public outcry over investigations and discipline of CAM providers, the FSMB sought to provide guidance. In the FSMB's view, the guidelines created a balance between the twin goals of "medical practices being evidence based while remaining compassionate and respectful of the dignity and autonomy of the patients...." Federation of State Medical Boards, Model Guidelines for the Use of Complementary and Alternative Therapies in Medical Practice (Approved by the House of Delegates of the Federation of State Medical Boards of the United States, Inc., as policy Apr. 2002). The proposed guidelines went beyond the stance of many boards at the time to recognize "that a licensed physician shall not be found guilty of unprofessional conduct ... solely on the basis of utilizing CAM." However, the harm evaluation guidelines proposed as a substitute for this presumption ask whether the CAM treatment at issue is effective and safe as measured by "having adequate scientific evidence of efficacy and/or safety or greater safety than other established treatment models for the same condition."

3. After a review of how New York courts interpreted that state's Medical Freedom Act, Joseph A. Barrette opined that the Act was not fulfilling its goal of protecting nonconventional physicians from being charged with and sanctioned for the practice of effective nonconventional medicine. Joseph A. Barrette, *The Alternative Medical Practice Act: Does It Adequately Protect the Right of Physicians to Use Complementary and Alternative Medicine?*, 77 ST. JOHN'S L. REV. 75, 112–13 (2003). Barrette wrote that true protection requires proof either "that the unconventional therapy is ineffective, that it poses a greater risk of patient injury than conventional medicine, or that it in fact caused injury rather than a mere designation of being unconventional in order for charges [of professional discipline] ... to be affirmed by the courts." Barrette proposed the following legislative "fix" which would (among other requirements) task the State Medical Board to 1) consult medical experts dedicated to the advancement of non-conventional medical treatment when a complaint against a CAM physician involves issues of clinical practice, and 2) demonstrate a prima facie case that the nonconventional medical treatment is ineffective before undertaking a formal investigation into the CAM provider. Barrette further proposed that CAM physicians under investigation be permitted to submit evidence from CAM journals to show the effectiveness and acceptance of unconventional therapies.

Does this legislative proposal adequately address any concerns raised by *Gonzalez v. New York State Depts. of Health*? How does it compare to the FSMB model guidelines addressed in the note above? For a description of one state's recent experience with medical freedom proposals, *see* Brenda Williams, *The CAM Controversy: Should Tennessee Embrace Complementary and Alternative Medicine?*, 98 TENN. MED. 165 (2005).

II. Striving for a Middle Ground on Regulation: Creation of Offices to Govern Unlicensed CAM Practitioners

The creation of the Office of Unlicensed Complementary Alternative Health Care Practice in Minnesota came about because of the culmination of a series of events in the mid to late 1990s.

- Media coverage of cases brought by health licensing boards against alternative practitioners.

- The push for licensure by CAM providers such as naturopaths, midwives and massage therapists.

- The licensure of Acupuncturists, effective in 1997.

- Creation of a Center for Spirituality in Healing by the University of Minnesota Academic Health Center in 1997.

- The 1997 directive from the legislature to the Department of Health to conduct a study on Complementary Medicine in Minnesota. The study was to include recommendations on possible regulation of CAM providers.

- Legislative interest in reforming occupational licensure driven by a 1998 taskforce on Health Care Workforce Regulation commissioned by the Pew Foundation.

In short, in the late 1990s Minnesota found itself in a place most other states could recognize. There were increased licensure requests from CAM providers, driven in part from fear of "unlicensed practice of medicine" civil lawsuits against them. There was a mounting recognition of the need to reform occupational licensure. Finally, there was a growing interest by citizens of being able to access and (hopefully) get insurance coverage for CAM treatments.

Against this backdrop, the Minnesota Department of Health issued its report to the Legislature on Complementary Medicine. The report made recommendations on general principles of regulation of Complementary Medicine providers. The report recognized "a need for legislation to allow licensed and unlicensed providers of Complementary Medicine to practice without fear of criminal or administrative prosecution from existing regulatory authority solely based on provision of alternative and complementary medicine." It raised the possibility of "a newly created unlicensed Complementary and Alternative Medicine Provider Act."

A year following the Complementary Medicine Report to the Legislature in 1998, a bill was introduced to create an Office of the Unlicensed Complementary and Alternative Health Care Practice. Under the new law, an office was created within the Department of Health. This office was charged with investigating complaints against CAM practitioners, creating and requiring a CAM Health Care Client Bill of Rights, establishing a set of "prohibited acts" which would be grounds for disciplinary action, and disciplining practitioners in some cases. The Act was particularly significant in its definition of CAM, its list of "prohibited conduct," and the bill of rights that, in part, sets a floor of what constitutes informed consent for CAM patients.

A. Defining CAM

As addressed in the Chapter One, most definitions of CAM are negative. CAM is not conventional. It is not Western medicine. It is a term with a fluid definition that acts as a catch-all. Review the Minnesota definition, which was subsequently adopted by Rhode Island, and compare it to the definition used by the National Center for Complementary and Alternative Medicine (NCCAM) set out on p. 7 of the text.

MINN. STAT. ANN. § 146A.01

Subd. 4. Complementary and alternative health care practices. (a) "Complementary and alternative health care practices" means the broad domain of complementary and alternative healing methods and treatments, including but not limited to: (1) acupressure; (2) anthroposophy; (3) aroma therapy; (4) ayurveda; (5) cranial sacral therapy; (6) culturally traditional healing practices; (7) detoxification practices and therapies; (8) energetic healing; (9) polarity therapy; (10) folk practices; (11) healing practices utilizing food, food supplements, nutrients, and the physical forces of heat, cold, water, touch, and light; (12) Gerson therapy and colostrum therapy; (13) healing touch; (14) herbology or herbalism; (15) homeopathy; (16) nondiagnostic iridology; (17) body work, massage, and massage therapy; (18) meditation; (19) mind-body healing practices; (20) naturopathy; (21) noninvasive instrumentalities; and (22) traditional Oriental practices, such as Qi Gong energy healing.

The statute further excludes certain health care practices from its definition of CAM, providing some delineation of when the practice of CAM crosses over into the practice of medicine, chiropractic and dentistry. The statute states that CAM practices *do not* include surgery, x-ray, radiation, administering or dispensing legend drugs and controlled substances, practices that invade the body by puncture of the skin, setting fractures, the use of medical devices, any practice included in the practice of dentistry, or the manipulation or adjustment of joints or the spine. Interestingly, the statute also states that marketing and distributing dietary supplements, educating customers about these products or explaining these products is not the practice of Complementary and Alternative Medicine as defined by the act.

B. Establishing Minimal Standards of Conduct

While the act does not set competency standards, by adopting a list of prohibited conduct it defines minimal standards of ethical and professional conduct. These include:

- Conviction of a crime reasonably related to engaging in CAM practices
- Engaging in sexual contact with a client
- False advertising
- Conduct likely to defraud or harm the public
- Adjudication as mentally incompetent
- Habitual overindulgence in intoxicating liquors
- Improper personal use of controlled substances
- Revealing a communication from a CAM client

- Engaging in abusive billing practices
- Failure to provide a client with his or her health care records
- Failure to provide a client with a copy of the CAM Patient Bill of Rights.

MINN. STAT. ANN. § 146A.08, subd. 1.

The list hedges into areas of competency when it proceeds to list "inability to engage in Complementary and Alternative Health Care Practices with reasonable safety" and "failure to provide a Complementary and Alternative Health Care client with a recommendation that the client see a health care provider who is licensed or registered … if there is a reasonably likelihood that the client needs to be seen by a licensed or registered health care provider" as prohibited conduct. The statute also provides that, even though a CAM practice may be "a less customary approach to health care," it shall not constitute the basis of disciplinary action per se.

C. Creating a Bill of Rights

The CAM Health Care Client Bill of Rights is to be posted in each provider's office as well as given to each heath care client. In addition, each client must sign a written statement stating that he or she has received the Bill of Rights. The Bill of Rights describes the training, experience and degrees of the practitioners, followed by the following statement: "The State of Minnesota has not adopted any educational and training standards for unlicensed Complementary Alternative Health Care Practitioners. This statement of credentials is for information purposes only." A sample Bill of Rights follows:

Complementary and Alternative Health Care Client Bill of Rights

R. Mathias, N.D. and J. Rudner, N.D.
Southeastern Health and Healing Medicine, Mayville Natural Care Center
(This statement is required by Section 146 A.11 of the Minnesota Statutes.)

Name and address of Licensed CAM Practitioner: R. Mathias, N.D. and J. Rudner; The Midway Holistic Healing Center, 940 Ashland Avenue, St. Paul, MN 55104; (651) 555-9348

Qualifications of Practitioner: B.S. Biology, the University of Minnesota (Minneapolis, MN) (1999); Massage Therapist Certificate (St. Paul, MN) (2001); Doctor of Naturopathic Medicine, University of Bridgeport (Bridgeport, CT) (2004).

THE STATE OF MINNESOTA HAS NOT ADOPTED ANY EDUCATIONAL AND TRAINING STANDARDS FOR UNLICENSED COMPLEMENTARY AND ALTERNATIVE HEALTH CARE PRACTITIONERS. THIS STATEMENT OF CREDENTIALS IS FOR INFORMATION PURPOSES ONLY.

Under Minnesota law, an unlicensed complementary and alternative health care practitioner may not provide a medical diagnosis or recommend discontinuance of medically prescribed treatments. If a client desires a diagnosis from a licensed physician, chiropractor, or acupuncture practitioner, or services from a physician, chiropractor, nurse, osteopath, physical therapist, dietitian, nutritionist, acupuncture practitioner, athletic trainer, or any other type of health care provider, the client may seek such services at any time.

Supervisor of practitioner: A. Olson, N.D., Owner of Southeastern Health and Healing Medicine, 1237 Seahawk Drive, St. Paul, MN (651) 555-9836.

Complaints. As a complementary and alternative health care client ("Client"), you have the right to file a complaint with the supervisor listed above or with the Minnesota Department of Health. Any such complaint should be directed to the attention of the supervisor, in writing, and should include supporting details sufficient to permit an investigation into the complaint to be commenced.

The Office of Unlicensed Complementary and Alternative Health Care Practice: Office of Unlicensed Complementary and Alternative Health Care Practice located in Minnesota Department of Health: P.O. Box 64882 St. Paul, MN, 55164-0882; 651-201-3728.

Fees: $225 for 110 minutes of consultation; $170 for 80 minutes of consultation; $120 for 50 minutes of consultation; and $90 for 40 minutes of consultation. For follow-up visits with existing patients: $130 for 80 minutes of consultation; $105 for 50 minutes of consultation; $90 for 40 minutes of consultation; and $70 for 25 minutes of consultation and $45 for 10 minutes of consultation; telephone consults: $15 per 5 minutes. No insurance companies have agreed to reimburse the Practitioner. The Practitioner does not contract with any health maintenance organization to provide service. The Practitioner does not accept Medicare, medical assistance or general assistance medical care. The Practitioner is not willing to accept partial payment, or to waive payment.

Notice of Change of Services and Charges: Clients have the right to reasonable notice of changes to the prices, services, or policies.

Theory and Approach of Treatment: In general, the Practitioner's choice of modalities depends on your needs as a client. The Practitioner typically uses one or more of the following combinations: ayurveda; cranial sacral therapy; culturally traditional healing practices; detoxification practices and therapies; energetic healing; folk practices; healing practices utilizing food, food supplements, nutrients, and the physical forces of heat, cold, water, touch, and light; herbology or herbalism; homeopathy; non-diagnostic iridology; body work, massage and massage therapy; meditation; mind-body healing practices; naturopathy; noninvasive instrumentalities; and traditional Oriental practices, such as Qi Gong energy healing.

Right to Current Information: As a Client, you have the right to complete and current information concerning the Practitioner's assessment and recommended service that is to be provided, including the expected duration of the services to be provided.

Personal Treatment and Interaction: As a Client, you may expect courteous treatment and to be free from verbal, physical, or sexual abuse by the Practitioner.

Right to Confidentiality: Client records and transactions with the Practitioner are confidential, unless release of these records is authorized in writing by you as the Client, or otherwise provided by law.

Right Access Records: As a Client, you have the right to be allowed access to records and written information from records in accordance with sections 144.291 to 144.298 of the Minnesota Statutes.

Other Available Treatment: Other services may be available in the community. Information concerning such services may be found in the Natural Care Center brochure.

Right to choose. As a Client, you have the right to choose freely among available practitioners and to change practitioners after services have begun, within the limits of health insurance, medical assistance, or other health programs.

Coordinated Records Transfer. As a Client, you have the right to coordinated transfer when there will be a change in the provider of services.

Right to Refuse Service. As a Client, you have the right to refuse service or treatment, unless otherwise provided by law.

Right of Nonretribution: You have the right to assert your rights without retaliation.

Patient Acknowledgement: I hereby acknowledge that I have received, read, and signed this copy of the Complementary and Alternative Health Care Bill of Rights in relation to the CAM services performed here.

PPa

Signature _____   Print Name _____   Date _____

Notes and Questions

1. Rhode Island adopted an Unlicensed Health Care Practices Act modeled in large part on the Minnesota law discussed above. In order to qualify as an unlicensed health care practitioner under either system, a provider must not have had a license revoked by a licensing board. Rhode Island's statute states that "in order to qualify as an unlicensed health care practitioner, an individual must satisfy the following criteria ... [including that he or she] has not had a license issued by health-related licensing board or the director of health revoked or suspended without reinstatement unless the right to engage in unlicensed health care practices has been established by order of the director of health." R.I. Gen. Laws §23-74-1(a)(4). This provision attempts to guard against the possibility of a formerly licensed practitioner, already the subject of disciplinary action, deciding to practice as an unlicensed CAM practitioner. For one state's experience with a similar situation, *see* John Dickerson, *Arizona's Homeopathic Board is the Second Chance for Doctors Who May Not Deserve One,* Phoenix New Times (Apr. 10, 2008) (describing how doctors who had lost their licenses in other states became homeopathic physicians licensed by the state of Arizona). The Rhode Island Department of Health addressed a similar situation shortly after adopting its Unlicensed Health Care Practices Act. Dr. Long A. Mai, an acupuncturist who engaged in the sale of herbs and Chinese herbology, sought refuge under the Act to continue the sale of herbal medicine after his acupuncture license was revoked when the Department found "that [Dr. Mai's] advertisement and drug therapy practices [were] designed to provide him with financial benefits to the physical, emotional, and financial detriments of his patients." *Mai v. Nolan*, No. 010166, 2005 WL 372047, at 2 (R.I. Super. Jan. 19, 2005). The Rhode Island Superior Court upheld both the decision to permanently revoke Dr. Mai's license to practice acupuncture and the Department's decision not to permit Dr. Mai to practice herbal medicine as an unlicensed practitioner.

2. One of the options available to the offices that receive complaints regarding unlicensed CAM practitioners is to alert law enforcement. In the case of John E. Curran, Rhode Island's Department of Health did just that. After an initial inquiry which forced the Department to suspend Curran's practice for falsely portraying himself as a physician and naturopath, Rhode Island's health department notified a Special Agent of the Food and Drug Administration. Together, they coordinated a joint investigation, which also included the United States Attorney's Office and the Internal Revenue Administration. A portion of the affidavit for a Search Warrant in the matter reads as follows:

The Scheme

A. Summary

12. The investigation has revealed that John Curran induces patients to purchase expensive treatment plans for alleged nutritional or therapeutic materials in order to cure them of alleged actual or imminent diseases that Curran claims to have diagnosed. Although he is not qualified to diagnose diseases, Curran advises his patients, among other things, that: (1) they have live parasites in their blood stream; (2) that they have a severely reduced number of blood cells; (3) that they have certain deficient "body functions;" (4) that they have worms in their blood; (5) that they have holes in their blood; and (6) that they have a life threatening disease. Curran provides the majority of his diagnoses by performing a "live blood analysis" or a "biomeridian test." As is further described below, neither test is designed to diagnose disease.

13. Upon providing a patient with the diagnoses, Curran promotes and sells the use of his treatment programs or alleged pharmacological materials, the cost of which ranges from approximately $200 to $10,000. Curran accepts cash, checks or credit cards, or, alternatively, promotes a credit service provided by GE Capital that will provide his patients with a line of credit to purchase his services. The line of credit is referred to as a "Credit Care Card." Examples of what he sells are products referred to as "E-water", and a super "green drink." Curran claims that E-water is therapeutic water, but the investigation has determined it is regular distilled water that Curran labels as "E-water." The "green drink" appears to be a compilation of ingredients with no therapeutic value.

In May of 2006, a federal jury found Curran guilty of fraud and money laundering. He was sentenced to two and a half years in federal prison as well as ordered to pay $1.4 million in restitution.

3. For additional information on Minnesota's CAM law *see* Alan Dumoff, *The Ins and Outs, Pros and Cons of Nonlicensed Practice: Report and Commentary on the Health Freedom Movement*, 12 ALTERNATIVE & COMPLEMENTARY THERAPIES 136 (June 2006); Tom McSteen, J.D. Maister, & Bernard Maister, *Physician Liability and Complementary Health Care: Minnesota's New Law that Sanctions the Practice of Complementary and Alternative Medicine has Implications for Physicians*, 84 MINN. MED. 43 (2001).

4. Minnesota's CAM laws specifically provide that marketing dietary supplements, educating customers about these products and explaining these products are not the practice of Complementary and Alternative Medicine. Why would the legislature have drawn this distinction? How would you advise a CAM provider who "educates" patients about dietary supplements in light of this provision?

5. While the failure to inform patients of the risks and benefits of CAM may subject practitioners to liability under negligence theories addressed in Chapter Four, California uses informed consent in the regulatory context as well. California does not take the additional steps of including this in a Bill of Rights and establishing an office to oversee unlicensed health care providers as done in Minnesota and Rhode Island. However, within its Business and Professions Code, California law states that its licensing boards "acknowledge the significant interests of physicians and patients alike in integrating preventative approaches and holistic-based alternatives into the practice of medicine." It directs each board to set specific standards for informed consent as well as standards for investigations involving the practice of alternative medicine. Cal. Bus. & Prof. Code § 2500-01.

III. Rethinking the Need for Regulation

The first thing we do, let's kill all the regulators.

Actually, stopping short of Shakespeare, Randall G. Holcombe advocates eliminating licensure and scope of practice restrictions. Without these restrictions, Holcombe argues, the market would develop quality measures and private regulatory agencies that would allow a wider variety of options and standards. For example, a deregulated environment would promote more than one standard. On the one hand, the system would allow patients who wanted higher quality to find it through boards that require higher qualifications. On the other hand, the system would allow those currently unlicensed to practice medicine (allowing lay midwives to deliver babies for example) and promote less expensive options by so doing.

In response to the argument that consumers are not knowledgeable enough to make informed, appropriate choices, Holcombe asserts that consumers need not be able to differentiate themselves. Rather, the market will create—and consumers rely upon—the knowledge of others, much as they look at Consumer Reports before buying a new washing machine. "An auto mechanic does not have to be a medical expert to use market information to find good health care, any more than a doctor has to be an automobile expert to find a good car," Holcombe writes. And if the consumer chooses a less-than-optimal treatment or provider, isn't that a permitted choice in a free society, much as we allow people to smoke, ride motorcycles and eat junk food? Consider the following excerpt:

> Deregulation not only provides incentives for patients to look for, and physicians to offer, better care, it permits all parties concerned the freedom to decide what is better care. For instance, in the debate over alternative medicine, such as herbal treatments, chiropractors, acupuncture, and so on, the question is not only whether alternative medicine is effective, but whether people should be allowed to use these alternatives even if their physical health may not improve or even suffer. Deregulation enables this freedom of choice. In a free country, people should be free to choose whatever health care options they want and for whatever purpose—for instance, to feel psychologically better—even if health care professionals believe that care is substandard. Because it is a certainty that eventually everyone's health will deteriorate and they will die, one must question whether the goal of the health care industry should be to only produce the best health possible.

Randall G. Holcombe, *Eliminating Scope of Practice and Licensing Laws to Improve Health Care*, 31 J.L. MED. & ETHICS 236, 242–43 (2003).

If traditional licensure was eliminated, what types of private sector quality organizations might fill the void? In his article, Holcombe suggests several possibilities including roles for organizations that sell information (such as Consumer Reports) and a larger role for insurance companies and the AMA. What business model would best address the market need? Who might be poorly served by this regulatory model?

Juxtaposed against Randall Holcombe's proposal to eliminate licensure and scope of practice laws is Peter Van Hemel's suggestion that NCCAM replace state licensing schemes with a uniform national system for CAM providers. Van Hemel writes as follows:

> The NCCAM, operating within the NIH, is institutionally competent to accept a role as a regulator. It is a centralized, federally funded research body, staffed with

experts and committed to the scientific investigation of CAM practices. The NCCAM occupies a middle ground where it currently dissatisfies both CAM advocates and CAM detractors—a desirable position for a regulator. With a clear congressional mandate and a stated intention to preempt state regulatory regimes, the NCCAM could assist the Secretary of HHS to draft universal licensure requirements and uniform legislation to describe scientifically acceptable and otherwise beneficial CAM practices. Under this mandate, the NCCAM could also identify safe practices outside of its regulation which do not conform to scientific testing, freeing those CAM practitioners from the threat of prosecution for practicing medicine without a license.

Peter J. Van Hemel, *A Way Out of the Maze: Federal Agency Preemption of State Licensing and Regulation of Complementary and Alternative Medicine Practitioners*, 27 Am. J.L. & Med. 329, 344 (2001).

What are the disadvantages of Van Hemel's idea of using federal standards instead of individual standards for each of the 50 states? Is something lost by removing health regulation from those closest to the area to an agency in Washington, D.C.? Would there be a concern that the NCCAM is too "pro-CAM" to effectively protect the public health?

Index

Bold page numbers indicate cases covered at length in the text and pages with boxes, tables or figures.

A

abusive billing practices, 274
acquisitions, 225
active pharmaceutical ingredient (API), 211
acts. *See* statutes
acupuncture, 3, 16–17
    AG scope of practice opinions, 88
    definition, 6
    Iowa, 112, 113
    licensure, 17, 42, **56 T2.1**, 273
additives (food), 200
adverse event reporting, 211
advertising (false/misleading), 41, 274
Aetna Health Plans of New York, Inc., Solla v., **242–47**
AIDS, 22
Alabama
    massage therapy, AG scope of practice opinions, 89
    midwifery legislation, 66–67, 74
Alaska Medical Freedom Act, 268
Alaska Stat. §08.64.326(a)(8)(A), 268
allopathy, 8
alternative medicine/therapies. *See also* individual therapies
    adult users, in 2002, **4 Fig. 1.1**
    definitions, 6, 9
    licensed provider users, 40–49
    risks, 21–24
    survey, physician users, 3–4
AMA. *See* American Medical Association (AMA)
American Chiropractic Association v. Trigon Healthcare, Inc., **258–60**
American Indian medicine, 18. *See also* traditional medicine
American Medical Association (AMA), 33–35
    on chelation therapy, 192n2
    chiropractic care *vs.*, 230–41
    homeopathy *vs.*, 241
American Medical Association, Wilk v., **82–83, 230–41**
American School of Osteopathy, 10
Ameringer, Carl, 40
Ames v. Washington State Health Department Medical Quality Health Assurance Commission, 51
Andrews, Lori, 101
Andrews (Arthur), Board of Medical Quality Assurance v., **60–63**
Angell, Marcia, 21–24
antitrust, 31, 223–66
    CAM practitioners as defendants, 260–66
    defenses, 226
    denial/cancellation of malpractice insurance, 254–57
    denials of clinical privileges, 248–54
    enforcement of laws, 225–26
    federal and state authorities, 224–26
    legal loss, Solla v. Aetna Health Plans of New York, Inc., **242–47**
    legal victory, Wilk v. American Medical Association, **82–83, 230–41**
    overview, 223–24
    policy argument, 227–29
    reimbursement caps/disparities in rates, 257–60

anxiety, **6 Fig. 1.2**
Ariff, Kamil M., 19
Arizona (scope-of-practice statute), 114
aromatherapy, 13
arteriosclerosis, 46, 114
arthritis, **6 Fig. 1.2**
assumption of risk (defense), 152–55, 187–88, 189
Athens Regional Medical Center, Sweeney v., 229
Atkins, Robert, 50, 54
Atkins diet, **15 Box 1.3**
attorney generals (AGs), 86–90
    Nebraska, chiropractic scope of practice opinion, 87–88
    opinion, midwifery for compensation, 76–77
    scope of practice, generally, 86
    scope of practice opinions, 88–90

B

back pain, **6 Fig. 1.2**
Baker, Moore v., **190–92**
Barnes, Patricia M., 15
Barrette, Joseph A., 54, 272
battery, 159–60
Bedford, Charlotte Fugett, 77–79
Beng, Khoo S., 19
Beth Israel Hospital (yoga in), **8 Box 1.2**
billing practices (fraudulent), 41
biologically based practices. *See* chelation therapy; dietary supplements; herbal medicine; vitamins; whole diets
black currant oil (BCO), 206
Blevins, Sue A., 40
Board of Medical Quality Assurance v. Arthur Andrews, **60–63**
Bohjalian, Chris, 77, 78
botanicals. *See* herbal medicine
boycotts
    CAM practitioners as antitrust defendants, 261–66
    in healthcare context, 230–41
breach, 116–40
    condition not amenable to CAM care, 128–29
    failure to diagnose, 131–40
    failure to refer, 122–28
    foregoing conventional care, 116–22
    incorrect diagnosis, 131–40
    malpractice defenses, 146–55
    negligent performance of CAM procedure, 129–31
Brewbaker III, William S., 230
Burg, Rebecca, 101
Byrd, Randolph C., 16

C

C. Maynard Guest, M.D., as Executive Secretary of the New York State Board for Professional Conduct v. Robert C. Atkins, M.D., **47–49**
California
    definition, practice of medicine, 36
    exception for religious practices, 63
    informed consent, Patient Bill of Rights, 278
    osteopathy in, 11
California State Board of Medical Examiners, Crees v., **95–99**
Calvert, Robert Noah, 13
CAM. *See* complementary/alternative medicine (CAM)
cancer
    CAM use and, **7 Box 1.1**
    chiropractic care, failure to diagnose, 138–40
    FDA qualified health claims, 218
    malpractice, failure to disclose, 179–83, 184–89
    malpractice, foregoing conventional care, 117–21
    unprofessional conduct, use of ozone therapy, 47–49
Canterbury v. Spence, **160–72**
Carroll, Wilcox v., **131–36**
Case, West Virginia University Hospitals, Inc. v., 90
Caspi, Opher, 194
causation, 141–46, 173
certification. *See* regulation
certified massage therapist (CMT), 13
certified midwives (CMs), 18
certified nurse midwives (CNMs), 18
    regulation, in Iowa, 227–29
certified professional midwives (CPMs), 18

Chan, Mabel M., 19
Chao, Maria T., 19
Charell v. Gonzalez, **117–21, 154–55, 179–83**
Chase-Lubitz, Jeffrey F., 34
chelation therapy, **46 Box 2.2**
   Arizona, scope of practice statute, 114
   medical malpractice, causal link, 141–42
   physician failure to inform, availability of, 190–92
   unprofessional conduct by physician, 45–47, 54
Chen, Moon S., 19
Chidester, Jones v., **146–51**
childbirth. *See also* midwifery
   midwifery litigation *vs.* physician-controlled childbirth, 66–67
   obstetric forceps, 17
   right to choose, regulation of midwifery in Iowa, 227–29
China (acupuncture in), 16
chiropractic care, 3, 11–12
   AG scope of practice opinions, 88–89
   alternative to conventional categories, 7–8
   AMA *vs.*, 230–41
   CAM practitioners as antitrust defendants, 261–66
   failure to refer, malpractice, 122–26
   failure to x-ray, negligence, 127–28
   Foster v. Georgia Board of Chiropractic Examiners, 91–95
   HMOs *vs.*, intra-enterprise conspiracy, 242–47
   Iowa Code, 113
   legislative intent, 95–99
   licensure, 41, **56 T2.1**, 267
   Louisiana Revised Statute, 112
   malpractice, 103–11, 114–16, 128–29, 130–31, 142–44, 144–46
   Nebraska, scope of practice opinion, 87–88
   Nevada Revised Statute, 113
   physical therapists *vs.*, 101
   practitioner education, 12
   practitioners as antitrust defendants, 261–66
   reimbursement caps/disparities in rates, 257, 258–60
   scope of practice, physical exams, 101
   Wilk v. American Medical Association, **82–83, 230–41**
cholesterol, **6 Fig. 1.2**
Christian Scientists, 34, 63, 64
circumcision (ritual), 63
Clayton Act, 224–25
clinical privileges (denials of), 248–54
clinical trials, 202–3
Code of Ethics (AMA), 34
Cohen, Amy F., 75
Cohen, Michael H.
   breach allegations made by plaintiffs, 121
   on CAM malpractice statistics, 140
   on CAM standards of care, 112
   on chelation therapy, **46 Box 2.2**
   on chiropractic standards of care, 111
   holistic health care, 55
   on informed consent, 195
   on medical freedom acts, 271
   on regulating spiritual healers, 64–65
   spiritual healing, 16
Cohen, Peter J., 211–12
Colella, Ugo, 137
Colorado, 86
competition, 225
   anticompetition and group boycott activities, 230–41
   CAM practitioners as antitrust defendants, 261–66
   geographic markets, 248–54
complementary/alternative medicine (CAM), 3–31
   adult CAM use, in 2002, **4 Fig. 1.1**
   cancer treatment and, **7 Box 1.1**
   conventional medicine *vs.*, 19–25
   in cultural context, 18–19
   definitions, 6–9, 7, 274
   diseases and conditions treated by, **6 Fig. 1.2**
   four domains, **10 T1.1**
   history of, 24
   informed consent in the CAM context, 178–96
   legal considerations, 26–29
   licensing requirement for select CAM practitioners, **56 T2.1**
   overview of modalities, 9–18
   rationale for using, 5–6

regulation of, emerging approaches, 31, 267–80
safety concern for use of, 24
in U.S., 3–5
Complementary and Alternative Health Care Client Bill of Rights, 275–77
Complementary Medicine Report, 273
condition not amenable to CAM care, 128–29
Connecticut
    CAM practitioners as antitrust defendants, 261–66
    Conn. Board of Naturopathic Examiners, Filkoff N.D. vs., 54–55
    FTC complaint, antitrust defendant, 261–66
conspiracies (in trade), 224
    denial/cancellation of malpractice insurance, 254–57
    denials of clinical privileges, 248–54
    health care insurance, reimbursement rate caps, 258–60
    intra-enterprise conspiracy doctrine, 242–47
    Wilk v. American Medical Association, **82–83, 230–41**
consumer protection (malpractice v.), 142–44
conventional medicine, 7. *See also* health care; nursing; physicians
    AG opinion, midwifery for compensation, 76–77
    aiding and abetting unlicensed person in, 41
    history, practice of medicine, 33–35
    licensed *vs.* unlicensed acts, **37 Box 2.1**
    professional standards of conduct, 41–42
    state statutory definitions, 36–37
    unlicensed exceptions, 36–37
    unlicensed providers, 56–63
    by unlicensed providers (faith healers), 60–63
coronary artery disease (CAD), 192n2
    chelation therapy, **46 Box 2.2**
    mind-body interventions, 58
covenants not to sue, 189–90
Crees v. California State Board of Medical Examiners, **95–99**

Cryns (Yvonne), People of the State of Illinois Ex Rel. Leonard A. Sherman, Director of Professional Regulation v., 67–71
Culbertson v. Mernitz, **174–78**
Curley v. State of Florida, **58–60**
Curran, John E., 277–78

D

Dana-Faber Cancer Institute
    Zalcim Center for Integrated Therapies, **7 Box 1.1**
Danforth, Sibyl, 77–79
defenses
    antitrust, 226
    assumption of risk, 152–55, 187–88, 189
    malpractice, 146–55
Delaware, 74
Del Toro, Miguel H., 218
dentistry, 274
Dent v. West Virginia, 34–35
Department of Health and Human Services (DHHS), 198
Department of Justice (DOJ), 223–24, 225, 229
DeSantis, Lauren, 271–72
DHHS, 198
Dickerson, John, 277
Dietary Supplement Health and Education Act of 1994 (DSHEA), 14, 206–14
    definition, dietary supplement, 206–7
    labeling requirements, 212–14
    safety standards, 207–11
dietary supplements (regulation of), 197–221
    active pharmaceutical ingredient (API), 211
    adverse event reporting, 211
    arguments, 219–21
    banning ephedra, 207–11
    DSHEA, 14, 206–19
    by the FDA of drugs, 202–4
    by the FDA of food, 198–201
    food *vs.* drugs, 204–6
    labeling requirements, 212–14
    in Minnesota, 278
    most commonly used, **198**

overview, 197–98
qualified health claims, 214–17
recommendations, 219–21
safety standards, 207–11
statistics, 197
unreasonable risk standard, 208–10
dietary therapy, 14–15
digitalis, 22
dilution, 13
direct entry midwives, 18, 227–29
disclosure, scope of, 168–69, 172
Dole, Robert, 38
Dossey, Larry, 16
doulas, 18, 267
drug/alcohol use, 41
drugs (regulation of), 202–4, 211–12
DSHEA, 14, 206–19
Dumoff, Alan, 278

E

Eckerly, M.D., Ireland v., **141–42**
eclectics, 34
EDTA therapy. *See* chelation therapy
Ehmann, Salazar v., **127–28**
Eisenberg, David M., 3–4, 12, 24, 121
electric stimulation, 11
energy medicine, 3, 15, 57–58, 64–65. *See also* acupuncture; reiki; therapeutic touch
engaging in unprofessional conduct. *See* unprofessional conduct
ephedrine alkaloids (ephedra), 207–11
risk-benefit analysis, 208–11
epilepsy (Hmong traditional healing of), **20 Box 1.4**
Ernst, Edzard, 195, 196
evening primrose oil, 206
exclusive dealings, 224–25
expert testimony
on causation, 144–46
in disciplinary complaint by medical board, 54
informed consent and, 160–72, 173
by physician, chiropractic standards of care, 103–11
two schools of thought defense, 146–51
on use of biofeedback machine, 51

F

Fadiman, Anne, **20 Box 1.4**
failure to diagnose, 131–40
failure to disclose risks of foregoing conventional medical care, 179–90
failure to inform
availability of CAM care, 190–92
risks of CAM care, 195–96
failure to refer, 122–28
false advertising, 41, 274
Fawell, Elizabeth B., 218
FDA. *See* Food and Drug Administration (FDA)
FDAMA, 199
FDCA. *See* Food Drug, and Cosmetic Act (FDCA)
Federal Trade Commission (FTC), 229
complaint, 261–66
Federal Trade Commission (FTC) Act, 224–26
Federation of State Medical Boards (FSMB), 272
felony conviction, 41
Filkoff N.D. v. Conn. Board of Naturopathic Examiners, 54–55
First Amendment, 19, 57, 226
Flexner, Abraham, 35
Flexner Report, 35–36
folic acid, 14
Food and Drug Administration (FDA), 30. 197–211
active pharmaceutical ingredient (API), 211
adverse events reporting, 211
clinical trials, 202–3
DSHEA, 14, 206–10
enforcement void, 218
food labeling, 200–201
"generally recognized as safe" (GRAS), 200
Good Manufacturing Practices (GMP), 200
mission, 199
overview of, 197–99
qualified health claims, 214–18
reform proposals, 199
regulation of dietary supplements, 204–6, 219–221

regulation of drugs, 202–4
regulation of food, 198–201
"significant scientific agreement" standard, 213
structure-function and health claims, 201
Food and Drug Administration Modernization Act of 1997 (FDAMA), 199
Food Drug, and Cosmetic Act (FDCA), 198
banning ephedrine alkaloids, **208**
definitions, 200, 202
foods, 198–201
foregoing conventional care, 116–22
Fosarelli, Pat, 16
Foster v. Georgia Board of Chiropractic Examiners, **91–95**

G

Ga. Code Ann. §43-34-38, 269
Garrison, Hinthorn v., **130–31**
Gellhorn, Walter, 34
"generally recognized as safe" (GRAS), 200
Georgia
chiropractic care, AG scope of practice opinions, 89
informed consent statute, 190–93
Official Code of Georgia Annotated (O.C.G.A.), 192–93
Georgia Board of Chiropractic Examiners, Foster v., **91–95**
Georgia Medical Freedom Act, 269
Gerson therapy, **7 Box 1.1**
Gevitz, Norman, 11
Gibbons v. Ogden, 26
ginseng, 22
GMP, 200
Goldstein, Michael S., 5
Gonzalez, Charell v., **117–21**, **154–55**, **179–83**
Gonzalez v. New York State Dept. of Health, **270–71**
Good Manufacturing Practices (GMP), 200
Gram, Hans, 13
GRAS, 200
Greaney, Thomas L., 229
Greenberg, Lauren A., 64
Guess, George A., 50
Guess, M.D., In re (George A.), **42–45**

H

Habeeb, W.R., 40
Hafner-Eaton, Chris, 75
Hahnemann, Samuel, 8–9
Halderman, Scott, 12
Hammer, Peter J., 229, 230
harm (to patient or public), 41, 274
religious healing, unlicensed practice of medicine, 58–60
Hartocollis, Anemona, **8 Box 1.2**
Hawaii, 88
HCQIA, 226, 254
head/chest cold, **6 Fig. 1.2**
healing touch, 57, 58
health care. *See also* nursing; physicians
application of antitrust laws, 229–30
denials of clinical privileges, 248–54
deregulation of, 279–80
HCQIA, 226, 254
HMOs, 242–47
medical staff bylaws, 248
"personal stake exception," 247
restraint of care in, 230–41
Health Care Quality Improvement Act (HCQIA), 226, 254
health claims (labeling), 213
health insurance. *See* insurance
health maintenance organizations (HMOs), 242–47
Healy, Helen, 84–85
Hemel, Peter Van, 279–80
herbal medicine, 3, 14–15
informed consent, 194
regulation of, in other countries, 211
risks, 21–24
Herfert, Wengel v., **114–16**
Hermer, Laura D., 66, 75
Hibbert, Nurse Midwifery Associates v., **254–57**
Hill, Morgan v., **144–46**
Hillard, James W., 101
Hinthorn v. Garrison, **130–31**
Hintz, Kerkman v., **103–11**
Hirtle, Robert L. (FTC complaint against), 261–66
History of Massage, An Illustrated Survey from Around the World, 13
Hmong traditional healing, **20 Box 1.4**

Hobson, Susan M., 112
Holcombe, Randall G., 279
holism, 5, 84–85
home births, 65–66, 67, 75
    opening statement, midwife's defense lawyer, 78–79
homeopathy, 13–14, 50
    AG scope of practice opinions, 89
    AMA *vs.*, 241
    definition, 6
    education, 14
    licensure, 42, **56 T2.1**
    medical profession *vs.*, 34
    Samuel Hahnemann, founder, 8–9
    statistics of practice, 35–36
    unlicensed physicians practicing as homeopathic physicians, 277
hospitals. *See* health care
Howell, Laura, 19
Hrbek, Andrea, 16
Huffman, Grace Brooke, 195
hydrotherapy (incorrect diagnosis), 131–36

I

Illinois (midwifery legislation), 74
incorrect diagnosis, 131–40
IND, 202
informed consent, 30, 157–96
    attitudes towards, 194–95
    available causes of action, 159–60
    binding arbitration clauses, 189–90
    in California, 278
    causation and, 173
    covenants not to sue, 189–90
    disclosures, objective *vs.* subjective, 172
    disclosure standards, 160–72, 174–78
    doctrine, 157–60
    expert testimony and disclosure, 173
    failure to disclose, 178–90
    failure to inform of CAM care risks, 195–96
    failure to inform patient of availability of CAM care, 190–92
    failure to obtain, burden of proof, 173
    Iowa Civil Jury Instruction, 173
    maintaining documentation, 194
    obligation to obtain, 194
    Official Code of Georgia Annotated (O.C.G.A.), informed consent, 192–93
    patient age and, 172–73
    required forms, 194
    sufficiency of consent form, 189
In re George A. Guess, M.D., **42–45**
insomnia, **6 Fig. 1.2**
insurance
    chiropractic care, reimbursement caps/disparities in rates, 257, 258–60
    health, "personal state exception," 247
    malpractice, denial or cancellation of, 254–57
    McCarran-Ferguson Act, 226
integrative medicine, **25 Box 1.5**
In the Matter of the Connecticut Chiropractic Association, the Connecticut Chiropractic Council, and Robert L. Hirtle, Esq., **261–66**
Investigational New Drug Application (IND), 202
Iowa
    informed consent, institutional *vs.* individual obligation, 194
    regulation of midwifery in, 227–29
    standards of care, 113
Iowa Acupuncture Practice Act, 112
Iowa Civil Jury Instruction, 173
Iowa Code, 113, 226
Iowa Competition Law, 226
Ireland v. Eckerly, M.D., **141–42**
irregulars, 6
Iyioha, Ireh O., 195

J

Jacobson v. Massachusetts, 26–29
Johnson, Marjorie B., 101
joint pain, **6 Fig. 1.2**
Jonas, Wayne, 24
Jones, White v., **142–44**
Jones v. Chidester, **146–51**
Josefek, Kristen J., 51
Jost, Timothy, 41
Juckett, Gregory, 19
jury instructions, 137, 173

K

Kaiser, Jona N., 212, 219
Kansas (AG scope of practice opinions), 88–89
Kaptchuk, Ted J., 12
Karan, Donna, **8 Box 1.2**
Kassirer, Jerome P., 21–24
Kaufman, D.W., 198
Kelly, J.P., 198
Kerkman v. Hintz, **103–11**
Kim, Jeongseon, 19
Kneipp, Sebastian, 14
Kronenberg, Fredi, 19
Kung, Christine C., 112

L

labeling
  "misbranding," 200–201
  overview, regulation by the FDA, 197
  qualified health claim summary, vitamin B and vascular disease, 217–18
Landry, Boyd, 85
Laos (traditional *vs.* conventional medicine), **20 Box 1.4**
lay midwives, 18, 75
Leary, Thomas B., 229
Lee, Emerson, 55
legislation. *See also* statutes
  chiropractic/acupuncture care standard, Iowa, 113
  chiropractic care, judicial canons interpreting intent, 95–99
  chiropractic care, regulation, 93–95
  chiropractic care standard, Louisiana, 112
  chiropractic care standard, Nevada, 113
  controlling lay midwives, 66–67
  medical practice acts, exceptions for religious practices, 63
  naturopathic registration law, Minnesota, 85–86
  North Carolina (legislation post-*Guess*), 50
  scope of practice, disputes, 83–85
  scope of practice, interpretation, 90–91
  support of alternative medicine, 50
Lerner, Maura, 84–85
leukemia, 22
licensed massage practitioner (LMP), 13
licensed massage therapist (LMT), 13
licensure, 30, 33–80
  chiropractic care, scope of practice, 91–95
  complaint and investigation process, 51–53
  deregulation of health care, 279–80
  distinguishing between providers, 37–39
  due process, 53, 55
  enforcement of unlicensed practice, 277–78
  medical school reform, 35–36
  physicians' use of CAM, 40–49
  practice of medicine, 33–37
  revocation of license, CAM providers, 54–55
  revocation/suspension of license, 52–53
  unlicensed providers and practice of medicine, 56–63
Ling, Hendrik, 13
Litoff, Judy Barrett, 18
Locke, Edwin A., 40
Louisiana, 89, 112
Lunstroth, John, 36
Lust, Benedict, 14

M

macrobiotic diet, **15 Box 1.3**
Madison, Kristin, 229
Mai, Long A., 277
Maister, Bernard, 278
Maister, J.D., 278
Mallory, Jill, **25 Box 1.5**
malpractice, 30, 103–55
  assumption of the risk, 152–55
  causal link to patient injuries, 141–44
  common law, 103–12
  condition not amenable to CAM care, 128–29
  consumer protection *vs.*, 142–44
  defenses, 146–151, 152–55
  expert testimony on causation, 144–46
  failure to diagnose, 131–40
  failure to refer, 122–28
  foregoing conventional care, 116–22
  incorrect diagnosis, 131–40

insurance, denial or cancellation of, 254–57
negligent performance of CAM procedure, 129–31
scope of practice statutes, 114–16
standards of care, 103–12, 114–16
statistics, CAM therapies, 140
statutes, 112–13
two schools of thought, 146–51
unprofessional conduct statutes, 114–16
manipulative, body-based practices. *See* chiropractic care; massage therapy; osteopathy
Marshall, John, 26
Marshall, William P., 86
Massachusetts, Jacobson v., 26–29
massage therapy, 3, 12–13
AG scope of practice opinions, 89
licensure, **56 T2.1**, 273
Matthews, Dale, 16
McCarran-Ferguson Act, 226
McDonagh, State Board of Registration for Healing Arts v., 54
McSteen, Tom, 278
meat, 200
medical boards
CAM use by licensed providers, 40–49
discipline by, 41
evidentiary nature of proceedings, 51–53
Federation of State Medical Boards (FSMB), 272
guidelines, 55
unlicensed providers and practice of medicine, 56–63
unprofessional conduct by physician (ozone therapy), **47–49**
Medical Freedom Acts, 268–72
medical records, 41, 194
medical schools, 4–5, 35–36
medical staff bylaws, 248
Meeker, William C., 12
Mehlman, Maxwell, 37–39
mental incompetence, 41, 274
mergers, 225
Mernitz, Culbertson v., **174–78**
midwifery, 17–18, 65–79
AG opinion, midwifery for compensation, 76–77
AG scope of practice opinions, 89–90

denial/cancellation of malpractice insurance, 254–57
history of, 65–66
licensure, in Minnesota, 273
practice of medicine *vs.*, 71–74
preference for physician-controlled childbirth, 66–67
public health *vs.* rights to privacy and choice, 75
regulation of, in Iowa, 227–29
state legislative conflicts over, 74–75
unlicensed practice of medicine, 67–71, 75
midwives, 3
different types of, 18
home birth by, opening statements, 77–79
Miller, Elizabeth, 211
mind-body interventions, 58. *See also* prayer; spirituality
"mindfulness mediation," 15
Minn. Stat. Ann. § 146A.01, 274
Minnesota
chiropractic care, performing physical exams, 101
Complementary and Alternative Health Care Client Bill of Rights, 275–77
doulas, 267
exemptions, religious practices, 63
marketing dietary supplements, 278
minimal standards of care, 274–75
Natural Health Legal Reform Project, 84
naturopathy, 84–85, 85–86
Office of Unlicensed Complementary Alternative Health Care Practice, 273–75
Minnesota Medical Association (MMA), 85
Minnesota Medical Freedom Act, 268
Minnesota Practice Act, 40
misdiagnosis. *See* failure to diagnose; incorrect diagnosis
Mississippi, 76–77
Missouri
Christian Science practitioners, 63
midwifery, AG scope of practice opinions, 89
midwifery legislation, 75
Missouri Healing Arts Practice Act, 54
mixers, 11

monopolies, 224
Montana, 88
Moore v. Baker, **190–92**
Morgan v. Hill, **144–46**
Mostrom v. Pettibon, **122–26**
musculoskeletal pain/injury, **6 Fig. 1.2**

N

National Center for Complementary and Alternative Medicine (NCCAM), 4, 279–80
natural childbirth, 66
naturopathy, 14
   definition, 9
   licensure, in Minnesota, 273
   licensure and education, 14, **56 T2.1**
   licensure controversy, 81
   licensure dispute, in Minnesota, 84–85
   Minnesota registration law, 85–86
   unprofessional conduct, 54–55
NCCAM, 4, 279–80
NDA process, 202–3
Nebraska, 87–88
neck pain, **6 Fig. 1.2**
negligence
   assumption of risk defense, 152–55
   defenses to, 146–55
   failure to diagnose, chiropractic malpractice, 138–40
   failure to disclose, 179–83
   failure to refer, chiropractic malpractice, 122–26
   failure to x-ray, chiropractic malpractice, 127–28
   foregoing conventional care, 116–22
   incorrect diagnosis and improper treatment, 137
   medical malpractice, breach, 116–40
   negligent performance of CAM procedure, 129–31
   trespass by physician, 157–59
neurocalometer, 12
Nevada, 89, 113
New Drug Application (NDA) process, 202–3
New York
   covenants not to sue, 189–90
   practice of medicine, definition, 36

New York Medical Freedom Act, 269–70, 272
New York State Department of Health, Gonzalez v., **270–71**
Nobel, Barry, 64
Noerr-Pennington doctrine, 226
North Carolina (legislation post-*Guess*), 50
North Carolina Medical Freedom Act, 268
not amenable to CAM care (patient), 128–29
notice, 53
Nurse Midwifery Associates v. Hibbert, **254–57**
nursing
   midwifery *vs.* practice of medicine, 71–74
   People and Sherman v. Cryns, 57
   scope of practice, spiritual healing therapies, 64
   unlicensed practice of medicine (lay midwife), 67–71
   unprofessional conduct, 53
Nutraceutical Corporation v. Von Eschenbach, **208–10**
nutrient content claims (labeling), 213
nutrition therapy. *See also* foods
   malpractice, foregoing conventional care, 117–21
   medical freedom act and, 270–71

O

OAM, 4
obstetrics, 17
   denial/cancellation of malpractice insurance, 254–57
   judicial canons interpreting legislative intent, 95–99
   unlicensed practice of medicine (lay midwife), 67–71
Office of Alternative Medicine (OAM), 4
Office of Unlicensed Complementary Alternative Health Care Practice (Minnesota), 273–75
Ogden, Gibbons v., 26
Ohio, 63
59 Okl. Stat. Ann. §492(F), 268–69
Oklahoma, 40, 268–69
opinions (attorney generals), 86–91
Ornish diet, **15 Box 1.3**

osteopathy, 9–11, 248–54
OTC Drug Review Program, 203–4
over-the-counter (OTC) drugs, 203–4
ozone therapy (unprofessional conduct by physician), **47–49**

P

Palmer, Bartlett Joshua (B.J.), 12
Palmer, David Daniel (D.D.), 11
Parker doctrine, 226
patient confidentiality, 274
patients
    Bill of Rights, 278
    Bill of Rights, Minnesota, 275–77
    CAM malpractice, not amenable to CAM care, 128–29
    cost of chronic conditions, 5
    doctor-patient relationship in integrative medicine, **25 Box 1.5**
    nondisclosure of CAM use to physicians, 24
    patient standard of disclosure, 160–72
    privileged communication, 41
    state medical freedom acts, 268–70
    unprofessional conduct by physicians, 41, 51
    use of CAM by, 5–6
    use of yoga by, **8 Box 1.2**
patient standard of disclosure, 160–72
Pearce, Laurie K., 75
Pearson v. Donna E. Shalala, Secretary, United States Department of Health and Human Services, **214–17**
penicillin, 22
People of the State of Illinois Ex Rel. Leonard A. Sherman, Director of Professional Regulation v. Yvonne Cryns, **67–71**
peptic ulcers, 22
Pethtel, Tschirhart v., **128–29**
Pettibon, Mostrom v., **122–26**
Pew Commission, 81
physical therapists, 101
physicians
    allopathic, standards of care, 146–51
    denials of clinical privileges, 248–54
    drug/alcohol use by, 41
    expert testimony, 103–11, 144–46
    gynecologist, professional standard of disclosure, 174–78
    history of practice of medicine, 33–35
    informed consent, 157–59, 160–72
    informed consent vs. assumption of risk, 179–83
    integrative medicine and, **25 Box 1.5**
    licensing boards' complaint and investigation process, 51–53
    malpractice, causal link, 141–42
    malpractice, failure to inform (availability of chelation therapy), 190–92
    malpractice, failure to obtain informed consent, 173
    malpractice, foregoing conventional care, 117–21
    malpractice, incorrect diagnosis, 131–36
    professional standards of conduct, 41–42
    unlicensed physicians practicing as homeopathic physicians, 277
    unprofessional conduct (sexual misconduct with patients), 41
    unprofessional conduct (using chelation therapy), 45–47
    unprofessional conduct (using homeopathy), 42–45
    unprofessional conduct (using LISTEN device), 51
    use of CAM, 40–49
physician's assistant (failure to supervise), 41
poultry products, 200
practice of medicine. See conventional medicine
prayer (healing through), 15, 63–64
pregnancy (vitamins supplements during), 14
price discrimination, 224
Pritikin diet, **15 Box 1.3**
privileged communication, 41, 54
prostitution, 13
public health, 26–29, 57

Q

qi, 5, 12, 16, 58
quackery, 3, 34, 37–39, 46
qualified health claims, 214–18
quinine, 22

R

Radin, Max, 90
Rao, Deepa, 19
reflexology, 13
regulation. *See also* licensure
   arguments for deregulation, 279–80
   Colorado regulation of mental health professionals, 86
   enforcement of unlicensed practice, 277–78
   innovations in CAM, overview, 267–68
   licensure *vs.* certification of CAM practitioners, 267–68
   scope of practice, 30
   of spiritual healers, 64–65
   state medical freedom acts, 268–72
   1998 Task Force on Health Care Workforce Regulation, 83
   of unlicensed CAM practitioners, 273–78
reiki imagery, 15, 58
relaxation techniques, 3
religious healing, 57–60
Reston, James, 16
Revici, Schneider v., **152–54, 184–89**
Rhode Island General Laws § 23-74-1(a)(4), 277
Rhode Island Medical Freedom Act, 268
Rhode Island Unlicensed Health Care Practices Act, 277
Rice, Thomas, 230
Richman, Barak D., 229
right to choose (birthing place and provider), 75, 227–29
Robert C. Atkins, M.D. v. C. Maynard Guest, M.D., as Executive Secretary of the New York State Board for Professional Conduct, **47–49**, 54
Rogers, M.D. (Robert J.) v. State Board of Medical Examiners of Florida, **45–47**
Rogers, Robert J., 50
Rosenbaum, Sara, 229
Rosenberg, L., 198
Ruebke (E. Michelle), State Board of Nursing and State of Kansas Ex Rel. State Board of Healing Arts v., **71–74**
Ruggie, Mary C., 112
Ruggio, Michael, 271–72
rule of reason analysis, 248–54
Rush, Benjamin, 38

S

Safriet, Barbara, 86, 100–101
Sage, William M., 230
Salazar v. Ehmann, **127–28**
Saltis, Cassandra A., 206
Scalia, Antonin, 90
Schloendorff v. The Society of New York Hospital, **157–59**
Schmidt, Greg, 84
Schneider v. Revici, **152–54, 184–89**
Schoenberg, Nancy E., 19
scope of practice, 81–102
   AG opinions, 86–91
   chiropractic care, judicial canons interpreting legislative intent, 95–99
   chiropractic care, legislative limiting, 100–101
   chiropractic care, malpractice, 114–16
   chiropractic care, physical exams, 101
   chiropractic care, unauthorized practice of medicine, 91–95
   judicial canons interpreting legislative intent, 90–91
   legislative disputes, 83–85
   Nebraska, chiropractic scope of practice opinion, 87–88
   overview, 81–83
   regulations, 30
sectarianism, 34
Sell v. Shore, **138–40**
sexual misconduct, 41, 54–55, 274
Shalala (Donna E.), Secretary, United States Department of Health and Human Services, Pearson v., **214–17**
Shalts, Edward, 241
shamanism, 18
Sherman Act
   § 1, conspiracies in restraint of trade, 224, 230–41, 242–47, 254–57
   § 1, conspiracies in restraint of trade (midwives), 228–29
   § 2, prohibiting monopolies, 224
   § 1 *vs.* § 2, 247
shiatsu, 12
Shore, Sell v., **138–40**
"significant scientific agreement" standard, 213
Sisco, Karen, 83
Sleath, Betsy, 19

Slessor, Caitlin, 227–29
Smith, Sandra J., 137
(The) Social Transformation of American Medicine, 33
Society of New York Hospital, Schloendorff v., **157–59**
Solla v. Aetna Health Plans of New York, Inc., **242–47**
Spence, Canterbury v., **160–72**
spinal manipulations, 11–12, 101
  reimbursement caps/disparities in rates for, 258–60
  risks, 195–96
SpineCare Medical Group, Inc, 159
spirituality, 15–16
  Center for Spirituality in Healing, 273
  definition, 5
  nursing and, 64
  regulation of spiritual healers, 64–65
standards of care
  chiropractic malpractice, expert testimony on causation, 144–46
  in common law, 103–12
  medical malpractice, breach of, 142–44
  minimal, in Minnesota, 274–75
standards of conduct (professional), 41–42, 42–49, 53
Starr, Paul, 33
state action doctrine, 226
State Board of Medical Examiners of Florida v. Robert J. Rogers, M.D., **45–47**
State Board of Nursing and State of Kansas Ex Rel. State Board of Healing Arts v. E. Michelle Ruebke, **71–74**
State Board of Registration for Healing Arts v. McDonagh, 54
state health licensing boards. *See also* licensure
  CAM use by licensed providers, 40–49
  complaint and investigation process, 51–53
State of Florida, Curley v., **58–60**
state police powers. *See also* regulation
  challenges to state medical practice acts, 39–40
  licensure, 34–35
  licensure *vs.* public health regulation, 40
  public health protection *vs.* Tenth Amendment, 40
regulation of CAM, 26–29
regulation of faith/spiritual healers, 60–65
unlicensed providers and practice of medicine, 56–63
statistics
  of adult chiropractic care, 12
  adverse event reporting, 211, 219–20
  of CAM malpractice, 140
  of CAM use, 3–4, 5
  home births, 65–66
  home births, in Europe, 75
  of Integrative Health Care Centers' use of spirituality, 16
  of mind-body interventions, 58
  of nondisclosure of CAM use, 24
  of non-M.D. practitioners (1928-1931), 35–36
  OAM budget, 4
  of practicing osteopaths, 11
  of prayer use, by CDC, 15
  scope of practice legislation, 81
  of traditional medicine, by WHO, 18
statutes
  15 U.S.C. §1, 224
  15 U.S.C. §2, 224
  15 U.S.C. §3, 225
  15 U.S.C. §13(a), 224
  15 U.S.C. §14, 224–25, 225
  15 U.S.C. §15, 225–26
  15 U.S.C. §18, 225
  15 U.S.C. §19(a)(1), 225
  15 U.S.C. §45(a)(1), 225
  15 U.S.C. §1011, 226
  42 U.S.C. §11111, 226, 254
  21 C.F.R. §119.1, 208
  42 C.F.R. §482.24(c)(2)(v), 194
  59 Okl. Stat. Ann. §492 (F), 268–69
  Alabama Act 499, 66–67
  Alaska Stat. §08.64.326(a)(8)(A), 268
  California Business and Professional Code, 36
  CAM definition, Minnesota statute, 274
  CAM standards of care, 112–13
  Clayton Act (15 U.S.C. §§12-27), 224–25
  Dietary Supplement Health and Education Act of 1994 (DSHEA), 14, 206–14

Food and Drug Administration Modernization Act of 1997 (FDAMA), 199
Food, Drug, and Cosmetic Act (FDCA), 198, 200, 202, **208**
FTC Act (15 U.S.C. §41), 224–26
Ga. Code Ann. §43-34-38, 269
Georgia informed consent, 190–93
Georgia Medical Freedom Act, 269
HCQIA, 226, 254
informed consent state statutes, 192–93
Iowa Acupuncture Practice Act, 112
Iowa Code, 113, 226
Iowa Competition Law, 226
Louisiana Revised Statutes, 112
McCarran-Ferguson Act, 226
Medicare Conditions of Participation, 194
Medical Freedom Acts, 268–72
Minn. Stat. Ann. §146A.01, 274
Minnesota Practice Act, 40
Missouri Healing Arts Practice Act, 54
N.C. Gen. Stat. Ann. §90-14(a)(6), 268
New York Education Law, 36
New York Medical Freedom Act, 269–70, 272
N.Y. Pub. Health Law §230(1), 269
Official Code of Georgia Annotated (O.C.G.A.), informed consent, 192–93
Rhode Island General Laws §23-74-1(a)(4), 277
Rhode Island Unlicensed Health Care Practices Act, 277
Sherman Act (15 U.S.C. §§ 1-7), 224, 228–47, 254–57
Texas Administrative Code, 193–94
Texas Civil Practice and Remedy Code, 159, 190–93
Texas Medical Disclosure Panel, 193
Stevinson, Clare, 195
Still, Andrew Taylor, 10
Still, Charles, 10–11
structure-function claims (labeling), 213
Studdert, David M., 121
Sugarbaker, Jeremy, 195
Sweeney v. Athens Regional Medical Center, 229

T

Tennessee, 89
Tenth Amendment, 26, 40, 57, 65
Texas (midwifery, AG scope of practice), 89–90
Texas Administrative Code, 193, 194
Texas Civil Practice and Remedy Code, 159, 190, 193
Texas Medical Disclosure Panel, 193
therapeutic touch, 15, 58
Thomsonianism, 34
Tibetan medicine people, 18
traditional medicine, 5, 18, 57
   tension with conventional medicine, **20** Box 1.4
Transcendental Meditation (TM), 15
Trigon Healthcare, Inc., American Chiropractic Association v., **258–60**
Tschirhart v. Pethtel, **128–29**
two schools of thought (defense), 135–36, 146–51
   jury instructions, 137
tying, 224–25

U

United States v. Nutrition Service, Inc., **204–6**
University of Arizona
   Program in Integrative Medicine, 4, **25** Box 1.5
University of Minnesota
   Center for Spirituality in Healing, 273
Unlicensed Health Care Practices Act (Rhode Island), 277
unlicensed providers, 56–63
   acts/instruments used by midwives, 75
   faith healers, 60–63
   "healing touch," 57
   lay midwives, 57
   religious healing, 57–60, 58–60
   spiritual providers, 57
   traditional medicine providers, 57
unprofessional conduct, 41
   Arizona statute (chelation therapy), 114
   by naturopathic doctor (sexual conduct with patient), 54–55
   by nurse, 53–54

by physician (chelation therapy), 45–47, 54
by physician (homeopathy), 42–45
by physician (ozone therapy), 47–49
unreasonable risk standard, 208–10

V

vaccines, 22, **26–29**
Van Hemel, Peter J., 34
vascular disease (and vitamin B), 217–18
vertebral arterial dissection, 195, 196
vibration, 11
vitalism, 5, 58
vitamins, 206–7
　"mega" doses, 211–12
　vitamin B and vascular disease, 217–18
　vitamin C, 14
Von Eschenbach, Nutraceutical Corporation v., **208–10**

W

Washington, 51
Washington State Health Department Medical Quality Health Assurance Commission, Ames v., 51
Weil, Andrew, **25 Box 1.5**
Wengel v. Herfert, **114–16**
Wertz, Dorothy, 17
Wertz, Richard, 17
West Virginia, Dent v., 34–35
West Virginia University Hospitals, Inc. v. Case, 90
White v. Jones, **142–44**
whole diets, 7 **Box 1.1**, 9, **15 Box 1.3**
Whorton, James C., 18
Wilcox v. Carroll, **131–36**
Wilk v. American Medical Association, 82–83, **230–41**
Williams, Brenda, 272
witchcraft. *See* midwifery

Y

yin-yang polarity theory, 17
yoga (in Beth Israel Hospital), **8 Box 1.2**
Young, Michael, 38

Z

Zone diet, **15 Box 1.3**
Zuk, Cary Elizabeth, 212, 219